Migrations in Jordan

Migrations in Jordan

Reception Policies and Settlement Strategies

Edited by
Jalal Al Husseini, Valentina Napolitano and
Norig Neveu

I.B.TAURIS
LONDON • NEW YORK • OXFORD • NEW DELHI • SYDNEY

I.B. TAURIS
Bloomsbury Publishing Plc, 50 Bedford Square, London, WC1B 3DP, UK
Bloomsbury Publishing Inc, 1359 Broadway, 12th Floor, New York, NY 10018, USA
Bloomsbury Publishing Ireland, 29 Earlsfort Terrace, Dublin 2, D02 AY28, Ireland

BLOOMSBURY, I.B. TAURIS and the I.B. Tauris logo are trademarks of Bloomsbury Publishing Plc

First published in Great Britain 2024
This paperback edition published 2026

Series design by Adriana Brioso
Cover image © Giles Clarke/Getty Images

A catalogue record for this book is available from the British Library.

Library of Congress Cataloging-in-Publication Data
Names: Husseini, Jalal, editor. | Neveu, Norig, editor. | Napolitano, Valentina, editor.
Title: Migrations in Jordan: reception policies and settlement strategies / edited by Jalal Al Husseini, Norig Neveu, Valentina Napolitano.
Description: London; New York: I.B. Tauris, 2024. | Includes bibliographical references and index. | Summary: "Jordan sheds important light on key issues around forced migration in the Middle East. This book is the first to study the long-term impact of multiple immigration flows on Jordanian society from 1948 to the present day. Part One investigates the criteria for integration and exclusion imposed by Jordan and international humanitarian organisations on different groups of refugees. Part Two analyses how state policy impacts the solidarity networks between different migrant communities and the different political, social, religious and family networks that are set up in camps and urban settings. Part Three turns to how migrants shape the Jordanian cityscape and geography themselves"– Provided by publisher.
Identifiers: LCCN 2023050998 (print) | LCCN 2023050999 (ebook) | ISBN 9780755606849 (hardback) | ISBN 9780755654406 (paperback) | ISBN 9780755606870 (epub) | ISBN 9780755606863 (ebook)
Subjects: LCSH: Refugees–Jordan. | Forced migration–Middle East. | Refugees–Government policy–Jordan. | Refugees–Jordan–Social conditions. | Jordan–Emigration and immigration. | Syria–History–Civil War, 2011—Refugees.
Classification: LCC HV640.4.J6 M54 2024 (print) | LCC HV640.4.J6 (ebook) | DDC 305.9/06914095695–dc23/eng/20240309
LC record available at https://lccn.loc.gov/2023050998
LC ebook record available at https://lccn.loc.gov/2023050999

ISBN: HB: 978-0-7556-0684-9
PB: 978-0-7556-5440-6
ePDF: 978-0-7556-0686-3
eBook: 978-0-7556-0687-0

Typeset by Deanta Global Publishing Services, Chennai, India

For product safety related questions contact productsafety@bloomsbury.com.

To find out more about our authors and books visit www.bloomsbury.com and sign up for our newsletters.

Contents

Contributors

Myriam Ababsa is a social geographer and urban planner. An associate researcher at the French Institute of the Near East (Amman) and Géographie-Cités (Paris 7), she has worked on urban planning and land governance in various countries of the Middle East (Jordan, Syria, Palestine). A former student of ENS Fontenay (1993–7), she holds a PhD from Tours University (2014), published in French: *Raqqa. Territoires et pratiques sociales d'une ville syrienne*, Ifpo 2009. She is the editor of the *Atlas of Jordan* (Ifpo 2013). She had co-directed *Popular Housing and Urban Land Tenure in the Middle East*, The American University in Cairo Press, 2012; and, with Rami Daher, *Cities, Urban Practices and Nation Building in Jordan*, Ifpo, 2011.

Jalal Al Husseini is an associate research fellow in political sociology at the French Institute of the Near East (Ifpo). He has also consulted with several United Nations agencies, including UNRWA and the ILO. Based in Amman since 1997, he has specialized in forced migration and labor market issues. Holder of a PhD obtained at the Graduate Institute of International Studies (Geneva), with a doctoral dissertation on the political dimensions of UNRWA's mandate, he has organized and contributed to academic and applied research programs, and has authored numerous publications. He is also the editor of several collective books, including *Palestinians between State and Diaspora: Uncertainty Times* (2011) and *Palestine in Networks* (2020).

Solenn Al Majali is a PhD candidate in anthropology, affiliated with the TELEMMe laboratory - Aix-Marseille University (France). She is also an assistant researcher at CNRS for the ITHACA Program (*Interconnecting Histories and Archives for Migrant Agency: Entangled Narratives Across Europe and the Mediterranean Region*) at the French Institute of the Near East (Ifpo) in Jordan. Her doctoral dissertation deals with the processes of exclusion and sociability among Yemeni and Somali refugee communities in a popular neighborhood of Amman.

Oroub El Abed is a researcher leading the Jordan research team for the Centre of Lebanese Studies (CLS) of the Lebanese American University (LAU) in Beirut, Lebanon. She researches refugee issues in the Middle East with a focus on socioeconomic and legal status and access to basic rights, and has published on Palestinians in Egypt and refugees in Jordan. Her PhD thesis (forthcoming publication) studies the rights of Palestinian refugees who are holders of the Jordanian citizenship. The work unpacks legal status, class stratification, and the discursive measures of the state in managing the heterogeneity of its people.

Ayham Dalal is an urban planner and architect working in the field of forced migration. He is the author of the book *From Shelters to Dwellings: The Zaatari Refugee Camp*, Transcript Verlag, 2022, and the co-editor of the book *Tempohomes*, TU Berlin University Press, 2022. He was a research fellow at CNRS-Migrinter, Ifpo Amman, TU Berlin, and the Refugee Studies Center at the University of Oxford. He has co-curated two exhibitions and co-directed an award-winning film on forced migration and camps in Germany and Jordan. Currently, he is an assistant professor at the Architecture and Urban Design Program at the German University in Cairo (GUC).

Kamel Doraï is a geographer and researcher at the CNRS (the French National Centre for Scientific Research) currently based at MIGRINTER, University of Poitiers (France). Since the early 2000s, he has held several researcher positions at the Ifpo in Damascus (Syria) and in Amman (Jordan). He also headed the Department of contemporary studies at Ifpo in Beirut (Lebanon) until 2020. His work focuses mainly on asylum and refugees in the Middle East, with a focus on migration and transnational practices within the Palestinian diaspora. He is currently conducting research on Syrian and Palestinian refugees from Syria in Jordan and Lebanon, as well as on the urbanization process of Palestinian refugee camps in Lebanon. He develops comparative studies between refugees residing in and out of camps, as well as analysis of their migratory experience and spatial practices to map the relationships between refugee camps and their urban environment in the Middle East.

Aline Fraikin is an urban planner and researcher and has her master's degree in urban and regional planning from the Technical University of Berlin (2020). She completed her master's thesis on micro-publics and studied a bottom-up initiated neighborhood park in Amman. At TU Berlin, she supervised several student projects on Berlin's refugee housing landscape. From 2018 to 2020, she was part of the research project "Architectures of Asylum" in the interdisciplinary Collaborative Research Center "Re-Figuration of Spaces," which took a comparative look at Jordan and Germany. She is currently working in the field of participatory urban planning in Berlin.

Lillian Frost is an assistant professor in the Department of Political Science at Virginia Tech. She specializes in forced migration, citizenship, and gender issues, particularly in the Arab World. She has held research fellow positions with the European University Institute, United States Institute of Peace, Harvard Belfer Center for Science and International Affairs, American Center of Research in Jordan, and Fulbright Program in Jordan. She also previously worked for the World Bank's Middle East and North Africa Social Protection unit. She received her PhD in political science from George Washington University.

Zoë Jordan is a postdoctoral researcher at the Centre for Development and Emergency Practice (CENDEP), Oxford Brookes University, UK, where she researches forced migration and humanitarianism, with a focus on how displaced populations respond to displacement in protracted and urban contexts. Her PhD (2020) addressed the act of refugee hosting among urban refugee populations in Amman, Jordan, primarily working with Sudanese refugees.

Anna Kvittingen is a PhD candidate in the Department of Social and Policy Sciences, University of Bath, UK. She previously worked as a humanitarian practitioner and has participated in academic and policy-focused research exploring humanitarian responses and refugees' experiences, most recently among ex-Gaza, Sudanese, and Yemeni refugees in Jordan. Through an exploration of governing practices in Jordan, her doctoral research seeks to further comprehend the way in which protection and assistance is negotiated and unequally rationed to different groups of refugees.

David Lagarde completed his PhD in geography at the University of Toulouse. His research investigates the links between social and spatial networks in Syrian refugees' journeys, focusing mainly on the conditions of movement at different scales of the Euro-Mediterranean space (local, regional, and transnational). His work makes ample use of cartography and visualization in order to represent the complexity and diversity of these spatial and social dynamics.

Valentina Napolitano is a sociologist, a researcher at the French National Research Institute for Sustainable Development (IRD), and a member of the Population Environment Development Laboratory (LPED). Her research deals with forced migrations, political violence, and family transformations in the Middle East, especially in Syria and Jordan. Her Phd deals with political commitments and mobilizations among Palestinian refugees in Syria. She is currently studying the effects of the Syrian war on the transformation and reconfiguration of refugee families in Jordan. She was a member of the "ANR Lajeh: Conflicts and Migrations" program and is actually member of the "H2020 ITHACA: Interconnecting Histories and Archives for Migrant Agency." Among her latest publications: "Managing Palestinian Refugees in Syria: A Sociohistorical Overview of UNRWA's Relationship with Syrian Authorities, 1950-70," *Jerusalem Quarterly*, 94 (2023): 48–64.

Norig Neveu is a research fellow at CNRS and a member of the Institute of Research and Study on the Arab and Muslim Worlds (IREMAM). Her research first focused on social dynamics around holy sites and religious politics in southern Jordan from the late Ottoman period. She is currently approaching a connected history of Christian and Muslim religious authorities in Jordan and Palestine between the nineteenth and twenty-first centuries. She contributed to different research programs on migration dynamics such as the Lajeh ANR and MAGYC (H2020). She is actually coordinating the PredicMo program "Grammars of preaching" (ANR). She has published several articles on religious tourism, transnational networks, and faith-based charities in Jordan and Palestine. She co-edited with Karène Sanchez Summerer and Annalaura Turiano, *Mission and Preaching: Connected and Decompartmentalised Perspectives from the Middle East and North Africa (19th–21st Century)*, Leiden: Brill, 2022.

Héloïse Peaucelle is a assistant professor of human geography at Aix-Marseille University (TELEMMe) and a PhD candidate at the University of Tours (Citeres/EMAM). She is an associate PhD student at the French Research Institute of the Near East (Ifpo), and a fellow of Institut Convergence Migration (policy). Her research focuses on urban geography in the Middle East where she investigates, through a qualitative approach, the migration issues, socio-spatial segregation, fragmentation in urban context, and right to the city for migrants and refugees. She has benefited from a doctoral grant offered by Ifpo within its partnership with the French Development Agency (2019/22). She conducted an ethnographic fieldwork in ʾIrbid city in Jordan among Syrian migrants including refugees and entrepreneurs. In her thesis, she focuses on the place of these groups of populations in the city, hence on their appropriation of space through practices and representations.

Yasmeen Shahzadeh was an intern community researcher at CLS-Jordan while completing graduate studies. She recently completed her MA in Education and Society with a focus on Gender and Women's Studies from the Department of Integrated Studies in Education at McGill University, Canada. Her research interests focus on access to education for women and vulnerable groups in Jordan.

Gaspard Vial Benamra has embarked on a PhD program in history at the University of Lyon 2. His doctoral research focuses on the history of the Chechens in Jordan from the beginning of the twentieth century to the present day. Based on private archives as well as official Ottoman and Mandate archives, he studies the modalities of settlement of this migrant community in Jordan and more specifically in al-Zarqāʾ. He also tackles the construction of a Chechen collective memory in Jordan.

Ann-Christin Zuntz is a British Academy Postdoctoral Fellow at the University of Edinburgh. She is an economic anthropologist, with a focus on the intersections of labor, forced migrations, and gender, in the Mediterranean. Since 2015, Ann has conducted fieldwork with displaced Syrians in Jordan, Turkey, Tunisia, and Bulgaria, and, remotely, in Iraq, Lebanon, and Syria. She conducts collaborative research with Syrian academics within the One Health FIELD Network.

Figures

Acknowledgments

This volume is an outcome of a collective multidisciplinary research program that has focused on refugee issues in Jordan (French national research agency—ANR *Lajeh*). Hosted at the Institut français du Proche-Orient (French Institute of the Near East, Ifpo) between 2016 and 2019, this program has also benefited from the support of the d'Alembert fund of the Institut français, which made it possible to organize a conference in Amman in 2018, in which all the contributors participated. We would like to thank the institutions that supported and made this project possible. We would also like to thank Isabelle Ruben for her invaluable work on the copy editing of the manuscript. We heartily thank Sarah Rolfo, who took care of the bibliography and the Arabic transliteration streamlining. A particular mention should be made of all those colleagues who proofread the chapters of the volume and whose suggestions were instrumental in enriching them and improving their quality. Last but not least, special thanks to Kamel Doraï (CNRS/Migrinter), who managed the *Lajeh* program and was at the origin of this research project.

Notes on Transliteration

In transliterating Arabic, this volume generally follows the International Journal of Middle East Studies (IJMES) system. There are, however, some exceptions to this rule: personal names where a specific spelling was preferred and used by the individual in question or has become recognized as the norm over time; and transliterations of colloquial Arabic (*'ammiyya*), where authors have used styles of transliteration which they feel best evoke the sounds and cadences of particular forms of the language. For the names of places, the English names have been kept only for the names of countries and capitals, while secondary cities and villages have been transliterated.

Introduction

Jordan, Conflicts, and Migrations: Rethinking Host Policies and Settlement Strategies from a Long-Term and Multiscale Perspective

Jalal Al Husseini, Valentina Napolitano and Norig Neveu

Jordan currently hosts the second highest number of registered refugees in the world relative to its population; only Lebanon hosts more. Three million out of its eleven million inhabitants[1] are refugees, including 2.31 million Palestinians registered with the United Nations Relief and Works Agency for Palestine Refugees in the Near East (UNRWA) since 1950,[2] and 750,000 refugees from other nationalities who are registered with the United Nations High Commissioner for Refugees, mainly from Syria (88 percent), but also from Iraq, Yemen, Sudan and Somalia.[3] Jordan's experience as a host country for refugees and migrants predates its independence as the Hashemite Kingdom in 1946. In the late nineteenth century, the territory that is currently Jordanian was part of the Ottoman *vilayet* of Syria and it welcomed Circassians and Chechens who had been ousted by Tsarist Russia after the Crimean War; Armenians fleeing Ottoman persecution in Anatolia were to follow (Ohannessian-Charpin 2007; Shami 1996b and 2009; Hamed-Troyansky 2017). After its creation in 1921 under the aegis of the British Mandate, the Emirate of Transjordan received other migrants, mainly Syrians fleeing persecution by the French Mandate authorities. Each of these refugee experiences has been unique, with its own specificities determined by various key factors. These include the country's general political context, the size of the refugee population, and the Jordanian polity's perceptions of the political and socioeconomic threats and opportunities each of these refugee populations might represent for the country. Accordingly, refugee inflows have been handled on a case-by-case basis, generating a multitude of reception policies, legal statuses, and contributions to Jordan's social fabric.

This may explain why most studies of migration to Jordan have focused on one refugee case at a time, with special emphasis on the larger Palestinian and Syrian

1 Data taken from the most recent census dating to September 2021. See the Jordanian Department of Statistics (DoS): http://dosweb.dos.gov.jo/

2 See the *UNRWA in figures*, December 31, 2021: https://www.unrwa.org/resources/about-unrwa/unrwa-figures-2020-2021/

3 See *UNHCR Factsheet- Jordan*, February 2021: https://reporting.unhcr.org/sites/default/files/Jordan%20country%20factsheet%20-%20February%202021.pdf/

refugee groups and on encampment policies. By analyzing most of the refugee experiences together, this volume constitutes a novel contribution to the existing literature and may be considered an observatory for the analysis of different migrations over time. It aims at stressing the cumulative and processual dimensions of Jordan's reception policies, as well as the refugees' settlement strategies and experiences. More precisely, the present volume focuses on migrations caused by conflicts, wars and crises, underlining their articulation around long-standing human mobility. This approach must be understood in the post-2011 period, in the aftermath of popular contestations, revolts, and the armed conflicts that sometimes followed, which have caused major population movements and given rise to a new interest in the study of migration from the Middle East and Maghreb. Academic research literature has scrutinized the question of legal and illegal migratory routes and itineraries, as well as the policies elaborated by the states and their international partners (the European Union for example) (Snel et al. 2021) to better manage so-called migration "waves'" or "crises" (Akoka 2016). Taking Jordan as a case study, this volume highlights the fact that the Middle East is the principal region from where refugees come and where the majority of them settle (Babar 2020). It also shows that these exceptional migratory episodes sit within a genealogy of older social networks and human mobilities that connect the overall region under various host state-specific reception policies and settlement strategies (Chatty 2010; Canefe 2017).

Geared to a multidisciplinary approach involving anthropology, architecture, geography, history, political science, and sociology,[4] this volume shows the multiple ways in which migrations have shaped the social, political, economic, and humanitarian landscape of contemporary Jordan. In so doing, it also highlights the type of interactive relations that have developed between migrant populations and their host society at local and national levels, showcasing how policies elaborated by the government and humanitarian agencies have deeply affected the migrants' daily lives and, conversely, how the latter's adaptation strategies, involving ancient family, economic, and religious solidarity networks and the creation of new ones, have shaped their host urban and social environment. Finally, the volume highlights how a localized, multiscale, and long-term approach contributes to broader epistemological changes in the understanding of migratory phenomena in a context of regional crises.

Localizing the Transnational: Adopting a Multiscale and Migrant-Centered Approach

This book tackles migration dynamics on a multiscale level. It combines, at one and the same time, the contributions of the transnational approach to migrations and those

[4] This volume is one of the outputs of a broader collective research project entitled "Lajeh: Conflicts and Migrations" that aimed at analyzing the forced migration phenomenon in the Middle East at large. Led by Kamel Doraï at the French Institute of the Near East (Ifpo), it was funded by the French National Research Agency (ANR) between 2016 and 2019. See the web page of the ANR Lajeh: https://lajeh.hypotheses.org/projet/programme-de-recherche

considering the agency of migrants (Van Liempt and Doomernik 2006; Triandafyllidou 2017). In this way, it suggests a slight swerve from the transnational approach to migration studies (Waldinger 2006; Schapendonk and Steel 2014; Mainwaring and Brigden 2016; Crawley and Jones 2021; Vogt 2018) by proposing to relocate the analysis in one national field. Transnational approaches, based on the observation that analyzing migrations solely in terms of the territories in which migrants settle, render invisible "the processes by which immigrants forge and sustain multi-stranded social relations that link together their societies of origin and settlement" (Basch et al. 1994: 6). By focusing on trajectories, networks, and ties, one can question notions such as transnational communities or social spaces. This effectively extends the analysis beyond the question of places of origin or destination and addresses cross-border experiences and livelihoods.

Drawing on empirical data and theoretical contributions, the chapters in this volume propose to reterritorialize the analysis by considering migrants fully-fledged actors in their relations with national and international institutions (Brun 2001; Loescher and Betts 2011) and by taking into account the effects of transnational dynamics (such as the externalization of European borders, the role of international humanitarianism, previous circulations, and mobilities) on their individual and collective strategies. By reterritorializing the analysis, the chapters also emphasize the decisive role of the host authorities in shaping the migrants' lives in Jordan, a country that is not a signatory to the UN Refugee Convention of 1951 and its 1966 Protocol, and to the UNHCR Statute of 1950. These instruments set universal standards for the refugees' legal status, access to the labor market, social protection and to public services in host states.[5] The production of state migration policies, including refugee policies, have therefore primarily responded to Jordan's evolving national needs and interests; moreover, its management has been dispersed between a multiplicity of "hands" at national and subnational levels (Ali 2021). The contributions of this volume combine state-centered and humanitarian perspectives with a multiscale and relational approach encompassing the multiple actors (governmental and international institutions, migrants' organizations, networks, families, and individuals) involved in the ongoing processes of negotiation at work in the management of migration. They also highlight the contribution of migrants to the host country's social, economic, political, and urban fabric.

In so doing, this volume extends recent work that has analyzed the interconnected ways migration governance shapes migrations, and migrations shape migration governance (Carmel, Katharina, and Regine 2021). Analyzing migrant reception policies from a migrant perspective makes it possible to meet three research objectives. Firstly, to provide new insight into host country and international organization settlement and humanitarian assistance by uncovering their social, economic, and political contingencies and by assessing the strategies migrants elaborate to manage and circumvent legal, political and social constraints. Secondly, to give voice to the

[5] For instance, refugees should enjoy rights to social protection, primary education, access to courts of justice on a par with citizens of the host country; and rights related to ownership, post-primary education, and employment on a par with foreign residents; see 1951 Convention: https://www.unhcr.org/fr/4b14f4a62

refugees' own representations and perceptions of host policies and of their local environment. Thirdly, to highlight the active role refugees play in keeping ties, activating or establishing solidarity networks, and developing long-term forms of settlement in the host country in spite of their legal and economic vulnerability. This perspective leads to a participatory conception of migrant governance, which challenges the traditional relegation of refugees to the position of objects to be governed and seeks to consider them as actors involved in shaping governance by including migrant-led initiatives in the field of social protection and humanitarianism (Pincock et al. 2020; Fiddian-Qasmiyeh 2016). Different contributions suggest that migrants are often the first to provide aid and assistance to other migrants, and that it is among family and solidarity networks that migrants are hosted before institutionalised responses are put in place.

Adopting a Long-Term Approach, Blurring the Dichotomic Approach to Migrations

Adopting a long-term approach to migrations in Jordan, this volume contributes to broader migration theories that aim to question the dichotomy often found in migration literature between forced and voluntary migrations (Snel et al. 2020; Crawley and Skleparis 2018; Erdal and Oeppen 2018; Castles et al. 2020). The terms used to qualify migration depend both on the categories used by the actors (states, international and humanitarian organizations, migrants) and on the reality of the migratory paths. The official label used to designate and categorize people as migrants, asylum seekers, refugees, or invited guests, and the consequent legal and socioeconomic status (access to public services, social protection and freedom of collective action) (Noiriel 1997; Cohen 2012; Kozma et al. 2014; Tejel and Oztan 2020) has varied widely depending on host country political and socioeconomic contexts and ensuing residence regulations (Malkki 1995). If these categories reflect different juridical statuses, with concomitant papers and social assistance access, they are often unable to capture the diversity of migrant trajectories, the evolutions over time of motivations and juridical status during a migratory path. At the same time, these categories have concrete effects on migrants' lives and rights (Crawley and Skleparis 2018; Snel et al. 2020; cf. Al Husseini and Kvittingen, Al Majali in this volume). For this reason, by adopting a long-term perspective and comparing different migratory waves, with multiple and varying statuses over time, this collective volume extends those studies that have gone beyond the dichotomy between forced and voluntary migration, refugees and economic migrants, in order to analyze them as a continuum (Snel et al. 2020; Crawley and Skleparis 2018; Erdal and Oeppen 2018; Castles et al. 2020). Over time one migrant population can be designated as guests, then become refugees, then workers. Others that see themselves as refugees fleeing war-torn countries can be treated as undesirable economic migrants. By analyzing the evolution and articulation of these categories, this volume provides an understanding not only of the policy production of these categories but also of the way migrants live them, appropriate and circumvent them during their trajectory.

Moreover, the long-term approach adopted in this volume confirms that migration routes and settlement processes of forced migrants are not always that spontaneous nor due to the proximity of a border; they have often been influenced by the existence of previous transnational migration networks based on family, tribal, or commercial ties, or on solidarity between former and new migrants of the same nationality (see Napolitano in this volume). Migrations connected to conflicts and crises also often build on previous experiences of mobility or migration, which may have been triggered by work, study, and training, as well as for religious reasons (see Lagarde and Doraï, Zuntz, Napolitano, and Neveu in this volume). For example, until the first half of the twentieth century, one of the major phenomena of mobility in the Middle East was the pilgrimage to Mecca (Chiffoleau 2015). Other symbolic spaces continue to attract thousands of visitors every year and create forms of knowledge of the territories of migration. Moreover, delving into migration processes often invites observers to replace them within the genealogy of older human or material mobilities that have for decades connected Jordan to its regional and international environment, thereby creating transnational—sometimes diasporic—entities that influence the present and future conditions of migrant groups. Thus, this volume considers the mechanisms of migration during violent conflicts and crises within older social networks and human mobilities. This allows not only for migratory experiences to be decompartmentalized, but also the genealogy of reception policies to be questioned and the migratory phenomenon to be put into perspective with forms of social organization built over time in Jordan and/or connecting it to the regional or even international scale.

Migrations and the Social, Political, and Urban Fabric of Contemporary Jordan

This collective volume argues that migrations have shaped Jordan's state/nation building process, namely the process conducted by the central and local authorities to foster a common national identity. So far, forced migration literature has mainly explored the way state formation has triggered displacements (De Bel-Air 2006; Doraï 2014; Stepputat and Nyberg Sørense 2014), and more rarely the way migrants have contributed to state/nation building itself (Chatty 2018) and to the shaping of cities (Hatziprokopiou 2016; Fawaz et al. 2018; Fawaz et al. 2021; Bontemps et al. 2018).

Jordan, between Long-Term Migration Policies and Long-Term Experience of Migrants

The contemporary history of the territory of Jordan is marked and shaped by migration, circulation, and mobility. Since the late nineteenth century, the Circassian migration is symptomatic of the role of migrants in shaping urban spaces, including Amman, which became the capital of the young Emirate of Transjordan in 1921: 7,000 Muslim Circassians and Chechens were expelled by Tsarist Russia from the Caucasus (Shami 2009; Hamed-Troyansky 2017, see Vial-Benamra in this volume). They were followed by a few hundred survivors of the Armenian genocide during

World War I (Ohannessian-Charpin 2007), as well as Syrian nationalists fleeing persecution in the French Mandate in the 1920s (Anderson 2005). These early migrants contributed to shaping the modern agricultural and economic life of Transjordan. They became full citizens of the Emirate of Transjordan (by virtue of the 1928 Nationality Law) and later the Kingdom of Jordan (by virtue of the 1954 Nationality Law); and while the return to their country of origin is not a legal claim (as in the case of the Palestinian refugees, for instance), their history and the conditions of their arrival in Jordan contribute to it's image as a "refugee haven" (Chatelard 2010c).

After the creation of the Hashemite Kingdom in 1946, Jordan, which extended its control over the West Bank during the First Arab-Israeli War (1948) and then annexed it in 1950, hosted 350,000 out of some 750,000 Palestinian refugees (70,000 in the East Bank and 280,000 in the West Bank), in addition to 462,000 indigenous West Bankers. Furthermore, some 350,000 Palestinians (one-third of them second-time refugees) were displaced from the West Bank and the Gaza Strip following Israel's occupation of these territories in 1967 (Abu Odeh 1999; De Bel-Air 2003; Al Husseini and Bocco 2009; Achilli 2015). Later, regional conflicts and crises in the Middle East and the Horn of Africa triggered the exodus of other refugee populations toward Jordan. Since the 1990s and the First Gulf War, several waves of Iraqi refugees have moved to Jordan, mainly to transit areas. As entrepreneurs, some of them marked the fabric of the Jordanian capital through their initiatives (Chatelard 2010a and b). After 2003 and the death of Saddam Hussein, thousands of Iraqi refugees arrived in Jordan, either in transit or for a longer period, often of waiting. This humanitarian crisis has been studied in its instrumental dimension, in particular through discussions on the counting of refugees, by international humanitarian aid institutions such as the UNHCR (Chatelard 2008). The reception and settlement policy were assessed in terms of the denominational restrictions applied (Chatelard and Doraï 2011) in a context of rising sectarianism in Iraq and terrorist attacks in Jordan in 2003. These first waves were joined by the arrival of new migrants fleeing the advances of ISIS after 2014.[6] As a consequence of long-running conflicts in Darfur and Somalia, since 2000 Jordan has hosted a small number of Sudanese (5,400) and Somalis (600) asylum seekers.[7] Arriving in the country with the help of smugglers, they considered Jordan only as a transit country but then remained stuck there without the possibility of being recognized as refugees or of accessing the job market and humanitarian aid (Davis et al. 2016; Al Majali 2020). An important number of Yemenis (nearly 12,000) and Syrians (660,000) arrived in Jordan with the advent of the Arab Spring and related conflicts in 2011,[8] joining those who were formerly resident in the country for educational, medical, commercial or political reasons (cf. Al Majali, Napolitano in this volume).

Migrants fleeing regional conflicts who settled in the country were not meant—from the state's perspective—to be fully assimilated and remain indefinitely in Jordanian society, whatever their different legal and humanitarian statuses. Only the

[6] In 2022, Jordan hosted nearly 66,000 Iraqi refugees according to the UNHCR. See: https://data2.unhcr.org/en/documents/details/91774

[7] Data issued by UNHCR in 2022. See: https://data.unhcr.org/en/documents/details/97304

[8] Data issued by UNHCR in 2022. See: https://data.unhcr.org/en/documents/details/97304

Palestinians that fled from Israeli forces during the 1948 and 1967 Arab-Israeli wars are officially recognized by Jordan as fully-fledged refugees or displaced persons with an unquestionable right of residence in the country pending the full resolution of the Palestinian-Israeli conflict, chiefly through the return of the refugees to their original homes.[9] However, the 1948 refugees (and their descendants) have been granted full citizenship as a means of involving them fully in the socioeconomic development of the country (see Al Husseini and Kvittingen; Frost in this volume). Moreover, as a result of the annexation of the West Bank and East Jerusalem, Palestinians played a crucial role in the establishment of the bureaucratic institutions of the independent Jordanian state (Anderson 2005) and also welfare and humanitarian institutions (Al Husseini 2000; Hanafi et al. 2014; Rioli 2020; Biancani and Rioli 2023; Neveu 2023). Jordan also underwent an important process of urbanization, especially in the capital Amman, which expanded with the arrival of Palestinians. The camps established close to the main cities provided a cheap workforce for the labor market and attracted funding from international aid (Achilli and Oesch 2016).

Status and Encampment Policies: Beyond the Unique Palestinian Experience

At the same time, the exceptionality of the Palestinian refugees' status as "refugee-citizens" has represented a real challenge to the country's stability because of their supposed hybrid identity and loyalty to the Jordanian state (Brand 1995; Massad 2008), as well as their social and political mobilization as a specific group within the host society (Achilli 2015; Gandolfo 2012; Latte Abdallah 2006). The Palestinian refugee experience is unique for understanding migrants' contribution to host state building. It is also decisive for grasping the reception policies developed later in Jordan (Kagan 2009). Unlike the Palestinian refugees, Iraqi, Syrian, Sudanese, Somali, and Yemeni refugees have been considered "invited guests" (El Abed 2014) who are temporarily tolerated on Jordanian soil pending return to their homes or resettlement in third countries. Categorized as "others" by the Jordanian state, these migrants have contributed to the definition by default of the borders of Jordanian national identity (Zaiotti 2006). Despite this temporary status, their presence has also shaped the social and urban landscape of contemporary Jordan. Al-Zaʿtarī camp, which in 2021 hosted nearly 70,000 Syrian refugees, constitutes the fifth largest "city" in Jordan (see Dalal and Fraikin in this volume). Moreover, the presence of Iraqis and Syrians, especially in northern Jordanian cities, has boosted local markets and given rise to new urban configurations (see Ababsa and Peaucelle in this volume).

From the end of the 1990s, studies on Iraqis, Syrians, and smaller migrant groups have led to consider new research approaches and themes, such as Jordan as a transit

[9] According to Resolution 194, adopted by the United Nations General Assembly in December 1948: "refugees wishing to return to their homes and live at peace with their neighbors should be permitted to do so at the earliest practicable date, and that compensation should be paid for the property of those choosing not to return and for loss of or damage to property which, under principles of international law or equity, should be made good by the Governments or authorities responsible."

country for forced migrants, especially Iraqi and African refugees (Chatelard 2003; Al Majali 2019), and its consequence on the types of assistance provided to them, their living conditions, as well as their prospects for the future, including through resettlement in third countries. These studies have also shed light on the long-term impacts of the Syrian and Iraqi refugees on the UNHCR's policy in the region, on entrepreneurship and on the urban development of Jordan, particularly in Amman (Chatelard 2009). Conversely, the protracted nature of the presence of Iraqi and Syrian refugees in Jordan has spawned a host of academic and policy-making publications documenting the effects of the policies of Jordan and its international partners on their access to the Jordanian territory. They have also highlighted their contribution (mostly informal) to the country's social and economic fabric, which has in some cases resulted in the tacit acceptance by the national authorities of their long-term residence and official status in Jordan, be it as temporary UNHCR-registered refugees, and of their improved access to public services, the labor market and humanitarian assistance (Ababsa 2015; Roussel 2015; Achilli 2015; Doraï 2016; Al Husseini and Napolitano 2019; Betts et al. 2021; Sheldon 2021). Conversely, studies have also pinpointed the hostility voiced by local host communities concerned by the impact of the refugees arrival on the local economy (Kuhnt et al. 2017; Lockhart and Barker 2018; see Ababsa in this volume).

Agency and Settlement Experience: Replacing the Migration Experience Back Center-Stage

Research on Iraqi and Syrian refugees has also tackled new issues that are part of a global trend toward a renewal of forced migration studies, underscoring the agency of the refugees and the linkages between labor migration and sudden conflict-related migration. In this respect, the role of family, social, and religious networks in determining and sustaining the refugees' migratory paths and their settlement process has been emphasized (Chatelard 2003; Lagarde and Doraï 2017; Lagarde 2018; Zuntz 2021), together with the role of refugees in shaping their livelihoods in constrained spaces, such as disadvantaged urban spaces (Peaucelle 2020) and refugee camps (Doraï and Piraud-Fournet 2018; Hart et al. 2018), in the face of modes of humanitarian governance that make increasing use of new coercive technologies, such as iris-scan technology (Hoffmann 2017; Macias 2019). At the stakeholder level, besides the traditional role played by local and international governmental and NGO actors in temporarily sustaining the living conditions of refugees (Hasselbarth 2014; Ababsa and Muhsen 2014; Tobin 2016), contributions have underlined the opportunities and challenges featured in the "Relief-Development nexus," a longer-term approach to forced migration situations promoted by international institutions worldwide, which have crystallized in Jordan around the issue of Syrian refugee inclusion in the labor market (Barbelet et al. 2018; Lenner and Turner 2018). Social transformations, such as marriage practices and gender relationships—including the growing number of faith-based charities initiatives—and the interaction of refugees with the host society command growing attention, especially in a context of prolonged Syrian displacement (Zbeidi 2020; Shanneik 2021; Sidhva et al. 2021).

Against this background, through the study of several migration cases, this volume shows that the actual situation of migrants often lies at (or results from), on the one hand, the intersection of stakeholder policies based on self-defined "national interests"; and on the other hand, their symbolic political significance (in the case of the Palestinian refugees, for instance) and migrants' agency as illustrated by their involvement in the country's economic, political, and social sphere. In all ways, migrants inevitably contribute in the medium to long run in shaping the national agenda, and transforming modes of governance, social practices, and popular imaginaries.

This book presents original empirical research based on a diversity of sources and modalities of investigation. These include the search for archival material and operational documents released by state institutions, international or local assistance institutions, and for the voice of the migrant groups themselves. In addition, the use of maps and architectural representations may also be considered innovative tools for analyzing host policies, space production, and solidarity networks. This volume features three main sections that highlight: firstly, the case-by-case host policies adopted over time by Jordan and humanitarian actors and their consequences on the everyday life of migrants; secondly, the way migration policies materialize in settlement spaces, both camps and urban spaces, and the way migrants themselves contribute to shaping their host environment and leaving their own marks on Jordanian territory; thirdly, the forms of solidarity, collective organization, and humanitarianism among migrants and the host society, showing the activation of historic family, economic, and religious ties, as well as the emergence of new ones.

1. Host Authorities and International Organization Policies

The first part of this volume examines Jordan's host policies of reception and integration of various groups of migrants: Palestinians, who came during the 1948 Arab-Israeli War, and those who left the Gaza Strip following the 1967 Six-Day War (the so-called ex-Gazans) (El Abed 2005; Pérez 2018); Yemeni refugees affected by the war in Yemen since 2015; and Syrians who have fled the war in their country since 2011. It argues that there is no one host policy but that different policies, which inform each other, have been shaped by precise social, economic, and political contingencies. Moreover, this chapter shows the concrete effects of these policies on migratory paths and life conditions, access to services, and to the job market.

Similar to other Middle Eastern host countries, Jordan has traditionally been spared in-depth analysis of its management of migration movements. While human rights groups and academics have underscored its discriminatory policies against migrants, whatever their status, little has been said of the motives underpinning those policies and their evolution caused by international, regional, and local developments (Ali 2021). The host authorities have thus often been handled analytically only as a contextual actor. This may be due to the fact that the attention of observers is primarily drawn to the situation of the refugees and the organizations that assist them. In addition, decision-making processes related to the management of sensitive issues affecting the country's security, such as refugee inflows, are difficult to decipher as they involve a variety of actors, such as the Royal Court, security services, the government, the donor countries, and international aid organizations, all of whom are endowed with responsibilities and powers that are not clearly delineated. Moreover, as refugees or even officials concur, the interpretation and application of legal frameworks has often been inconsistent, adding to the confusion.

The four chapters of this part endeavor, with different methodologies, to clarify the debate about Jordan's migrant management policies. The authors place these policies within their evolving socio-political contexts and highlight the set of normative and bureaucratic labeling tools mobilized by the state apparatus and international organization partners (UNHCR, and UNRWA for Palestine refugees) in order to control migrant populations and institutionalize their legal/humanitarian status, based on perceptions of the effects such populations may have on the host society. Far from being limited to access to humanitarian aid and public services, these tools (from eligibility regulations to narratives emphasizing the difference between nationals, citizens, and foreigners) also aim to instill a "bureaucratic refugee identity" among migrant groups and, more broadly, to impose a line between those who are considered Jordanians and those who are not (Zetter 2007).

In her chapter, Lilian Frost highlights how migration and reception policies may contribute to constraining legal/regulatory frameworks, but can also be the source of claims and forms of citizenship. By tackling the case of Palestinian refugees, her study describes actual non-citizenship and demonstrates its importance in explaining state-society relations. Specifically, she considers non-citizenship through both the input of academic literature on this concept and the Arabic distinctions between political and social citizenship, namely *muwāṭana* and *jinsiyya*. In addition, Frost looks at evidence from Jordan's policies over time toward two non-citizen refugee groups, the ex-Gazans and the Syrian refugees. These case studies highlight the fact that the types of rights the Jordanian government grants to non-citizen protracted refugees reflect by default those offered to its own citizens. They also reveal that, to some extent, lines between citizens and non-citizens may in practice get blurred overtime not without raising internal debates within the Jordanian polity.

Focusing on the "ex-Gazans," Anna Kvittingen and Jalal Al Husseini examine the way the Jordanian polity has legally and administratively governed them since 1967. They show how Jordan's decision to maintain them as non-citizens (contrary to the 1948 refugees) has durably defined them collectively, under the guise of non-assimilation in the name of the preservation of their UN-backed right of return, as a marginalized socioeconomic and political group shuffled between ad hoc regulatory decisions, limited in their access to socioeconomic rights and restricted in their political voice. The fact that such discrimination has been officially predicated on a professed positive discrimination principle aimed at preserving their "right of return" has also effectively contributed to imposing it while stifling the ex-Gazans' voice and UNRWA advocacy efforts. Be that as it may, the chapter also shows that Jordan's apparently principled ex-Gazan policy has also responded to past and/or present challenges perceived as directly threatening the country's stability, including the consolidation of a separate Palestinian national identity in Jordan, and Israel's aggressive policies in the Palestinian Occupied Territories aimed to trigger the displacement of the latter's population towards Jordan.

Solenn Al Majali's chapter tackles the reception policies implemented by the Jordanian government toward Yemeni forced migrants, who currently constitute the third largest UNHCR-registered refugee population in Jordan, in order to decipher the "non-reception" strategy of the state. To do so, she considers the humanitarian treatment of Yemenis as "non-Syrian refugees," as categorized by the UNHCR, and its consequences. Her research shows how the Jordanian government established new conditions to restrict the arrival of Yemenis in the kingdom after 2015. While Jordan led an open-door policy for Yemenis until April 2015, they had thereafter to obtain a visa before arrival, and those already settled in the country without the appropriate documentation have been threatened with deportation. Thus, Yemenis have faced new forms of institutional violence in Jordan due to the non-reception policies they had to deal with because their situation has been made illegal. Through this case study, she highlights how the legal labeling applied by governmental and humanitarian institutions impacts on the social and financial resources of migrants and their everyday life.

David Lagarde and Kamel Doraï reconstruct the path toward Jordan of Syrian street traders who fled the civil war after 2011, analyzing the evolution of migration routes and strategies according to the progressive closure of the borders. They show how family, friend, and professional networks that supported Syrians during the first steps of their migration have been gradually replaced in the context of the locking of borders and the hardening of the Jordanian host policy in 2014. "Weak ties," established with smugglers and local institutional actors more especially, have subsequently played a more relevant role in refugee trajectories and settlement practices.

2. Urban Dynamics, Intermingling, and Space Production

The second part of the book analyzes the effects of host policies in terms of the territorial distribution and settling of migrants in Jordanian territory, and explores the way such policies have contributed to shaping new urban spaces and even entire cities. This "space approach" allows us to observe the interaction between different categories of migrants and the host society according to the degree of integration allowed by the host state. The contributions in this part focus on the creation of camps and urban spaces. For a long time, refugee camps, their evolution and their gradual insertion into urban spaces were the yardstick for understanding migration issues in the Middle East. Over the last twenty years, research on migration has attempted to focus on refugees' spatial footprints within urban spaces, where the majority of them are settled (Sassen 2001; Ridgley 2013; Villazor 2009). Understanding the contribution of migrants to contemporary urban development has thus become a major challenge for the social sciences, both in terms of architectural and cultural legacies and of the investment policies implemented in their settlement spaces. It is within these spaces that social dynamics, reception policies, and co-constructed spaces are studied in the four articles of this section.

Gaspard Vial-Benamra's chapter adopts a historical perspective to address migratory phenomena that predated and followed the formation of the Emirate of Transjordan (1921). The author underlines the role of confessional, kinship, and ethnic networks in the settling strategies of the Chechens in the Late Ottoman Empire, and their role in the development of the city of al-Zarqā' through agricultural development projects, a topic still understudied for this period. He then examines the forms of organization of the Chechen populations, their role within municipal structures, and their interaction with local political powers as they also developed communal and local modes of organization in al-Zarqā' (e.g., schools). Lastly, he reveals the major role of these migrant groups within the emergence of several Jordanian villages and towns during the Mandate period and their place in the state-building process. Within this framework, religious figures and institutions played a central role in maintaining community ties as well as in developing networks with other migrant groups, in al-'Azraq for instance, and with local political representatives.

The issue of strategies for the production and settlement of space is particularly central when dealing with refugee camps. Drawing on Michel Foucault's concept of "bio-power" (1993) and Giorgio Agamben's "state of exception" (2003), refugee camps have been seen as specific places of control and coercion where "undesirable populations" are transferred (Agier 2008). In Jordan, Palestinian camps embody the quintessential refugee experience and their inhabitants have been in the public glare. Scholars have highlighted how the camps have gradually evolved and been integrated within neighboring towns, while remaining a dubious symbol of the plight of Palestinians after 1948 and the preservation of their "right of return" (Destremau 1994; Al Husseini 2011; Berg 2014; Achilli and Oesch 2016). The camp option was not adopted for Iraqi refugees, out of a concern not to encourage their long-term settlement, a choice that hampered fundraising efforts required for the humanitarian response (Turner 2015). In 2012, when faced with the massive arrival of Syrian refugees, the Jordanian authorities decided to set up numerous camps and reception centers in the border region. These spaces became showcases of Jordan's reception policy. Their forms and organization evolved over time, depending on the different actors involved in the construction and administration, and their respective interests, as shown by Ayham Dalal and Aline Fraikin in their chapter. The space lens adopted by the authors offers an unprecedented perspective on Jordanian reception policy, showing how space reflects the labeling of the refugee as a specific social and juridical category. While the Syrians were initially welcomed as guests and initially settled in urban spaces and in small "open" camps and reception centers built within and around towns and villages close to the Syrian border, the formalization of their refugee status went hand in hand with the establishment of "closed" camps. Moreover, these were established in geographically isolated locations in order to ensure that the Syrians are kept away from the labor market.

Also based on the case study of Syrian refugees, Myriam Ababsa's contribution shifts the gaze to urban spaces that have hosted the largest number of Syrian refugees and assesses the impact of housing programs promoted by international organizations in the 'Irbid region. The author discusses the way these programs foster social cohesion between local populations and refugees in a context of pressure on public services and the labor market. Moreover, she shows how housing policies are a part of the developmental turn adopted by Jordan in its response to the refugee crisis and how they shape longer-term urban policies. This approach is also adopted by Héloïse Peaucelle's chapter that sheds light on the way Syrian refugee mobility, ways of living, and social and professional practices have produced new spaces of sociability and urban life in the case of the northern city of ʾIrbid. Tracing the evolution of a neighborhood in south ʾIrbid, she analyzes Syrians' modes of settlement in the city, showing more particularly how refugees concentrated in a district formerly inhabited by students that became known as "Little Darʿā," from the name of the main Syrian city from which they came from. The Syrian presence changed the standing of this neighborhood, causing the departure of Jordanian citizens and international students, and the relocation of businesses to other areas in the east of the city. It is now considered abandoned by the authorities and is marginalized in the city urban development plans.

3. Social Reconfigurations: Solidarity Networks and Humanitarianism

The third part of the volume sheds light on the capacity of refugees to activate and set up, (re)build, and intersect different types of solidarity networks. It considers the forms of ties that unite refugees of different nationalities in Jordan at political, social, religious and family levels. Network analysis of migration developed in the 1990s as a legacy of the Chicago School (Massey et al. 1993; Faist 2000), according to which networks develop when social capital functions, not only on a local scale but also as a transnational transmission system (Shami 1996a). The intersection of the network approach with a transnational perspective makes it possible to understand the strategies of installation, reception and departure in all their complexity, giving full scope to the agency of actors and actresses (Snel et al. 2020). For instance, kinship ties are essential in hosting and providing assistance in the early days of migration. Moreover, using matrimonial strategies can help to (re)establish solidarity links with family members belonging to the host country. They represent means to improve subsistence resources in the host country and to recreate modes of belonging and sociability, as is shown in Ann-Christin Zuntz's chapter. This chapter analyses the migration path of a rural Syrian refugee family, particularly its female members, who found shelter in the north of Jordan. The chapter shows how former circular mobilities in the local farmer circles provided this family with access to transnational support networks, shaping their trajectories and livelihood strategies during their migratory path. Zuntz also provides a much-welcomed perspective on gender dynamics during displacement situations, as she studies how women provide a substantial part of the family income through work in the agriculture sector and marriage strategies.

A second major insight of this section concerns the refugee contribution to assistance and humanitarianism. After 2011, the arrival of hundreds of thousands of Syrian refugees in Lebanon, Turkey, and Jordan has brought the question of hospitality to the forefront (Boudou 2017; Şenoğuz and Carpi 2018; Naïli et al. 2022; Zamam 2016). New civil society actors have emerged, in particular Islamic NGOs, recalling both the importance of assistance within the religious sphere (Ager and Ager 2011) and the emergence of South-South or even South-North dynamics and models, which have been added to, and sometimes supplanted, the more classic and long-standing North-South humanitarian dynamics (Fiddian-Qasmyieh 2016). Moreover, during the last decade one of the major inputs in migration studies has consisted in the growing acknowledgment of refugee agency. An increasing number of studies have pointed out the ways in which refugees not only live displacement, but also their own responses to it (Fiddian-Qasmyieh 2020). This includes the individual's capacity to mobilize resources during their journey and to develop economic livelihood strategies (Jacobsen 2006), installation practices, and home-making (Hart, Paszkiewicz, and Albadra 2018; Dalal 2023). On a collective level, refugees also exhibit solidarity and support within their own community and toward other migrants and displaced communities (Fiddian-Qasmiyeh 2016, Pincock et al. 2020).

Extending this literature, Valentina Napolitano shows that a number of associations and humanitarian organizations have been founded by Syrians to help other needy refugee Syrians. In this case, the existence of Syrian migrant networks before 2011, mainly of students and political opponents who arrived in Jordan in the 1980s, has represented a key resource in organizing local responses to the arrival of refugees as a consequence of the war, given the limitations on refugee activism and forms of independent assembly imposed by the Jordanian authorities. The author also highlights how these initiatives allow Syrians with different migratory paths to gather together and provide alternative opportunities of involvement and employment for educated refugees who have limited access to the formal labor market.

Religious belonging can be a shaping factor of refugee solidarities and forms of gathering, as is the case for Christian Iraqi migrants studied by Norig Neveu through the lens of faith-based charities in Jordan and Christian clerical transnational networks. Since 2014, in response to an official call by King Abdullah II to take refuge in Jordan, thousands of Christian Iraqi refugees have settled in the country where previous waves of Iraqis had already migrated since the 1990s and especially after 2006. The author shows how different initiatives have been launched by priests and confessional charities, not only to provide basic services to needy refugees, but also to prepare them either for resettlement in North America, Australia and Europe or, alternatively, for their establishment in Jordan or for their return to Iraq. The chapter also lays stress on the strategies developed by priests to establish local reception policies informed by former migration experiences, and based on religious and associative networks. In so doing, it reveals the strategies used by faith-based charities to adapt to local realities and the ways in which their representatives have managed to establish themselves as key local interlocutors of international organizations.

The fourth contribution in this final section shows that migration can also produce, in the short or longer-term, new spaces of social mixing, sociability and solidarity, where refugees of different origins and citizens of the host country come together. This is the case of the youth associations and cultural spaces founded in Amman in recent years and studied by Oroub El Abed, Zoë Jordan, and Yasmeen Shahzadeh. By providing social activities and services in the fields of education, employment and culture, these youth organizations aim to give voice to the needs and aspirations of young people in a context where they face difficult access to such services. They represent spaces where young people, refugees and Jordanian citizens can develop and build long-term projects in the host country, including spaces for intellectual development. Their analysis offers the opportunity, through the study of the profile of the creators of these structures, to understand how different waves of migration contribute to the genealogy of local assistance projects for migrants.

Bibliography

Ababsa, Myriam (2015), "De la crise humanitaire à la crise sécuritaire. Les dispositifs de contrôle des réfugiés syriens en Jordanie (2011–2015)," *Revue européenne des migrations internationales*, 31 (3–4): 73–101.

Ababsa, Myrian, and Mamoon Muhsen (2014), "Gulf Donors and NGOs Assistance to Syrian Refugees in Jordan," *UNHCR Gulf Report*. Available online: http://data.unhcr.org/syrianrefugees/country.php?id=107/.

Abu Odeh, Adnan (1999), *Jordanians, Palestinians and the Hashemite Kingdom in the Middle East Peace Process*, Washington, DC: US Institute of Peace Press.

Achilli, Luigi (2015), *Palestinian Refugee and Identity: Nationalism, Politics and the Everyday*, London: I.B. Tauris.

Achilli, Luigi, and Lucas Oesch (2016), "Des espaces d'ambiguïté: les camps de réfugiés palestiniens en Jordanie," *A Contrario*, 23 (2): 17–36.

Agamben, Giorgio (2003), *Homo sacer*, Paris: Éditions Seuil.

Ager, Alastair, and Joey Ager (2011), "Faith and the Discourse of Secular Humanitarianism," *Journal of Refugee Studies*, 24 (3): 456–72.

Agier, Michel (2008), *Gérer les indésirables*, Paris: Flammarion.

Akoka, Karen (2016), "Crise des réfugiés, ou des politiques d'asile?," *La vie des idées*. Available online: https://laviedesidees.fr/Crise-des-refugies-ou-des-politiques-d-asile.html.

Al Husseini, Jalal (2000), "UNRWA and the Palestinian Nation-Building Process," *Journal of Palestine Studies*, 114 (2): 51–64.

Al Husseini, Jalal (2011), "The Evolution of the Palestinian Refugee Camps in Jordan: Between Logics of Exclusion and Integration," in Myriam Ababsa and Rami Daher (eds.), *Cities, Urban Practices and Nation Building in Jordan*, 181–204, Beirut: Ifpo.

Al Husseini, Jalal, and Riccardo Bocco (2009), "The Status of the Palestinian Refugees in the Near East: The Right of Return and UNRWA in Perspective," *Refugee Survey Quarterly*, 28 (2–3): 260–85.

Al Husseini, Jalal, and Napolitano Valentina (2019), "La politique jordanienne à l'égard des réfugiés syriens: entre hospitalité et protection des intérêts nationaux," *Confluences Méditerranée*, 3 (110): 127–42.

Ali, Ali (2021), "Disaggregating Jordan's Syrian Refugee Response: The 'Many Hands' of the Jordanian State," *Mediterranean Politics*. Available online: https://doi.org/10.1080/13629395.2021.1922969.

Al Majali, Solenn (2019), "Interactions et altérités des réfugiés subsahariens en Jordanie," *Civilisations*, 68: 95–115.

Al Majali, Solenn (2020), "L'intégration des réfugiés subsahariens à Amman (Jordanie)," in Wissal Anir, Hassan Faouzi, and Mohamed Khachani (eds.), *Migrations, représentations sociales et stéréotypes*, 263–71, Paris: L'Harmattan.
Anderson, Betty (2005), *Nationalist Voices in Jordan: The Street and the State*, Austin: University of Texas Press.
Babar, Zahra (ed.) (2020), *Mobility and Forced Displacement in the Middle East*, London: Hurst & Co.
Barbelet, Veronique, Jessica Hagen-Zanker, and Dina Mansour-Ille (2018), *The Jordan Compact – Lessons Learnt and Implications for Future Refugee Compacts*, Policy-briefing, ODI.
Basch, Linda, Nina Glick Schiller, and Cristina Szanton Blanc (eds.) (1994), *Nations Unbound: Transnational Projects, Postcolonial Predicaments, and Deterritorialized Nation-States*, Switzerland: Gordon and Breach.
Berg, Kjersti (2014), "From Chaos to Order and Back: The Construction of UNRWA Shelters and Camps, 1950–1970," in Sari Hanafi, Leila Hilal, and Lex Takkenberg (eds.), *UNRWA and Palestinian Refugees: From Relief and Works to Human Development*, 109–28, London: Routledge.
Betts, Alexander, Ali Ali, and Memişoğlu Fulya (2021), *Local Politics and the Syrian Refugee Crisis*, Oxford: University of Oxford Refugee Studies Centre.
Bontemps, Véronique, Showra Makaremi, and Sarah Mazouz (eds.) (2018), *Babels, Entre accueil et rejet: ce que les villes font aux migrants*, Lyon: Le Passager clandestin, coll. Bibliothèque des frontières.
Boudou, Benjamin (2017), *Politiques de l'hospitalité*, Paris: CNRS Editions.
Brand, Laurie (1995), "Palestinian and Jordanians: A Crisis of Identity," *Journal of Palestine Studies*, 24 (4): 46–61.
Brun, Catherine (2001), "Reterritorializing the Relationship Between People and Place in Refugee Studies," *Geografiska Annaler: Series B, Human Geography*, 83 (1): 15–25.
Canefe, Nergis (2017), *States of Exile: Rethinking Forced Migration in Contemporary Middle East*. Available online: https://www.academia.edu/33435814/States_of_Exile_Rethinking_Forced_Migration_in_Contemporary_Middle_East.
Carmel, Emma, Lenner Katharina, and Paul Regine (2021), "The Governance and Politics of Migration: A Conceptual-Analytical Map," in Emma Carmel, Katharina Lenner, and Regine Paul (eds.), *Handbook on the Governance and Politics of Migration*, 1–23, London: Elgar.
Castles, Stephan, Hein De Haas, and Mark Miller (2020), *The Age of Migration. International Population Movements in the Modern World*, New York: The Guilford Press.
Chatty, Dawn (2010), *Displacement and Dispossession in the Modern Middle East*, Cambridge: Cambridge University Press.
Chatty, Dawn (2018), *Syria: The Making and Unmaking of a Refugee State*, Oxford: Oxford University Press.
Chatelard, Geraldine (2003), "Iraqi Forced Migrants in Jordan: Conditions, Religious Networks, and the Smuggling Process," paper presented at the Wider Conference on Poverty, International Migration and Asylum, September 27–28, 2002, Helsinki.
Chatelard, Geraldine (2008), "Jordan's Transient Iraqi Guests: Transnational Dynamics and National Agenda," in *Viewpoints*, Special Issue, *Iraq's refugee and IDP crisis: Human toll and implications*, online Middle East Institute, Washington, DC.
Chatelard, Géraldine (2009), *Migration from Iraq between the Gulf and the Iraq wars (1990-2003): Historical and Sociospatial Dimensions*, Centre on Migration, Policy and Society Working Paper No. 68, University of Oxford.

Chatelard, Geraldine (2010a), "Cross-Border Mobility of Iraqi Refugees", *Forced Migration Review*, Special Issue *Adapting to Urban Displacement*, 34: 60–1.
Chatelard, Geraldine (2010b), "What Visibility Conceals. Re-embedding Refugee Migration from Iraq," in Dawn Chatty and Bill Finlayson (eds.), *Dispossession and Displacement: Forced Migration in the Middle East and North Africa*, 17–44, New York: Oxford University Press.
Chatelard, Geraldine (2010c), "Jordan: A Refugee Haven," *Migration Information Source*. Available online: http://www.migrationinformation.org/Feature/display.cfm?id=236.
Chatelard, Geraldine, and Kamel Doraï (2011), "Les Irakiens en Syrie et en Jordanie: régimes d'entrée et de séjour et effets sur les configurations migratoires," *CERISCOPE Frontières*. Available online: http://ceriscope.sciences-po.fr/content/part2/les-irakiens-en-syrie-et-en-jordanie.
Chiffoleau, Sylvia (2015), *Le voyage à La Mecque. Un pèlerinage mondial en terre d'Islam*, Paris: Belin.
Cuison Villazor, Rose (2009), "'Sanctuary Cities' and Local Citizenship," *Fordham Urban Law Journal*, 37 (2): 573–98.
Cohen, Daniel (2012), *In War's Wake: Europe"s Displaced Persons in the Postwar Order*, New York: Oxford University Press.
Crawley, Heaven, and Katherine Jones (2021), "Beyond Here and There: (re) Conceptualising Migrant Journeys and the 'In-between'," *Journal of Ethnic and Migration Studies*, 47 (14): 3226–42.
Crawley, Heaven, and Dimitris Skleparis (2018), "Refugees, Migrants, Neither, Both: Categorical Fetishism and the Politics of Bounding in Europe's 'Migration Crisis'," *Journal of Ethnic and Migration Studies*, 44 (1): 48–64.
Dalal, Ayham (2023), *From Shelters to Dwellings: The Zaatari Refugee Camp*, Bielefeld: Transcript Verlag.
Davis, Rochelle, Abbie Taylor, Will Todman, and Emma Murphy (2016), "Sudanese and Somali Refugees in Jordan: Hierarchies of Aid in Protracted Displacement Crises," *Middle East Report*, 279: 2–10.
De Bel-Air, Françoise (2003), *Population, politique et politiques de population en Jordanie, 1948–1998*, Doctoral thesis in Demography and Social Sciences under the supervision of Philippe Fargues, Paris: EHESS.
De Bel-Air, Françoise (2006), *Migration and Politics in the Middle East. Migration Policies, Nation Building and International Relations*, Beirut: Ifpo.
Destremau, Blandine (1994), "L' espace du camp et la reproduction du provisoire: les camps de réfugiés palestiniens de Wihdat et de Jabal Hussein à Amman," in Riccardo Bocco and Mohammad-Reza Djalili (eds.), *Moyen-Orient: Migrations, démocratisations, médiations*, 83–98, Paris: PUF.
Doraï, Kamel (2014), "State, Migrations and Border"s Fabric in the Middle East," *Fontrera Norte*, 26 (3): 119–39.
Doraï, Kamel (2016), "La Jordanie et les réfugiés syriens," *La Vie des idées*. Available online: https://laviedesidees.fr/La-Jordanie-et-les-refugies-syriens.html.
Doraï, Kamel, and Pauline Piraud-Fournet (2018), "From Tent to Makeshift Housing," in Mona Fawaz, Ahmed Gharbieh, Mona Harb, and Dounia Salamé (eds.), *Refugees as City-Makers*, 136–9, Beirut: AUB Issam Fares Institute (IFI) Social Justice and the City Publication.
El Abed, Oroub (2005), "Immobile Palestinians: The Impact of Policies and Practices on Palestinians from Gaza in Jordan," in Hana Jaber and Françoise Métral (eds.), *Mondes en mouvements. Migrants au Moyen-Orient au tournant du XXIe siècle*, 81–92, Beirut: Ifpo.

El Abed, Oroub (2014), "The Discourse of Guesthood: Forced Migrants in Jordan," in Anita Fabos and Riina Isotalo (eds.), *Managing Muslim Mobilities. Religion and Global Migrations*, 82–100, New York: Palgrave Macmillan.

Erdal, Marta Bivand, and Ceri Oeppen (2018), "Forced to Leave? The Discursive and Analytical Significance of Describing Migration as Forced and Voluntary," *Journal of Ethnic and Migration Studies*, 44 (6): 981–98.

Faist, Thomas (2000), *The Volume and Dynamics of International Migration and Transnational Social Spaces*, Oxford: Oxford University Press.

Fawaz, Mona, Carla El-Hage, and Mona Harb (2021), *Spatial Patterns, Gray Spacing and Planning Policy Implications: The Urbanization of Forced Population Displacement in Lebanon*, London: Routledge.

Fawaz, Mona, Ahmad Gharbieh, Mona Harb, and Dounia Salamé (eds.) (2018), *Refugees as City-Makers*, Beirut: AUB Issam Fares Institute (IFI) Social Justice and the City Publication.

Fiddian-Qasmiyeh, Elena (2016), "Refugees Hosting Refugees: Local Communities: First and Last Providers of Protection," *Forced Migration Review*, 53: 25–7.

Fiddian-Qasmiyeh, Elena (ed.) (2020), *Refuge in a Moving World. Tracing Refugee and Migrant Journeys Across Disciplines*, London: UCL Press.

Fiddian-Qasmiyeh, Elena, Gil Loescher, Katy Long, and Sigona Nando (eds.) (2014), *The Oxford Handbook of Migration and Refugee Studies*, Oxford: Oxford University Press.

Foucault, Michel (1993), *Surveiller et punir*, Paris: Gallimard.

Francesca, Biancani, and Rioli Maria Chiara (2023), "Special Issue: UNRWA Archives (Part 1)," *Jerusalem Quarterly*, 93: 6–13.

Gandolfo, Luisa (2012), *Palestinians in Jordan: The Politics of Identity*, London: Bloomsbury Academic.

Hamed-Troyansky, Vladimir (2017), "Circassian Refugees and the Making of Amman, 1878–1914," *International Journal of Middle East Studies*, 49 (4): 605–23.

Hanafi, Sari, Leila Hilal, and Lex Takkenberg (eds.) (2014), *UNRWA and Palestinian Refugees: From Relief and Works to Human Development*, London: Routledge.

Hart, Jason, Natalia Paszkiewicz, and Dima Albadra (2018), "Shelter as Home: Syrian Home-making in Jordanian Refugee Camps," *Human Organization*, 77 (4): 371–80.

Hasselbarth, Sarah (2014), *Islamic Charities in the Syrian Context in Jordan and Lebanon*. Available online: https://library.fes.de/pdf-files/bueros/beirut/10620.pdf.

Hatziprokopiou, Panos, Yannis Frangopoulos, and Nicola Montagna (2016), "Migration and the City," *City*, 20 (1): 52–60.

Hoffmann, Sophia (2017), "Humanitarian Security in Jordan's Azraq Camp," *Security Dialogue*, 48 (2): 97–112.

Jacobsen, Karen (2006), "Editorial Introduction. Refugees and Asylum Seekers in Urban Areas: A Livelihood Perspective," *Journal of Refugee Studies*, 19 (3): 273–86.

Kagan, Michael (2009), "The (Relative) Decline of Palestinian Exceptionalism and Its Consequences for Refugee Studies in the Middle East," *Journal of Refugee Studies*, 22 (4): 417–38.

Kozma, Liat, Schayegh Cyrus, and Wishnitzer Avner (eds.) (2014), *A Global Middle East: Mobility, Materiality and Culture in the Modern Age, 1880–1940*, London: I.B. Tauris.

Kuhnt, Jana, Ramona Rischke, Anda David, and Tobias Lechtenfeld (2017), *Social Cohesion in Times of Forced Displacement - The Case of Young People in Jordan*, Econstor, Discussion paper 243.

Lagarde, David (2018), "Prélude. De Damas à Dortmund: le Parcours d'une famille syrienne," in Véronique Bontemps, Showra Makaremi, and Sarah Mazouz (eds.), *Entre accueil et rejet : ce que les villes font aux migrants*, 7–10, Paris: Le passager clandestin.

Lagarde, David, and Doraï Kamel (2017), "De la campagne syrienne aux villes jordaniennes. Un réseau marchand transfrontalier à l'épreuve du conflit syrien," *Espace, Populations, Sociétés*. Available online: http://journals.openedition.org.inshs.bib.cnrs.fr/eps/7212; https://doi-org.inshs.bib.cnrs.fr/10.4000/eps.7212.

Latte Abdallah, Stéphanie (2006), *Femmes réfugiées palestiniennes*, Paris: PUF.

Lenner, Katharina, and Lewis Turner (2018), "Making Refugees Work? The Politics of Integrating Syrian Refugees into the Labor Market in Jordan," *Middle East Critique*, 28: 1–31.

Lockhart, Dorsey, and Katrina Barker (2018), *Syrian Refugees and Social Cohesion in Jordan*, Amman: West Asia-North Africa Institute (WANA).

Loescher, Gil, and Betts Alexander (2011), *Refugees in International Relations*, Oxford: Oxford University Press.

Malkki, Liisa (1995), *Purity and Exile: Violence, Memory and National Cosmology Among Hutu Refugees in Tanzania*, Chicago: University of Chicago Press.

Macias, Léa (2019), "Entre contrôle et protection: ce que les technologies de l'information et de la communication font au camp de réfugiés," *Communications*, 2019/1 (n°104): 107–17.

Mainwaring, Cetta, and Noelle Brigden (2016), "Beyond the Border: Clandestine Migration Journeys," *Geopolitics*, 21 (2): 243–62.

Massad, Joseph (2008), "Producing the Palestinian as Other Jordan and the Palestinians," in Roger Heacock (ed.), *Temps et espace en Palestine: flux et résistances identitaires*, 273–92, Beirut: Ifpo.

Massey, Douglas, Arango Joaquin, and Hugo Graeme (1993), "Theories of International Migration: A Review and Appraisal," *Population and Development Review*, 19 (3): 431–66.

Naïli, Falestin, Valentina Napolitano, and Pauline Piraud-Fournet (2022), "Introduction: Charity, Relief and Humanitarianism as a Means of Maintaining Social and Political Stability in the Middle East. A Longue Durée Analysis of Actors, Categories and Practices," *Endowment Studies*, 6 (1–2): 1–31.

Neveu, Norig (2023), "The Palestinian Refugees, Christian Humanitarianism, and the Remaking of the Melkite Church in Jordan," *BRISMES*. Available online: https://www.tandfonline.com/doi/full/10.1080/13530194.2023.2233220.

Noiriel, Gérard (1997), "Représentation nationale et catégories sociales. L'exemple des réfugiés politiques," *Genèses*, 26 (1): 25–54.

Ohannessian-Charpin, Anna (2007), "Les Arméniennes de Ma'ân, entre oubli et mémoire," in Raymond Kévorkian, Lévon Nordiguian, and Vahé Tachjian (eds.), *Les Arméniens 1917–1939, La quête d'un refuge*, 241–54, Beirut: Presse de l'Université de Saint Joseph.

Peaucelle, Héloïse (2020), "La présence syrienne à Irbid (2). Transformations paysagères et migrations," *Les carnets de l'Ifpo. La recherche en train de se faire à l'Institut français du Proche-Orient*. Available online: https://ifpo.hypotheses.org/10821, September 7, 2020. hypotheses.org.

Pincock, Kate, Alexander Betts, and Evan Easton-Calabria (2020), *The Global Governed? Refugees as Providers of Protection and Assistance*, Cambridge: Cambridge University Press.

Pérez, Michael Vicente (2018), "The Everyday as Survival among Ex-Gaza Refugees in Jordan," *Middle East Critique*, 27 (3): 275–88.

Ridgley, Jennifer (2013), "Cities of Refuge. Immigration Enforcement, Police, and the Insurgent Genealogies of Citizenship in US Sanctuary Cities," *Urban Geography*, 29 (1): 53–77.

Rioli, Maria Chiara (2020), *A Liminal Church: Refugees, Conversions and the Latin Diocese of Jerusalem, 1946–1956*, Leiden: Brill.

Roussel, Cyril (2015), "La frontière syro-jordanienne dans le conflit syrien: enjeux sécuritaires, gestion frontalière," *L'Espace Politique*, 27 (27). http://journals.openedition.org.inshs.bib.cnrs.fr/espacepolitique/3658.

Sassen, Saskia (2001), *The Global City. New York, London, Tokyo*, Princeton: Princeton University Press.

Schapendonk, Joris, and Griet Steel (2014), "Following Migrant Trajectories: The Im/Mobility of Sub-Saharan Africans En Route to European Union," *Annals of the Association of American Geographers*, 104 (2): 262–70.

Şenoğuz, Pınar, and Estella Carpi (2018), "Refugee Hospitality in Lebanon and Turkey. On Making 'the Other'," *International Migration*, 57 (2): 126–42.

Shami, Seterney (1996a), "Transnationalism and Refugee Studies: Rethinking Forced Migration and Identity in the Middle East," *Journal of Refugee Studies*, 9 (1): 3–26.

Shami, Seterney (1996b), "The Circassians of Amman. Historical Narratives, Urban Dwelling and the Construction of Identity," in Jean Hannoyer and Seteney Shami (eds.), *Amman, Ville et Société*, 303–22, Beirut: CERMOC.

Shami, Seteney (2009), "Historical Processes of Identity Formation: Displacement, Settlement, and Self-Representations of the Circassians in Jordan," *Iran and the Caucasus*, 13 (1): 141–59.

Shanneik, Yafa (2021), "Displacement, Humanitarian Interventions and Gender Rights in the Middle East: Syrian Refugees in Jordan as a Case Study," *Journal of Ethnic and Migration Studies*, 47 (15): 3329–44.

Sheldon, Zachary (2021), "Nationality, Class, and Iraqi Migrants in Jordan," *ACOR*. Available online: https://acorjordan.org/2018/01/02/nationality-class-iraqi-migrants-jordan/.

Sidhva, Dina, Ann-Christin Zuntz, Ruba al Akash, Ayat Nashwan, and Areej Al-Majali (2012), "In Exile, the Woman Became Everything," *Journal of Humanitarian Affairs*, 3 (1): 4–15.

Snel, Erik, Özge Bilgili, and Richard Staring (2021), "Migration Trajectories and Transnational Support within and beyond Europe," *Journal of Ethnic and Migration Studies*, 47 (14): 3209–25.

Stepputat, Finn, and Ninna Nyberg Sørensen (2014), "Sociology and Forced Migrations," in Elena Fiddian-Qasmiyeh, Gil Loescher, Katy Long, and Nando Sigona (eds.), *The Oxford Handbook of Refugee and Forced Migration Studies*, 86–99, Oxford: Oxford University Press.

Tejel, Jordi, and Ramazan Oztan (eds.) (2020), "The Special Issue 'Forced Migration and Refugeedom in the Modern Middle East' Towards Connected Histories of Refugeedom in the Middle East," *Journal of Migration History*, 6 (1): 1–15.

Tobin, Sarah (2016), *Everyday Piety: Islam and Economy in Jordan*, London: Cornell University Press.

Triandafyllidou, Anna (2017), "Beyond Irregular Migration Governance: Zooming in on Migrants' Agency," *European Journal of Migration and Law*, 19 (1): 1–11.

Turner, Lewis (2015), "Explaining the (Non-)Encampment of Syrian Refugees: Security, Class and the Labour Market in Lebanon and Jordan," *Mediterranean Politics*, 20 (3): 386–404.

Van Liempt, Ilse, and Jeroen Doomernik (2006), "Migrant's Agency in the Smuggling Process: The Perspectives of Smuggled Migrants in the Netherlands," *International Migration*, 44 (4): 165–90.

Vogt, Wendy A. (2018), *Lives in Transit. Violence and Intimacy on the Migrant Journey*, Oakland: University of California Press.

Waldinger, Roger (2006), "'Le 'transnationalisme' des immigrants et présence du passé," *Revue européenne des migrations internationales*, 22 (2): 23–41.

Zamam, Tahir (2016), *Islamic Traditions of Refuge in the Crises of Iraq and Syria*, London: Palgrave MacMillan.

Zaiotti, Ruben (2006), "Dealing with Non-palestinian Refugees in the Middle East: Policies and Practices in an Uncertain Environment," *International Journal of Refugee Law*, 18 (2): 333–53.

Zetter, Roger (2007), "More Labels, Fewer Refugees: Remaking the Refugee Label in an Era of Globalization," *Journal of Refugee Studies*, 20 (2): 172–92.

Zuntz, Ann-Christin (2021), "'Refugees' Transnational Livelihoods and Remittances: Syrian Mobilities in the Middle East Before and After 2011," *Journal of Refugee Studies*, 34 (2): 1400–22.

Zbeidy, Dina (2020), "Marriage, Displacement and Refugee Futures: Marriage as Aspiration among Syrian Refugees in Jordan," *Etnofoor*, 32 (1): 61–76.

Part 1

Host Authorities and International Organization Policies

1

Beyond Citizenship

Unpacking Jordan's Relationship with Palestinian Protracted Refugees

Lillian Frost

Jordan hosts the world's most refugees per capita (UNHCR 2019a).[1] As of 2019, these refugees include 747,080 refugees registered with the Office of the United Nations High Commissioner for Refugees (UNHCR), including 656,512 Syrian, 67,286 Iraqi, 14,703 Yemeni, and 6,126 Sudanese refugees (UNHCR 2019b). These more recent groups add to the 2.2 million Palestinian refugees Jordan started hosting after the 1948 and 1967 wars. These Palestinians are registered with the United Nations Relief and Works Agency for Palestine Refugees in the Near East (UNRWA 2019).[2]

Registered refugees constitute 30 percent of Jordan's population (World Bank 2019),[3] and nearly all these refugees are protracted. The United Nations (UN) defines a protracted refugee group (PRG) as a group of refugees from the same nation living in the same host country for at least five years without immediate prospects for a durable solution (Loescher and Milner 2006). Durable solutions include repatriation to the refugee group's home country, resettlement to a third country (e.g., Germany), and full local integration in the group's host country (e.g., Jordan).

While in a protracted refugee situation, a PRG interacts with their host state, and this host state must decide how to treat that PRG. This is particularly the case because, unlike economic migrants, host countries cannot deport PRGs legally. However, host states do have control over the sets of rights and legal statuses they offer to a PRG. For example, host states can enable a PRG to nationalize, or host states can block a PRG from nationalizing indefinitely.[4]

1 Note that, unlike this UNHCR report, I include the UNRWA Palestinians in Jordan's total refugee population. As such, Jordan hosts a total of 2,989,659 registered refugees.

2 Jordan is the largest per capita host of refugees when considering the Palestinians registered with UNRWA. UNHCR typically does not factor UNRWA figures into its totals.

3 Jordan's total population (including refugees and all other residents), according to the November 2019 World Bank estimates, is 9,956,011.

4 For refugees registered with UNHCR, receiving legal citizen status constitutes full local integration and ends that person's refugee status. However, this is not the case for Palestinian refugees

The dividing line between which PRGs receives access to legal citizen status in a host country often depends heavily on when the group arrived and the political context surrounding that arrival. For example, in Jordan, all Palestinian refugees who arrived after the 1948 War could obtain Jordanian nationality. However, after the 1967 War, not all Palestinian refugees had access to Jordanian nationality. Specifically, Palestinians from Gaza who arrived on Jordan's East Bank in 1967 could not obtain nationality. However, Palestinians who came to the East from the West Bank maintained their Jordanian nationality, despite Jordan losing control over the West Bank.

This divergent treatment of refugees coming from the same nation highlights how contingent access to legal citizen status is. Although decisions about who can become a citizen are linked to nation- and state-building processes, these initial decisions can block a PRG from accessing legal citizen status in the long term. At the same time, PRGs can remain in host states for decades. During this protracted stay, regardless of access to nationality, PRGs can acquire both formal and informal rights, as well as a sense of belonging in their host states.

This chapter asks how we can describe the relationship between host states and their PRGs. Jordan is not alone in hosting PRGs. As of 2016, UN data reveal that 74 percent of all refugees are protracted, living in fifty-one host states (UNHCR 2016).[5] In addition, the number of protracted refugees and PRG host states has been increasing. For example, in 1993, only 59 percent of all refugees were protracted, living in thirty-one host states. This trend means that refugees are spending more time in host states, often without access to legal citizen status in that host state.

This chapter uses citizenship as a framework for analyzing the relationship between a PRG and its host state. In doing so, this chapter provides a more comprehensive definition of citizenship that goes beyond legal citizen status and includes the sets of rights and feelings of belonging groups have with a state. This analysis builds on Arabic distinctions between *muwāṭana* (citizenship) and *jinsiyya* (nationality) to break down citizenship into four components. The analysis also uses original interview data from Jordan to unpack these different dimensions of citizenship as well as the tensions between them. Overall, this analysis uses rich empirical data from Jordan to demonstrate how PRGs can challenge traditional boundaries of state citizenship and operate as citizens, regardless of their legal status.

1. Pushing the Boundaries of Citizenship: The State and the Rights of All Residents

Citizenship is the relationship between a state and its citizens and non-citizen residents (Frost and Shteiwi 2018), as designated by the statuses, rights, and loyalties established

registered with UNRWA. These PRGs can receive legal citizen status and maintain their registration as Palestinian refugees.

5 If we add the UNRWA Palestinian refugees to these calculations, 78 percent of the world's refugees are in a protracted refugee situation and the average duration of a protracted refugee situation would increase substantially, given that most Palestinians have been displaced for 50–70 years.

between the state and a group.[6] This definition breaks down citizenship into four main areas: (1) legal status, (2) de jure rights, (3) de facto rights, and (4) senses of belonging to a state.[7] The first two represent legal categories that are often clear-cut, and the second two indicate practiced categories that are typically difficult to identify and measure.

Specifically, nationality is a dimension of citizenship and describes access to legal citizen status (Ebright 2018). De jure and de facto rights include a group's civil, political, social, and economic rights. De jure rights refer to the formal laws stipulating a group's rights, which states typically specify in constitutions, laws, and international agreements. De facto rights describe the implementation of these de jure rights in practice.

Governments may specify de facto rights in administrative decisions, instructions, or regulations that officials distribute to relevant agencies. In this form, de facto rights qualify as a lower level of law, but they are distinct from the de jure laws discussed here because the state can conceal them from the public and change them without public notice. De facto rights may not materialize until someone tries to access a legal right or enters a government office. As such, in addition to the affected individuals, bureaucrats, development workers, journalists, and activists can provide accounts of that group's rights in practice.

Both de jure and de facto rights can vary over time and across groups. In addition, rights can reflect legal status divides clearly, e.g., when only those with nationality can vote, or rights can blur this dividing line, e.g., when all residents, regardless of nationality, have access to public grade schools. Likewise, senses of belonging in or to a state can emerge among residents with and without nationality. Further, those with and without nationality may also not feel like they belong or have loyalty to a state.

This four-pronged approach aims to unite and expand the vast citizenship literature, where studies tend to focus on only one aspect of citizenship. These aspects include citizenship as *identity and beliefs*, particularly liberal beliefs (Kymlicka 2011; Joppe 1999), as an *activity* or *participatory practice* (Tully 2001) and as *acts* that shift established practices and represent claims to new rights (Isin and Nielsen 2008). Others associate citizenship with certain *sets of rights* (Marshall 1950) or *legal statuses* (Howard 2006). Still others view citizenship as a *contract*, representing a form of resource distribution (Butenshøn 2000), certificate regulating state-society relations (Davis 2000) or a social practice (Ong 1996).

This more nuanced definition of citizenship also builds on the historic trajectory of changes in "who" citizenship includes. Specifically, conceptualizing citizenship as including residents with and without nationality is one shift of many over time and place. For example, in ancient Greece, citizenship concerned only arms-bearers who could defend the territory, and in the Roman Empire, citizenship applied only to property owners. For much of history, citizenship also only applied to free men, as opposed to women, children, and slaves. Further, colonial holdings applied

6 Although I examine citizenship at the group level, individuals can co-exist in different groups, leading to complex and heterogeneous forms of citizenship at the individual level.

7 *Jinsiyya* describes legal status, while different forms of *muwāṭana* reflect the other three dimensions.

citizenship only to the Caucasian Europeans residing in those colonies (Shafir 1998: 1-30).

In addition, this definition defends and includes the rights of residents without nationality. This comprehensive view helps to expand the boundaries of citizenship studies by offering a conceptual tool with which to "examine the gray areas of citizenship" (Chung 2017: 448). These gray areas include "precarious" citizenship forms, where people "inhabit ad hoc and temporary legal statuses for protracted periods" (Lori 2017: 744).

Methods and Case Selection

Jordan provides a particularly clear and sustained example of these four different dimensions of citizenship. Specifically, despite the textual consistency over time in the constitution's treatment of nationality, in practice, debates over "who" is Jordanian have fluctuated and often occupied a prominent position in public discourse. This makes Jordan an ideal site to unpack these discrepancies between citizenship as legal status, de jure rights, de facto rights, and senses of belonging.

This chapter unpacks these four main dimensions of citizenship by assessing the tensions between them. To do so, this analysis draws in part from archival files I compiled on Jordan's internal politics from 1946 to 1973 from the British and US National Archives. The analysis also draws from 200 interviews with over 150 individuals that I conducted in Jordan from 2016 to 2019 with a wide variety of people, from prime ministers, ministers of interior, and ministers of foreign affairs to registered refugees and non-citizen children of Jordanian mothers and non-Jordanian fathers. These interviews primarily took place in Amman, but some occurred in 'Irbid, Jerash, al-Mafraq, al-Zarqā', and al-Balqā'. I note when interviews did not take place in Amman; otherwise, where no location is noted, the interview occurred in Amman.

I used snowball sampling techniques, where current interviewees recommended and connected me to new interviewees. Most interviewees chose to conduct the interview in English, but roughly a third selected Arabic. I conducted all interviews, but for some interviews conducted in an Arabic dialect (versus Modern Standard Arabic), I brought along a research assistant to help translate. I de-identified my interviewees to protect their anonymity. As such, I describe them with as much information as possible to contextualize their position and expertise without providing enough information to specify the exact person.

2. History of Citizenship in Jordan

Jordan gained independence in 1946 as the Hashemite Kingdom of Transjordan from the British, after being under Mandate since 1921 (as the Emirate of Transjordan). The British designated Emir Abdullah—the second son of Sharīf Husayn bin ʿAlī, the leader who led the Arab Revolt against the Ottomans—as the head of Jordan, which comprised the territory east of the Jordan River, now referred to as the East Bank (Salibi 1998).

Jordan's population skyrocketed in 1948 and 1949, following the First Arab-Israeli War. This war led to Jordan's annexation of the West Bank and brought a flood of refugees into both the East and West Banks. Altogether, these demographic shifts increased Jordan's population by about 900,000 Palestinians (Brand 1988). The state welcomed these refugees with the 1949 addendum to the 1928 Law of Nationality, which granted equal citizenship to all people holding "Palestinian nationality" and residing in "Transjordan or the Western Territory administered by the Hashemite Kingdom of Jordan" in 1949 (Frost 2022).

A public referendum, under Emir Abdullah, followed these legal changes in 1950 and created the union of the East and West Banks as the Hashemite Kingdom of Jordan. This union institutionalized equal rights as Jordanian citizens for everyone living on both banks, including Jordanians of Transjordanian and Palestinian descent (Abu Odeh 1999). The 1954 Law of Jordanian Nationality, passed under King Hussein (the grandson of Emir Abdullah), updated the earlier laws and extended citizenship to Palestinians who arrived in Jordan after the 1949 addendum (Massad 2001: 39).

The Second Arab-Israeli War in 1967 led to Jordan's loss of the West Bank and East Jerusalem to Israeli occupation. This devastating war brought 250,000–300,000 new Palestinian refugees to the East Bank who needed emergency outlays of food and shelter (Brand 1988). Most of these Palestinians came from the West Bank as internally displaced persons or as second-time refugees (i.e., uprooted in 1948 to the West Bank and again in 1967 to the East Bank). These Palestinian-Jordanian groups maintained their full Jordanian citizenship.

Other Palestinian refugees, approximately 30,000–50,000, came from the Gaza Strip.[8] Many of these Palestinians were not from the Gaza Strip originally but had fled there after the 1948 War, making them refugees again in 1967. For this reason, scholars describe this group as the "ex-Gazans" rather than the "Gazans," though in practice Jordanians often do not make this distinction (Pérez 2011). The Jordanian government considered these Palestinians as Gazan because previously they had been under Egyptian rule. As such, they did not have, nor did they receive, access to Jordanian nationality.[9] The ex-Gazan refugees are Jordan's oldest non-citizen PRG. Most official estimates suggest that, as of 2018, there are around 150,000 ex-Gazans in Jordan (Al Sharif 2018).

Jordan did not broadly denationalize any of its citizens of Palestinian descent after losing control of the West Bank in 1967 or following violent clashes between the Palestine Liberation Organization (PLO) and the Jordanian government from 1970 to 1971. However, in 1988, King Hussein announced Jordan's legal and administrative

[8] Airgram from the American Embassy in Tel Aviv to the Department of State, July 12, 1968, 1967–69 Subject Numeric File, File REF Jordan A-1038; Airgram from the American Embassy in Amman to the Department of State, May 16, 1968, 1967–69 Subject Numeric File, File REF Jordan A-341, The US National Archives College Park.

[9] This contrasts with Palestinians coming from the West Bank in 1967 or from anywhere in Palestine in 1948, both of whom became Jordanian citizens after Jordan annexed the West Bank under the 1950 Unity of the Banks (which formally lasted until Jordan's disengagement with the West Bank in 1988).

disengagement from the West Bank and removed Jordanian nationality from everyone living on the West Bank at that time.

The disengagement aimed to distinguish between Jordan and Palestine. This was important in part to combat right-wing rhetoric in Israel that "Jordan is Palestine" or the "alternative homeland" for Palestinians. The disengagement also stemmed from the PLO gaining recognition as the sole representative of the Palestinians in 1974, rather than recognizing King Hussein as a representative as well. In addition, the disengagement reflected the failure of Jordan's final status peace negotiations with Israel and the PLO since 1967, the PLO's growing influence in the West Bank, the outbreak of the first Intifada in, as well as increasing measures to "Transjordanize" the public and security sectors after the conflict in 1970 and 1971, by filling these positions with citizens of Transjordanian, not Palestinian, descent.

Jordan received its next wave of approximately 200,000–300,000 Palestinians after the Iraqi invasion of Kuwait in 1990. Most of these Palestinians were Jordanian citizens who had left for the Gulf decades earlier, but who were forced to return because of Jordan's and the PLO's support for Iraq during the war. This group arrived amid increasingly discriminatory policies toward Palestinian-Jordanians. These policies included electoral laws to reduce the number of Palestinians in parliament as well as waves of nationality revocations (Abu Odeh 1999). These nationality revocations occurred during administrative procedures, such as renewing a driver's license. For example, during these procedures, government staff would remove Palestinian-Jordanians' nationality based on internal ministry instructions about implementing the disengagement (Lynch 1999; Frost and Brown 2020).

Given these massive waves of Palestinians entering Jordan, the Jordanian government has suggested that its citizens are divided roughly in half between Palestinian-Jordanians and Transjordanian-Jordanians (i.e., those originating from the East Bank or at least residing there prior to the 1948 War). However, the actual demographic breakdown of Jordanians of Palestinian and Transjordanian descent remains unknown, or at least unpublished. Regardless, UNRWA reports that there are over 2 million registered Palestinian refugees living in Jordan. These figures do not include the many Palestinian-Jordanians who are not registered with UNRWA or the Palestinians who lost their Jordanian nationality in 1988 but currently live on the East Bank.

This demographic division between Palestinian-Jordanians and Transjordanian-Jordanians has constituted an identity crisis in Jordan. This identity crisis became more salient after the 1970–1 conflict between the PLO and the Jordanian army, as well as following the 1988 disengagement. These events have brought questions about citizenship and who is truly Jordanian to the core of Jordan's politics and policy-making.

Another partial by-product of this identity confusion is that Jordan did not sign the 1951 Geneva Convention and its 1967 Protocol. Jordan also did not sign the 1954 Convention relating to the Status of Stateless Persons or the 1961 Convention on the Reduction of Statelessness. Furthermore, Jordan does not have a domestic law on refugees. Instead, Jordan applies its Law No. 24 of 1973 on Residence and Foreigners' Affairs to non-citizen refugees. These decisions stem from concerns with the Palestinian right of return as well as from maintaining a distinct Jordanian identity, while hosting Palestinian as well as other refugee populations.

Regardless, Jordan still is bound to respect customary international law, including non-refoulement. Non-refoulement stipulates that states should not return refugees "to the frontiers of territories" where their lives or freedom would be threatened (NRC 2016). In addition, Jordan has signed other human rights conventions that afford refugees rights, including the International Covenant on Civil and Political Rights (1966) and the International Covenant on Economic, Social, and Cultural Rights (1966) (Jastram and Achiron 2001). These international agreements have helped push Jordan to grant refugees, regardless of their citizen status, social rights, including access to education and health care.

Jordan is also party to two regional conventions concerning refugees: the Declaration on the Protection of Refugees and Displaced Persons in the Arab World (1992) and the Arab Convention on Regulating Status of Refugees in the Arab Countries (1994). These agreements, however, tend to focus on the conditions under which a country does not have to grant an individual refugee rights, including when governments deem such actions as threats to national security. On the other hand, these documents highlight the importance of protecting refugee women and children, as well as treating refugees no worse than foreign residents.

Jordan's complicated history with Palestinians as well as its various legal obligations to refugees has generated tensions between legal status and belonging as well as between de jure and de facto rights. The following sections use examples from Jordan to unpack these tensions. These examples include linguistic distinctions between nationality and citizenship as well as specific accounts of tensions between these dimensions of citizenship.

3. Legal Status versus Belonging

Jordanian distinctions in Arabic between *jinsiyya* (translated as nationality) and *muwāṭana* (translated as citizenship) can help illuminate the tension between notions of citizenship as legal status versus belonging. My interviewees broadly agreed that *jinsiyya* is legal and gives individuals citizen status through official documents, like passports and national identity numbers. This definition aligns with Davis' translation of *jinsiyya* as "passport citizenship" (Davis 1995, 2000), which represents legal status as a citizen and the right to abode in a state based on this status.

Muwāṭana is less clear-cut. Davis defines it as "democratic citizenship," including equal access to the civil, political, social, and economic resources of the state (Davis 1995, 2000). However, my interviewees described other aspects of *muwāṭana*. For example, many interviewees described *muwāṭana* as feelings of duty and belonging. Some examples included *muwāṭana* as civic duty in terms of "how you are participating in political life,"[10] "your obligation as a good person,"[11] or "showing generosity even with limited resources."[12] Others included *muwāṭana* as patriotism, specifically as a "commitment to a homeland,"[13] "a feeling,"[14] and "being linked to tribes and land."[15]

10 Author interview with Jordanian lawyer, February 2017.
11 Author interview with Jordanian lawyer, December 2016.
12 Author interview with Jordanian consultant and former parliamentarian, December 2016.
13 Author interview with Jordanian consultant and former advisor to the king, February 2017.
14 Author interview with Palestinian (non-Jordanian) development worker, December 2016.
15 Author interview with Jordanian professor, February 2017.

The conceptual distinction between citizenship as legal status and senses of belonging and duty highlights that legal citizen status is not a requirement for a resident to feel like a member of the state. Thus, citizen and non-citizen groups could share overlapping conceptions of their membership, identity, practices, and acts as individuals in a state. For instance, I spoke with many non-citizen, lifelong residents of Jordan who felt a sense of belonging to Jordan (a form of *muwāṭana*), despite never having legal status (*jinsiyya*) as a Jordanian.

Ex-Gazans are one case of this phenomenon, where some ex-Gazans share a strong sense of Jordanian identity and belonging with their Jordanian citizen peers. One development worker I spoke with, whose mother is Jordanian and father is ex-Gazan, described her views on Jordanian citizenship:

> Citizenship means growing up in Jordan. My mom is Jordanian, and I am helping Jordan's development. . . . I feel like a Jordanian citizen even though I don't have a national number. Some situations make me remember that I am not a citizen, but I feel Jordanian. . . . I feel *muwāṭina* but I do not have *jinsiyya*.[16]

As alluded to in the example above, another prominent group of resident non-citizens is the children of Jordanian mothers and non-Jordanian fathers. Only Jordanian men can pass their nationality onto their spouses and children, which means that the children of Jordanian mothers and non-Jordanian fathers cannot obtain Jordanian nationality, even if they have only ever lived in Jordan (Frost 2022). One of these children, a Jordanian mother and Syrian father, who is now in his 30s and has kids of his own, described how it felt to realize he was not Jordanian:

> When you turn 18, you realize you are a stranger, but I don't know Syria. People told me I am not Jordanian. . . . Many of my friends do not know that I am not Jordanian; I try not to bring it up. It is embarrassing when everyone thinks you are Jordanian and you have this different colour identity card. . . . I went to a bank and wanted to talk to an employee about cashing my paycheck. When I showed my passport, they were surprised I was Syrian because I have a Jordanian accent. . . . I will do anything the government asks; I pay taxes.[17]

Like many other children of Jordanian mothers, this interviewee feels confused about his identity. Until he was 18, he thought he was Jordanian, and he still considers himself Jordanian—just like those he interacts with but who do not know his legal status. He possesses a sense of belonging to Jordan, but he does not have legal citizen status. This discrepancy challenges the simple alignment of legal and practiced citizenship identities.

Representing the inverse of these cases, I spoke with Jordanians of Palestinian descent who identify as having a Jordanian passport but being Palestinian. In

[16] Author interview with ex-Gazan development worker, December 2016.

[17] Author interview with a lifelong resident of Jordan with a Jordanian mother and Syrian father, February 2017.

these cases, people have Jordanian *jinsiyya* but Palestinian *muwāṭana*, even if they grew up on Jordan's East Bank. As one such interviewee explained: "My nationality is from Jordan, but I feel Palestinian. Palestine is my homeland; the homeland of my ancestors . . . *muwāṭana* is about feelings and *jinsiyya* is about documents."[18]

A high-ranking former government official offered a similar description of Jordanian-Palestinians with these feelings. He noted "[Jordanian-]Palestinians are like those nationalized in another country—they have not melted down into the Jordanian melting pot. Deep in their hearts, they are Palestinian." He then added that *muwāṭana* is about "belonging" and *jinsiyya* is about having a "passport."[19]

Other cases like this include those with Jordanian nationality, but who have not spent their lives in Jordan. For instance, one Jordanian-Palestinian who heads a non-profit organization explained how "maybe only half of Palestinian-Jordanians feel like citizens"; she added, in particular, "the Palestinians who came back from the Arab Gulf in the 1990s, they have full rights but do not have feelings of being a citizen. . . . These Palestinian-Jordanians have not been engaged in Jordan's life, and most of them do not vote and they are not represented politically."[20]

However, these cases are not limited to Jordanians of Palestinian descent. As one high-level, long-serving government official noted, "There are Jordanian-Palestinians with the same attachment to Jordan as East Bank Jordanians. . . they appreciate Jordan."[21] Other interviewees pointed out that there are Jordanians of East Bank descent who have spent their lives in the United States and feel more attached to their American culture and identity. One government official commented that some of his children who have dual nationality feel closer to the United States.[22] A Jordanian journalist also shared how she has struggled to convince her children to speak Arabic, even while living in Jordan, after spending time in the United States.[23]

This distinction between legal citizen status and feelings of belonging challenges a clear explanation of who has citizenship. Although it is straightforward to demarcate who has nationality, individuals with nationality may not feel like citizens, just as individuals without nationality may feel like they are citizens. As the next section details, these blurry boundaries of citizenship also manifest in the fuzzy lines between the rights residents have in law versus in practice.

4. De Jure versus De Facto Rights

In addition to *muwāṭana* as belonging and duty, many interviewees discussed *muwāṭana* in theory versus practice. In theory, and in line with Davis' definition (Davis

18 Author interview with Palestinian-Jordanian former government bureaucrat, January 2019.
19 Author interview with former East Bank Jordanian minister, December 2016.
20 Author interview with Jordanian-Palestinian non-profit organization head, December 2016.
21 Author interview with former East Bank Jordanian minister, October 2019.
22 Author interview with former East Bank Jordanian minister, October 2019.
23 Author interview with East Bank Jordanian journalist, October 2019.

1995, 2000: 53), *muwāṭana* represents democratic citizenship, where all citizens enjoy equal rights, including political rights. Yet, most interviewees noted that this form of *muwāṭana* does not exist in Jordan and instead would describe *muwāṭana* in practice. This description often concerned the varying sets of rights the state grants to different groups, such as women, religious minorities, and ethnic groups.

Specifically, one interviewee, who is a women's rights activist, described *muwāṭana* as the "relationship between you and your country; your acts and its actions toward you . . . a give and take relationship." She distinguished, however, between how citizenship should be, that is "rights to good education and healthcare" as well as feeling respected with "a real parliament that reflects your will," and how citizenship is in practice. She provided an eight-point scale of citizens in Jordan, where Muslim men of East Bank descent enjoyed the most rights, and Christian women of West Bank descent enjoyed the fewest rights.[24] She added the caveat that if one belongs to the "ruling club," then you immediately move up the list to number one and enjoy the most rights while in that club.[25]

This form of *muwāṭana* in practice highlights that citizens do not necessarily enjoy all the democratic rights traditionally associated with citizenship or the rights spelled out in the state's constitution and laws. Likewise, this description emphasizes that people with the same legal status as citizens may experience rights and belonging differently, including based on their ethnicity, gender, and religion.

For example, although Jordanians of Palestinian descent have equal political and economic rights as Jordanians of East Bank descent, in practice, there are far fewer Palestinian-Jordanians in the government and security services. As one former high-ranking government official observed: "There are no Palestinian[-Jordanians] in the administration any more. . . . There are only Palestinians in the Cabinet and Senate—in visible institutions with no real power. . . . It has become normal that Palestinians are not in the government now."[26] A former member of parliament and government official similarly noted: "After 1974, the number of Palestinian[-Jordanians] in the Senate, House, and Cabinet has been reduced, and there are very few in the army and security positions. Palestinians are underrepresented in the public sector and it is hard to change."[27]

In addition, Palestinian-Jordanians are underrepresented in the parliament because rural, predominantly Transjordanian areas receive proportionally more seats. As a political analyst familiar with Palestinian-Jordanian issues elaborated:

[24] Her specific breakdown of citizens in Jordan, ranked according to most to fewest rights:
1. Male, East Bank descent, Muslim
2. Male, West Bank descent, Muslim
3. Male, East Bank descent, Christian
4. Male, West Bank descent, Christian
5. Female, East Bank descent, Muslim
6. Female, West Bank descent, Muslim
7. Female, East Bank descent, Christian
8. Female, West Bank descent, Christian

[25] Author interview with East Bank Jordanian women's rights activist, February 2017.

[26] Author interview with Palestinian-Jordanian former government official, January 2016.

[27] Author interview with East Bank Jordanian former parliamentarian, March 2017.

> There is officially no discrimination to Palestinian-Jordanians in law with political rights. However, since 1993, when you look at the [election] laws and the distribution and proportion of seats, Amman is under-represented... All designing of electoral institutions is with two obsessions in mind (1) the demographics of Palestinians and (2) the Muslim Brotherhood. The government wants to limit both.[28]

A former senior government official similarly noted:

> With citizenship, there is a disconnect between law and practice because the law says Jordanians are equal regardless of ethnic origins, but there is legal and cultural discrimination toward Palestinians. Most of the army and intelligence is made up of East Bank Jordanians. The electoral law also ensures that Palestinians make up no more than 10–15 per cent of the parliament . . . the government did this to make sure Palestinians and Islamists have weak influence.

However, he added that: "In some ways, since there is so much intermarriage, blocking Palestinian-Jordanian citizenship is more about blocking real reforms and new forms of citizenship."[29]

Another example of discrepancies between law and practice occurs among Jordanian women married to non-Jordanians. As of 2014, they have several civil rights, or "privileges," they can pass to their children. These privileges include access to public education, public healthcare, work professions, driver's licenses, as well as to investment and ownership opportunities. The privileges also include access to special identification (ID) cards to facilitate obtaining these services.

However, many of these privileges have not been enforced (Frost and Brown, 2020). One woman married to a non-Jordanian stated "the privileges are not effective... they are not enforced... you get nothing, just an ID card that says my mother is Jordanian."[30] A former parliamentarian also claimed: "the bureaucracy is not responding well; there are weak institutions. Much is not being implemented. Ministers come in and do their vision - sometimes good, sometimes bad."[31]

A high-ranking government official also observed that "the government approved the privileges, or civil rights, but they have not really been implemented. Implementation is an issue . . . There is pushback at many levels, like policymaking, with different members of parliament, and implementation . . . where [staff] interpretation comes in."[32] A lawyer familiar with this issue simply stated: "The privileges are not law so it is easy not to implement them."[33]

On the other hand, some groups have more de facto than de jure rights. For example, the ex-Gazans in practice have had access to temporary Jordanian passports and many

28 Author interview with Palestinian-Jordanian political analyst, October 2019.
29 Author interview with East Bank Jordanian former government official, January 2016.
30 Author interview with East Bank Jordanian women's rights activist, February 2017.
31 Author interview with East Bank Jordanian former parliamentarian, October 2019.
32 Author interview with former East Bank Jordanian minister, December 2017.
33 Author interview with Jordanian lawyer, October 2019.

work sectors, despite lacking citizen status and the absence of any laws specifying these rights (Frost and Brown 2020).

First, Jordan's Ministry of Interior (MOI) eased the ex-Gazans' mobility and legalized their residency by issuing them temporary passports, starting in 1968 (El-Abed 2005). The temporary passports look like regular passports on the outside, but on the inside, they do not include a national number and identify the carrier as an ex-Gazan. Although this passport does not provide ex-Gazans with nationality, nor access to most of the legal rights associated with citizen status, ex-Gazans can use it to travel abroad,[34] register in schools, obtain work, and prove their legal residency in Jordan (El-Abed, Husseini and Al-Rantawi 2014).

These temporary passports exist in practice, but the Jordanian government never passed any official laws about these documents. This is surprising because Jordan has laws concerning passports and these laws do mention other travel documents, such as those needed for pilgrimages (Jordan Ministry of Interior).[35] News articles, on the other hand, discuss the temporary passports for ex-Gazans by name and serve as one of the main sources of information about them. A recent example includes reporting that ex-Gazans, as of February 2017, can renew these passports every five years (Jordan Times 2017; Al-Ghad 2017). The candid discussion of them in newspaper articles stands in stark contrast to their absence in legal documents, particularly in registered laws. This legal quandary highlights how the ex-Gazans enjoy the right to a Jordanian temporary passport in practice but not in law (Frost and Brown 2020).

In addition, before 2016, ex-Gazans did not need work permits in practice, though as non-citizens they technically did by law. A Jordanian citizen and political leader from Gaza noted: "Before the 1990s, more work sectors were open to Gazans."[36] An ex-Gazan teacher also described this situation: "Since last year [2016] Gazans need a work permit—this is for foreign workers, like the Egyptians—the government ignores us living here for 50 years . . . since last year, the government closed 54 professions to Gazans."[37]

One ex-Gazan UNRWA teacher described how "Gazans have never been able to work in the Jordanian government, but in the 1980s, the government let them work in public schools because they needed teachers."[38] Another ex-Gazan teacher corroborated this anecdote: "I taught for UNRWA and at a public high school . . . From 1977 to 1980, I taught in a public school, but in 1980, they introduced the family book for Jordanian families. As a Gazan, I only had a two-year passport. After four years of being with the Ministry of Education, they fired me."[39]

As these rights highlight, the ex-Gazans in Jordan largely have de facto rights, including rights in practice that other non-citizen groups do not receive. These rights are based on ministry instructions and newspaper articles rather than published

34 However, some countries do not accept these temporary passports as international travel documents.
35 Note that for this and all other references to Arabic sources in the bibliography, the titles reflect the author's translations into English.
36 Author interview with Jordanian political leader and journalist, February 2017.
37 Author interview with ex-Gazan refugee living outside of a camp, February 2017.
38 Author interview with ex-Gazan refugee living in a camp, Jerash, May 2017.
39 Author interview with ex-Gazan refugee living outside of a camp, February 2017.

laws.[40] However, ex-Gazans' access to de facto, rather than de jure, rights places them in a precarious situation and exposes them to a lower quality of life and standard of living than Jordanian citizens (Kvittingen et al. 2019). As such and considering the over 50 years they have lived in Jordan, the ex-Gazans want de jure rights that secure their de facto rights. By breaking apart the different dimensions of citizenship, it is clear that states can grant PRGs de facto rights without granting them nationality (i.e., legal citizenship status).

Conclusion

The conceptual distinctions between citizenship as legal status, de jure rights, de facto rights, and senses of belonging highlight that legal citizen status is not a requirement for a resident group, such as a PRG, to have access to other dimensions of citizenship. Specifically, legal citizen status does not necessarily generate feelings of belonging to a state. A group could have legal citizen status but lack a sense of belonging to the state. Likewise, a group may feel a sense of belonging to the state, despite lacking nationality in that state.

In addition, a group may have de jure rights that are not implemented in practice or de facto rights that are not provided in law. This attention to rights in practice highlights how, despite legal differences, citizen and non-citizen groups may have the same rights in practice. Similarly, this conceptualization recognizes that there are many citizenship rights, duties, practices, and feelings that concern residents with and without nationality (Frost and Shteiwi 2018). These include access to public elementary schools, paying taxes, protesting injustice, and feeling loyalty to the state. These findings highlight the blurry boundary at times between the experience of citizenship for residents with and without legal citizen status.

Further, this conceptualization of citizenship enables comparisons of the rights and duties of all resident groups over time and across space. It also offers a logical approach to studying the "rights, participation and recognition" of residents without nationality in a state (Bosniak 2017: 326). This is an important point because legal citizen status is not a necessary requirement for a group to enjoy de jure rights in a state or "the right to have rights" (Arendt 1951). As such, host states should be able to offer all PRGs basic rights in law and practice, without having to nationalize these groups. A clear example of states, such as Jordan, granting non-citizens de jure rights is the distribution of passports, as specified in law, to non-citizen investors (Frost 2021).

Overall, this chapter provides a conceptual framework for understanding the relationship between a PRG and its host state, by focusing on Jordan's relationship with different Palestinian PRGs. In doing so, this chapter expands the citizenship literature and contributes to debates about how states treat refugees and non-citizens. In addition, this analysis adds to a growing literature that examines citizenship and migration policies beyond Western Europe and North America. This analysis engages in-depth

[40] In terms of *de jure* rights, the ex-Gazans largely fall under the terms of the 1973 Residency and Foreigner Affairs Law and its amendments, which treat the ex-Gazans like other non-citizen Arabs.

empirical data from Jordan to demonstrate the different components of citizenship as well as how PRGs challenge traditional notions of state citizenship. Jordan's policies toward Palestinian PRGs reveal that citizenship concerns more than legal citizen status and includes both non-citizens and citizens.

Bibliography

Abu Odeh, Adnan (1999), *Jordanians, Palestinians, and the Hashemite Kingdom in the Middle East Peace Process*, Washington, DC: United States Institute of Peace Press.

Al-Ghad (2017), "Approval of Raising the Length [of Validity] of Passports and Identity Cards for Ex-Gazans to 5 Years," (in Arabic), February 22. Available online: https://bit.ly/2WA3RpA (accessed November 19, 2019).

Al Sharif, Osama (2018), "Jordan Moves to Improve Lives of Gazan Refugees," *Al-Monitor*, December 13. Available online: https://www.al-monitor.com/pulse/originals/2018/12/jordan-gaza-refugees-palestinian-settlement.html (accessed March 20, 2019).

Arendt, Hannah (1951), *The Origins of Totalitarianism*, London: George Allen & Unwin.

Bosniak, Linda (2017), "Status Non-Citizens," in Ayelet Shachar, Rainer Bauböck, Irene Bloemraad, and Maarten Vink (eds.), *Oxford Handbook of Citizenship*, 314–36, Oxford: Oxford University Press.

Brand, Laurie (1988), *Palestinians in the Arab World: Institution-Building and the Search for State*, New York: Columbia University Press.

Butenschøn, Nils (2000), "State, Power, and Citizenship in the Middle East: A Theoretical Introduction," in Nils Butenschøn, Uri Davis, and Manuel Hassassian (eds.), *Citizenship and the State in the Middle East: Approaches and Applications*, 3–27, Syracuse: Syracuse University Press.

Chung, Erin (2017), "Citizenship in Non-Western Contexts," in Ayelet Shachar, Rainer Bauböck, Irene Bloemraad, and Maarten Vink (eds.), *Oxford Handbook of Citizenship*, 431–52, Oxford: Oxford University Press.

Davis, Uri (1995), "Jinsiyya versus Muwatana: The Question of Citizenship and the State in the Middle East: The Cases of Israel, Jordan and Palestine," *Arab Studies Quarterly*, 17 (1–2): 19–50.

Davis, Uri (2000), "Conceptions of Citizenship in the Middle East: State, Nation, and People," in Nils Butenschøn, Uri Davis, and Manuel Hassassian (eds.), *Citizenship and the State in the Middle East: Approaches and Applications*, 49–69, Syracuse: Syracuse University Press.

Ebright, Katherine (2018), "Nationality and Defining 'The Right to Have Rights,'" *Columbia Journal of Transnational Law*, 56: S855–97.

El-Abed, Oroub (2005), "Immobile Palestinians: The Impact of Policies and Practices on Palestinians from Gaza in Jordan," in Jaber Hana and Métral France (eds.), *Mondes en mouvements, migrants et migrations au Moyen-Orient au tournant du XXIe siècle*, Beirut: Ifpo.

El-Abed, Oroub, Jalal Al Husseini, and Oraib Al-Rantawi (2014), "Listening to Palestinian Refugees/Displaced Persons in Jordan: Perceptions of Their Political and Socio-economic Status," Communication in Amman: Al Quds Center for Political Studies, January 2014.

Frost, Lillian (2021), "Formalizing Rights: The Case for Linking Legal Rights to Non-Citizen Statuses," *Digest of Middle East Studies* 30 (4): 270–7.

Frost, Lilian (2022), "Report on Citizenship Law: Jordan," Global Citizenship Observatory (GLOBALCIT) Country Report, 2022/2, European University Institute. Available online: https://cadmus.eui.eu/handle/1814/74189 (accessed February 26, 2024).

Frost, Lillian, and Nathan Brown (2020), "Constitutions and Citizens," in Roel Meijer, James Sater and Zahra Babar (eds.), *Handbook of Citizenship in the Middle East and North Africa*, 130–43, London: Routledge Press.

Frost, Lillian, and Musa Shteiwi (2018), "Syrian Refugees and Citizenship," in Roel Meijer and Nils Butenschøn (eds.), *The Middle East in Transition: The Centrality of Citizenship*, 292–315, Cheltenham: Edward Elgar Publishing.

Howard, Marc Morjé (2006), "Comparative Citizenship: An Agenda for Cross-National Research," *Perspectives on Politics*, 4 (3): 443–55.

Isin, Engin, and Greg Nielsen (2008), *Acts of Citizenship*, London: Zed Press.

Jastram, Kate, and Marilyn Achiron (2001), "Refugee Protection: A Guide to International Refugee Law," UNHCR. Available online: https://www.refworld.org/docid/3cd6a8444.html (accessed February 26, 2024).

Joppke, Christian (1999), "How Immigration is Changing Citizenship: A Comparative View," *Ethnic and Racial Studies*, 22 (4): 629–52.

Jordan Ministry of Interior. "Legislations: Laws," (in Arabic). Available online: https://bit.ly/2JBFkwE (accessed November 19, 2019).

Jordan Times (2017), "Validity of Gazans' Temporary Passports Extended to 5 Years," February 22. Available online: http://www.jordantimes.com/news/local/validity-gazans%E2%80%99-temporary-passports-extended-5-years (accessed November 19, 2019).

Kvittingen, Anna, Age A. Tiltnes, Ronia Salman, Hana Asfour, and Dina Baslan (2019), "'Just getting by' – Ex-Gazans in Jerash and Other Refugee Camps in Jordan," Fafo Report 2019: 34.

Kymlicka, Will (2011), "Multicultural Citizenship Within Multination States," *Ethnicities*, 11 (3): 281–302.

Loescher, Gil, and James Milner (2006), "Protracted Refugee Situations: The Search for Practical Solutions," in UNHCR (ed.), *The State of the World's Refugees 2006: Human Displacement in the New Millennium*, 105–27, Oxford: Oxford University Press.

Lori, Noora (2017), "Statelessness, 'In-Between' Statuses, and Precarious Citizenship," in Ayelet Shachar, Rainer Bauböck, Irene Bloemraad, and Maarten Vink (eds.), *Oxford Handbook of Citizenship*, 743–66, Oxford: Oxford University Press.

Lynch, Marc (1999), *State Interests and Public Spheres: The International Politics of Jordan's Identity*, New York: Columbia University Press.

Marshall, T. H. (1950), "Citizenship and Social Class," in T. H. Marshall (ed.), *Citizenship and Social Class and Other Essays*, 1–85, Cambridge: Cambridge University Press.

Massad, Joseph (2001), *Colonial Effects: The Making of National Identity in Jordan*, New York: Columbia University Press.

NRC (2016), "The Obligations of States Towards Refugees Under International Law: Some Reflections on the Situation in Lebanon." Available online: https://www.nrc.no/globalassets/pdf/reports/obligations-of-state.pdf (accessed December 1, 2017).

Ong, Aihwa (1996), "Cultural Citizenship as Subject-Making: Immigrants Negotiate Racial and Cultural Boundaries in the United States," *Current Anthropology*, 37 (5): 737–62.

Pérez, Michael Vicente (2011), "Human Rights and the Rightless: The Case of Gaza Refugees in Jordan," *The International Journal of Human Rights*, 15 (7): 1031–54.

Salibi, Kamal (1998), *The Modern History of Jordan*, New York: I.B. Tauris.
Shafir, Gershon (1998), *The Citizenship Debates*, Minneapolis: University of Minnesota Press.
Tully, James (2001), "Introduction," in Alain G. Gagnon and James Tully (eds.), *Multinational Democracies*, 1-34, Cambridge: Cambridge University Press.
UNHCR (2014), "Protracted Refugee Situations," UNHCR Report EC/54/SC/CRP, June 14, 2004.
UNHCR (2016), "In Search of Solutions: Addressing Statelessness in the Middle East and North Africa," UNHCR Middle East and North Africa Bureau.
UNHCR (2019a), "Global Trends: Forced Displacement in 2018," June 20. Available online: https://www.unhcr.org/5d08d7ee7.pdf (accessed November 19, 2019).
UNHCR (2019b), "Jordan - Factsheet (September 2019)," UNHCR Operational Portal. Available online: https://data2.unhcr.org/en/documents/details/71536 (accessed November 19, 2019).
UNRWA (2019), "In Figures 2018–2019," February 2019. Available online: https://www.unrwa.org/sites/default/files/content/resources/unrwa_in_figures_2019_eng_sep_2019_final.pdf (accessed November 19, 2019),
World Bank (2019), "Population, Total – Jordan." Available online: https://data.worldbank.org/indicator/SP.POP.TOTL?locations=JO (accessed November 19, 2019).

2

Sacrosanct Rights, National Interests, and Insecure Status

Governing Ex-Gazans in Jordan

Jalal Al Husseini and Anna Kvittingen

This chapter explores how Jordan has governed the presence of a specific group of Palestinian residents on its territory: the so-called "ex-Gazans" (in Arabic: *ʾabnāʾ qiṭāʿ Ghazza*—people from the Gaza Strip). Ex-Gazans are former residents of the Gaza Strip (henceforth "Gaza") who made their way to the East Bank (present-day Jordan) during, or in the wake of, the June 1967 Arab-Israeli War and the subsequent Israeli occupation of Gaza, the West Bank, Golan Heights, and Sinai. Compared to the 350,000 Palestinians displaced from the West Bank, ex-Gazans were a relatively small population of approximately 47,000 in 1968. Today these ex-Gazans and their descendants comprise some 200,000 persons. Around 160,000 belong to families that were not indigenous Gazans but rather refugees from territories seized by Israel during the 1948 Arab-Israeli War.[1] These families have been registered as "Palestine refugees" with the United Nations Relief and Works Agency for Palestine Refugees in the Near East UNRWA, making up some of the 2.2 million refugees registered with UNRWA in Jordan today.[2]

Palestinians residing in the West Bank (of the Jordan river) following the 1948 Israeli-Arab conflict, be they refugees from Israel/former Palestine or indigenous West Bankers, came under Jordanian rule and were naturalized with the reunification of the East and West Banks under Hashemite rule in 1950. Thus, the vast majority of those arriving at East Bank border crossings in the wake of the 1967/8 Israeli-Arab conflict were simply considered to be (internally) "displaced persons" from the West Bank holding Jordanian citizenship. Ex-Gazans, however, who had lived since 1948 in a territory administered by Egyptian authorities and held Egyptian travel documents, were not incorporated into Jordan's polity through citizenship. Nor were they

1 UNRWA, *Protection in Jordan*, March 2018, https://www.unrwa.org/activity/protection-jordan

2 "Palestine refugees" in Jordan comprises refugees registered with UNRWA who established themselves in Jordan in 1948 ("1948 refugees") and other 1948 refugees displaced for a second time from the West Bank to the East Bank in 1967/8. https://www.unrwa.org/sites/default/files/content/resources/unrwa_in_figures_2019_eng_sep_2019_final.pdf. 00

categorized as migrants, whose stay is determined by specific residence legislation. Instead, Jordanian authorities have considered ex-Gazans a transient displaced population entitled to temporary residence pending their return to Palestine—be it to their original villages in Israel/Palestine or to Gaza.

The situation of ex-Gazans has long eschewed significant public attention. Available publications highlights protection and service provision gaps associated with their inferior legal status as stateless Palestinian refugees (El-Abed 2005; Palestinian Return Center 2018; Perez 2010; Kvittingen et al. 2019). A few notable ethnographic accounts explore ex-Gazans' lived experience and the particular ways in which their statelessness is navigated when seeking to claim more rights (Feldman 2012; Perez 2010, 2018). To our knowledge there has been little comprehensive analysis of the rationale behind Jordan's ex-Gazans policies, namely, how Jordan has governed this population that does not fit neatly within any of its regulatory frameworks (Frost 2020). This is no easy task. Since their arrival, the status accorded to ex-Gazans has been influenced simultaneously by various actors, including the king himself, the government, parliament, civil society organizations, and UNRWA. Moreover, their access to rights and entitlements has been formalized through a panoply of ad hoc decrees, regulations, and public statements that have often appeared confusing, inconsistent, and unsettling to ex-Gazans.

Geared to a historical methodology, this chapter is primarily concerned with the rationales and dynamics involved in perpetuating a distinctive mode of governing ex-Gazans that differs from that which has been applied to other Palestinians or any other foreigner category. It shows that while Jordan's ex-Gazan regime was created to label ex-Gazans as temporary residents holding a sacrosanct, albeit elusive, "right of return" to Palestine, the regime's evolution has predominantly responded to the aim of maintaining Jordan's political and socioeconomic stability. This aim has been articulated either in relation to the emergence of the Palestinian national movement and its internal repercussions within Jordan or in relation to the role ex-Gazans could play in the country's economy. Through analyzing how Jordan has governed ex-Gazans, this chapter also offers insight into decision-making processes concerning the degree to which ex-Gazans should be integrated into the country's social and economic fabric.

The chapter is divided into three sections. The first section focuses on the key initial year of displacement (1967–1968) when the status of those displaced from Gaza shifted from that of temporary residents *stricto sensu* to ex-Gazan residents. The second section turns to how Jordan has regulated the status of ex-Gazans through a hybrid regime comprising residence status and basic socioeconomic entitlements. It explores how this regime has evolved from 1967/1968 to the present day in line with fluctuating Jordanian internal and external policies and the needs and claims of ex-Gazans. The third section describes the way ex-Gazans have tried to address the resulting challenges; notably through coping strategies supported by Jordanian and international advocacy entities.

The analysis draws predominantly on interviews with over 200 ex-Gazans of different ages and walks of life (workers, students, businessmen, community leaders) undertaken during several periods of fieldwork between 2015 and 2020. Most interviews took place in Jerash camp (locally known as Gaza camp) in northern Jordan where the vast majority of residents are ex-Gazan, but also in other places with concentrations of ex-Gazans, including Mārkā refugee camp northeast of Amman and the capital's southern suburbs. Interviews were also conducted with key information holders, including current or retired government officials and UNRWA staff. Additionally, research in UNRWA's archives pertaining to ex-Gazans and a review of Jordanian laws and regulations were undertaken to trace formal shifts in government regulation of ex-Gazans, as well as to understand the modalities of their settlement in Jordan. The overall analysis draws on a wide cross-section of interviews; hence, we only cite specific interviews when directly quoting individuals or particular details.

1. Turning Displaced Gazans into "Ex-Gazans" (1967-1968)

1.1. Welcoming Displaced Gazans: Early Assumptions and Policies

First generation ex-Gazans generally concur that the main trigger for movement toward Jordan in 1967-1968 was the need to flee the brutality of Israeli occupation in Gaza. Jordan, then accessible through Israel and the West Bank, was the closest safe haven.[3] Socioeconomic considerations also mattered. Many were poor, unemployed men (Segev 2007), and Jordan was believed to be a welcoming country with job opportunities as well as generous provisions of humanitarian aid by both UNRWA and Jordanian authorities (see Section 1.2).[4] Eager to decrease the demographic pressure in Gaza, Israeli authorities contributed to the migration process by making its public transportation facilities available, and by providing chartered buses and petty cash to poor emigrating families (Lesch 1984).[5] In addition, some 400 Gazans affiliated with anti-occupation resistance groups were expelled to Jordan between 1968 and 1974 (Lesch 1979). From a trickle of a few hundred in August 1967, the number of displaced Gazans had reportedly reached 47,000 a year later. Of these, 38,500 were Palestine refugees who had registered with UNRWA in Gaza in 1950 and 8,500 were indigenous Gazans.[6]

Jordanian authorities were initially undecided as to what policy to follow. Buckling under the arrival of hundreds of thousands of citizens formerly residents of the West Bank, they were unwilling to address the longer-term status of those coming from Gaza. When pressured by UNRWA to elaborate a clear ex-Gazan policy in October 1967,[7] they replied that they did "not see the necessity of obtaining residence permits for them, because their residence [would] be temporary until their return." Therefore, similar to the dozens of Gazans that had temporarily resided in Jordan during the

[3] Egyptian travel documents Gazans carried at the time specified that these did not allow access to Egypt without a visa. Such visas were difficult to acquire.

[4] *Letter from John Reddaway, Deputy Commissioner-General, to Director of UNRWA Affairs*, Jordan, March 27, 1968 (UNRWA, Central Registry Archives).

[5] Ex-Gazans also noted that those escorted by Israeli authorities had to sign papers of non-return.

[6] *Letter from Chief Relief Operations Division to Deputy Commissioner General*, August 1, 1967; *Number of Refugees DPs on East Bank*, August 1968 (UNRWA, Central Registry Archives); and *Report of the Commissioner General of UNRWA, 1 July 1967 - 30 June 1968*, (A/7213), par.10.

[7] *Note for the Record—DUA Meeting with Chairman of Supreme Ministerial Committee for DPS*, 11 October 1967 (UNRWA, Central Registry Archives).

first Israeli occupation of Gaza in 1956–7, mere humanitarian assistance was deemed necessary pending their return.[8] Political reasons may also have rendered Jordanian authorities reluctant to engage in the longer-term settlement of Gazans and grant them a similar citizen status to the 1948 refugees: they shared a Palestinian nationality with the latter but not the same history and political identity. While the 1948 refugees had been merged into the Jordanian polity as citizens, Gazans had lived as stateless persons under the administrative authority of Egypt, a country that had established itself as Jordan's rival regional power, carrying out leftist pan-Arab nationalist policies that opposed the pro-Western approach championed by the Hashemite regime (Shlaim 2008). Consequently, the only Jordanian documentation issued to displaced Gazans during the early years of their stay in Jordan was the Displacement Attestation issued by the border authorities upon their arrival at the Allenby or al-Dāmiya bridges—the two main formal entry points to Jordan.

Eventually, Israel's continuing occupation of Gaza and the West Bank, its reluctance to allow the repatriation of substantial numbers of displaced persons, as well as mounting calls within Jordan itself to prevent Israel from expelling more Palestinians (Lesch 1979) led Jordanian authorities to close its border to displaced Palestinians from the West Bank in March 1968 and from Gaza in July 1968. In the following years, Gazans would only be accepted into Jordan as temporary visitors under strict conditions, including the payment of a financial guarantee that increased from 100 Jordanian dinars (henceforth, JD) in 1968 to JD1,000 in July 1969.[9]

1.2. Accommodating Displaced Gazans: Toward a Hybrid Integration Regime

During the first year of their stay in Jordan, displaced Gazans were primarily considered recipients of humanitarian assistance delivered by UNRWA and the host authorities.[10] However, they were not restricted from working in the growing construction and services sectors, or as free entrepreneurs or businessmen. The latter were among the first to benefit from Jordanian temporary passports issued to facilitate their travels abroad in late 1967 (see Section 2.2). Moreover, until February 1968, displaced Gazans were relatively free to establish themselves where they wished. Some were hosted by relatives and integrated relatively easily in the country's fast-expanding urban centers of Amman, al-Zarqā', Mārkā, al-Ruṣayfa, and al-ʿAqaba. Less well-connected Gazans lacking local support or means of livelihood were sent to makeshift reception centers

[8] *Letter from the Ministry of Development and Reconstruction to Director of UNRWA Affairs*, Jordan, 8/10/1967 (UNRWA, Central Registry Archives).

[9] "Jordan Tightening Restrictions Imposed on Gaza Inhabitants," *al-Quds*, July 14, 1969 (UNRWA, Central Registry Archives). Nevertheless, Jordan continued to allow a limited number of Gazans as residents, including militants deported by Israel, and persons from Gaza joining their spouses in Jordan.

[10] In line with UN General Assembly resolution 2252 (ES-V) of July 1967, the Agency also delivered temporary basis relief assistance to non-registered displaced persons "in serious need of immediate assistance."

established in the Jordan Valley.[11] These centers were gradually dismantled because of frequent skirmishes between the Jordanian army and Palestinian *fedayeen* militias on the one hand, and between the militias and the Israeli Defense Forces on the other. From early 1968, most of these displaced Gazans were rehoused in an especially erected emergency camp near the small town of Jerash in northern Jordan.[12]

The establishment of the Jerash camp bore witness to Jordan's realization that the displaced Gazans had effectively become *ex-Gazans*, a term initially coined by UNRWA aptly representing their situation: they were in Jordan to stay. However, the location of the camp in a rural area far from Jordan's main urban centers, together with their status as non-Jordanian residents, has in retrospect been viewed by ex-Gazans as harbingers of their relative marginalization, combining elements of integration (residence) and discrimination (limited civil rights and livelihood opportunities). Initially made up of tents, Jerash camp first hosted some 4,500 people, mainly transferred from reception centers in the Jordan Valley, later to be joined by ex-Gazans who had initially settled elsewhere and wished to be reunited with relatives in Jerash camp.[13] By December 1970, Jerash camp had reached its designated capacity of around 11,500, comprising half the ex-Gazan population at that time. At present, around 30,000 ex-Gazans are registered with UNRWA in Jerash camp,[14] although only around half or so live within its official borders. To this day, the camp remains one of the main concentrations of ex-Gazans. With its population suffering alarmingly dismal conditions compared to other camp refugees (Kvittingen et al. 2019), it is also the key symbol of their vulnerable status, as will be explored in Section 3.

2. The Making of an "Ex-Gazan" Regime

2.1. The Ex-Gazans within Jordan's Palestinian Framework

By being ultimately accepted as semi-permanent residents, ex-Gazans were incorporated into Jordan's Palestinian framework; a governing framework grounded in and officially sustained by an ostensible commitment to Palestinian refugees' right to return to their homes in pre-1948 Palestine, in line with UN General Assembly resolution 194 (III) of December 1948.[15] Reaffirmed by UN General Assembly

11 Gazans shared these camps with other displaced persons from the West Bank and Bedouins from the Sinai. *Summary of Gaza Arrivals via Ghor Nimrin Reception Center, 12 February -31 July 1968*, (UNRWA, Central Registry Archives).

12 The Mārkā camp in the North-East of Amman has also hosted a substantial number of ex-Gazans (about 40 percent of the 53,000 refugees registered there). Other so-called "emergency camps" were set up in 1967-1968 to accommodate those displaced, predominantly from the West Bank, in the governorates of Amman (al-Baqaʿa, prince Hassan (unofficial camp), and al-Ṭālbiyaa), al-Zarqāʾ (Sukhna), ʾIrbid (ʿAzmī al-Muftī), and Jerash (Sūf).

13 *Note—Increased Need for Assistance to Displaced Persons*, March 11, 1968; and *Emergency Camps Established after June 1967* (UNRWA, Central Registry Archives).

14 https://www.unrwa.org/where-we-work/jordan/jerash-camp

15 Paragraph 11 of this resolution states that "refugees wishing to return to their homes and live at peace with their neighbors should be permitted to do so at the earliest practicable date, and that compensation should be paid for the property of those choosing not to return".

Resolution 3236 (1974) as an inalienable right of the Palestinian people, the "right of return" has represented a pillar of Palestinian political consciousness (Sayigh 1979). It has also constituted the basis of a professed "positive" discrimination regime promoted by the Arab League preventing, save few exceptions, refugees from acquiring host country citizenship, ostensibly to preserve their Palestinian nationality in exile. Arab League recommendations have concurrently aimed to counterbalance the impact of Palestinian refugees' statelessness by providing socioeconomic rights (residency, travel documents, employment, and freedom of movement) on a par with the host population, it being clear that they keep their Palestinian nationality.[16] In practice, however, such rights have never been fully granted by Arab host countries, usually justified by the imperative to preserve their "right of return" (Al Husseini and Bocco 2009: 5).

Jordan's approach seemingly differed from that of other Arab states by granting the 1948 refugees full citizenship. But this step aimed to associate the refugees with Jordan's modernization drive pending the realization of their "right of return" (Mishal 1978), and not as a substitute for it. Indeed, Jordanian authorities have continuously promoted that right and preserved its most potent symbols, namely the refugee camps and UNRWA, thus attesting to refugees' citizenship being framed as temporary assimilation not affecting their status as refugees (Al Husseini and Bocco 2009: 4). However, it has remained difficult for Jordan to showcase the same level of commitment to the "right of return" as other Arab host countries precisely because, as citizens, the 1948 refugees could not be officially treated differently. By this token, the ex-Gazans have become the benchmark Palestinians against which Jordan's commitment to the principle of the "right of return" to Palestine has been continuously tested at national and regional levels. A refusal to assimilate ex-Gazans through citizenship, with all the implications this has in terms of reduced rights and access to services, remains for Jordan the primary symbol of such a commitment.

The ensuing substandard socioeconomic status that was to affect ex-Gazans (see next subsections) was reinforced by the complex nature of relations between Jordan and the Palestine Liberation Organization (PLO) after the latter's takeover by guerrilla movements and their relocation to Amman and other cities of (East) Jordan after the 1967 Arab-Israeli conflict. In retrospect, such relations have been marked, on the Jordanian side, by concerns over the regime's survival and stability as the PLO emerged as a military and political actor in Jordan in the late 1960s. While the military threat posed by the Palestinian guerrillas that controlled large swathes of Jordanian territory was thwarted through army intervention during the Black September events of 1970–1971,[17] the perceived menace of a possible Palestinian political takeover of Jordan remains vivid to this day. Several factors have fueled such a perception. First, Arab League and UN General Assembly recognition, in 1974, of the PLO as the sole political

[16] As specified in the Arab League "Protocol on the Treatment of Palestinian Refugees" (the Casablanca Protocol) of 1965 that Jordan formally ratified without reservations; in https://unispal.un.org/DPA/DPR/unispal.nsf/0/E373EB5C166347AE85256E36006948BA

[17] The Black September events of 1970 (and 1971 in the region of Jerash) was a conflict between the Jordanian army loyal to the Hashemite regime and PLO-affiliated factions.

representative of the Palestinian people[18] launched competition between Jordan and the PLO regarding representation of Jordan's Palestinian residents in international fora (Brand 1995). Second, from the early 1980s, insistent voices from within Israel's right-wing parties have proposed that Jordan become Palestinians' alternative homeland.[19]

Seeking to distance itself from the Palestinian question and its inherent dangers, the Jordanian authorities pandered more openly to their nationalist Transjordanian base; that is, to those citizens who lived in the East Bank prior to the arrival of Palestinian refugees and who, wary of any expression of an alternative Palestinian identity in Jordan, have championed a "Transjordanian" identity as the sole legitimate foundation of the Jordanian state (Abu-Odeh 1999; Massad 2001; Nanes 2008). As the Palestinian uprising against the Israeli occupation of Gaza and the West Bank (the *Intifāḍa*) of 1987 rapidly threatened to spill over into Jordan (Shlaim 2008: 454), King Hussein took a spectacular step. In July 1988, under the motto "Jordan is not Palestine,"[20] he unilaterally severed the legal and administrative links Jordan had maintained with the West Bank since 1967. In 1991, the Jordanian National Charter further emphasized the political threat the Palestinians constituted to the country's stability: "The Jordanian-Palestinian relationship must not be understood or exploited . . . to lead to a weakening of the Jordanian state from the inside or to create conditions leading to the realization of Zionist designs to make Jordan an alternative to the Palestinian homeland."[21] Such a threat, voiced to this day under the slogan "no to an alternative homeland, no to [permanent] resettlement,"[22] has led Jordanian authorities to stifle any manifestation of Palestinian nationalism on its territory, as well as to limit the representation of Jordanians of Palestinian origin in parliament and their recruitment into the higher echelons of public administration (Abu-Odeh 1999). In parallel, they have underscored the temporariness of ex-Gazans' stay in Jordan and opposed any significant influx of Palestinian populations from the occupied Palestinian territories, Iraq, or Syria (Al Husseini and Signoles 2009; Erakat 2014), it being clear, as a governmental official stated, that "The Palestinians from outside Jordan, be they from the occupied Palestinian territories or the Diaspora, should not be enticed to come over to Jordan because of comparatively better treatment of Palestinians."[23] These views effectively ruled out any prospect of access to citizenship for ex-Gazans, resulting in their continuing to

[18] UN Resolution 3210 (XXIX), October 14, 1974, and text of the Rabat's Summit Resolution on Palestine, http://www.monde-diplomatique.fr/cahier/proche-orient/rabat74-en

[19] For example: Al-Najjar, Abdel Nasser, "The Promotion of an 'alternative homeland' is an odious Israeli plot," *MEMO*, January 20, 2020, https://www.middleeastmonitor.com/20200120-the-promotion-of-an-alternative-homeland-is-an-odious-israeli-plot/

[20] The royal decision, which entailed the withdrawal of Jordanian citizenship from West Bankers (their citizen ID being replaced by a travel document) was taken eight months after the outbreak of the first Palestinian uprising (*Intifāḍa*) in December 1987; see: *Address to the Nation*, July 31, 1988, http://www.kinghussein.gov.jo/88_july31.html

[21] The National Charter is a document prepared by a royal commission tasked to lay the foundations of national public activity following the disengagement from the West Bank in 1988 and the resumption of democratic life in 1989, with the first multi-party parliamentary elections since 1956.

[22] "King says Jerusalem a red line, no to alternative homeland; affirms history of Arab Army in Palestine," March 27, 2019, https://kingabdullah.jo/en/news/king-says-jerusalem-red-line-no-alternative-homeland-affirms-history-arab-army-palestine

[23] Interview with representatives of the Ministry of Labor and Jordan Investment Commission, September 2018.

face obstacles in accessing civil rights and entitlements. However, as will be seen in Sections 2.2 and 2.3, other contextual factors have at times played a more positive role in shaping the ex-Gazan regime. First, lulls in Jordanian-PLO tensions, such as on the conclusion of a partnership institutionalized through the Amman Accords in February 1985,[24] have contributed to decisive and durable improvements in the ex-Gazans' status and living conditions, notably in terms of identification documents. Second, ex-Gazans' contribution to the local economy as workers, investors/entrepreneurs, or simply as tax/fee payers has been seen to benefit the local economy and earned them (limited) access to economic entitlements. Third, pressure from UNRWA or Jordanian entities traditionally favorable to the improvement of Palestinian refugees' status, such as the Palestine Parliamentary Committee[25] or the king himself,[26] has at times led the government to improve the terms of ex-Gazans' integration.

Against this background, the following sections analyze the evolution of two key aspects of the ex-Gazan legal regime: first, the granting of Jordanian Identity Documents (IDs) as documents to be used by ex-Gazans as travel documents, proxy residence permits, and to access public services. Second, access to public services in the fields of education, health, employment, and ownership according to criteria specific to each of these fields.

2.2. Identification Documents: Toward Long-Term Integration Short of Assimilation

The issuance of Jordanian IDs to ex-Gazans has usually been accompanied by an official narrative asserting their purely functional or humanitarian purpose. Notwithstanding, the issuance of IDs has still spurred controversial debates about their significance and the long-term impact on both the "right of return" and on Jordan's political and socioeconomic fabric.

2.2.1. The One-Year Temporary Passport Experiment (1967–1974): Jordan's Economic Interests versus Arab Concerns

As alluded to above, Gazan displaced persons were still considered temporary residents until early 1968; however, their inclusion into the labor market (with the exception of professional occupations and the public sector reserved for Jordanians) was tolerated, and indeed encouraged as an economic asset, in particular for entrepreneurs and

[24] The Amman Accords between Jordan and a weakened PLO (following Israel's invasion of Lebanon in 1982 and the loss of its military bases there) promoted the principle of land for peace (with Israel) and self-determination for Palestinians within the framework of an Arab Confederal Union between Jordan and Palestine. The Accords were abrogated in 1986 following the refusal of the PLO's left-wing parties to endorse them.

[25] This Committee is one of the Parliament's permanent Committees. It informs and provides recommendations on any issue concerning the "Palestine issue."

[26] Until the late 1980s, the King (Hussein) managed Jordan's ex-Gazan policy. With the resumption of democratic life in 1989 and the first multi-party elections held since 1956, the King has limited his involvement to offering recommendations. For example, in 2005, King Abdullah recommended facilitating ex-Gazans' access to universities and to treatment for acute and chronic diseases.

businessmen, some of whom also operated in the Gulf countries. Following complaints about the cumbersome procedures involved in traveling back and forth to Jordan with Egyptian travel documents,[27] King Hussein decided in late 1967 to facilitate their travels by granting them, by royal decree, a renewable one-year Jordanian temporary passport (TP1) in exchange for their Egyptian documents. The distribution of the TP1 was extended through 1968 to ex-Gazans in need of specific medical or educational services abroad, a trend that was institutionalized in the Passports Law of 1969, of which article 13 stipulates that temporary passports of one-year maximum not conferring citizenship may be issued in special cases.

However, in the early 1970s, several Arab countries, including Egypt, expressed concern that a generalized issuance of TP1 might lead to the unrestrained settlement of ex-Gazans across the Middle East. This led Jordan to distribute the TP1 sparsely and on an ad hoc basis for exceptional medical and educational purposes until about 1974.

2.2.2. The 1974 Identification Card for Ex-Gazans: A Limited Inclusion and Security-Oriented Step

By 1974 it had become clear that ex-Gazans were unlikely to return to Gaza following the regional status quo resulting from the 1973 Arab-Israeli War. Jordan then granted them a special personal ID card, the Identification Card for [ex-Gazans], to facilitate security checks and daily commercial transactions in Jordan. With no time limit, it offered for the first time proof of open-ended residence in the kingdom pending a possible future return to Palestine.[28] However, it was made clear that the granting of this ID card was not to be interpreted as a step toward formal citizenship. Ex-Gazans continued to be considered protracted temporary foreign displaced persons and holders of Egyptian travel documents. The security lens through which the Jordan authorities viewed Palestinian residents at large following Black September seemed to preclude any further integration in the country (Abu-Odeh 1999). Moreover, the PLO's successful bid to impose itself regionally and internationally as the sole representative of the Palestinian people during the same year buttressed this security approach.

2.2.3. Temporary Jordanian Passports since 1986: Reconciling Long-Term Integration and Temporary Status

The rapprochement in February 1985 between Jordan and the PLO around the Amman Accords somewhat tempered Jordan's security approach toward Palestinians. It resulted in King Hussein's decision to grant temporary passports of three years (TP3) to ex-Gazans who had resided in Jordan for a minimum of ten years. The most comprehensive document granted to the ex-Gazans so far, the TP3 was meant to replace all previous Egyptian and Jordanian identification documents. However, its issuance faced opposition from the PLO which viewed the TP3 as paving way to ex-Gazans' assimilation in Jordan, thereby undermining its own representation of this

[27] It necessitated, for those ex-Gazans who wished to return to Jordan, a Permission to Return Document by the Ministry of Interior; interview with Civil Registration and Passports Department, Amman, April 5, 2017.

[28] Interview with Civil Status Department, Amman, February 25, 2016.

segment of the Palestinian people.[29] Thus, distribution first started on a small scale in 1986, after the PLO's rejection of the Amman Accords and the new breakdown of Jordan-PLO relations. As a Jordanian minister then tersely commented, "Now we [the government] can be more relaxed in our attitudes towards the Gaza refugees."[30]

Jordan's dismantling of its legal and administrative links with the West Bank in 1988 put an end to the "liberal" TP3 experiment. While West Bankers lost their Jordanian citizenship, ex-Gazans' TP3 was reduced to 2 years (TP2), and issuance was restricted. For example, TP2s that were expired for a year or more were not to be renewed,[31] and ex-Gazan women marrying a resident of Gaza lost their TP2.[32] The discrimination faced by ex-Gazans also concerns the modalities of issuance of the TP2. Commonly described by ex-Gazans as humiliating, the process of issuing the TP2 underlines their sub-resident status. First, it is relatively costly: JD100 per issuance, double the cost of a Jordanian national passport. Some poor ex-Gazans cannot afford the TP2 at all, and others are reluctant to obtain it despite the adverse consequences: lacking a TP2 can complicate registration in UNRWA and public schools, opening bank accounts, and acquiring contract loans (see Section 2.3). It is also a relatively long process, taking 7-10 days, while a Jordanian citizen gets his/her passport within a matter of hours. This time includes security clearance steps which can lead to withdrawal of IDs from ex-Gazans suspected of misconduct or of unlawful political activities. The unilateral withdrawal of ID documents, "one of the main tools used by the Jordanian authorities to deter or punish wrongdoing ex-Gazans,"[33] can deprive them of access to Jordanian or UNRWA services and limit their freedom of movement by exposing them to the risk of arrest at any police roadblock. In such situations, ex-Gazans can institutionally reconnect with their Palestinian identity by acquiring a proof of Identity Certificate from the Palestine Embassy in Amman. This eases movement within Jordan; however, the document remains, somewhat ironically, "the least of an ID a Palestinian may have in Jordan."[34]

2.2.4. The Temporary Residency Card of 2004: Managing the Integration of Ex-Gazans Amid Protests within Jordanian Society

While the issuance of the TP3 and TP2 for ex-Gazans was uncontroversial, that of the Temporary Residence Card (TRC) issued some 15 years later (in 2004) sparked controversial debates around the legal and political status of ex-Gazans in Jordan. The government's decision to issue the TRC was a response to popular ex-Gazan protests against an earlier decision to increase the fee for the TP2 from JD20 to JD50. Highlighting the fact that many ex-Gazans could no longer afford the TP2, the Palestine

[29] Interview with a former member of Jordan's Ministry of Foreign Affairs, Amman, June 2019.

[30] *Note for the Record—Meeting with the Minister of Occupied Territories Affairs on 8 July 1986* (UNRWA, Central Registry Archives).

[31] Articles 8 and 9 of *the Disengagement Regulations for the Year 1988*, https://www.refworld.org/docid/43cd04b94.html

[32] Their children are not granted TP2s. In: Interview at Civil Registration and Passport Department, Amman, April 5, 2017, and *Summaries of Jordanian Press* detailing the Royal decision of 1991 (UNRWA, Central Registry Archives).

[33] Interview with lawyer working on human rights issues in Jordan, Amman, June 2019.

[34] Interview with Palestine Embassy official, January 2018.

Parliamentary Committee suggested that an alternative, cheaper, identification document be issued for daily transactions. The TRC was thus made available to all ex-Gazans over the age of sixteen at a lower cost (JD2). This administrative measure provoked fear, mainly among "Transjordanian" circles that, given the absence of any durable solution to the Palestinian refugee issue, the TRC might de facto represent an acknowledgment of ex-Gazans' permanent settlement outside Palestine. In the words of one member of parliament, "[g]iving Gazans residence cards is unacceptable. By doing this, the government is allowing for permanent settlement of the refugees and thus it waives their 'right of return.'"[35] The government quickly clarified that the TRC had "no political implications," being a purely humanitarian gesture aimed to facilitate transactions for those unable to afford the two-year temporary passport.[36] For that matter, as the ex-Gazans were quick to notice, unlike the 1974 Identification Card that had no time limit, the TRC had a (renewable) validity of one year only.

In this balancing act, the Jordanian government maintained the TRC as a recognition of the ex-Gazans' right to reside in the country, while preserving their legal status as temporary residents awaiting their return to Palestine. In so doing, it secured its standing as a defender of that right in the eyes of the Arab World and the Palestinian refugees at large. It also bolstered its internal standing as the ultimate guarantor of internal stability by mitigating on the one hand the political concerns of part of Jordanian society wary of a rampant "palestinization" of Jordan, and on the other hand the residency and livelihood concerns of the ex-Gazans.

2.3. Variegated Access to Services and Entitlements: Fragmenting Ex-Gazans' Lives

While the IDs made available to the ex-Gazans granted them residency in Jordan, it did not delimit their access to education, health, employment and ownership. Also here, access has been determined by political, economic and administrative considerations tied to Jordan's internal and external stability. In sum, while they in principle have been eligible for basic services provided by UNRWA or the Jordanian government, higher education, access to employment and ownership have been restricted in the name of either the preservation of the "right of return," the interests of the economy or to pander to segments of Jordanian society.

2.3.1. Public Education and Medical Services: Ex-Gazans as Semi-citizens

Jordanian authorities and ex-Gazans have generally considered UNRWA the main provider of basic services, in particular primary education and medical services, as well as relief and social services since Jordan's National Aid Fund for the poor is earmarked for Jordanian citizens. However, the UNRWA welfare system has shown its limits. Firstly, some 40,000 individuals not previously registered with UNRWA in

[35] "No political implications for Gazans' residence cards—Habashneh," *Jordan Times*, October 5, 2004.
[36] *Idem.*

Gaza are in principle ineligible to register with UNRWA and benefit from its services, except on an ad hoc basis when they live in camp catchment areas. Furthermore, due to UNRWA's inability to keep pace with the increasing demand for its services due to population growth, refugees (especially those living outside camps) have increasingly resorted to the Jordanian basic services system.

In the field of primary education, Jordan has officially adopted an inclusionary policy, whereby ex-Gazans have been able to access the (10) years of basic schooling in public schools without fees normally paid by non-nationals. However, closer inspection indicates that this is not a given. For instance, the decision to exempt ex-Gazan children from school fees is formally renewed yearly. Even the principle of enrollment itself has been questioned by the Ministry of Education at various times since the late 1990s. The enrollment of Iraqi and, later, Syrian refugees in public schools led to overcrowded classrooms, prompting the Ministry to state that other non-Jordanian children, such as ex-Gazan children, would only be enrolled based on the schools' (limited) capacity.[37] More recently, in 2020, the Ministry required that ex-Gazan students hold the (relatively expensive) TP2 to enroll in public schools, despite a 2018 government decision specifying that the less expensive TRC would be sufficient. In most cases, intervention by the Palestine Parliamentary Committee and/or the Royal Court has enabled ex-Gazans to (re)enroll in public schools free of charge.[38] Yet, the government's earlier decisions have exacerbated uncertainty among ex-Gazans with respect to their status and access to public services, thus fueling feelings of estrangement within Jordanian society.

Ex-Gazans' access to the Jordanian public health system has followed a similar trend. For decades, they could only rely on UNRWA's primary medical services[39] and were excluded from the national medical insurance system. Expensive treatment costs were covered on an ad hoc, humanitarian, basis by the government or the Royal Court. In 2007, increasing pressure from ex-Gazans prompted UNRWA to approach Jordanian authorities to request that they be integrated into the country's Civil (Health) Insurance Programme that covers government employees, Jordanian poor and disabled persons, as well as all Jordanians under 6 years of age. Jordan's government responded positively—but partially and typically as a humanitarian gesture devoid of any "mischievous political objectives."[40] It agreed to fully include ex-Gazan children under 6 years of age but to treat those over 6 years as "uninsured Jordanians" who are subsidized at 40/50 percent in government hospitals.[41] Yet, ex-Gazans remain vulnerable to chronic diseases not covered by the Civil Insurance Programme, such as

[37] "Nothing new regarding the admission of the Ex-Gazans in governmental schools," May 2, 2015, http://royanews.tv/news/39212/%D9%84%D8%A7;.

[38] "Exemption of the holders of temporary passports from the decision to raise fees in governmental schools to non-Jordanians," *al-Ghad,* August 29, 2006.

[39] UNRWA does not provide hospitalization services but operates a referral service to public hospitals for the poorest registered refugees (about 3 percent of the total registered refugees—https://www.unrwa.org/sites/default/files/content/resources/unrwa_in_figures_2020_eng_v2_final.pdf).

[40] Instruction No.11 of the year 2007 on the Treatment of Gazans in Ministry of Health Hospitals and Centres (published in Official Gazette, No. 3827, May 16, 2007, p. 3611 (free healthcare for children up to 6) and p. 3612 (subsidized fees equivalent to uninsured Jordanians).

[41] Poor ex-Gazans were also exempted from cancer treatment and dialysis costs; see 2007 Cabinet Decision No. 4827 (May 16, 2007); and Cabinet Decision No. 116 on Mechanism for the Treatment of Cancer Patients (June 19, 2018).

heart and brain diseases, and very few are insured through private insurance schemes (Kvittingen et al. 2019: 73).[42] As government or Royal Court sources of financial support for the ex-Gazans' medical needs have dried up in the past few years, early deaths due to lack of adequate treatment are said to have taken place.[43]

2.3.2. Higher Education and Employment: From Quasi-citizen to International Status

The evolution of access to higher education and employment embodies for many ex-Gazans Jordan's arbitrary decisions they have been subjected to since their arrival in Jordan.

Until 1986/7, ex-Gazans had been allowed to access university through the competitive registration process (*tanāfusī*) available for Jordanians. Since then, ex-Gazan students have been transferred to the registration system for foreign students (*mūwāzī dawlī*), where the more expensive tuition fees are comparable to those of private universities.[44] To explain this change, ex-Gazans refer to a possible consequence of Jordan's disengagement from the West Bank/Palestine and/or to a need to buffer university budgets. To access higher education, ex-Gazans with little means have depended on community financial support,[45] and on the discretionary support offered by the Royal Court or the Palestine Embassy in the form of subsidized university places.[46] Nevertheless, it is believed that a majority of ex-Gazan university candidates are effectively prevented from enrollment at university.

Employment is another area where ex-Gazans' entitlements have been limited and/or drastically diminished, seriously eroding their trust in the government and feeling of integration in Jordan. Until 2016 ex-Gazans, in contrast to migrant workers, could freely access and work in sectors not strictly reserved for Jordanian citizens. This included most menial, vocational, and technical jobs, and a handful of professional occupations open to foreigners when specialized Jordanian labor is not available, or based on reciprocity agreements between Jordan and the Palestinian Authority.[47] The

[42] As found by Fafo in 2011, only 30 percent of ex-Gazans living outside camps and 17 percent of ex-Gazans living inside camps had health insurance (Tiltnes and Zhang 2013: 100), as compared to 70 percent amongst Jordanians. See "55% of population, 68% of Jordanians covered by health insurance," *The Jordan Times*, February 22, 2016.

[43] The few beneficiaries of such exemptions are only allowed to attend public hospitals that are ill equipped to treat such diseases; interview with President of the Jerash Camp Services Committee, May 20, 2017.

[44] Fees for the foreign students are from four times (computer science) to nine times (English) higher than that of Jordanian students eligible through the competitive registration process.

[45] For instance, the Jerash camp committee mobilizes a pool of private donors that cover the costs of university fees and other administrative fees, including for security clearance and valid identification documents.

[46] The Royal Privilege quota provides 350 university places at *tanāfusī* fees to camp refugees. The Palestine Embassy quota provides 189 places, limited to literary and scientific streams, for all Palestinian applicants from both inside and outside Jordan.

[47] For instance, ex-Gazans can practice as engineers and doctors but cannot establish their own contracting business/practice and are not entitled to retirement pensions. Nurses and specialized doctors are tied to the specific health facility where they are employed. Ex-Gazans, as other foreigners, face difficulties in establishing businesses, especially those who do not hold the TP2, as most commercial banks only grant loans to ex-Gazans holding the TP2.

singularity of ex-Gazans' situation (working without a working permit) was widely interpreted by them as a recognition of their resident status as a displaced population unable to return to their homeland. Since 2016, within the framework of a reform of the labor market aimed at promoting the employment of Jordanian nationals (and Syrian refugees)[48] at the expense of foreign workers, ex-Gazans have been required to obtain work permits akin to those imposed on migrant workers, which has resulted in fewer jobs available to them, including within technical/vocational sectors.[49] Explaining this abrupt change in the ex-Gazans' employment status, the Ministry of Labor merely stated that there had never been any deliberate policy to treat ex-Gazans differently to other foreign workers; their situation had simply not (yet) been regulated.[50] Again, this decision triggered a controversial political debate. On the one hand, "Transjordanian" political circles not only supported the decision but suggested that since ex-Gazans were subject to work permits, they, like other migrant workers, should also be required to obtain yearly residence permits.[51] On the other hand, ex-Gazans supported by the Palestine Parliamentary Committee attacked the government's disregard for the financial burden imposed on ex-Gazans by its decision (the cheapest agricultural work permits cost JD300—about a month's wage), and the symbolic downgrading of ex-Gazans' status from protracted refugees/displaced persons to migrant workers.[52] The government emerged again as a balancing actor. It upheld its decision but waived the work permit fee,[53] and, more importantly, reassured ex-Gazans that their residence rights would remain unaffected by the shift in their employment status.[54]

2.3.3. Real Estate Ownership: Ex-Gazans as Sub-foreigners

Real estate ownership arguably best manifests the attachment of individuals to their place of abode, and ex-Gazans' ownership rights have remained severely restricted. Real estate ownership for non-Jordanians is governed by a 2002 law that grants them the right to purchase residential property within municipal zoned areas upon approval of the Prime Minister and the Ministry of Finance. In 2006, the law was revised so that "holders of temporary passports" also have to secure the agreement of the Ministry of

48 In 2016, Jordan and its main international donors signed a Compact, whereby Jordan accepted to facilitate Syrian refugees' access to the labor market in exchange for increased international assistance and trade incentives.

49 The occupations closed to foreigners have recently expanded to include all administrative and clerical occupations, warehouse and sales, in addition to electricity, mechanical and car repair professions, guards, and servants. In other occupations, a quota is imposed; https://data2.unhcr.org/en/documents/details/59816

50 "Statement from the Ministry of Labor regarding ex-Gazans holders of temporary passports," January 9, 2016, http://www.petra.gov.jo/Public_News/Nws_NewsDetails.aspx?lang=1&site_id=2&NewsID=231963&Type=P.

51 "Weakening of the rights of the holders of temporary passports . . . and an MP demands their deportation towards Palestine," *al-Quds*, January 20, 2016

52 "Campaign lobbying against work permits for temporary passport holders," *Jordan Times*, January 14, 2016.

53 Ex-Gazans are only required to pay the administrative fee of JD10 that is also imposed on Syrian refugees; see "Temporary passport holders exempted from work permit fees," *Jordan Times*, January 10, 2016.

54 According to the Interior Minister's speech at the Parliament, in "No residency permits required for Gazans with temporary passports," *The Jordan Times*, January 23, 2016.

Interior.[55] In practice, however, access to real estate ownership for ex-Gazans has from the outset only been granted on an ad hoc basis by decrees, the rationale of which is not necessarily shared with the public administration in charge of land registration and transactions. In July 1986, when King Hussein authorized the issuance of the TP3 for ex-Gazans, he also permitted them to purchase up to one dunum (=1,000 m^2) of housing property per household for private use.[56] There are no estimates of the number of properties acquired by ex-Gazans at that time, but it is believed to have been massive, with some families said to have accumulated up to fifteen dunums before the authorization was lifted about a year later.[57] Since then, opportunities for acquiring property have been provided twice to help revitalize a stagnant real estate sector, but with heavy restrictions that betray the Jordanian authorities' inherent reluctance. In 2009, ownership opportunities were opened for a mere three months. Since 2019, property ownership has again been open to ex-Gazans, but only to heads of households who can register either a residence or land not exceeding one dunum, and inheritance is in principle limited to the usufruct of the property.[58]

2.3.4. A Functional Citizenship for Ex-Gazan Children of Jordanian Women?

In 2002, Queen Rania recommended at the Arab Women's Summit that Jordanian women married to non-Jordanians, including ex-Gazans, should pass on their citizenship to their children. The government initially approved of Queen Rania's initiative before withdrawing its support under pressure from "Transjordanian" political circles fearful that such a step would entail the naturalization of hundreds of thousands of Palestinian children and encourage the idea of Jordan as an alternative homeland for Palestinians.[59] In 2014, the government, supported by King Abdullah himself, again adopted a compromise solution. It continued to deny those children citizenship but decided to grant them civil rights on a par with Jordanian citizens, notably in the fields of real estate ownership, higher education, health services, and employment. This could have potentially benefited a population of 155,000 children of Palestinian temporary passport holders—including 42,000 children of ex-Gazan fathers. However, by 2018 only 72,000 yellow Identification Cards for the Children of Jordanian Women had been granted.[60] Many ex-Gazans claim that it remains difficult to obtain, requiring security clearance, and is not recognized by most local administrations.[61]

55 Law No. 47 of 2006 on the Rent and Selling of Immovable Properties to Non-Jordanians and Legal Persons, par. 7.

56 *Note for the Record—Meeting with the Minister of Occupied Territories Affairs on 8 July 1986* (UNRWA, Central Registry Archives).

57 Interview with Land Authority, Amman, May 2019; focus group discussions in Jerash, April 10, 2017.

58 "Details about land ownership for ex-Gazans in Jordan," *Al-Wakil News*, January 16, 2020.

59 *Foreigners in Their Own Land Jordanian Women & Hereditary Citizenship*, December 28, 2007, http://black-iris.com/2007/12/28/foreigners-in-their-own-land-jordanian-women-hereditary-citizenship/

60 Out of a total population of children of Jordanian women estimated at 350,000; interview with Civil Registration and Passports Department, Amman, April 5, 2017.

61 Interviews with ex-Gazans in Mārkā camp, April 17, 2017; Human Rights Watch, "'*I Just Want Him to Live Like Other Jordanians' – Treatment of Non-Citizen Children of Jordanian Mothers*," April 24, 2018, https://www.hrw.org/report/2018/04/24/i-just-want-him-live-other-jordanians/treatment-non-citizen-children-jordanian#

3. A Population in Limbo?

3.1. Variable Layers of Vulnerability

Since the mid-2000s, in a context marked by the demise of the Israeli-Palestinian peace process and the rise of radical Islamism across the Middle East, several international stakeholders, including the European Union, have expressed concern for the situation of ex-Gazans and their future in Jordan. Due to the restrictions placed on their access to employment, ownership, and services, ex-Gazans social and political marginalization could constitute a breeding ground for political destabilization.

A 2011 socioeconomic study conducted by the Norwegian research foundation Fafo among the inhabitants of Jordan's thirteen refugee camps confirmed that, across a series of poverty lines, ex-Gazans are poor about twice as often as Palestinian refugees holding Jordanian citizenship (Tiltnes and Zhang 2013: 257).[62] As a consequence of grinding poverty, poor ex-Gazans have resorted to negative coping strategies, including accruing debts, not renewing the TP2, and reducing food, educational, and medical expenditures, which have further contributed to undermining their economic, social, and physical status.

Nevertheless, ex-Gazans of all walks of life stress that the main challenge they face is their particular legal situation and the sense of uncertainty this generates. They resent the fact that more than half a century after their arrival in Jordan, they still live as stateless persons with limited economic and social rights, especially in the fields of employment and ownership, and are subject to unfair and unsubstantiated changes in legislation, and frequent security checks. The experience of uncertainty is a pervasive feature of prolonged displacement in which the granting of liminal status to refugees or reactive and ad hoc policies may be explicit governance strategies and/or result from weak governance (Horst and Grabska 2015; Nassar and Stel 2019). However, unlike many other refugee populations, ex-Gazans' sense of uncertainty has been difficult to face since the hallmarks of their legal regime, statelessness, and reduced civil rights continue to be officially presented positively as a means of preserving their Palestinian nationality. This is reflected in ex-Gazans' narratives which rarely contest the official positive discrimination discourse. Rather, they question more generally Jordan's staunch stance not to treat them on a par with the 1948 refugees, whose "right of return" is in principle also preserved, and castigate the volatility and increasingly discriminatory nature of decisions regarding their status. Being ex-Gazan, most concurred, has become a social stigma.

Nonetheless, ex-Gazans do usually recognize the support they have received from various domestic entities, including the Palestine Parliamentary Committee and the Royal Court, which have at times intervened when government decisions were deemed arbitrary and unfair. As for UNRWA, ex-Gazans agree that its assistance has extended beyond the delivery of humanitarian services to include their preferential recruitment

[62] The overall poverty rates of ex-Gazans are primarily due to the alarmingly dismal conditions of the remote Jerash refugee camp, where the impact of their status is particularly accentuated (52.3 percent of its residents report incomes under the national poverty line) (Kvittingen et al 2019: 67).

as local staff doctors, nurses, teachers, administrators, and menial workers. Although employment by UNRWA does not cover all their employment needs, it represents one of few available secure sources of income (Perez 2010: 7; Kvittingen et al. 2019: 89).[63] Moreover, the Agency is often portrayed by ex-Gazans as their only effective representative (though limited to the socioeconomic sphere), as the PLO has remained conspicuously silent about their predicament. Yet, ex-Gazans concur that so far positive interventions have mitigated some effects but failed to address the core issue: their lack of citizenship or equivalent rights. Dwindling hopes of any return to Palestine and estrangement from the Palestinian state-building process in the West Bank and Gaza Strip have reinforced ex-Gazans' sense of abandonment.[64]

3.2. Windows of Opportunity?

It would be inaccurate to depict ex-Gazans merely as a passive community subject to an unfair and arbitrary legal regime. First, as Perez (2018) has argued, in the context of precarious situations, the ability to repeat ordinary daily activities in work and at home possesses its own form of agential effort. Second, ex-Gazans have resourcefully deployed various strategies to circumvent their legal restrictions. For example, they have resorted to informal, or uncertified, land transfer agreements or given power of attorney to other close Jordanian citizen proxies (in-laws, business partners, acquaintances) to purchase property for them. More radically, ex-Gazans have sought to escape their legal regime altogether, including through work migration to the Gulf countries or through marriage of ex-Gazan women to Jordanian men (ex-Gazan women can obtain citizenship after three years' marriage). Yet, here again, far from challenging the ex-Gazan regime, these strategies have often just underlined ex-Gazans' vulnerability. For instance, purchasing property through a Jordanian proxy entails risking the latter, or his/her descendants, breaching the informal agreement: many ex-Gazans are said to have lost their property or paid for it more than once.[65] Meanwhile, job opportunities in the Gulf have diminished in recent years, and marriage arrangements are necessarily limited (Kvittingen et al. 2019).

Whereas ex-Gazans have individually and as families sought to improve their material conditions and opportunities, their record on collective action is limited. As stateless non-citizens deprived of the right to vote, to be elected to parliament or to register in any political party and, moreover, under constant threat that their IDs might

[63] In recognition of the challenges they face in finding employment, UNRWA has prioritized the employment of ex-Gazans: they represent about 20 percent of UNRWA's local staff in Jordan although they make up only around 7 percent of the Palestine refugee population; interview with UNRWA official, January 2020.

[64] Ex-Gazans have generally maintained contacts with their relatives in Gaza through phone calls and social media. Marriages between ex-Gazans and Gazans also take place occasionally, leading to migrations. From 2010 to April 2017, 2,075 ex-Gazans newly married to Gazans migrated to Gaza, compared with 465 that migrated from Gaza to Jordan; interview with UNRWA official, Amman, May 2018.

[65] Interview with Land Authority, Amman, March 2017; focus group discussions in Jerash and Mārkā camps (February–April 2017) and Amman (January 2020).

be withdrawn, they have been deprived of powerful collective mobilization tools.[66] Even grassroots social or cultural initiatives, through which appeals for sympathy and rights might be articulated and members mobilized, have been strictly controlled—if not banned—for fear that they are motivated by underlying political goals contrary to national interests.[67] In retrospect, their main endeavor was a petition signed by 100,000 persons asking the government to grant them citizenship in 2001. The government refused to address the petition in the name of the "right of return" and opposition to permanent resettlement in Jordan.[68] Since then, during sit-ins organized close to Ministries or the Royal Palace, or through statements in the media, ex-Gazans have rather focused on the protection of sectoral interests or on the acquisition of full civil rights (see Perez 2010; Feldman 2012). While such claims have sometimes been endorsed in principle by Jordanian officials, they have ultimately been shelved under the pretense that the cause of the "right of return" is of higher importance than improved living conditions.[69]

In recent years, ex-Gazans have also established committees to give more political voice to their claims, such as the Committee for Gazans Living in Jordan and the Follow-up Committee for the Rights and Issues of the ex-Gazans in Jordan. Very active in the media, they have used internet tools such as Facebook and the blogosphere to convey information about the situation of ex-Gazans to a wider Jordanian audience.[70] While critical of the government, they have tended to promote a spirit of coexistence between ex-Gazans and the Jordanian people. However, they have so far failed to coalesce into an effective ex-Gazan political or social front likely to truly influence the government.

Conclusion

This chapter has sought to analyze how Jordan has legally and administratively governed ex-Gazans since 1967/1968. As a displaced population, ex-Gazans share key commonalities with the main refugee group residing in Jordan, the 1948 Palestinian refugees: a UN-recognized right to return to their original homes in Palestine, be it Gaza or lands under Israel sovereignty since 1948; a right to reside in Jordan pending the implementation of such return; and ethnic/national ties with a "Palestinian people"

66 Even the main opposition political party, the Islamic Action Front, has been lukewarm in its support for the ex-Gazans. Focus group discussion with Jerash camp notables, May 20, 2017.

67 This includes the establishment of volunteer social clubs, the organization of book fairs, theater events, etc. Focus group discussion with ex-Gazan men, Jerash camp, April 17, 2017.

68 See "The government refuses to accord citizenship to one hundred thousand Gazans in line with the Jordanian position related to the preservation of the right of return and compensation," *al-Rai*, October 16, 2002.

69 Interview with ex-Gazans entrepreneurs having met with government officials, Amman, January 2020. Some wealthy ex-Gazan entrepreneurs having thrived in the Gulf countries have received Jordanian citizenship as royal entitlements following meetings with Kings Hussein or Abdullah II.

70 For instance, www.facebook.com/mltakagazajordan, https://ar-ar.facebook.com/CitizenoftheGazaStripinJordan; https://ar-ar.facebook.com/gazafreejo/); or Gaza Camp (https://www.facebook.com/Gazarefugees/.../1505439442822761:0); and the news blog "Gaza Jordan" (https://gazajordan.wordpress.com/)

that has been promised full self-determination in the occupied territories of the West Bank and Gaza. However, it is their key difference from the 1948 refugees—their status as non-citizens—that has defined them as a marginalized socioeconomic and political group shuffled between ad hoc regulatory decisions, limited in their access to socioeconomic rights and restricted in their political voice. The fact that such discrimination has been officially predicated on a professed positive discrimination principle aimed to preserve their "right of return," together with Jordan's security approach to Palestinian affairs in general, has also effectively contributed to stifling their voice. The situation of the ex-Gazans in Jordan raises several issues that question their relationships with host authorities and the latter's mode of governance.

The main issue pertains to the responsibilities of the state toward ex-Gazans and Palestinian refugees in general. Despite the development of universal humanitarian protection instruments that have set standards for the legal and social protection of refugees, state sovereignty remains key to their implementation. Because states often fear that abiding by existing international legal frameworks may be detrimental to their sovereignty and interests, they ultimately decide who is a "refugee" and what his or her rights and entitlements are (e.g. Arar 2017, Janmyr 2017). This is the case in Jordan. Like most other Middle Eastern countries, Jordan is not signatory to the 1951 UN Refugee Convention and its treatment of the Palestinian refugees, be they 1948 refugees or ex-Gazans, has been less underpinned by normative or legal considerations than by internal political and economic considerations, sometimes in the face of opposition of other Arab host countries (e.g., the granting *en masse* of citizenship to the 1948 refugees) or of refugees and their advocates (e.g., maintaining ex-Gazans as a stateless population).

However, the ex-Gazans' case amply shows how access to daily rights and entitlements have also been influenced by interventions of various internal and external parties, at times preventing Jordan from pursuing a coherent ex-Gazan policy. Some interventions have sought to limit the integration of ex-Gazans: the PLO as a means of "keeping a grip" on them (until the mid-1980s) or, more recently, "Transjordanian" political circles aiming to contain an alternative Palestinian identity in Jordan and stem the Israeli-supported "Jordan as a Palestinian homeland" scenario. Conversely, other institutional actors have attempted to improve the status and living conditions of ex-Gazans on humanitarian and/or political-civic grounds, including the Parliament Palestine Committee, the king, and UNRWA. In the face of such divergent forces, the government has had to engage in an often-awkward balancing act to mitigate resulting tensions while preserving Jordan's national interests. However, far from resulting in a balanced and informed agenda, this exercise has chiefly consisted of ad hoc corrective measures designed to cushion the detrimental impact of governmental measures on the most vulnerable ex-Gazans. Reducing the cost of ex-Gazans' work permits to compensate for the fact that they had been relegated to the status of migrant workers in 2016 is a case in point.

Two further issues concern the political and legal limbo the ex-Gazans find themselves in. The first relates to the absence of political authority responsible for their daily legal protection. While Jordan considers itself a host state offering them residence and basic services, the PLO, internationally recognized as their legitimate formal representative, has never been vocal about their situation, and the Palestine Embassy in Amman has to date been denied any representational role for ex-Gazans, limiting its assistance to minimal administrative and material services. The second issue relates to the current significance of the discrimination ex-Gazans have been subjected to in the name of their "right of return" to Palestine.

This right is still proclaimed as sacrosanct by ex-Gazans at large; however, the younger generations increasingly question the way such discrimination is unilaterally imposed on them. What they call for is a progressive ex-Gazan policy reconciling the positive discrimination principle justified by their status with their human rights and aspirations for their future, notably through their being granted Jordanian citizenship or full civil rights. This claim is not new. In other host countries calls to dissociate the right of return from efforts to durably improve living conditions have been made by Palestinian refugees, social activists, and even the Palestinian Authority which, in 2005, went so far as to say that granting Palestinian refugees' functional citizenship (as in Jordan for the 1948 refugees) did not harm the validity of the right of return (Shiblak 2011; Al Husseini and Bocco 2009). The opposition of Arab host states, including Jordan, to endorse such a proposal, exposed for ex-Gazans and other refugees how, with the passing of time, the "right of return" had been squarely appropriated by the state for the sake of preserving national interests.

Bibliography

Abu-Odeh, Adnan (1999), *Jordanians, Palestinians and the Hashemite Kingdom in the Middle East Peace Process*, Washington, DC: US Institute of Peace Press.

Al Husseini, Jalal, and Riccardo Bocco (2009), "The Status of the Palestinian Refugees in the Near East: The Right of Return and UNRWA in Perspective," *Refugee Survey Quarterly*, 28 (2–3): 260–85.

Al Husseini, Jalal, and Aude Signoles (2009), "Construction nationale territorialité, et diasporisation: le cas palestinien," *Maghreb-Machrek*, 199 (1): 23–42.

Arar, Rawan (2017), "Leveraging Sovereignty: The Case of Jordan and the International Refugee Regime," *Refugees and Migration Movements in the Middle East*, Pomeps/ University of Southern California.

Brand, Laurie A. (1995), "Palestinians and Jordanians: A Crisis of Identity," *Journal of Palestine Studies*, 24 (4): 46–61.

El-Abed, Oroub (undated), "Jordan Today: An Open Border Country or a Nationalist One? The Case of the Palestinians." Available online: https://www.academia.edu/206918/Jordan_Today_An_open_border_country_or_a_nationalist_one.

El-Abed, Oroub (2005), "Immobile Palestinians: The Impact of Policies and Practices on Palestinians from Gaza in Jordan," in Hana Jaber and Françoise Métral (eds.), *Mondes en mouvements. Migrants au Moyen-Orient au tournant du XXIe siècle*, 81–92, Beirut: Ifpo.

Erakat, Noura (2014), "Palestinian Refugees and the Syrian Uprising: Filling the Protection Gap During Secondary Forced Displacement," *International Journal of Refugee Law*, 26 (4): 581–621.

Feldman, Ilana (2012), "The Humanitarian Condition: Palestinian Refugees and the Politics of Living," *Humanity: International Journal of Human Rights, Humanitarianism and Development*, 3 (2): 155–72.

Frost, Lillian (2020), *Ambiguous Citizenship: Protracted Refugees and the State in Jordan*, Ph.D. Dissertation, Faculty of The Columbian College of Arts and Sciences, The George Washington University.
General Assembly (1968), *Report of the Commissioner-General of the United Nations Relief and Works Agency for Palestine Refugees in the Near East July 1, 1967 - June 30, 1968*, 23rd Session Supplement 13 (A /7213).
Horst, Cindy, and Katarzyna Grabska (2015), "Flight and Exile—Uncertainty in the Context of Conflict-Induced Displacement," *Social Analysis*, 59 (1): 1–18.
Janmyr, Maja (2017), "No Country of Asylum: 'Legitimizing' Lebanon's Rejection of the 1951 Refugee Convention," *International Journal of Ref Law*, 29 (3): 438–56.
Kvittingen, Anna, Åge A. Tiltnes, Ronia Salman, Hana Asfour, and Dina Baslan (2019), *Just Getting by - Ex-Gazans in Jerash and Other Refugee Camps in Jordan*, Oslo: Fafo Report: 34.
Lesch, Ann M. (1979), "Israeli Deportation of Palestinians from the West Bank and the Gaza Strip, 1967–1978," *Journal of Palestine Studies*, 8 (2), Winter: 101–31.
Lesch, Ann M. (1984), *The Gaza Strip: Heading Toward a Dead End. Part I: History and Politics*, UFSI Reports, 10, Africa/Asia [Aml-1-'84].
Massad, Joseph (2001), *Colonial Effects: The Making of National Identity in Jordan*, New York: Columbia University Press.
Mishal, Saul (1978), *West Bank/East Bank: The Palestinians in Jordan, 1947–1967*, New Haven: Yale University Press.
Nanes, Stefanie (2008), "Choice, Loyalty, and the Melting Pot: Citizenship and National Identity in Jordan," *Nationalism and Ethnic Politics*, 14 (1): 85–116.
Nassar, Jessy, and Nora Stel (2019), "Lebanon's Response to the Syrian Refugee Crisis – Institutional Ambiguity as a Governance Strategy," *Political Geography*, 70 (August): 44–54.
Palestinian Return Centre (2018), *Decades of Resilience – Stateless Gazan Refugees in Jordan*. Available online: https://prc.org.uk/upload/library/files/DecadesOfResilience2018.pdf.
Perez, Michael Vicente (2010), "Human Rights and the Rightless: The Case of Gaza Refugees in Jordan," *The International Journal of Human Rights*, 15 (7): 1031–54.
Perez, Michael Vicente (2018), "The Everyday as Survival among Ex-Gaza Refugees in Jordan," *Middle East Critique*, 27 (3): 275–88.
Sayigh, Rosemary (1979), *Palestinians: From Peasants to Revolutionaries*, London: Zed Books.
Segev, Tom (2007), *1967: Israel, the War, and the Year that Transformed the Middle East*, New York: Metropolitan Books, an imprint of Henry Holt and Company, LLC.
Shiblak, Abbas (2011), "Passport for What Price? Statelessness Among Palestinian Refugees," in Are Knudsen and Sari Hanafi (eds.), *Palestinian Refugees – Identity, Space and Place in the Levant*, 113–27, New York: Routledge.
Shlaim, Avi (2008), *Lion of Jordan - The Life of King Hussein in War and Peace*, London: Penguin Books.
Tiltnes, Åge A., and Huafeng Zhang (2013), *Progress, Challenges, Diversity: Insights into the Socio-Economic Conditions of Palestinian Refugees in Jordan*, Oslo: Fafo Report 2013: 42.

3

Non-reception Policies and Restricted Humanitarian Assistance

The Case of Yemeni Refugees in Jordan

Solenn Al Majali

By early 2021, Jordan was hosting around 14,000 Yemeni refugees.[1] The majority of Yemeni nationals residing in Jordan fled their country of origin because of the current conflict, which started in autumn 2014. As a consequence of Houthi forces[2] taking over the capital, Ṣanʿāʾ, from government control in September 2014 and the intervention of Saudi Arabia in 2015, the war in Yemen has provoked a devastating economic and humanitarian crisis. Nearly 3.65 million Yemenis have been displaced inside the country and around 600,000 fled to neighboring countries in the region, such as Egypt and Djibouti, and to Malaysia.

The number of Yemenis registered with the UNHCR in Jordan has kept growing, as Yemenis have gradually become familiar with asylum procedures and aware of the humanitarian aid to be obtained from the UNHCR, including cash assistance and resettlement in a third country. As Yemen entered its seventh year of conflict in 2021, Yemenis in Jordan no longer plan to return to Yemen and are waiting to be granted refugee status, thereby opening up the possibility of resettlement. However, not all Yemenis register as refugees within the UNHCR. For example, businessmen and students[3] who live in Jordan temporarily and who have not been able to go back to

1 13,902 Yemeni refugees have registered with the UNHCR in Amman (source: February 2021, UNHCR Fact sheet).

2 The Houthis are from the Zaydi branch of Shiʿism (different from Twelver Shiʿism in Iran or in Iraq). There have been several Zaydi imamates in the mountains of northern Yemen since the ninth century. As an example, the Mutawakkilite imamate was established in North Yemen after the collapse of the Ottoman Empire in 1918. In the 1990s, the Houthis, led by the charismatic figure of Hussein al-Houthi, became a major opposition force to former President Ali Abdullah Saleh. In 2004, the president launched military campaigns to fight the Houthi resistance in the northern Yemeni province of al-Saʿāda. During the Arab uprisings, the Houthis were one of the political forces that stood up against Saleh. Saleh's replacement by ʿAbd Rabbuh Manṣūr Hādī, vice-president of Saleh, was rejected by the Houthis, who seized Ṣanʿāʾ in 2014, causing ʿAbd Rabbuh Manṣūr Hādī exile to ʿAdan (Southern Yemen).

3 According to our interviews with the Yemeni ambassador in Jordan (August 2020, Amman), there are fewer than 1,000 Yemeni students in Jordan. They study at the Jordan University, Yarmouk University in ʾIrbid, and Muʾta University in al-Karak.

Figure 3.1 A Yemeni man of Somali origin in Jabal Amman. Source: S. Al Majali, Amman, 2021.

their country since the outbreak of the war, have not registered.[4] Since 2015, they have been joined by members of the middle classes who started to seek refuge in Jordan after being personally threatened by the Houthi militias following their takeover of Ṣanʿāʾ in September 2014. Young Yemeni men were also targeted for forced conscription by Houthi forces and by their ideological indoctrination. In the context of the war, it is important to note that mainly middle- and upper-class Yemenis have been able to travel by airplane with legal visas and to settle abroad. In this chapter, the expression "Yemeni refugees" does not refer to all Yemenis in Jordan, but only to those who have applied for the status granted by the UNHCR. Once in Jordan, Yemenis do not receive the same humanitarian and legal treatment as Syrian refugees by the different reception actors involved, including the Jordanian government, specifically the Ministry of Interior and the Ministry of Labour, as well as the UNHCR Refugee Status Determination section. These stakeholders grant protection to refugees according to the Memorandum of Understanding that was concluded between the Jordanian government and the UN agency since 1998 and amended in 2014.[5] The aim of this chapter is to assess the impact of the formal and actual legal status granted to Yemeni asylum seekers. It examines the reception policies for Yemeni refugees and their legal,

4 However, these students and workers may be recognized as "refugees *sur place*" according to UNHCR categorization.

5 Memorandum of Understanding between UNHCR and the Jordanian government, April 5, 1998.

economic and social inclusion. Since the 1990s, in migration studies, researchers have studied the reception policies of states through the lens of inhospitality (Fassin, Morice and Quiminal 1997; Boudou 2017; Agier 2018; Berg and Fiddian-Qasmiyeh 2018; Stavo-Debauge 2018). Concepts of hospitality and inhospitality are intimately interlinked. Indeed, hospitality has the inherent power to delimit the place that is being offered to the other (Derrida 2000; Derrida and Dufourmantelle 2000 cited by Berg and Fiddian-Qasmiyeh 2018). Although these researches tend to focus on the hosting policies in the Global North, the case of the reception of Yemeni refugees in Jordan illustrates a policy of statutory, economic, and social inhospitality. Thus, I propose to explore reception policies concerning Yemeni refugees from the perspective of inhospitality and non-reception. As Claudio Bolzman shows, state policies have an influence on the "social destiny" of refugees (Bolzman 2001: 139).[6] The sociologist argues that the situation of refugees in a country will largely depend on the reception policies and on the legal status granted. The hosting policies for refugees in Jordan have been the subject of extensive research, particularly concerning Palestinian citizens (Brand 1995; De Bel-Air 2003; Al Husseini 2004), Iraqi refugees (Chatelard and Doraï 2009) as well as Syrian forced migrants (Ababsa 2015; Doraï 2016; Al Husseini and Napolitano 2019). However, few studies have been carried out on the hosting policies of forced migrants of other nationalities. In doing so, this chapter aims to document, by comparison, the reception policies managing other refugee groups. Earlier works on the situation of refugees in Jordan indicate a progressively more precarious status and reduction of life prospects. Yemeni refugees have arrived very recently, since 2015, and are also much less numerous in Jordan than the other refugee populations (such as the Palestinians, Syrians, and Iraqis). Moreover, because of the socioeconomic origin of Yemeni refugees in Jordan, who come mainly from the middle class arriving legally by air, it makes it difficult for the reception actors to determine their status in Jordan. For all these reasons, Yemeni refugees receive little attention from humanitarian actors and researchers.

However, this case study, on the periphery of the large migratory movements, highlights a default hosting policy, a non-reception policy by humanitarian actors that includes both the non-granting of refugee status by the UNHCR to Yemenis, and administrative decisions by the Jordanian Ministry of Interior and Ministry of Labour to limit the socioeconomic integration of Yemenis. This chapter suggests a different approach to Jordan's reception policy from that found in academic literature, in light of Yemeni migratory movements, which also informs the situation of other East-African refugees in Jordan, including Somali and Sudanese forced migrants.[7] It is based on ethnographic fieldwork carried out from January to July 2019 and from June 2020 to September 2020, as part of doctoral research on the processes of exclusion and

6 The exact quote in French is: "Les États récepteurs disposent en fait d'un pouvoir considérable sur les destinées des exilés, qui sont définis par les institutions de la société d'arrivée comme des demandeurs d'asile : par leurs politiques, ils définissent le champ des possibles qui s'ouvre à eux" (Bolzman 2001: 136).

7 6,024 Sudanese and 718 Somalis were registered with UNHCR by February 2021 (UNHCR, February 2021, Fact sheet). Regarding their numbers, they are also considered as "minorities" refugees in Jordan.

sociability within Yemeni refugee groups. This fieldwork includes several semi-directed interviews conducted with female and male Yemeni refugees from 18 to 60 years old living mainly in relatively impoverished neighborhoods of Jabal Amman (in the center of Amman), al-Jbayha (in the north of Amman), and the industrial city of Saḥab on the outskirts of Amman. The dispersed settlement of Yemenis in Amman (also settled in other governorates of Jordan such as ʾIrbid and Maʿān) allows a plurality of social categories to be taken into account. Indeed, in al-Jbayha, Yemenis are composed of

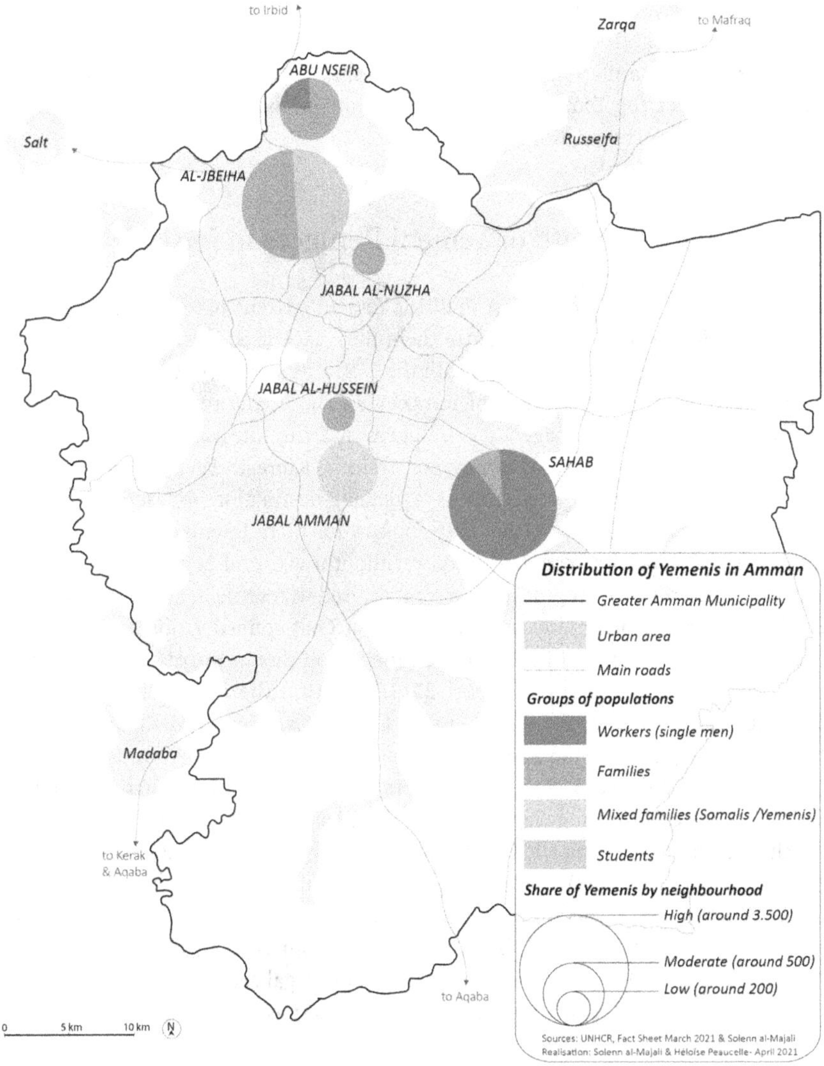

Figure 3.2 A map showing the demographic distribution of Yemeni asylum seekers in the Greater Amman area. By: Solenn Al Majali and Héloïse Peaucelle. April 2021. Sources: UNHCR, Fact sheet February 2021 and interviews with Yemeni respondents.

families and students from middle-class backgrounds coming from the central and northern governorates of Yemen. In Saḥab, the majority are single men working in factories, mainly from the central governorates of Yemen such as ʿIbb and Taʿizz. In Jabal Amman, Yemeni families are of Somali origin, speak Somali and Yemeni dialects, and used to live in ʿAdan in the south of Yemen. They are mainly from middle-class backgrounds but are largely impoverished because of their refugee status in Jordan.

In the first part of this chapter, I will show how the migratory paths that Yemenis took to reach Jordan, who first came as medical migrants, have shaped the policies of the Jordanian ministries and the UNHCR, resulting in an ambiguous status and categorization. Next, I will show how these policies of non-reception have restricted their access to humanitarian and public services. Finally, I will discuss how the non-reception policies for Yemeni asylum seekers hinder their economic insertion and undermine their social relations.

1. The Path of Yemeni Refugees to Jordan

Before the outbreak of the conflict in 2015, Yemeni citizens used to come to Jordan temporarily for medical reasons. Since then, they have used this medical migration as a mobility strategy to seek asylum with the UNHCR in Jordan. Here I use the term "strategy" to refer to the agency[8] of refugees. In the literature on migration, some studies have looked at the agency of refugees and the integration of displacement as strategies to bypass public policy constraints (Kibread 1993; Monsutti 2004). The Hashemite Kingdom was seen as a default destination for Yemeni refugees because, administratively, it was an easy country for them to enter. Until April 2015, Yemenis were allowed to come to Jordan without a visa and generally they did not envisage a long-term stay in this country but aspired to resettle in a Western country.

For many Arab foreigners, such as citizens of Gulf countries, Jordan is seen as a leading destination for medical tourism in the region due to the qualified physicians and well-equipped hospitals (Crouzel 2013: 318–19). The institutions working in this industry are notably the King Hussein Cancer Center, the Al Khalidi Hospital, the Jordan Hospital and the Speciality Hospital, among others. We must also recall that during the 2011 conflict, Syrian fighters were treated in Jordanian hospitals, in particular in the northern governorates and in Amman (Roussel 2015: 227). Also, in March 2018, the Hashemite Kingdom of Jordan eased medical visa procedures for foreign patients to strengthen medical care in the country.[9] These measures were applied to several nationalities such as Syrians, Sudanese, and Yemenis. Previously, there had been restrictions on people of these nationalities from entering Jordan for medical purposes. The visa restrictions were due to fear of illegal settlement in Jordan. After Saudi Arabia's raids on Ṣanʿāʾ in March 2015, Yemenis started to escape the country but

8 In order to refute the image of "refugees" deprived of any choice or will, the concept of "agency" allows us to highlight the strategies that refugees use when facing a reduced range of possibilities.

9 *The Jordan Times*, March 14, 2018. Available online: http://www.jordantimes.com/news/local/medical-tourism-visa-procedure-changes-still-need-additional-steps (accessed July 31, 2021).

faced visa restrictions in countries that had had open-door policies prior to the conflict in Yemen, such as Jordan and Egypt. In April 2015, Jordan required Yemenis to obtain an entry visa, and the easiest way for them to achieve this was by obtaining a medical visa prior to arrival from some specific tourist agencies in Yemen. According to my interviewees, most vulnerable Yemeni families have sold land and personal property to be able to reach Jordan by air. This strategy of mobility has enabled them to enter Jordan and to undergo the Refugee Status Determination process (RSD) conducted by the UNHCR. In this way, they are allowed to stay legally in Jordan for two months. The story of Fahima, a 35-year-old Yemeni woman, is a case in point. She visited Jordan repeatedly for medical treatments before 2015 because her mother had cancer. At that time, Yemenis could enter Jordan without visas, which facilitated their mobility to medical destinations such as Amman. When she was in Jordan in 2015, she realized that she could not go back to Yemen because of the Civil War.[10] Living in Jabal al-Ḥusayn with her family and coming from the middle class, she mobilized her knowledge of the country to settle in Amman. She decided to stay in Jabal al-Ḥusayn because she was familiar with the area and had connections with other Yemeni families. However, with the new policies for Yemenis in Jordan, her status has changed. While she could come to Jordan without a visa before 2015, she now had to regularize her status and therefore applied for refugee status at the UNHCR in Amman. However, this is not the case for all Yemenis in Jordan who were not aware of the asylum procedure when they arrived in 2015/2016. For the medical migration of Yemenis abroad, Beth Kangas prefers not to use the term "medical tourism" as it suggests frivolity and leisure. Instead, she uses the expressions "international medical travel" or "medical migration": "Referring to journeys for life-prolonging treatments as 'tourism' trivializes the health conditions and the lack of services within Yemen and makes the travel seem frivolous. People travel in search of medical care because they cannot access it at home" (Kangas 2010: 353). Local healthcare facilities in Yemen are indeed very limited (Kangas 2007: 296). Yemenis sought medical treatment abroad in different countries such as India, Jordan, Saudi Arabia, and in Western countries for a few wealthy businessmen or high-level government officials. According to anthropologist Kangas, most of the Yemeni patients and the Yemeni community that settled in Amman were from governorates of North Yemen, such as Ṣanʿāʾ and the central governorates (Kangas 2007: 302).

However, since the war in 2015, according to my fieldwork, other members of Yemeni society have settled in Jordan. This is, for instance, the case of the so-called *muwalladīn*, Yemenis of Somali origin who obtained Yemeni nationality[11] and mostly hail from southern governorates, especially from ʿAdan. Hamada, a single

[10] Interview with Fahima, Amman, Jabal al-Ḥusayn, January 2019.

[11] The term *muwallad (muwalladīn*, plural) refers to individuals with an African mother and a Yemeni father. Here we must recall the old links between Somalia and Yemen. Firstly, in the late nineteenth century, under the British protectorate of South Yemen, Somali traders settled in ʿAdan and some of them obtained Yemeni nationality. This emigration was perpetuated with skilled workers who fled from the repressive Somali government of Siad Barre. After the fall of Siad Barre's regime in January 1991, needy Somalis were exiled in Yemen as they claimed Yemeni origins and family networks. Since Somalia's political instability, those who were half Somali/half Yemeni established themselves in Yemen and obtained citizenship, with the new regulation of the late Yemeni president Ali Abdullah Saleh (Pérouse de Montclos 2003: 141).

man of 29 years and a *muwallad* originally from ʿAdan, came to Jordan in 2014.[12] He worked as an electrician in a factory in ʿAdan. As a *muwallad* in Yemen, he faced social discrimination[13] in accessing the job market and he felt his prospects of life in Yemen were further diminished by the conflict. He decided to travel to Jordan, temporarily benefiting from the open-door policies at that time, until Jordan imposed visa restrictions on Yemenis in April 2015. He decided to settle in Jabal Amman where a Somali female friend of his mother hosted him. After the situation deteriorated in Yemen, he decided, in 2018, to bring his mother and brothers to Jordan using medical visas that they obtained from a travel agency in ʿAdan.[14] Unlike Fahima, Hamada was a first-time visitor to Jordan and did not come for medical treatment. Plus, these medical visas allowed his family to ensure their mobility in Jordan and to find refuge there. To regularize their situation in Amman, they registered with the UNHCR as Somali asylum seekers and not as Yemenis (even though they have both passports). Indeed, during my fieldwork, I have found that most mixed Yemeni-Somalis register as Somalis with the UNHCR, as it is known among their communities that Yemeni citizens are struggling to obtain refugee status for reasons I will address below.

There has been no significant arrival of Yemeni refugees in other countries due to the geographical position of Yemen and the impossibility of applying for asylum in border countries (such as Saudi Arabia) because of the lack of humanitarian institutions there. The strategy of medical mobility allows Yemenis to come legally to Jordan. Applying for asylum with the UNHCR subsequently is a process of regularizing their presence in Amman.

However, this mobility strategy of using medical visas to come to Jordan, adopted by Fahima and Hamada and many other Yemenis, has had an impact on their categorization as refugees by the UNHCR and the hosting authorities as well as on their eligibility for humanitarian assistance.

2. The Blurring of Legal Status

Given the complexity of Yemeni refugee migratory patterns, the Jordanian government and humanitarian workers are more likely to view them as "economic migrants." This highlights the limits of the legal category of "refugee" since it does not take into account the economic motivations that led the asylum seekers to leave (Shami 1993; Monsutti 2004). At first, in 2015/2016, Yemenis were perceived by the UNHCR and International Non-Governmental Organizations (INGOs) (that flourished in Jordan

12 Interview with Hamada, Amman, Jabal Amman, January 2019.

13 Regarding the topic of social discrimination against *muwalladīn*, see: Peutz 2019: 357–76.

14 Mobility from South Yemen is easier than from North Yemen as the only accessible airports are in Sayʾūn and ʿAdan (Ṣanʿāʾ airport has been closed since 2016). The only options for North Yemenis to travel abroad are to reach ʿAdan or Sayʾūn to access the airports. Yet because of the war, the journey from the North to the South takes around 20 hours and is interrupted by many checkpoints. The hostility of South Yemenis toward North Yemenis has also increased with the conflict, which makes traveling from north to south more challenging.

mainly in 2013/2014 as a response to the Syrian crisis) as labor migrants who overstayed their visas. Consequently, these institutions were not registering Yemenis as potential beneficiaries. When Yemenis became aware of their rights as persons displaced by war, they started to apply for asylum in order to legalize their presence in Amman, as they could not afford residency permit costs.

After the Saudi-led coalition intervention in March 2015 in Ṣanʿāʾ, the designation of the conflict in Yemen, between Civil War and proxy-war, remained unclear. The UNHCR office in Amman then faced a new influx of refugees from Yemen where the legitimate government of President ʿAbd Rabbuh Manṣūr Hādī, supported by the Saudi-led coalition countries, remained in place.[15] However, the 1951 Geneva Convention considers that the status of "refugee" shall apply to any person who has "a well-founded fear of being persecuted for reasons of race, religion, nationality, membership of a particular social group or political opinion, is outside the country of his nationality and is unable or, owing to such fear, is unwilling to avail himself of the protection of that country."[16] From the beginning of the conflict until 2016/2017, the government of ʿAbd Rabbuh Manṣūr Hādī, considered legitimate by the international community, was still in power in most of the Yemen territory, before the spread of the Houthi forces from the north to the west coast of the country and the arrival of the secessionist groups in the south of Yemen. To consider Yemenis coming from these areas as refugees thus seemed contradictory.[17] Ossama, co-owner with a Jordanian of a Yemeni restaurant in Jabal Amman, recalls the ambiguous status of Yemenis in Jordan, because at the beginning of the conflict they used to return regularly to Yemen, especially to relatively stable areas, thinking that the war would not last.[18] This, of course, contradicts the principle of impossibility of return according to the UNHCR definition of a refugee. Ossama, who is 46 years old, came to Jordan in 2017, directly from Saudi Arabia. Originally from Dhamār, to the south of Ṣanʿāʾ, he studied agriculture at the University of ʿAdan. After being an employee of the Ministry of Agriculture in Ṣanʿāʾ, he completed his doctoral studies in Saudi Arabia and moved to Jordan as a consequence of increasingly restrictive Saudi policies against foreign workers. In Jordan, he decided not to register with the UNHCR because of advice from his fellow citizens who found the procedure "useless." He plans to leave Jordan by seeking asylum through one of the European embassies. Therefore, Yemenis were at first considered ineligible to apply for asylum because they hailed from government-controlled areas; instead, they were perceived as temporary migrants in Jordan, fleeing a conflict that would probably end soon.

Indeed, the definition of a refugee established by the 1951 Geneva Convention is based on a distinction between immigration and asylum (Akoka 2020). This distinction is not shaped by the needs of the populations concerned but rather by geopolitical issues. As an example, during the Cold War, political exiles from communism were immediately considered as refugees by European countries. It was also during this

15 However, ʿAbd Rabbuh Manṣūr Hādī's government was in exile in Saudi Arabia from 2015.

16 UNHCR, 2019, "Handbook and Guidelines on Procedures and Criteria for Determining Refugee Status under the 1951 Convention and the 1967 Protocol Relating to the Status of Refugees."

17 Interview with a female Yemeni researcher in October 2021, based in Amman since 2016.

18 Interview with Ossama, Amman, Jabal Amman, July 2021.

period that a refugee was defined as someone persecuted by an authoritarian regime (such as communism). This shows the hierarchy of values in liberal democracies where civil rights predominate over socioeconomic rights (Akoka 2020: 43–4). It explains the strict distinction between economic migrants and refugees by the UNHCR (Bhabha 1996; cited by Akoka 2020: 43). However, Jordanian anthropologist Seteney Shami pointed out that these displacement categories are related (Shami 1993). Involuntary migration has to be considered on a large scale linking political, economic, and social factors. As Shami explains: "In summary, population displacement and resettlement needs to be seen as a process, conditioned by historically shaped social, economic and political forces, and not as a single event taking place at a moment in time" (Shami 1993: 11). War and outbreaks of violence, coupled with the lack of economic opportunities, lead refugees to settle in a new country. Therefore, forced migrants who reached Jordan are also seeking new life opportunities to build their future. Indeed, most of the Yemeni refugees claimed asylum in Jordan in order to apply for resettlement and therefore consider the country as a transitory step on their journey, due to the limited career and life prospects in Jordan.

I have shown that the definition of the status of Yemeni exiles is complex due to geopolitical factors internal to the conflict in Yemen. Moreover, as Karen Akoka demonstrates, the Refugee Status Determination procedure conducted by the UNHCR is, for historical reasons, built on a strict distinction between "refugee" and "migrant" categories. Non-hosting policies are therefore primarily based on the lack of legal status and on the deprivation of refugee status for Yemenis in Jordan.

3. Non-recognition of Yemenis as Refugees

As I have explained above, since 2015, the Jordanian government has established new specific conditions related to legal status to reduce refugee arrivals into the kingdom. Moreover, different measures have been taken by Jordanian ministries that aim to make the legal status of Yemenis precarious. These policies were firstly manifested by the non-recognition of Yemenis as refugees fleeing a war.

Between 2016 and 2018, Yemenis, like Somalis and Sudanese, were categorized as restricted nationalities regarding their possibilities for medical treatments in Amman, a way to restrain the refugee influx due to national security concerns.[19] The Jordanian government had decided to designate Yemeni nationals among the restricted nationalities in line with the 1973 Residence and Foreigners' Affairs Law, which establishes the requirements for the entry and residence of foreign nationals in Jordan. Thus, Yemeni nationals were required to obtain an entry permit prior to arrival and to be sponsored by a Jordanian citizen.[20] Those already in the country without the appropriate documentation were liable to deportation. However, the 1973

[19] For more information on the security approach to refugees since the arrival of Syrians, consult: Al Husseini 2013: 282–8.

[20] Ardd-Legal, August 2018. See also the official page of the Jordanian Ministry of the Interior: http://moi.gov.jo/Pages/viewpage.aspx?pageID=196 (accessed July 5, 2021).

law established some exceptions for persons who are eligible for political asylum.[21] It suggests that Yemeni individuals are denied their right to political asylum. There are several reasons for the non-recognition of Yemenis as statutory refugees by both the Jordanian Ministry of Interior and the UNHCR. I explain it first by external geopolitical factors related to the dynamics of the conflict in Yemen. Indeed, Jordan was one of the members of the Saudi-led coalition and its military campaign entitled Operation Decisive Storm, which targeted the Houthi forces in Ṣanʿāʾ in April 2015. Consequently, recognizing Yemenis as refugees would mean recognizing Saudi Arabia as responsible for the departure of Yemeni civilians. This geopolitical situation recalls that of the Sudanese refugees in Egypt in September 2005. The UN agency in Cairo decided to suspend the granting of refugee status and the resettlement process for Sudanese, including South Sudanese or refugees from the Sudanese Darfur region. Talks between the current Southern Sudan and the central government in Khartoum were indeed taking place. Continuing to recognize the Sudanese as refugees would have implied that the conflict was ongoing. Therefore, the UNHCR froze all procedures related to forced displacement for the Sudanese. They were no longer considered refugees seeking protection (Brücker et al. 2019). Similarly, my hypothesis, confirmed by many interviews, shows that granting the status of refugee to Yemenis would mean that they are fleeing a conflict in which Saudi Arabia is one of the main responsible parties. Other factors related to the internal situation of Jordan may explain the non-recognition of Yemenis as refugees. Indeed, when the number of Yemenis seeking refuge in Jordan started to markedly increase in early 2016, prompting the UNHCR to consider them as asylum seekers as from April 2016,[22] the Jordanian authorities put in place a new visa regulation for Yemenis that strictly restricted their possibilities of residence in the country. Fearing a new refugee crisis, Jordanian authorities only tolerated specific categories of Yemenis, such as women and their children, and medical patients with medical visas. Young Yemeni men who came for medical treatment were treated as "suspicious cases" subject to intensive interrogations and checks at the Amman International Airport upon their arrival in Jordan.

Moreover, internal factors have to be taken into account. Jordan authorities' fear of a "Syrianization" of the Yemeni arrival within the kingdom since 2015 grew,[23] as Yemenis increasingly sought refuge in Jordan and UNHCR humanitarian reports began to consider them as a refugee category due to their growing numbers. The introduction of a new visa system for Yemenis at the start of the conflict can be seen as a way for the Jordanian government to limit the arrival of Yemeni exiles. Therefore, Jordan's reception policy was being shaped once again by its previous experiences, particularly the Syrian crisis.

Furthermore, since 2015, the UNHCR has tried to homogenize the individual Refugee Status Determination (RSD) procedure and make it more efficient. In this case, it has established "country guidelines" for more than fifteen countries (UNHCR

[21] The Residence and Foreigners' Affairs Law, article 29, Available online: https://www.refworld.org/docid/3ae6b4ed4c.html (accessed July 5, 2021).

[22] UNHCR Jordan Fact Sheet, April 2016. Available at: Document - UNHCR Jordan - Jordan Fact Sheet - April 2016 (accessed on April 16, 2023).

[23] Ardd-Legal, May 2016.

2016: 5).[24] For each country, the UNHCR has a document defining the "vulnerable" individuals according to the national, ethnic, or racial origin of the applicants (Brücker et al 2019: 138). Categories such as "single women" and "persecuted individuals," from a "vulnerable" tribe, clan, or ethnic group, are more likely to be recognized by the UNHCR as "refugees" according to established standards. Indeed, the policy on migration relies upon the labeling of particularly vulnerable persons or groups. Vulnerability is a criterion for special protection or assistance in a migration context. Using labels and categories structures interactions between service providers and beneficiaries within the bureaucracy of the UNHCR. However, the UNHCR's categorizations of vulnerability seem to have a policy-making approach for "vulnerable groups" rather than an individual approach (Flegar 2018: 381).

According to my research, the UN agency has no document related to asylum procedures for Yemeni citizens seeking refuge abroad. It simply considers that "as the situation in Yemen remains highly fluid and uncertain, the UNHCR calls on all countries to allow civilians fleeing Yemen access to their territories" (UNHCR April 2015: 4). The framework for granting status to Yemeni asylum seekers remains very unclear and is related to 'the suspension of forcible returns of nationals' and to the regional refugee protection frameworks (UNHCR 2016: 4). In comparison to Jordan, for instance, Djibouti has accepted Yemeni refugees on a *prima facie* basis (Peutz 2019: 7), which means that they are immediately considered as refugees because of their large number and the known situation in the country of departure. In Jordan, the lack of knowledge and definition of the conflict in Yemen makes it difficult for the UNHCR to conduct RSD interviews for Yemenis. Consequently, it leaves them in legal limbo which also impacts their access to humanitarian and public services.

4. Differential Humanitarian Treatment

It is important to recall that the UNHCR uses different registration processes for Syrian and "other" refugees, shaping the categorization of beneficiaries within the UN agency. Syrian forced migrants in Jordan are recognized as refugees *prima facie* and must register with both the Jordanian Ministry of Interior and the UNHCR. In fact, Syrians are not required to undergo the RSD process and are thus accorded protection and access to primary health care and other essential services. Other nationalities have to have an interview with a UNHCR lawyer who determines their situation on a case-by-case basis (Davis et al. 2016: 6). First, they must obtain the document certifying their registration as asylum seekers. Then they have to go through the RSD process, which involves several interviews and home visits. According to my interviews with Yemeni informants, this procedure often takes years and is particularly difficult to access for Yemeni citizens in Jordan. This is the case for Mohammed, 28 years old, a Yemeni asylum seeker from a middle-class background who lived and studied in the Taʿizz governorate. There is a great number of Yemenis coming from the Taʿizz governorate

[24] These "country guidelines" are available online at: https://www.refworld.org/publisher,UNHCR,COUNTRYPOS,,,0.html (accessed June 1, 2021).

as it is on the front line between loyalists and Houthi forces. Since his arrival in Jordan with his sisters and brothers in 2016, Mohammed has been waiting to be recognized as a refugee by the UNHCR.[25] The same is true for Ibtissam, who arrived in Jordan in September 2015, after having worked as a school director in Ṣanʿāʾ.[26] She and her family were personally persecuted by the Houthis because they were not collaborating with them.[27] They therefore decided to find refuge in Jordan, thinking that the war would end soon. Ibtissam's file at the UNHCR is still pending. While waiting for a decision from the UNHCR, Yemeni asylum seekers cannot obtain any humanitarian assistance. However, in some neighborhoods, such as Jabal Amman or Abū Nsayr, they can rely on local charities that offer occasional assistance, such as food baskets during religious events (Ramadan). Therefore, the non-access of Yemenis to the registration process of the UNHCR amplifies the categorization of beneficiaries according to their nationalities. It also hinders their access to humanitarian services such as monthly financial assistance by UNHCR and access to resettlement. While Ibtissam and Mohammed live in Jordan on their savings and on support from relatives abroad, their waiting for refugee status prevents their access to economic resources to meet their daily needs.

This is an exceptional situation if compared with that of Syrians who register as refugees within the UNHCR and obtain a specific service card from the Residence and Border Administration of the Ministry of Interior for the Syrian community, valid for one year and renewable (Doraï 2016). First, Syrian refugees have to get the Asylum Seeker Certificate from the UNHCR to obtain the document from the Ministry of Interior. The Ministry of Interior card (MoI card) gives them access to Jordanian public health care and education services (Achilli 2015: 5). This grant of rights attests to a certain degree of recognition by the Jordanian Government of Syrian refugees. However, other refugees do not possess such cards. It shows that they are not recognized by the Jordanian Ministry of Interior and that they are left without any legal status, in an administrative limbo. Moreover, by the end of 2019, the Ministry of Interior amplified these non-reception policies by ordering the UNHCR to not register any new asylum seekers, leaving many Yemeni refugees in Jordan as illegal residents, without any recognition from the UNHCR.[28]

As can be seen, non-reception policies for Yemeni refugees result in the production of different categories of Yemenis at the UNHCR depending on their access to UN agency status and their year of arrival in Jordan. The construction of these categories is shaped by the policies of the Jordanian Ministry of Interior and the RSD section of the UNHCR. In fact, the conflict has escalated in Yemen, leading to new refugee arrivals in Jordan, Djibouti, and Egypt.[29] This new regulation by the Jordanian Ministry of Interior is creating new categories among the Yemeni asylum seeker community.

The non-recognition of Yemenis as refugees in Jordan and their categorization as "non-Syrian" refugees lead to a lack of access to humanitarian services. In addition, the

25 Interview with Mohammed, Amman, al-Jbayha, October 2020.

26 Interview with Ibtissam, Amman, Jabal al-Ḥusayn, October 2020.

27 Since the Houthis took control of Ṣanʿāʾ in September 2014, they have implemented a new school curriculum that promotes their political and religious ideologies.

28 See Al Majali and Verduijn 2020.

29 See Al-Absi 2020.

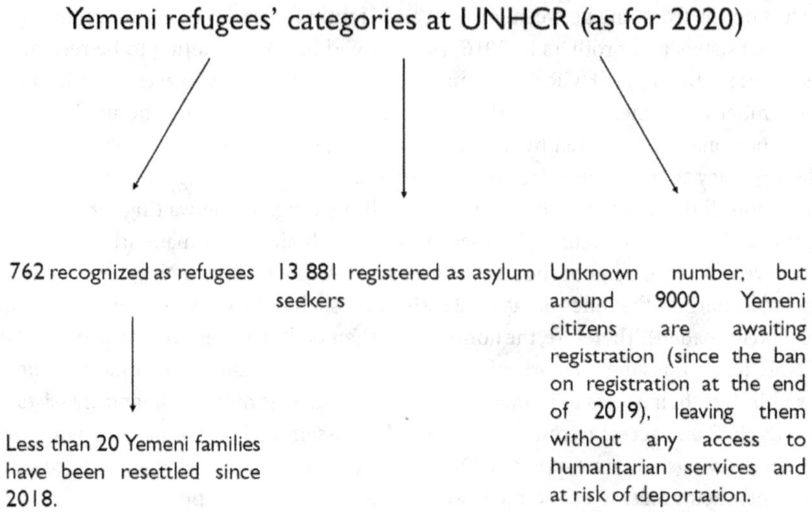
Yemeni refugees' categories at UNHCR (as for 2020)
762 recognized as refugees
13 881 registered as asylum seekers
Unknown number, but around 9000 Yemeni citizens are awaiting registration (since the ban on registration at the end of 2019), leaving them without any access to humanitarian services and at risk of deportation.
Less than 20 Yemeni families have been resettled since 2018.

Figure 3.3 Figure explaining the different categories of Yemenis at the UNHCR. Source: UNHCR 2020, Refugee Statistics. Diagram by: S. Al Majali, 2021.

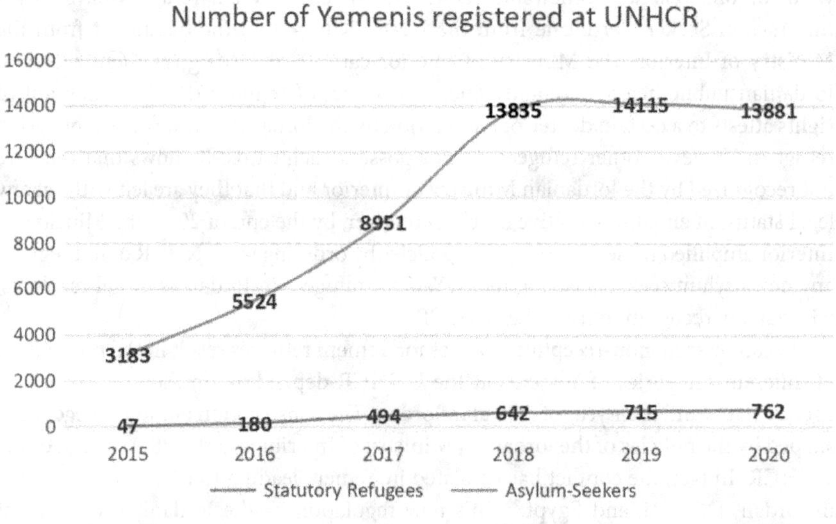
Number of Yemenis registered at UNHCR
16000
14000
12000
10000
8000
6000
4000
2000
0
3183
5524
8951
13835
14115
13881
47
180
494
642
715
762
2015
2016
2017
2018
2019
2020
Statutory Refugees
Asylum-Seekers

Figure 3.4 Graph showing the number of Yemenis who have been granted refugee status (statutory refugees). Yemeni asylum seekers are still awaiting a status determination interview by the UNHCR. It can be seen that since 2015, most Yemenis are awaiting this interview and are simply registered as asylum seekers. Their registration peaked in 2015. Since January 2019, when the UNHCR suspended the registration of new asylum seekers, the number of Yemeni asylum seekers has not really increased. Source: UNHCR 2020, Refugee Statistics. Diagram by: S. Al Majali, 2021.

evolving policy of the Jordanian ministries has resulted in the construction of several categories among Yemeni asylum seekers. In what follows, I will demonstrate how this lack of legal status leads in a process of illegalization of Yemenis in Jordan.

5. Restricted Access to Public Services: A Process of Illegalization

As all Arab foreigners in Jordan, Yemenis are allowed to work in the specific sectors of construction, agriculture, and food services. Nevertheless, they have to apply for a work permit, which is very expensive and is conditional on obtaining a Jordanian sponsor under the *kafāla* system.[30] It explains why most Yemenis in Jordan are working in cleaning sectors, factories, and Yemeni restaurants. Unequal access to work between refugees amplifies the respondent's perception of a discriminatory policy.[31] Indeed, in February 2016, Jordan reached an agreement, the Jordan Compact, with the international community in order to make the work market more accessible to Syrian refugees within certain sectors of the Jordanian job market (Al Husseini and Napolitano 2019). This agreement can be explained in the context of the Syrian crisis in the region. The Syrian crisis has led to a huge displacement of people to Egypt, Iraq, Jordan, Lebanon, Turkey, and other countries in the region, and has attracted a great deal of attention from donor countries. These southern host countries are becoming spaces of remote containment for Western countries, hindering the movement of refugees (Le Houérou 2007: 17). However, the Jordan Compact is exclusive in that it supports the inclusion only of Syrian refugees in the labor market.

Concerning Yemeni refugees, their exclusion from the job market has been increased by the new regulation adopted by the Ministry of Interior in January 2020. Yemenis residing in the country can no longer obtain a work permit and have the UNHCR asylum seeker documents at the same time. This reinforces the status of a legal vacuum for Yemenis, who are confined in a legal in-between. This situation has led, in 2020, to several deportations of Yemenis who had work permits and the UNHCR documents at the same time, which shows that the Jordanian Ministry of Interior does not recognize Yemenis as asylum seekers protected by the UNHCR under the principle of non-refoulement.[32] According to respondent Ibtissam,[33] for Yemenis life opportunities in Jordan have been considerably reduced. Either they have to wait for recognition from the UNHCR and resettlement, a procedure which takes years, particularly for Yemenis; or they reside in Jordan as foreign workers with work

30 I refer to Gilbert Beaugé's text (1986) for the definition of the *kafāla* system. The *kafāla* system has its roots in Muslim customary law, where a foreigner was given particular protection by the tribe. In the *kafāla* system, migrant workers cannot enter and stay in the host country legally without being sponsored by a national (the employer). The worker's immigration status is tied to the employment contract. He cannot change jobs nor leave the country without first obtaining explicit, written permission from the employer.

31 Mennonite Central Committee 2017: 16.

32 Human Rights Watch, March 2021.

33 Interview with Ibtissam, Amman, Jabal al-Ḥusayn, October 2020.

permits and therefore with residency permits. Since 2020, having both documents is considered illegal for Yemenis according to the Jordanian Ministry of Labour. Non-reception policies consist here of a gradual illegalization of Yemenis in Jordan. Indeed, as the researcher Yamamoto underlines (quoted by De Bel-Air 2008: 8):

> The process of immigrant integration is simultaneously one of the class formation. The State greatly influences this process through its capacity to determine what rights and entitlements migrants can obtain. In this sense, unauthorized immigration represents the power of the State to illegalize a certain group of people. Rendering them illegal means depriving them of rights and the protection that the government would otherwise provide. In other words, unauthorized immigrants are constructed by the State as a rightless class of people through the making of immigration laws and policies. Being "illegal", unauthorized immigrants comprise extremely vulnerable and exploitable members of the society. (Yamamoto 2007)

The Jordanian state has the power to leave a group in illegality and therefore without rights. The non-recognition of Yemenis by the government leaves them as non-citizens having limited or no access to fundamental rights and basic services. At the same time, the state forms a class, a part of society without rights, vulnerable and exploitable (Bolzman 2001: 145). Françoise De Bel-Air also believes that this reinforces the segmentation between local and foreign populations, between protected and unprotected workers (De Bel-Air 2008: 8): "Enjoying basic human rights thus becomes a citizen's privilege. More specifically, illegal manpower becomes extremely flexible, perfectly adapted to a deregularized economy's demands in terms of (short

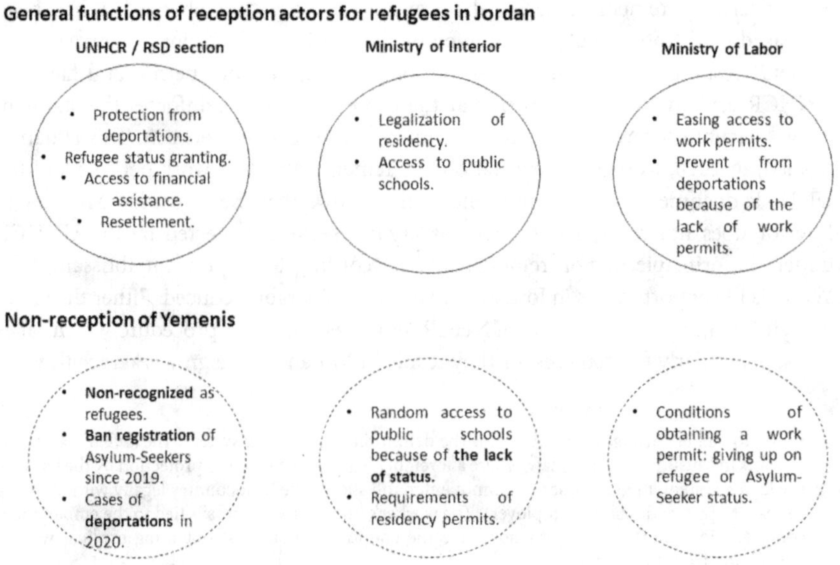

Figure 3.5 Process of refugee inclusion in Jordan at different institutional levels. Diagram by: S. Al Majali, 2021.

term) maximal profits for investors, or as a private commodity as opposed to a public responsibility as is the case with undocumented domestic workers."

The hosting of refugees in Jordan involves several actors responsible for the attribution of a juridical status from which other rights derive. In the case of Yemeni refugees, the functions of the RSD section of the UNHCR are not fulfilled. This lack of status for most Yemenis confines them to illegality. The lack of status hinders their access to public services such as schools and the labor market. In the first case, they are deprived of their rights as refugees. In the second case, the Ministry of Labour tends to confine Yemenis to the category of "migrants" and denies their rights as refugees.

The illegalization of Yemenis in Jordan also has major consequences on their everyday life and social relations.

6. Life in Jordan: An Ambiguous Status and Social Marginalization

The direct consequence of non-recognition of Yemenis as refugees by the UNHCR and Jordanian ministries leads to their socioeconomic marginalization and has important social consequences, whether in terms of interactions with Jordanians or with other fellow citizens and migrants.

Refugees in Jordan are caught between several temporalities,[34] which have significant consequences on their social destiny. The latter is influenced by different factors corresponding to different time scales. The temporality of politics, dictated by political and immediate events, has a significant influence on their lives in Jordan. As an example, in March 2017, former US President Donald Trump implemented the "Muslim Ban." This policy resulted in the suspension of applications for the resettlement of many refugees who were in Jordan, whether Syrian, Iraqi, Somali, Sudanese, or Yemeni. Amid growing uncertainty, their wait was renewed.

The second temporality in which refugees in Jordan are embedded is social because their presence in Jordan becomes permanent. Indeed, social relations are built up with other refugees and with the local populations, they come to think of the temporary as permanent. Non-reception policies regarding Yemeni refugees in Jordan have several consequences on their social relationships. They add to the widespread racism they have to face in Jordan, which amplifies their feelings of being foreigners.[35] However, Yemenis in Jordan do not form one community in the country. As I have shown above, the status of Yemenis in Jordan differs from one place to another. Therefore, the feeling of racism from local populations may change from one area to another. For example, according to my observations in one neighborhood in Jabal Amman, interactions between Jordanians and Yemeni refugees can be difficult. This is related to the Somali origins of the *muwalladīn* and their black skin color. But it is above all the internalization of a precarious legal status that prevents Yemeni refugees from

[34] The historian Fernand Braudel distinguished three historical scales: a long-term timescale (social), a medium-term timescale (economic), and a short-term timescale (politics) (Braudel 1949).

[35] Baslan et al., 2019.

establishing relationships with Jordanians. The status of a refugee is interpreted as a status of subordination, without rights, vis-à-vis Jordanian citizens. The fear of deportation in case of dissension with Jordanians was thus very prevalent in my interviews with informants and observations in a neighborhood in Jabal Amman, where most Somalis and Yemenis of Somali origin live. Young men often play football together on Saturday afternoons, and soccer matches are organized according to the nationalities of the players. For instance, while Yemenis of Somali origin will play against Somalis, Jordanian youths play in a different place. Informants told me that for fear of tension during soccer games with Jordanians, groups of young men of different origins never play together.

Moreover, the vulnerable legal status influences the social capital of Yemeni refugees. Indeed, social relations between well-off and middle-class Yemenis are relatively weak. My fieldwork shows the sense of embarrassment that informants may feel about their situation hinders their communication with wealthy members of the Yemeni community. As an example, the informant Ibtissam, who was a school director in Ṣanʿāʾ, explains that her social relations have been greatly reduced as her situation deteriorates in Jordan.[36] At first, Ibtissam had many acquaintances among Yemeni groups in Jordan. She used to go to many events such as Yemeni weddings where she would meet women from wealthy classes. Then, very soon, she realized that her savings from Yemen were running out and that she could no longer pay the rent for her apartment. At the same time, her husband and son could not work because of the impossibility of obtaining work permits. If they were caught, they could be sent back to Yemen. Now Ibtissam lives on the occasional help of a Yemeni friend and on UNHCR financial aid that they give to all asylum seekers in December every year. Ibtissam shared with me that she would almost feel "ashamed" if she had to see her old friends again, because of her socioeconomic situation. Let us also recall that the organization of Yemeni society into "castes," into very narrow social classes, makes it difficult for a Yemeni man or woman to accept his refugee status and to beg for humanitarian aid. We can thus observe a progressive deterioration of social capital among Yemenis of both the middle and working classes.

Conclusion

While fleeing the outbreaks of violence of war in their own country, Yemeni forced migrants face new forms of institutional violence in Jordan as a consequence of the non-reception policies to which they are confronted. Sociologist Pierre Bourdieu has conceptualized symbolic institutional violence which results from hierarchies and categorizations of social institutions (Bourdieu and Passeron 1970). Bourdieu establishes that these categorizations and hierarchies imposed by the dominant on the dominated are internalized by the subjects of such symbolic violence and perceived as legitimate. The status of refugee or asylum seeker is similarly internalized by forced

36 Interview with Ibtissam, Amman, October 2020.

migrants as a status of non-rights, of social powerlessness in Jordan. In the case of Yemeni refugees, this symbolic violence manifests itself in different forms: the long-institutionalized wait for a status, the ban on working, a non-recognition of their rights as refugees, and social downgrading.

Based on Bolzman's paradigm about policies of exclusion of refugees, this chapter has tried to demonstrate how legal labeling by governmental and humanitarian institutions shapes the social and financial resources of forced migrants. I have shown that these policies of non-reception by the Jordanian Ministry of Interior and the UNHCR result in a process of illegalization of Yemeni asylum seekers. This is made manifest by the non-granting of refugee status to Yemenis by the UN agency. Furthermore, even if they register as asylum seekers with the UNHCR, again the Jordanian government does not recognize their rights and limits their access to public services. The Ministry of Interior confines Yemeni asylum seekers to the status of foreign workers without having their rights. The Jordanian government has actually refused to allow them to obtain two statuses at the same time: asylum seeker status from the UNHCR and work permit status. Moreover, refugees in Jordan are caught in different temporalities: the first is that of their everyday life in Jordan and the second is their wait for resettlement. This chapter also shows the way their illegal status in Jordan or their legal vacuum impacts on social resources. Their gradual interiorization of a rightless status hinders their interactions with local populations and their fellow citizens. The internalization of an illegal status by Yemenis in Jordan reproduces the categories of the dominant local and the dominated refugee. In the same way, relations with their fellow citizens create the categories of donor and beneficiary.

Bibliography

Ababsa, Myriam (2015), "From a Humanitarian Crisis to a Security Crisis. Control Measures for Syrian Refugees in Jordan (2011–2015)," *Revue européenne des migrations internationales*, 31: 73–101. Available online: https://journals.openedition.org/remi/7380 (accessed January 1, 2020).

Achilli, Luigi (2015), "Syrian Refugees in Jordan: A Reality Check," *Migration Policy Centre, Policy Briefs*: 1–12. Available online: https://cadmus.eui.eu/handle/1814/34904 (accessed January 7, 2020).

Agier, Michel (2018), *L'Étranger qui vient*, Paris: Éditions du Seuil.

Akoka, Karen (2020), *L'asile et l'exil. Une histoire de la distinction entre réfugiés/migrants*, Paris: La Découverte.

Al-Absi, Qabool (2020), "The Struggle Far from Home: Yemeni Refugees in Cairo," Sanaa Center for Strategic Studies. Available online: https://sanaacenter.org/publications/main-publications/12286 (accessed December 18, 2020).

Al Husseini, Jalal (2004), "La question des réfugiés palestiniens en Jordanie entre droit au retour et implantation définitive," *Cahiers de l'Orient*, 75: 31–50. Available online: https://halshs.archives-ouvertes.fr/halshs-00411839/document (accessed December 12, 2019).

Al Husseini, Jalal (2013), "La Jordanie face à la crise syrienne," in François Burgat and Bruno Paoli (eds.), *Pas de Printemps pour la Syrie. Les clés pour comprendre les acteurs et les défis de la crise*, 282–8, Paris: La Découverte.

Al Husseini, Jalal, and Valentina Napolitano (2019), "The Jordanian Policy Toward Syrian Refugees: Between Hospitality and Protection of Interests," *Confluences Méditerranée*, 3: 127–42. Available online: https://doi-org.inshs.bib.cnrs.fr/10.3917/come.110.0127 (accessed July 29, 2021).

Al Majali, Solenn, and Simon Verduijn (2020), "Somalis and Yemenis of Mixed Origin Stranded and Struggling in Jordan's Capital," *Mixed Migrations Platform*. Available online: http://www.mixedmigration.org/articles/somalis-and-yemenis-of-mixed-origin-stranded-and-struggling-in-jordans-capital/ (accessed July 23, 2020).

Ardd Legal Aid (May 2016), "Hidden Guests: Yemeni Exiles in Jordan." Available online: https://ardd-jo.org/sites/default/files/resource-files/hidden_guests_yemeni_exiles_in_jordan.pdf (accessed September 6, 2018).

Ardd Legal Aid (August 2018), "Recent Development and Main Challenges of Yemeni Refugees Situation in Jordan: 1–10." Available online: https://ardd-jo.org/sites/default/files/resource-files/recent_development_and_main_challenges_of_yemeni_refugees_situation_in_jordan-_legal_paper_0.pdf (accessed September 6, 2018).

Baslan, Dina, Anna Kvittingen, and Rochelle Johnston (2019), "Realizing the Rights of Asylum Seekers and Refugees in Jordan from Countries Other than Syria with a Focus on Yemenis and Sudanese," *NRC*. Available online: https://reliefweb.int/report/jordan/realizing-rights-asylum-seekers-and-refugees-jordan-countries-other-syria-focus (accessed May 5, 2019).

Beaugé, Gilbert (1986), "La kafala: un système de gestion transitoire de la main-d'œuvre et du capital dans les pays du Golfe," *Revue européenne des migrations internationales*, 2 (1): 109–22. Available online: https://www.persee.fr/doc/remi_0765-0752_1986_num_2_1_998 (accessed December 1, 2019).

Berg Mette, Louise, and Elena Fiddian-Qasmiyeh (2018), "Hospitality and Hostility Towards Migrants: Global Perspectives – An Introduction," *Refugee Hosts*. Available online: https://refugeehosts.org/2018/10/31/hospitality-and-hostility-towards-migrants-global-perspectives-an-introduction/ (accessed June 1, 2021).

Bhabha, Jacqueline (1996), "Embodied Rights: Gender Persecution, State Sovereignty, and Refugees," *Public Culture*, 9 (1): 3–32.

Bolzman, Claudio (2001), "Politiques d'asile et trajectoires sociales des réfugiés : une exclusion programmée. Les cas de la Suisse," *Sociologie et sociétés*, 33 (2): 133–58. Available online: https://www.erudit.org/en/journals/socsoc/2001-v33-n2-socsoc730/008315ar.pdf (accessed September 10, 2020).

Boudou, Benjamin (2017), *Politique de l'hospitalité*, Paris: CNRS Éditions.

Bourdieu, Pierre, and Jean Claude Passeron (1970), *La Reproduction. Éléments pour une théorie du système d'enseignement*, Paris: Éditions de Minuit.

Brand, Laurie (1995), "Palestinians and Jordanians: A Crisis of Identity," *Journal of Palestine Studies*, 24 (4): 46–61. Available online: https://www.paljourneys.org/sites/default/files/Palestinians_and_Jordanians_A_Crisis_of_Identity-Laurie_A._Brand.pdf (accessed September 1, 2020).

Braudel, Fernand (1949), *La Méditerranée et le monde méditerranéen à l'époque de Philippe II*, Paris: Armand Colin.

Brücker, Pauline (2019), "Le guichet du HCR, entre standardisation bureaucratique et ethos humanitaire: le cas du HCR-Caire," *Politique et Sociétés*, 38 (1): 129–55. Available online: https://www.erudit.org/fr/revues/ps/2019-v38-n1-ps04467/1058293ar.pdf (accessed January 14, 2020).

Brücker, Herbert, Philipp Jaschke, Yuliya Kosyakova (2019), *Integrating Refugees and Asylum Seekers into the German Economy and Society - Empirical Evidence and Policy*

Objectives, Transatlantic Council on Migration, Migration Policy Institute, Available online: https://www.migrationpolicy.org/sites/default/files/publications/TCM_2019_Germany-FINAL.pdf.

Chatelard, Géraldine, and Kamel Doraï (2009), "La présence irakienne en Syrie et en Jordanie: dynamiques sociales et spatiales, et modes de gestion par les pays d'accueil," *Maghreb-Machrek*, 199: 43–60. Available online: https://hal.archives-ouvertes.fr/hal-00338403v2/document (accessed January 5, 2020).

Crouzel, Isabelle (2013), "Medical Tourism," in Myriam Ababsa (ed.), *Atlas of Jordan, History, Territories and Society*, 318–19, Beirut: Ifpo.

Davis, Rochelle, Emma Murphy, Abbie Taylor, and Will Todman (2016), "Sudanese and Somali Refugees in Jordan," *Middle East Research and Information Project (MERIP)*, 279. Available online: http://www.merip.org/mer/mer279/sudanese-somali-refugees-jordan (accessed January 22, 2019).

De Bel-Air, Françoise (2003), "Migrations internationales et politique en Jordanie," *Revue européenne des migrations internationales*, 19: 3. Available online: http://journals.openedition.org/remi/2651 (accessed October 22, 2019).

De Bel-Air, Françoise (2008), "Irregular Migrations to Jordan: Socio-Political Stakes," CARIM Analytic and Synthetic Notes (Cooperation Project on the Social Integration of Immigrants, Migration, and the Movement of Persons). Available online: https://cadmus.eui.eu/bitstream/handle/1814/10511/CARIM_AS%26N_2008_78.pdf?sequence=1&isAllowed=y (accessed October 22, 2019).

Derrida, Jacques (2000), "Hospitality," *Angelaki*, 5 (3): 3–18. Available online: https://www.tandfonline.com/doi/abs/10.1080/09697250020034706 (accessed June 1, 2021).

Derrida, Jacques, and Anne Dufourmantelle (2000), *Of Hospitality*, Stanford: Stanford University Press.

Doraï, Kamel (2016), "La Jordanie et les réfugiés syriens," *La Vie des idées*. Available online: http://www.laviedesidees.fr/La-Jordanie-et-les-refugies-syriens.html (accessed October 23, 2019).

Fassin, Didier, Morice Alain, and Catherine Quiminal (1997), *Les Lois de l'inhospitalité. Les politiques de l'immigration à l'épreuve des sans-papiers*, Paris: La Découverte. Available online: https://www.cairn.info/les-lois-de-l-inhospitalite--9782707127433.htm (accessed June 1, 2021).

Flegar, Veronika (2018), "Who Is Deemed Vulnerable in the Governance of Migration?" *Asiel- & Migrantenrecht*, 8: 374–83. University of Groningen Faculty of Law Research Paper No. 50/2019.

Human Rights Watch (March 2021), "Jordan Yemeni Asylum-Seekers Deported." Available online: https://www.hrw.org/news/2021/03/30/jordan-yemeni-asylum-seekers-deported#:~:text=The%20authorities%20handed%20down%20most,Commissioner%20for%20Refugees%20(UNHCR) (accessed March 31, 2021).

Kangas, Beth (2007), "Hope from Abroad in the International Medical Travel of Yemeni Patients," *Anthropology and Medicine*, 14 (3): 293–305. Available online: https://www.researchgate.net/publication/244888268_Hope_from_Abroad_in_the_International_Medical_Travel_of_Yemeni_Patients (accessed March 3, 2020).

Kangas, Beth (2010), "Traveling for Medical Care in a Global World," *Medical Anthropology*, 29 (4): 344–62.

Kibread, Gaim (1993), "The Myth of Dependency Among Camp Refugees in Somalia (1979–1989)," *Journal of Refugee Studies*, 6 (4): 321–49. Available online: https://www.researchgate.net/publication/240320756_The_myth_of_dependency_among_camp_refugees_in_Somalia_1979-1989 (accessed October 23, 2019).

Le Houérou, Fabienne (2007), "Migrations Sud-Sud. Les circulations contrariées des migrants vers le monde arabe," *Revue des mondes musulmans et de la Méditerranée*, 119–120: 9–21. Available online: https://journals.openedition.org/remmm/4083 (accessed December 20, 2019).

Memorandum of Understanding Between UNHCR and Jordanian Government (April 5, 1998). Available online: https://www.rescuerefugees.eu/wp-content/uploads/2017/09/LE2JOR002_AREN.pdf (accessed July 31, 2021).

Mennonite Central Committee (November 2017), "On the Basis of Nationality: Access to Assistance for Iraqi and Other Asylum Seeker and Refugees in Jordan: 1–51." Available online: https://reliefweb.int/sites/reliefweb.int/files/resources/On%20the%20Basis%20of%20Nationality.pdf (accessed September 7, 2018).

Monsutti, Alessandro (2004), *War and Migration: Social Networks and Economic Strategies of the Hazaras of Afghanistan*, Neuchâtel: Editions de l'Institut d'Ethnologie de Neuchâtel.

Pérouse de Montclos, Marc-Antoine (2003), *Diaspora et terrorisme*, Paris: Presses de Sciences Po.

Peutz, Nathalie (2019), "'The Fault of Our Grandfathers': Yemen's Third-generation Migrants Seeking Refuge from Displacement," *International Journal of Middle East Studies*, 51 (3): 357–76.

Roussel, Cyril (2015), "Comment gérer le conflit syrien depuis la Jordanie?" *Outre-Terre*, 44: 226–36. Available online: https://www-cairn-info.inshs.bib.cnrs.fr/revue-outre-terre2-2015-3-page-226.htm (accessed October 13, 2019).

Shami, Seteney (1993), "The Social Implications of Populations Displacement and Resettlement: An Overview with a Focus on the Arab Middle East," *International Migration Review*, 101: 4–33.

Stavo-Debauge, Joan (2018), "L'oubli de ce dont c'est le cas. Critique, circonstances et limites de l'hospitalité selon Derrida," *SociologieS*. Available at: http://journals.openedition.org/sociologies/6796 (accessed June 1, 2021).

UNHCR (April 2015), "UNHCR Position on Returns to Yemen." Available online: https://www.refworld.org/publisher,UNHCR,COUNTRYPOS,YEM,5523fdf84,0.html (accessed June 1, 2021).

UNHCR (2016), "UNHCR Guidelines on International Protection No.12-HCR/GIP/16/12," Available online: https://www.unhcr.org/fr-fr/en/media/unhcr-guidelines-international-protection-no-12-hcr-gip-16-12-02-december-2016.

UNHCR (2019), "Handbook and Guidelines on Procedures and Criteria for Determining Refugee Status Under the 1951 Convention and the 1967 Protocol Relating to the Status of Refugees." Available online: https://www.unhcr.org/publications/legal/5ddfcdc47/handbook-procedures-criteria-determining-refugee-status-under-1951-convention.html (accessed March 6, 2021).

UNHCR (2020), "Refugee Statistics." Available online: https://www.unhcr.org/refugee-statistics/download/?url=Wl57Td (accessed June 1, 2021).

UNHCR (February 2021), "Fact Sheet." Available online: https://reporting.unhcr.org/sites/default/files/Jordancountryfactsheet-February2021.pdf (accessed March 5, 2021).

Yamamoto, Ryoko (2007), "Crossing Boundaries: Legality and the Power of State in Unauthorized Migration," *Sociology Compass*, 1 (1): 95–110.

4

Host State Policies and the Changing Role of Social Networks for Syrian Refugees in Jordan

David Lagarde and Kamel Doraï

Following an "open-door" policy toward Syrian asylum seekers, running from 2011 to the beginning of 2013, the growing number of people fleeing Syria to Jordan has led the Jordanian government to implement drastic restrictions to the entry and stay of this population in the kingdom. The national authorities took four main decisions regarding the entrance of Syrian asylum seekers to Jordan:

(i). At the beginning of 2012, they started setting up transit and refugee camps in northern Jordan, in order to select people authorized to enter and to decide where they were allowed to settle.

(ii). In May 2013, the growing number of arrivals led Jordan to close all the official border crossing points to new Syrian asylum seekers.

(iii). By summer 2013, due to the growing flow of Syrians entering the country irregularly and the emerging influence of different Islamist rebel groups on the territory of Southern Syria, the Jordanian authorities decided to close the western informal border crossings used by most asylum seekers to enter Jordan since the beginning of the crisis.

(iv). In June 2014, when the Islamic State organization took over al-Mawṣul in Iraq, Jordan finally implemented drastic restrictions on the number of new entries at the last two operating informal border crossing points of al-Ḥadalāt and al-Rukbān. Following this decision, only tens of Syrian refugees per day were allowed to enter the country.

The role of states in shaping refugee mobility and the different modes of border control versus migrants' strategies to circumvent these constraints has already been analyzed in the European and North American contexts (Koslowski 2000; Koser 2007; Collyer and King 2015). On the other hand, network analysis of migration is a long-standing field of research (Fawcett 1989; Kritz and Zlotnik 1992; Massey et al. 1993; Koser 1997; Faist 2000). Nevertheless, while a growing part of literature focuses on the role of social networks in migrants' decision-making and settlement in host societies (Boyd 1989; Koser 1997; Portes 1997; Collyer 2005; Ryan et al. 2008), few studies to date have questioned their influence on the journeys of migrants and asylum seekers (Schapendonk 2012, 2015).

As previously evidenced in the Middle East (Chatelard 2005) and other regional situations such as Europe (Clochard 2010) or North America (El Colegio de la Frontera Norte 2011), during our fieldwork in Jordan we have noticed that the progressive closure of the Jordanian borders to Syrian nationals directly affected their ability to rely on their personal networks in order to access resources. Indeed, at the beginning of the crisis, strong kin and friendship ties played a key role in their access to information, mobility, employment, housing, or health care, both on the road and in their places of settlement in Jordan. With the reinforcement of Jordanian migration regulations, Syrians were forced to rely on weak ties (Granovetter 1973)[1] and became much more dependent on migration management professionals (such as the IOM, UNHCR, Jordanian border guards, local and international NGOs) as well as on smugglers, which has had deep impacts both in terms of migratory itineraries and coping strategies. In light of these observations, this chapter aims to highlight the evolution and the diversity of actors (Krissman 2005; Muanamoha et al. 2010) that have shaped the trajectories of Syrian refugees to/in Jordan since 2011.

From a humanitarian perspective, refugees are usually deemed a vulnerable population in need of assistance (Zetter 1991; Malkki 1996). In an attempt to counter this approach, this chapter, which is based on field research carried out by David Lagarde as part of his doctoral thesis, intends to emphasize the autonomy and self-decision-making of refugees (Ma Mung 2009) from a long-term perspective. For this purpose, we have chosen to focus our research on a community of Syrian street peddlers (and their relatives) coming from the Syrian village of Dayr Muqaran, who have settled in Jordan since 2011. Most of them were already familiar with Jordan, as they used to come and work in the kingdom before the beginning of the uprising. As we will see in the rest of this chapter, this case study highlights how earlier Syrian migrations to Jordan helped determine the current polarization of flows toward specific locations of the country. It also underlines the central role of family and village networks in order to access certain niches of the Jordanian labor market, in particular farm works, catering, the food industry as well as street vending. Moreover, these observations lead us to share the conclusions of authors who criticize the strict distinction generally made between economic migrants and refugees (Richmond 1994; Long 2013). While most studies on Syrian migration focus only on the post-2011 refugee crisis, we consider that a *continuum* exists between what is considered as "voluntary migration" prior to 2011 and the current "forced migration." We assume that refugee movements resulting from conflicts are often influenced by previous migration flows and correlated networks that are re-mobilized during the humanitarian crisis (Gehrig and Monsutti 2003; Doraï 2011). Therefore, mapping long-term mobility can help better understand the current forced migration processes and their connections with other forms of social organization built over time in a regional area (e.g., commercial mobility, family strategies). Shami and McCann (Shami and McCann 1993) suggest that displacement

1 Following Granovetter, we consider that strong ties consist in close family members and friends, when weak ties are connections outside the closest social circles.

often leads to labor migration as a coping strategy. But conversely, as will be highlighted in this chapter, labor migration may also shape and structure forced displacement patterns of dispersion and settlement. In the remainder of this article, we will try to highlight the social, temporal, and spatial dynamism of Syrian networks in Jordan by showing (i) how the reinforcement of migration controls has reshaped the itineraries of asylum seekers and thereby the characteristics of migration networks; (ii) what kind of social support and ties asylum seekers and refugees rely on in order to access resources.

1. Syrians in Jordan: Historical and Current Migration

Traditionally known as an emigration country, Jordan is also a settlement and a transit space for economic and forced migrants (De Bel Air 2015). Contemporary refugee movements can thus only be understood in light of two correlated contexts: long-term migratory circulations in a cross-border environment sustained by the existence of well-established transnational networks. The current Syrian crisis has shed light on the growing presence of Syrians in Jordan and the ancient migratory links that exist between Southern Syria and Northern Jordan. Although Syrian migration toward Jordan is not a new phenomenon, the presence of Syrian nationals in this country pre-2011 is difficult to evaluate. Indeed, before the start of the uprising only about 3,000 Syrian nationals had a residence permit in Jordan (Pitea 2010). Nevertheless, it is known that several tens of thousands of Syrians worked irregularly in Jordan, traveling back and forth between the two countries using their passport to cross the border.[2] Since 2011, the number of Syrian nationals in Jordan has skyrocketed. Indeed, in January 2020, about 650,000 Syrian refugees were registered with the UNHCR in this country, 82 percent of whom lived outside refugee camps.[3]

In this context, we suggest analyzing the current Syrian exodus in a long-term perspective, using the case study of the commercial network of a group of street peddlers and their relatives from Dayr Muqaran.[4] The fieldwork was conducted during October 2014 (in Amman, ʿAjlūn and ʾIrbid) and October–November 2015 (in Amman, ʾIrbid and al-Zarqāʾ). Twenty-four qualitative, in-depth interviews, ranging from half an hour to four hours, were conducted to gather data for this chapter. All the people interviewed were born in Dayr Muqaran (eighteen men working as street peddlers and six women, who were all the wives or relatives of the peddlers). Most, if not all of the respondents used to come to Jordan before the beginning of the 2011 Syrian uprising and they all moved permanently to the Hashemite Kingdom after 2012 for two main reasons: the degradation of public safety conditions and the lack of job opportunities in Syria. From the late nineteenth century until the end of the 1980s, most of the Dayr Muqaran population made a living from agricultural activities. But since the 1970s, a

2 Before the implementation of new entry restrictions toward Syrian nationals in Jordan and Lebanon since the beginning of the conflict, Syrians were only required a valid passport and a visa free of charge that could be obtained at the border to enter the Hashemite Kingdom territory.

3 https://data2.unhcr.org/en/situations/syria/location/36

4 This village, located in the Baradā valley, between Damascus and the Lebanese border, hosted around 5,000 to 7,000 inhabitants before the beginning of the uprising.

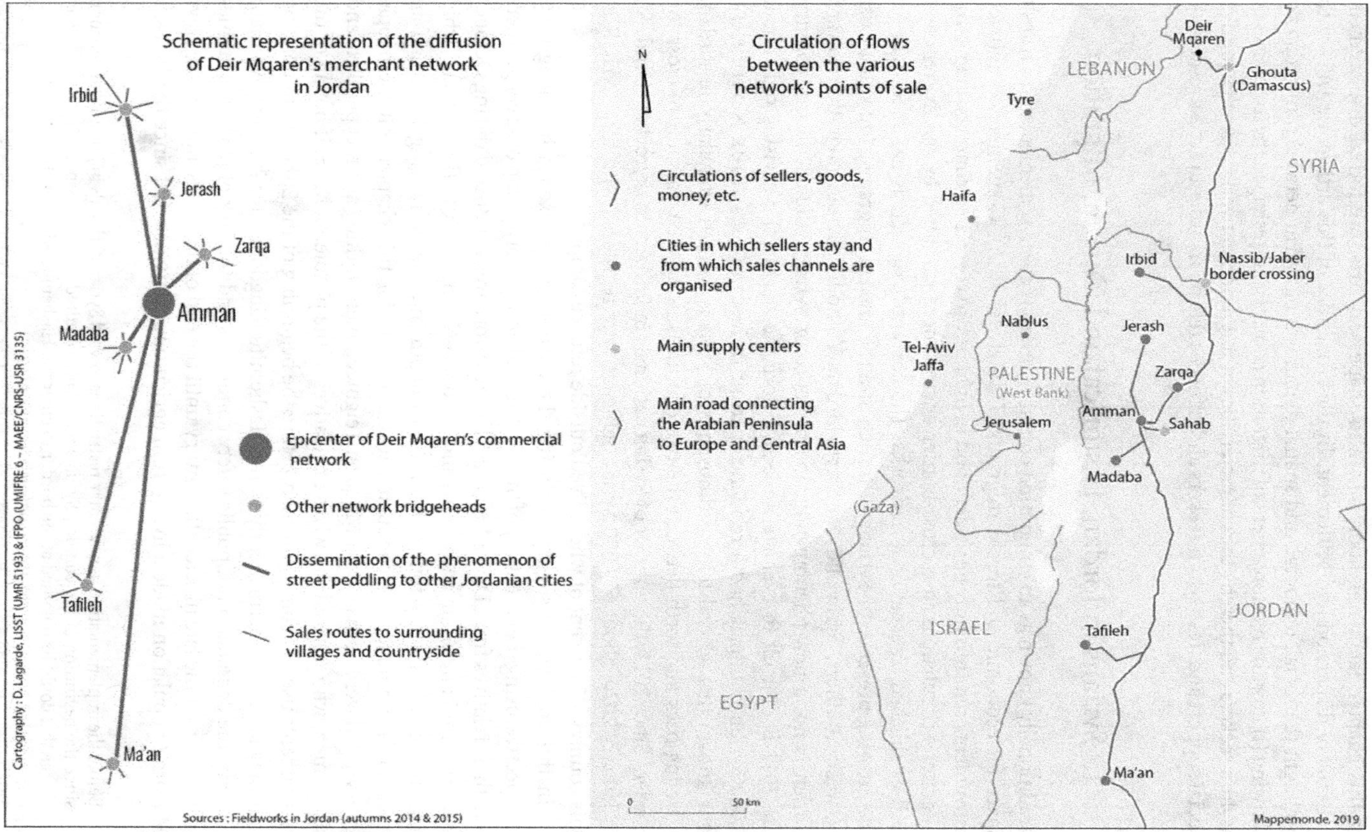

Schematic representation of the diffusion of Deir Mqaren's merchant network in Jordan
Irbid
Jerash
Zarqa
Amman
Madaba
Tafileh
Ma'an
Epicenter of Deir Mqaren's commercial network
Other network bridgeheads
Dissemination of the phenomenon of street peddling to other Jordanian cities
Sales routes to surrounding villages and countryside
Cartography : D. Lagarde, LISST (UMR 5193) & IFPO (UMIFRE 6 – MAEE/CNRS-USR 3135)
Sources : Fieldworks in Jordan (autumns 2014 & 2015)
Circulation of flows between the various network's points of sale
N
Circulations of sellers, goods, money, etc.
Cities in which sellers stay and from which sales channels are organised
Main supply centers
Main road connecting the Arabian Peninsula to Europe and Central Asia
0
50 km
Deir Mqaren
LEBANON
Ghouta (Damascus)
Tyre
SYRIA
Haifa
Irbid
Nassib/Jaber border crossing
Nablus
Jerash
Tel-Aviv Jaffa
PALESTINE (West Bank)
Zarqa
Amman
Sahab
Jerusalem
Madaba
(Gaza)
JORDAN
ISRAEL
Tafileh
EGYPT
Ma'an
Mappemonde, 2019

Figure 4.1 Merchant networks between Syrian and Jordan.

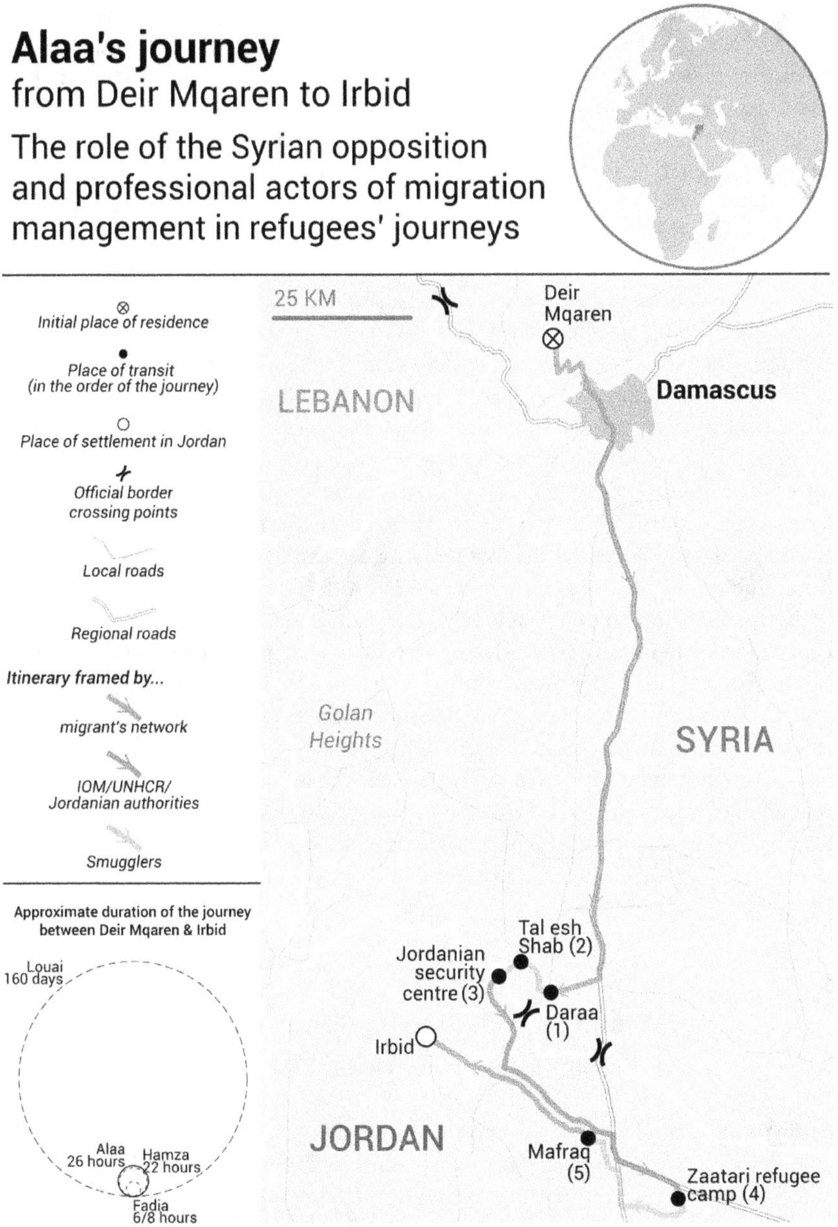

Figure 4.2 Example of a migration trajectory.

combination of demographic, political, and environmental changes gradually dried up the river that used to cross the village, which deeply affected the agricultural sector in the valley (de Châtel 2014). Large-scale government land expropriations conducted in the 1970s and 1980s to create military zones left many farmers of the Baradā valley without land, causing a steep rise in unemployment. At the same time, with the growth of the urban population of the neighboring Syrian capital, the demand for water rose considerably, causing the rapid drying-up of the river. This situation drove some men from Dayr Muqaran to launch trans-border commercial activities between Syria, Jordan, and Lebanon. They thus started to buy dried fruits, nuts, and sweets, either from Damascene traders in the capital or directly in the duty-free shops located in the border areas. Playing on price and information differentials created by state boundaries, in the early 1990s they began to develop a lucrative trans-border activity that, in addition of being one of the only job opportunities in the village, became the main source of income for its inhabitants (Lagarde 2019).

As Syrian nationals, they were free to travel as often as they wished to Jordan and Lebanon. The majority of them did it every month, taking a stock of foodstuffs bought in Syria, and stayed abroad as long as they needed to sell it, generally no more than three to five weeks. Going through cities and villages, they first stayed in hotels and gradually developed good relations with the local population, be they owners of the rooms they stayed in, customers they met in the streets, or local wholesalers they were supplying. By the mid-2000s, the number of street peddlers from Dayr Muqaran operating abroad became so large that the vast majority decided to rent and share apartments. According to the interviews we conducted in northern Jordan, before the beginning of the uprising, around 500 people from this village regularly traveled to Jordan and Lebanon to sell foodstuffs. In the Hashemite Kingdom alone, they rented around thirty apartments in all the major towns (see Figure 4.1) in which they established a turnover system, allowing them to stay with their friends and relatives from the village at a lower cost during their circular migration through Jordan.

But when the first clashes in Southern Syria started in 2011, the mobility of the vendors was rapidly affected. By the end of the year, it became nearly impossible for Dayr Muqaran street peddlers to continue their trans-border activities because of the emergence of criminal gang activity on the road and the rise of security checks at the border.

2. Open-Door Policy and the Prominent Role of Village Networks (2011–2013)

During the first two years following the beginning of the Syrian uprising in March 2011, regional borders were still open to Syrians, facilitating their circulation between different locations within neighboring countries. Some people started to leave Syria, often for short periods of time, in order to escape fighting or to work abroad. This open-border policy enabled Syrians to easily access resources such as housing, employment, and financial or emotional support at a transnational scale.

Fadia's case is representative of this early-conflict situation. She was born in Dayr Muqaran in 1986 from a Syrian mother born in this same village, and a Palestinian father who came to Syria from Jordan in 1970. When she was 10, she moved to the Palestinian refugee camp of Yarmouk, located in the suburbs of Damascus, where her father was working as an English teacher. Later on, in the early 2000s, her parents separated and Fadia moved again with her mother, her brother, and her three sisters to the central neighborhood of Muhājirīn. In the following years, her brother and sisters all moved to different European countries where they settled and obtained secure working positions. By the end of 2011, when the uprising started to turn into an armed conflict, her brother and sisters all beseeched Fadia and their mother to join them in Europe. But it was only when the first violent clashes occurred in a central neighborhood of Damascus that the two women finally took the decision to leave. Within only two days, they fled to Lebanon in order to get a visa for Denmark where one of Fadia's sisters had been living since 2005. As the Danish consulate in Damascus was closed due to the uprising, they decided to go to the closest one, in Beirut, and to stay in Baḥamdūn, a location where some of their relatives from Dayr Muqaran were already working and living.

Nevertheless, when they went to the Danish consulate to apply for a visa a couple of days later, the officials who recorded their application intimated them that their request would not be granted. Considering that they would not be able to reach Europe through legal channels, Fadia and her mother decided to return to Syria. But because Fadia was afraid to go back to Damascus, they chose to go and stay with some of their family members in Dayr Muqaran. Once in the village, Ghalib, Fadia's cousin, hosted them. In addition to being provided with practical support, being surrounded by their close relatives was also important for them. But despite this emotional support, Fadia felt too unsafe to stay in the village, fearing getting trapped in this remote area as violent clashes were occurring in the upper valley. Since 2010, her cousin Ghalib had often been working as a street peddler in the ʾIrbid Governorate, but because of the situation in Syria, he had made fewer commercial trips to Jordan in the past six months and within a few months, he ran out of money. Together with his cousin Fadia, Ghalib decided to leave Syria for Jordan. As a Jordanian citizen on her father's side and with her mother's wedding contract, Jordan appeared to Fadia and her mother as the best available option in the region. Moreover, being with Ghalib, they could stay in the apartment he usually stayed in when he came to work in ʾIrbid. Once again, relying on strong family ties, the two women easily entered Jordan through an official border crossing point and found accommodation in ʾIrbid.

After a week spent in ʾIrbid, Fadia chose to move to Amman, where her boyfriend was living. "I met him at the University in Damascus where he was studying in 2010. When we arrived in Jordan, he suggested to us to stay with his parents' who, like my dad, are Jordanians from Palestine." Even if she admits that when she first arrived in Jordan, she felt Syrian before being Jordanian or Palestinian, she always had strong emotional connections with the Palestinian history and diaspora. Her Palestinian origin also largely facilitated the attitude her boyfriend's family had toward her. It also reinforced the solidarity they showed Fadia and her mother when they first arrived in Jordan and stayed with them in Jabal al-Ḥusayn, a historically Palestinian neighborhood of the Jordanian capital (Oesch 2020). As well as hosting them until they found their own flat, her boyfriend and his siblings provided them with useful information about the Jordanian rental market prices and the best places to live in with respect to their budget. Meanwhile, they could also count on Fadia's brother's financial support. "When we moved in the Ṭabarbūr neighbourhood, my brother, who lives in Belgium, immediately sent us some money via Western Union to buy furniture for the apartment. After that, he kept on helping us financially until I finally earned enough money to make a living for my mum and I."

When the demonstrations started in Syria in March 2011, Fadia was enrolled in a Bachelor's degree in English at the University of Damascus and was also working as an Arabic teacher for foreigners, most of them employed in NGOs or IOs in Syria. But after the summer of 2011, with the ongoing crisis in the country, her students started to leave. When she arrived in Amman a year later, she contacted, through Facebook, some of her students who had also recently moved to Jordan. Some of their friends and colleagues, from the "newly settled expatriate community" in Jordan, were looking for an Arabic teacher. Thanks to a snowball effect, Fadia rapidly enlarged her professional network with NGO and IO workers and rapidly improved her standard of living.

Being an educated woman of Palestinian origin and speaking English, Fadia has a sociologically and spatially diversified network.[5] Indeed, she can rely on strong family ties connecting her locally with her relatives in her native village and transnationally with her siblings in Europe, as well as weak ties she developed with international workers before the beginning of the uprising in Syria and maintained through social networking tools such as Facebook. Moreover, even if she had never lived in Jordan before the conflict, having Jordanian nationality enabled her and her mother (thanks to her wedding contract) to bypass the confines imposed on Syrian refugees by the Jordanian government in the months following their arrival in the country.

The role of the pre-2011 cross-border trade networks is crucial to circumvent blockages at the official border crossing points. During the summer of 2012, clashes spread to most parts of the Syrian territory, including central neighborhoods of Ḥalab and Damascus, the country's two major cities. This situation forced tens of thousands of people to flee their homes. The size of the refugee influx transiting through the *Nassib-Jaber* official border crossing point between Syria and Jordan was such that it had a deep impact on border dynamics. Indeed, Syrian border officers started to take advantage of this situation by forcing asylum seekers to pay bribes to stamp their passports before leaving Syria and entering Jordan. Moreover, on the other side of the border, a growing number of Syrians were being pushed back by the Jordanian border guards. In this context, only few Syrians kept on trying to enter legally into Jordan, while going back and forth on a regular basis between the two countries became almost impossible.

With the difficulties of finding job opportunities in his country, Hamza, another of Fadia's cousins from Dayr Muqaran, decided to move to 'Irbid in January 2013 in order to work as a street peddler, as he had been used to doing since 2007 and until the uprising started in Syria in 2011:

> When I decided to leave the village, it was already almost impossible to enter Jordan through an official border crossing point. So with five other people from the village, we asked my brother-in-law to help us enter the country. He is also from Dayr

[5] In our sample, Fadia is the only one to have a Palestinian background and who carries Jordanian citizenship.

> Muqaran and often came to work in Jordan since 1998, but not as a street peddler like me. Indeed, he used to buy tonnes of goods in Damascus to export them to Jordan by truck and sell them to grocers and retailers in all parts of the Jordanian territory. Thanks to his business, he knew influential tribal leaders and border officers who helped many people from the village to enter the country with their help.

Hamza's testimony underlines the centrality that some specific inhabitants from the village network started to gain from their commercial relations as soon as the Jordanian borders started to close off. Being an important trader, Hamza's brother-in-law was familiar with the Syrian-Jordanian border environment and with some of its officials. Nevertheless, with the growing number of blockages encountered at the border, Jordanians that were able to help Syrians to bypass these constraints started to expect payment in return for their services:

> When we had decided to leave the village, my brother-in-law called one of his contacts in Jordan, told him when we were planning to be at the border, and in return, he was supposed to phone a border officer to let us through. The deal was to give the intermediary a hundred dollars once in Jordan for each person that would be allowed to enter. But once we got there, only three of us were able to go through, and I was not part of the lucky few.

Therefore, Hamza decided to rely on his own acquaintances from ʾIrbid. He thus phoned one of his regular customers who works for the Jordanian secret police and asked him if he would be able to help him enter the country:

> When I called him, he promised to find a solution as soon as possible. So I spent the night at a hotel located on the Syrian side of the border and the following morning, he called me saying that a border officer was waiting for me to stamp my passport and let me enter Jordan. And in the end, I didn't even have to pay for this.

Even if Hamza's personal network at that time was not composed of such influential people as his brother-in-law's, personally knowing the people he solicited finally ensured him their trust and loyalty. When he arrived in ʾIrbid half an hour after crossing the border, he stayed in the same apartment he had always stayed in with his friends and cousins from Dayr Muqaran since he first came to work in Jordan in 2007. Two days later, Hamza met with Karam, a Jordanian wholesaler who used to buy goods from Hamza's father back in the late 1990s (Lagarde 2019). Hamza thus started buying sweets, dried fruits, and nuts from Karam and took up his peddling activities again.

Hamza's example is particularly relevant to emphasize the emerging importance of weak ties such as professional relations or acquaintances in the itineraries and coping strategies of Syrians before the complete closure of the two official Jordanian border crossing points. Compared to his cousin Fadia, though Hamza was only able to rely on his village and commercial network, it was still sufficient in January 2013 to enter Jordan legally and circumvent the al-Zaʿtarī refugee camp through which all asylum seekers entering Jordan irregularly were forced to transit since its opening in

July 2012. He was then also free to rely on his previous kinship connections to find accommodation and work in 'Irbid. Moreover, he often sent money to his wife and children back home via Haram Exchange, a long-established money transfer company with offices located in central Damascus.

While Jordanian authorities began to tighten their entry policy, Syrian refugees had to cross via informal border crossings before transiting through al-Zaʿtarī refugee camp. They were no longer allowed to cross through the official entry points and settle directly where they wanted. By the spring of 2013, increasingly frequent and violent clashes and bombings in and around Dayr Muqaran drastically limited the daily mobility of the village inhabitants. It thus became difficult for women living alone with their children to go to Damascus in order to collect the money sent by their husbands working in Jordan in one of the Haram Exchange offices. Furthermore, some families had now been separated for several months. As a result, a growing number of women decided to reunite with their husbands in Jordan. But during the same period, the ongoing situation on the ground in Southern Syria pushed Jordan to close its official border crossing points to Syrian asylum seekers.

In June 2013, Hamza's wife, Alaa, decided to leave the village with their two children. But as they were not able to reach Jordan through legal channels, Hamza organized their trip from Jordan, once again relying on his own kinship connections. Hamza explains that one of his customers in 'Irbid managed to find a solution to get his family into Jordan:

> In June 2013, one of my customers told me that he knew people in Darʿā who could help my family out of Syria. This person is part of a tribe whose members are mainly settled in the Ḥawrān region, straddling Southern Syria and Northern Jordan. He was in touch with the Free Syrian Army who was still in charge of helping people to cross the border into Jordan. For 15,000 Syrian pounds[6] (SYP), this guy was able to get Alaa and the people she had planned to travel with into Jordan, and for an extra 150 dollars, to get them out of al-Zaʿtarī camp. (. . .) During the following months, other friends and relatives from the village asked me to help them to enter Jordan and leave al-Zaʿtarī. Sometimes, people I didn't even know also called me on my mobile phone because they heard I was able to help them. But some people started to talk and gossip about me saying that I was making money out of this, so I preferred to stop helping people to cross the border.

Once Alaa and her children managed to cross the border, the Jordanian police checked their identity papers before placing them on board of an IOM bus that took them to al-Zaʿtarī camp. As Hamza had already planned everything before his friends and family arrived in Jordan, Alaa received a phone call from a Jordanian smuggler who was waiting for them in the camp. He took them to his car that was parked a few hundred meters away and then took a back road to leave without a glitch. After a half-hour drive through the desert and on the main road linking Amman and the Syrian border, the smuggler dropped them off in front of the town hall in al-Mafraq. Hamza

6 About US$100.

was waiting for them with Yasser, one of his friends from the village also working as a street peddler in Jordan. Alaa's friend who had traveled with her left directly from 'Irbid to Amman with the four children she was traveling with while Alaa went to 'Irbid. The couple and their two children stayed at Yasser's for nine days, until they rented their own apartment near a shopping mall in the vicinity of which Hamza sold his merchandise.

This example stresses the consequences of the closure of the Jordanian borders on Syrian asylum seekers' access to mobility and the itineraries they follow to reach the Hashemite Kingdom. First, it is evident that the closure of borders and the implementation of transit centers and refugee camps in Jordan forces Syrian asylum seekers to follow longer but also more dangerous itineraries. Secondly, it also underlines the operation of social networks on three different spatial scales. In the sending areas, families, relatives and friends provide social support. Indeed, in a context of conflict where women must sometimes travel alone with their children, family and friendship ties are essential to understanding the bonding of groups of travelers. Family members also provide financial support from the desired destination to sending areas *via* money transfers and information. They manage to organize their relatives' trips from a distance by using their kinship connections in Jordan.

At the borders, four actors assist asylum seekers: (i) smugglers/facilitators organizing the trips; (ii) Syrian rebel groups in charge of directing the flows of asylum seekers in cooperation with the Jordanian authorities; (iii) border police on the Jordanian side of the border; (iv) professional agents of migration management (e.g., the IOM and the UNHCR) supervising asylum seekers' mobility and settlement in Jordan. As a result of the progressive closure of the Jordanian borders, Syrian asylum seekers' access to mobility is becoming increasingly dependent on weak ties.

3. Reinforcement of Border Controls and Changing Itineraries: The Central Role of Weak Ties

By the end of June 2013, Jordan completely closed its western border with Syria. This event coincided with the end of the cooperation between the FSA and Jordan in managing the flow of asylum seekers. Syrians fleeing their country are now forced to take the road east to enter *via* the informal crossing points of al-Ḥadalāt and al-Rukbān, the last two entry points still operating between the two countries. The itinerary now crosses the governorate of al-Suwaydā' partly controlled by the Syrian regime, and the Syrian Desert. The trips are thus more dangerous, expensive, and fragmented (Collyer 2007; Schapendonk 2012). This last case study intends to highlight: (i) how Syrian asylum seekers and refugees use social networks in a context of strict migration controls in Jordan and (ii) their increased dependence on migration management professionals and on the humanitarian sector.

Louai and his wife have two daughters. The youngest, Loubna, suffers from a heart disease and must undergo regular medical treatment. With the worsening of the security situation in Syria, it was becoming nearly impossible for her parents to take her to Damascus for her treatment. Moreover, Louai, who worked as a chef in a village located a few kilometers away from Dayr Muqaran, lost his job in 2013. After his dismissal, he tried six times to go to Jordan to work as a street peddler, but even with the help of his friends and relatives, he never succeeded in legally entering the country. As Louai explained, he finally decided to enter Jordan with the help of a smuggler:

> In August 2014, we decided to leave the village with one of our friends and her three kids. We got in contact with Fatima, a girl from Dayr Muqaran married to a man from Kiḥīl, a village located in Southern Syria. I didn't know her that well, but I knew her husband helped people from the village to get in touch with smugglers. So I decided to phone her and ask her husband to help us. At that time, Fatima and her husband were already living in Jordan. But they told us to go to their place in Kiḥīl where their son was still living. So one of our friends from Dayr Muqaran drove us to Damascus and from the bus station, we took a microbus for Kiḥīl. We stayed for a week at Fatima's until a smuggler came to get us. Then the smuggler kept us at his place for another week until the road was safe and he gathered enough people wishing to enter Jordan to cross the border. The day we left, each family had to pay 40,000 SYP[7] before boarding the smuggler's van.

Even if people from Dayr Muqaran can still rely on their village network's weak ties to find smugglers or housing on their way to Jordan, trustworthiness seems to crumble as social proximity declines. Indeed, when Louai and his relatives were forced to solicit assistance outside of their own personal networks, certain problems arose. Only a couple of hours after they left the smuggler's place, he left them stranded in the middle of the desert. Louai's only solution was to phone Fatima's husband in Jordan who promised him that he would manage to send someone to pick them all up. Finally, twelve hours later, two other smugglers arrived and demanded that each family pay an extra 10,000 SYP[8] to continue toward the border. After a night-long drive, Louai and the other families he was traveling with finally made it to the al-Ḥadalāt informal border crossing. Since June 2014, when the Islamic State organization took over al-Mawṣul, only tens of asylum seekers have been allowed to enter the country everyday under strict supervision, most of them being sent back to Syria when they arrive at the Rabāʿ al-Sarḥān registration center.[9] Those accepted into the Jordanian territory are in most cases forced to reside in the al-ʾAzraq refugee camp, which opened in April 2014. Due to the heightened supervision of the entry and stay of Syrians in the Hashemite Kingdom and the development of tools designed to strictly frame the refugees' mobility within

[7] About US$270.

[8] About US$68.

[9] In July 2013, in order to better organize, filter, and document the flow of asylum seekers coming from Syria, the UNHCR and the Jordanian government opened the Rabāʿ al-Sarḥān reception center where any asylum seeker entering Jordan *via* an informal crossing point is now required to go through for registration. Four transit centers opened at the same period in the eastern border region north of the city of al-Ruwayshīd. Controlled by the Jordanian authorities, the International Committee of the Red Cross (ICRC) is in charge of health and housing services in these places, where asylum seekers are waiting for several days while they go through interviews conducted by the Jordanian security in order to make sure newcomers do not pose a threat to national security.

the country (Ababsa 2015; Roussel 2015), the effects of the migrants'social networks on access to mobility in Jordan were considerably weakened. But with Loubna's medical certificate attesting that she was suffering from a heart disease, Louai and his family did not have to wait much at the border. They then went through two transit centers where they spent twenty days in the first one and two days in the second in order to undergo heavy security interviews. They then went to Rabāʿ al-Sarḥān registration center before being sent to al-ʾAzraq refugee camp.[10] Unlike Louai and his wife, the friend from Dayr Muqaran that they were traveling with got blocked for more than a month with her three children before finally entering the Jordanian territory and follow the same security checks.

Once in al-ʾAzraq refugee camp, Louai's family rapidly got authorization from the Jordanian authorities to leave the camp on a regular basis because of Loubna's health problems. In total, the family spent four months going back and forth every ten to fifteen days between al-ʾAzraq, the Al Bashir hospital in Amman where Loubna was getting her treatment, and their friends and relative's homes where they were staying outside the camp. Meanwhile, Louai started a legal procedure to definitively leave the camp. As Louai explained, despite the strict migration controls toward Syrians in Jordan, Dayr Muqaran's village network has been efficient in enabling the family to leave the al-ʾAzraq refugee camp and to find work and accommodation in Jordan:

> While we were going back and forth between the camp and our family and friends' house in Jordan, I asked Shafiq, my brother-in-law, to see with Karam if he would accept to start administrative procedures to get us an authorization to leave the camp and settle in ʾIrbid. With the mediation of Shafiq, Karam accepted to become our sponsor and the 27th of October 2014, we finally left the camp for ʾIrbid. We found an apartment with the help of my friend Hamza (see 3.2 above) who knew a Jordanian grocer who had an apartment to rent in the town centre. And the day after we arrived in ʾIrbid, I got foodstuffs from Karam and started to work for the first time in my life as a street peddler, following advice that my friends gave me about how and where to sell.

As shown previously, the tight village network of Dayr Muqaran can give its members access to many resources such as information about mobility, housing, job opportunities, and emotional support. Nevertheless, except in the case of Fadia, who can rely on older transnational Palestinian networks, the social capital inherent to this village network only seems to operate at a regional scale in Syria, Jordan, and Lebanon. Yet, specific resources such as access to health or mobility to remote locations can only be reached through transient acquaintances. The rest of Louai's family migration journey highlights the growing influence of humanitarian organizations on the most vulnerable Syrian refugees in Jordan. Indeed, during the first months they spent in Jordan, Loubna's health quickly deteriorated. Only an expensive operation that none

[10] Al-ʾAzraq refugee camp was opened in April 2014 by the UNHCR, in a desert area 20 km away from the town of al-ʾAzraq. It can accommodate up to 130,000 refugees, but in 2019 it hosted only 35,000. The camp is isolated and disconnected from its local environment.

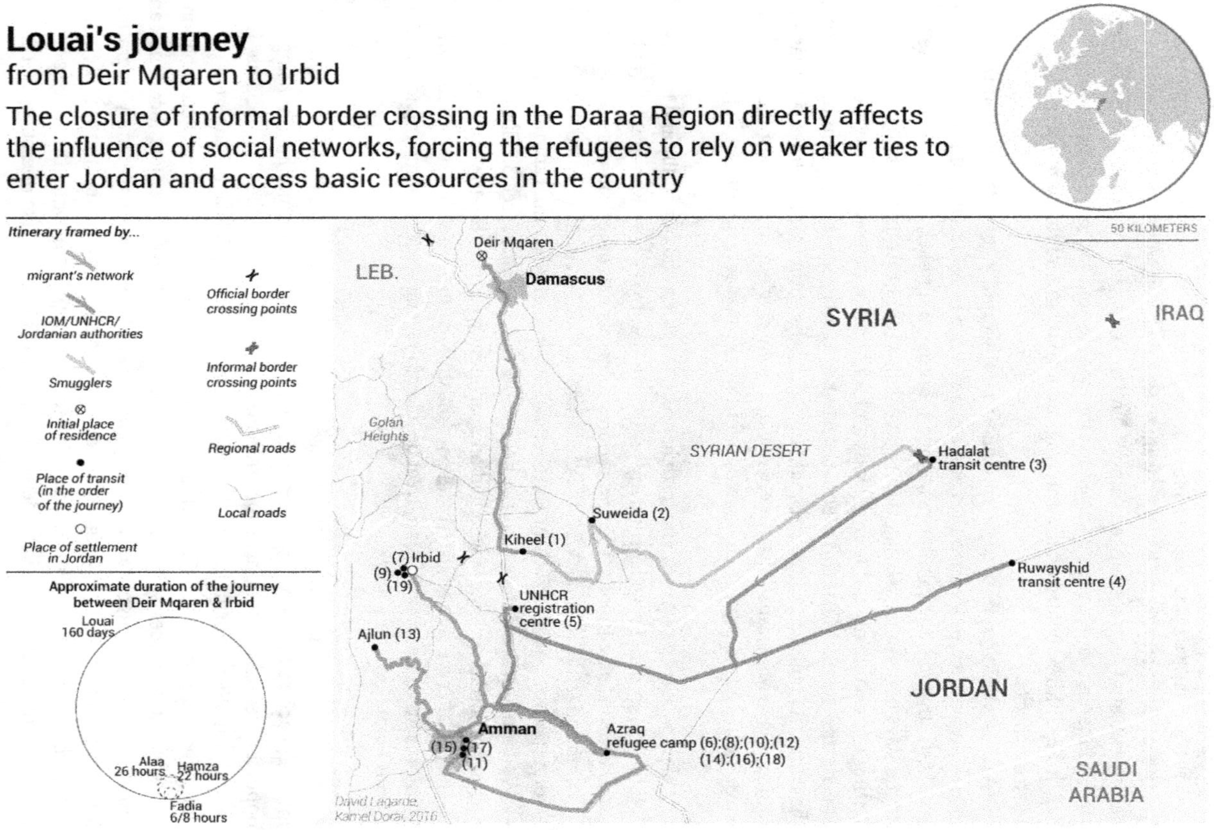
Louai's journey
from Deir Mqaren to Irbid
The closure of informal border crossing in the Daraa Region directly affects the influence of social networks, forcing the refugees to rely on weaker ties to enter Jordan and access basic resources in the country
Itinerary framed by...
migrant's network
IOM/UNHCR/ Jordanian authorities
Smugglers
Initial place of residence
Place of transit (in the order of the journey)
Place of settlement in Jordan
Official border crossing points
Informal border crossing points
Regional roads
Local roads
Approximate duration of the journey between Deir Mqaren & Irbid
Louai 160 days
Alaa 26 hours
Hamza 22 hours
Fadia 6/8 hours
50 KILOMETERS
Deir Mqaren
Damascus
LEB.
SYRIA
IRAQ
Golan Heights
SYRIAN DESERT
Hadalat transit centre (3)
Suweida (2)
Kiheel (1)
(7) Irbid
(9)
(19)
UNHCR registration centre (5)
Ruwayshid transit centre (4)
Ajlun (13)
JORDAN
Amman
(15)
(17)
(11)
Azraq refugee camp (6);(8);(10);(12) (14);(16);(18)
SAUDI ARABIA
David Lagarde, Kamel Doraï, 2016

Figure 4.3 Example of a migration trajectory.

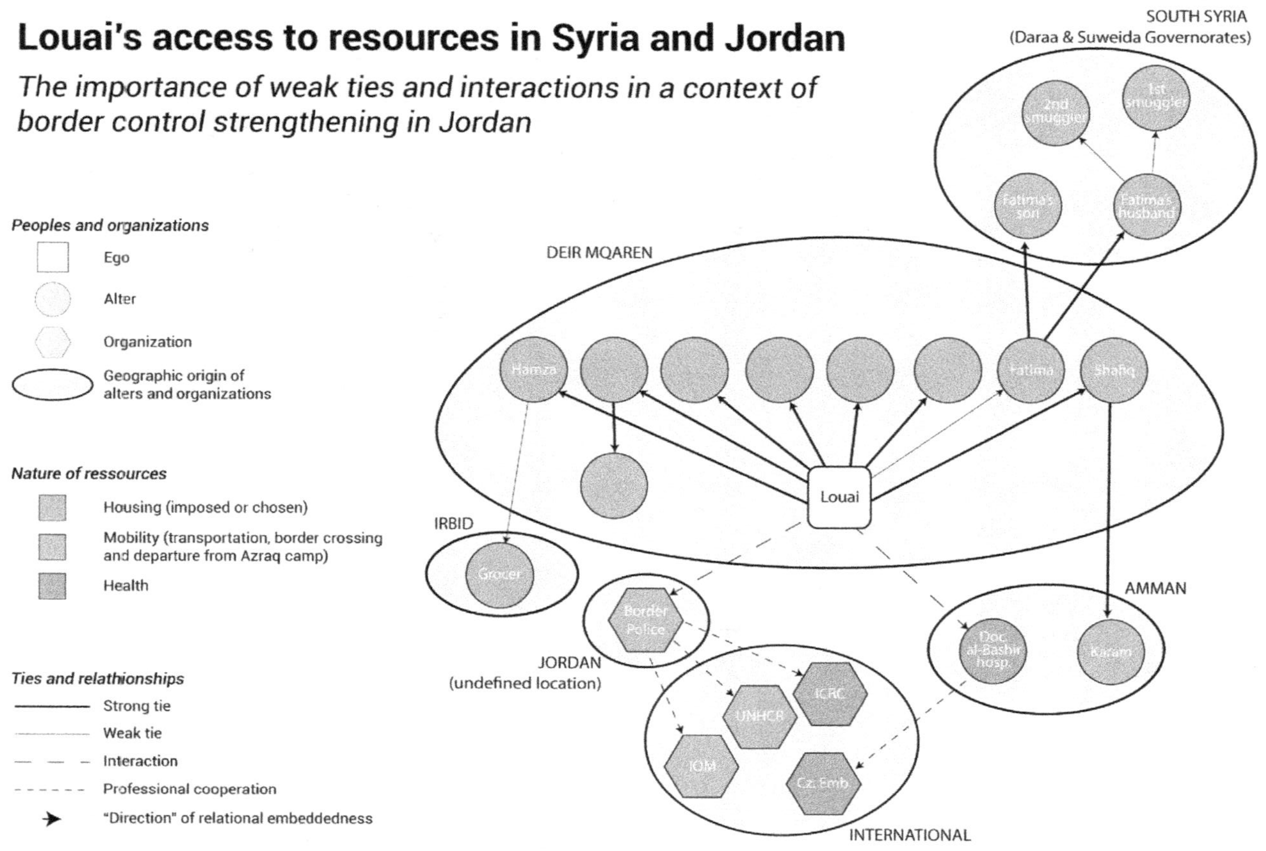

Louai's access to resources in Syria and Jordan
The importance of weak ties and interactions in a context of border control strengthening in Jordan
Peoples and organizations
Ego
Alter
Organization
Geographic origin of alters and organizations
Nature of ressources
Housing (imposed or chosen)
Mobility (transportation, border crossing and departure from Azraq camp)
Health
Ties and relathionships
Strong tie
Weak tie
Interaction
Professional cooperation
"Direction" of relational embeddedness
SOUTH SYRIA
(Daraa & Suweida Governorates)
2nd smuggler
1st smuggler
Fatima's son
Fatima's husband
DEIR MQAREN
Hamza
Fatima
Shafiq
Louai
IRBID
Grocer
Border Police
JORDAN
(undefined location)
AMMAN
Doc. al-Bashir hosp.
Karam
UNHCR
ICRC
IOM
Cz. Emb.
INTERNATIONAL

Figure 4.4 Access to resources in Syria and Jordan.

of the international NGOs or IOs in Jordan willing to pay for could improve her health. During one of their visits to the Al Bashir hospital, Louai and his wife met with a Jordanian doctor who told them about an annual grant provided by the Czech Embassy in Amman to finance operations for sick children living in Jordan. Louai decided to apply for it and Loubna finally underwent the operation she needed. In such a context, the role of state policies, IOs as well as local and international NGOs, is becoming essential to understand the shaping of migrants' spatial trajectories. To carry on with Louai's example, at the end of 2015, the UNHCR offered him the possibility of taking part in a resettlement program that could give him the opportunity to move to the United States. After undergoing three interviews, the family finally left for America at the beginning of 2016. But as Louai explained a couple of months before the departure, his family does not have much influence on the rest of its own migration journey:

> Despite the (. . .) interviews we had with officials, the UNHCR doesn't let us know more about the process. We don't even know when we would move if our request is accepted, nor to which city we would be sent in the U.S. In these conditions, I must admit that I am sometimes a bit afraid to leave my friends and family behind me to settle in a country where I don't know anybody. But at least, I know that my two daughters will get a much better future it we move to the US rather than staying here.

Conclusion

Since 2014, Jordan has almost closed its northern border to newcomers. While Syrians were allowed to circulate between the two countries before 2011, developing trans-border trading activities and family networks, the current Syrian crisis has completely reshaped this migration pattern. At the beginning of the Syrian uprising, refugees could rely on already existing networks to enter Jordan and settle freely in one of the main cities in the northern part of the kingdom. Restrictions on entries and the creation of refugee camps have generated constraints, with two main consequences: first, the lengthening and the growing complexity of the journey, and second, the reduced efficiency of already existing migrant social networks. Syrians who first entered Jordan after mid-2012 have faced huge constraints to enter and settle outside refugee camps. They became much more dependent on external actors, be they formal (UNHCR, Border Police, etc.) or informal (smugglers in particular). The current Syrian experience, and more specifically those groups who were circulating between Jordan and Syria, contributes to a better understanding of the role of social networks in the migration process during the crisis. Whereas most of the studies on the relationship between forced migration and transnational networks focus on South-North movement, this contribution has emphasized the role of such networks in South-South migration. As shown by the example of the Dayr Muqaran street peddlers, forced migrations are articulated with other forms of long-term mobility that developed over time at a regional level. Nevertheless, political and security constraints tend to limit the role of such social networks in the case of protracted conflicts. Indeed, regarding the often-changing policies toward Syrian migration in recent years, asylum seekers and refugees have been forced to draw upon different kinds of ties that can include relatives, friends, professional actors of migration management, and acquaintances. In this sense, they appear to be much more dependent on weak ties as compared to economic migrants. So even if networks are used differently, we observed that they still play a key role on the spatial trajectories of asylum seekers and refugees.

Bibliography

Ababsa, Myriam (2015), "De la crise humanitaire à la crise sécuritaire. Les dispositifs de contrôle des réfugiés syriens en Jordanie (2011–2015)," *Revue européenne des migrations internationales*, 31 (3): 73–101.

Boyd, Monica (1989), "Family and Personal Networks in International Migration: Recent Developments and New Agendas," *The International Migration Review*, 23 (3): 638–70.

Chatelard, Géraldine (2005), "Iraqi Asylum Migrants in Jordan: Conditions, Religious Networks and the Smuggling Process," in George J. Borjas and Jeff Crisp (eds.), *Poverty, International Migration and Asylum*, 341–70, London: Palgrave Macmillan.

Clochard, Olivier (2010), "Le contrôle des flux migratoires aux frontières de l'Union européenne s'oriente vers une disposition de plus en plus réticulaire," *Carnets de géographes*, (1) October.

Collyer, Michael (2005), "When Do Social Networks Fail to Explain Migration? Accounting for the Movement of Algerian Asylum-Seekers to the UK," *Journal of Ethnic and Migration Studies*, 31 (4): 699–718.

Collyer, Michael (2007), "In-Between Places: Trans-Saharan Transit Migrants in Morocco and the Fragmented Journey to Europe," *Antipode*, 39 (4): 668–90.

Collyer, Michael, and Russell King (2015), "Producing Transnational Space: International Migration and the Extra-territorial Reach of State Power," *Progress in Human Geography*, 39 (2): 185–204.

De Bel Air, Françoise (2015), "Jordanie," in Gildas Simon (ed.), *Dictionnaire des migrations internationales: Approche géohistorique*, 260–65, Paris: Armand Colin.

De Châtel, Francesca (2014), "The Death of the Garden of Eden," in Terje Tvedt and Terje Oestigaard (eds.), *A History of Water, Series III, Vol. 1, Water and Urbanization*, 305–27, London: I.B. Tauris.

Doraï, Kamel (2011), "Iraqis in Exile: Migratory Networks as a Coping Strategy," *International Journal of Contemporary Iraqi Studies*, 5 (2): 215–29.

El Colegio de la Frontera Norte (2011), *Encuesta sobre migración en la frontera Norte de México*, Mexico. Available online: http://gobernacion.gob.mx/work/models/SEGOB/Resource/1746/1/images/EMIF%20NORTE%202011.pdf.

Faist, Thomas (2000), *The Volume and Dynamics of International Migration and Transnational Social Spaces*, Oxford: Oxford University Press.

Fawcett, James T. (1989), "Networks, Linkages, and Migration Systems," *The International Migration Review*, 23 (3): 671–80.

Gehrig, Tina, and Alessandro Monsutti (2003), "Territoires, flux et représentations de l'exil afghan: le cas des Hazaras et des Kaboulis," *A contrario*, 1 (1): 61–78.

Granovetter, Mark S. (1973), "The Strength of Weak Ties," *American Journal of Sociology*, 78 (6): 1360–80.

Koser, Khalid (1997), "Social Networks and the Asylum Cycle: The Case of Iranians in the Netherlands," *The International Migration Review*, 31 (3): 591–611.

Koser, Khalid (2007), "Refugees, Transnationalism and the State," *Journal of Ethnic and Migration Studies*, 33 (2): 233–54.

Koslowski, Rey (2000), "The Mobility Money Can Buy: Human Smuggling and Border Control in the European Union," in Timothy Snyder and Peter Andreas (eds.), *The Wall around the West: State Borders and Immigration Controls in North America and Europe*, 203–18, Lanham: Rowman & Littlefield.

Krissman, Fred (2005), "Sin Coyote Ni Patrón: Why the 'Migrant Network' Fails to Explain International Migration," *International Migration Review*, 39 (1): 4–44.

Kritz, Mary M., and Hania Zlotnik (1992), "Global Interactions: Migration Systems, Processes, and Policies," in Mary M. Kritz, Lin Lean Lim, and Hania Zlotnik (eds.), *International Migration Systems: A Global Approach*, 177–89, Oxford: Clarendon Press.

Lagarde, David (2019), "Syrian Street Vendors and Globalisation," *Mappemonde. Revue trimestrielle sur l'image géographique et les formes du territoire*, (126) April.

Long, Katy (2013), "When Refugees Stopped Being Migrants: Movement, Labour and Humanitarian Protection," *Migration Studies*, 1 (March): 4–26.

Ma Mung, Emmanuel (2009), "Le point de vue de l'autonomie dans l'étude des migrations internationales: 'penser de l'intérieur' les phénomènes de mobilité," in Françoise Dureau and Marie-Antoinette Hily (eds.), *Les mondes de la mobilité*, 25–38, Rennes: Presses de l'Université de Rennes.

Malkki, Liisa H. (1996), "Speechless Emissaries: Refugees, Humanitarianism, and Dehistoricization," *Cultural Anthropology*, 11 (3): 377–404.

Massey, Douglas S., Joaquim Arango, Graeme Hugo, Ali Kouauci, and Adela Pellegrino (1993), "Theories of International Migration: A Review and Appraisal," *Population and Development Review*, 19 (3): 431–66.

Muanamoha, Ramos Cardoso, Brij Maharaj, and Eleanor Preston-Whyte (2010), "Social Networks and Undocumented Mozambican Migration to South Africa," *Geoforum*, 6 (41): 885–96.

Oesch, Lucas (2020), "An Improvised Dispositif: Invisible Urban Planning in the Refugee Camp," *International Journal of Urban and Regional Research*, 44 (2): 349–65.

Pitea, Roberto (2010), "Transit Migration: Challenges in Egypt, Iraq, Jordan and Lebanon," CARIM Research Reports 2010/02, Robert Schuman Centre for Advanced Studies, San Domenico di Fiesole (FI): European University Institute.

Portes, Alejandro (1997), *Globalization from Below: The Rise of Transnational Communities*, University of Oxford Transnational Communities [Programme], 52.

Richmond, Anthony H. (1994), *Global Apartheid: Refugees, Racism, and the New World Order*, Toronto and New York: Oxford University Press.

Roussel, Cyril (2015), "La frontière syro-jordanienne dans le conflit syrien: enjeux sécuritaires, gestion frontalière," *L'Espace Politique. Revue en ligne de géographie politique et de géopolitique*, (27) September.

Ryan, Louise, Rosemary Sales, Mary Tilki, and Bernadetta Siara (2008), "Social Networks, Social Support and Social Capital: The Experiences of Recent Polish Migrants in London," *Sociology*, 42 (4): 672–90.

Schapendonk, Joris (2012), "Turbulent Trajectories: African Migrants on Their Way to the European Union," *Societies*, 2 (December): 27–41.

Schapendonk, Joris (2015), "What if Networks Move? Dynamic Social Networking in the Context of African Migration to Europe," *Population, Space and Place*, 21 (8): 809–19.

Shami, Seteney, and Lisa McCann (1993), "The Social Implications of Population Displacement and Resettlement in the Middle East," *International Migration Review*, 27 (2): 425.

Zetter, Roger (1991), "Labelling Refugees: Forming and Transforming a Bureaucratic Identity," *Journal of Refugee Studies*, 4 (January): 39–62.

Part 2

Urban Dynamics, Intermingling and Space Production

5

Questing for Land

Chechen[1] Villages in the Shaping of Transjordan,[2] an Overview

Gaspard Vial-Benamra

The settlement of Chechen populations in the Middle East dates back to the second half of the nineteenth century. Among them, around 200 families had settled in southernmost Ottoman Syria—today's Jordan—by 1903. They founded the villages of al-Zarqā', Ṣuwayliḥ, Sukhna, and al-'Azraq al-Shīshān. Chechens of Jordan are still predominantly living in the historical hearts of these towns and now represent a population of approximately eleven thousand.[3]

Historiography dedicated to the North Caucasian diasporas in the Middle East focuses mainly on the resettlement of Muslims from Russia in the Ottoman Empire.[4] Recently, there has been increased academic interest in reconsidering the colonial nature of Ottoman rule[5] and Caucasian settlers are being rethought as imperial colonists whose resettlement was meant to counterbalance demographics, constitute loyal armed forces, and improve the agricultural sector (Fratantuono 2019). Taking the

1 She self-designation or endonym is Nakh (inclusive) and Nakhcho (exclusive). Nakh designates an ancient macro-ethnic group of the North-Central, Northeastern Caucasus, while Nakhcho designates the eastern portion of it, known by the exo-ethnonym Chechen, and the western portion, the self-designated Ghalghaï, is known as Ingush. For a comprehensive view on the matter see Nichols (2004). In our case study, Chechen villages also hosted Dagestani families of Avar ethnicity who migrated along with the Chechens, as well as a few Ingush families. There were, for example, five Dagestani families and four Ingush families living in Ṣuwayliḥ in the late 1930s (Faḫrī and Al-Tall 1939: 23, Peake 1958 :224).

2 Although the toponym Transjordan or the French equivalent, Transjourdain, was already used in the late Ottoman era by Western observers, it does not reflect any territorial or political reality until 1921. The term is chosen for ease of reading because of the intricacy of administrative divisions of the area during the Ottoman era.

3 According to a field study for a Master thesis in Geography that focuses on the Chechens' geographical distribution, there were 8,776 Chechens in Jordan in 1996. See (Al-Bashāyra 1999: 159-60). Based on his calculations, there were, theoretically, 11,303 Chechens in Jordan in 2019.

4 For the first academic studies about the Circassians and Chechens in Ottoman Transjordan, refer to (Abujaber, 1989; Lewis 1987; Rogan, 1999; Chatty, 2010: 91-133).

5 For an overview statement see (Türesay, 2013). For a nuanced analysis of Ottoman imperialism see (Aymes, 2013).

Chechens as a case study, this chapter aims to assess particular internal group dynamics among migrants and question the existence of a North Caucasian ethnotype created by the primary sources that has still not been deconstructed in Ottoman and Middle Eastern studies. This, additionally, is a starting point to consider the socioeconomic dynamics of the Chechen settlers as an aspect of the emergence of the Jordanian nation. In fact, this chapter does not take into account a separated periodicity between the late Ottoman era and the Mandate era. Chechens, like many of the Transjordanians living on the fringes of state-administrated areas, experienced similarly limited interactions with statehood from the time of their settlement during the last years of Ottoman rule until the mid-to-late 1920s. By the same token, spatial integration of the migrants was subject to the same dynamics throughout this period, which is not restricted to the fall of the Ottoman Empire.

As for the Chechens in Transjordan and Jordan, their history is generally under-assessed by academic studies.[6] The main reason for that is the apparent paucity of sources. The fact is that until the late 1920s, Chechens had very limited contacts with legal institutions, hence they are not to be found in Ottoman sharia court archives for example, in contrast with the Circassians.[7] The latter formed the local Ottoman *Jandarma* and engaged in trading activities on a regional scale and so were, logically, better acquainted with institutions and quicker to formalize their social and economic activities.[8] Chechens, on the other hand, formed smaller village units, were more inclined toward subsistence agriculture and relied extensively upon their own Sufi leadership, which to a great extent regulated both internal and external interactions. To address this archival challenge, special attention is given to the private papers retained by Jordanians of Chechen descent.[9] Such archives are of different types, such as personal memoirs and testimonies, correspondence, and official letters which, combined with later state archives, provide us with a more comprehensive insight into the community life of the migrants and settlers.

6 The very first academic production on the Chechen/Ingush diasporas in the Middle East is a PhD thesis which was published as a monograph, see (Badaev 1998). Recent Russian-language articles also treated the subject but with a broader approach on the migration itself and the different places of settlement of the Chechen, mostly in Turkey, Syria, and Jordan; for an overview, see (Israilov) Jordan Chechen minister Said Bino also published a book on the history of Jordanian Chechens (2007).

7 They are, for example, barely mentioned in the recent *Palgrave Handbook of the Hashemite Kingdom of Jordan* (2019), which contained a chapter entitled "Circassians." The chapter, however, accurately noted that the opening of Tsarist archives by Georgia in 2008 boosted Circassian activism for the recognition of a Circassian genocide perpetrated by Tsarist forces. In our view, the vitality of Circassian activism, added to the fact that the Circassians are indeed more numerous than other Caucasians in the areas concerned, had an impact on the reading grid adopted by many researchers who studied the Caucasian diasporas in the Middle East.

8 For a recent study on the issue, refer to Hamed-Troyansky (2017).

9 Many of the manuscripts and documents related to the Transjordan Chechens were collected by Jordanian researcher Abdulghani Hassan some decades ago but these materials were scattered following his death. Such valuable sources have remained almost entirely unexploited in the academic field and are to be found in Jordan where descendants of migrants conserve original documents or copies of them in the private sphere.

1. *Hijra*: Sufi Networking and Demographic Engineering

North Caucasian migrations toward the Ottoman lands have long been studied by historians and consist of two waves of migration. The first concerns the forced migrations during the final years of the Russian conquest of the Caucasus and its aftermath (1857-1865) and as a consequence of the Russian-Ottoman War of 1876-1878: more than one million North Caucasians were to be resettled in the Ottoman lands, the vast majority of whom were Circassians.[10] The second wave was the post-conflict voluntary migrations that took place during the establishment of the Tsarist colonial administration in the North Caucasus from the late 1870s to the 1910s (Ibragimova 2006; Jersild 2002). North Caucasians were widely labeled as *muhājir* or faith migrants (t. *muhācir*) by the Ottomans, a socio-cultural designation retained by the migrants and their descendants.[11] Academic research on the subject tends to deconstruct this designation, even in the case of voluntary migration, by putting forward more complex socioeconomic dynamics. For example, G. Chochiev took the case of Ossetian *muhājirs*—which could be enlarged to include the Kabardians—to point out that Tsarist colonial rule threatened the power and prestige of local Muslim aristocracies (Chochiev 2015).

Agrarian reforms and compulsory military service or financial compensation indeed transformed the societal landscape. However, migratory dynamics have to be put into perspective with the plurality of North Caucasian societies. Chechens formed a casteless peasant society[12] in which Sufi orders—both the Naqshbandiyya-Khālidiyya and Qādiriyya[13]—played a major role in ethnic cohesion and were embedded into the clan structure to become a sort of ethno-Sufism (Zelkina 1993, 2000). Following the last uprising against Russian presence organized by Sufis in both Chechnya and North Daghestan in 1877, local scholars began to articulate the Islamic concept of *hijra*—voluntary migration, hence *muhājir*—in context. Colonial rule as a whole, and not, for example, religious freedom alone, was perceived as a theological issue (Kemper 2002).[14] Thus, it questioned the opposition between a poorly defined religious cause and socioeconomic causes for migration. In the case of the Chechens, it could be stated

10 For statistics on the North Caucasian migrations see notably Karpat (1985), Fisher (1987), McCarthy (1995).

11 In Turkey, they were labeled as Circassian *muhājirs*, a homogenizing collective designation for North Caucasians which did not take into account ethnic plurality and different ethno-religious dynamics; see, for example, Ryan Gingeras (2011).

12 For recent works on Chechen historical anthropology, see Dettmering (2005), Nataev (2010), and Nataev (2015).

13 The Naqshbandiyya order is named after the fourteenth-century "Tadjik mystic figure Bahā' al-Dīn Naqshband al-Buḫārī." The Khālidiyya is a suborder created by the late eighteenth-century North Iraqi Kurd Khālid al-Baghdādī and soon penetrated into Dagestan. Qādiriyya refers to late eleventh-century "Iraqi Islamic scholar Abd al-Qādir al-Jilānī." Structurally, the Naqshbandiyya was a more centralized Sufi order than the Qādiriyya, while in matters of cult practices the Naqshbandī Sufis recite liturgies silently (*dhikr sirrī*) whereas the Qādirī are known for their loud recitation (*dhikr jahīrī*); see Alexander Knysh, *Islam in Historical Perspective* (Routledge, 2016: 236).

14 Many writings of the Naqshbandī shaykhs of Northern Dagestan were transcribed in their hagiographies, notably in Durkilī (2004 [1935]); Kabbani, Haqqani and Nasr (2004 [1995]).

that the 1901 migration was an ethnoreligious reaction of a stateless and sufist society to the establishment of a non-Muslim statehood.

That being stated, the Ottoman government considered these *muhājirs* a loyal and industrious element meant to be relocated in strategic buffer areas.[15] In 1865–1866, for example, more than ten thousand Chechen migrants were settled in Ra'ʾs al-ʿAyn and its surroundings, in today's northeastern Syria, to form an Ottoman stronghold in the heart of a Kurdish-Bedouin land.[16] At the beginning of Sultan Abdülhamid II's reign, during the 1870s and early 1880s, Circassians were relocated to found several villages in Southern Syria: al-Qunayṭra, Jarash, Amman, and Wādī al-Sīr. Their relocation to Southern Syria was part of Ottoman policies to incorporate the area both economically and administratively.[17] They soon formed the local *Jandarma* to settle tribal discords, decrease the local power of Druze and Bedouin, collect taxes, and protect the newly settled administration while also contributing to intensive agriculture to integrate the regional grain market. At the turn of the twentieth century, Caucasian migrants were supposed to answer two demographic issues: replace Armenian villagers in Eastern Anatolia, many of whom had been dispossessed by the authorities during the 1890s, and increase the settled population in Southern Syria to accompany the building of the Hejaz Railway, a flagship project of the pan-Islamic and modernist Hamidian era (1900–1908).[18]

But only considering demographic engineering would underestimate the influence of group dynamics on the very conduct of the migration. Chechen migrants made up a total of around 700 families in late 1901, belonging to various socioeconomic units or clans (ch. *teypnash*) living in adjacent rural areas in Chechnya. The migration project was led by a Sufi master named Tawsultān—called Muḥammad al-Nūrānī al-Naqshbandī in manuscripts—and his close disciples. The memoirs of migrant Salmīrzā, Mīrzā, written around 1913, indicate that the initial project was to settle in *Shām* or Greater Syria, considered as a sacred land in Islamic theology.[19] The itinerary toward Southern Syria was also scheduled and coordinated by pathfinders among the migrants who had probably already made a pilgrimage to Mecca and therefore knew how to reach stopping places like al-Zarqāʾ and Maʿān along the *hajj* route typically used by the Northeastern Caucasians.[20] The migrants' projects, however, did not reflect the Ottomans' initial plans since the latter immediately settled the newcomers in multiple Armenian villages throughout the provinces of Erzurum and

15 On the Ottoman perception of North Caucasian migrants and more precisely the Hamidian support for their immigration see notably Karpat (2002).

16 At first, the Ottomans built a fortified village for the Chechen settlers as testified by a British observer in George Taylor, "Journal of a Tour in Armenia, Kurdistan and Upper Mesopotamia, with Notes of Researches in the Deyrsim Dagh, in 1866," *The Journal of the Royal Geographical Society* 308 (1868): 346–7.

17 On the relation between grain export, intensive farming, and land registration in Ottoman Transjordan, see Carroll (2008).

18 On the subject refer to Özyüksel (2014).

19 *Mudhakkirāt Mirzā Ibn Sālmirzā Ibn Shaḥmirzā* (1913), 2, Private Archives of Layla Arslan.

20 Before their integration into the Russian Empire, Dagestanis and Chechens used to travel through Georgia and Eastern Anatolia to join the main Syrian *hajj* route (*ṭarīq al-Shāmī*); see, for example, Kane (2015: 32). Places like al-Zarqāʾ and al-ʾAzraq had been renowned halts on the Syrian *hajj* route ever since the early Ottoman period; see, for example, Banī Yūnus (2011: 2).

Bitlis,[21] while at the same time organizing the settlement of Circassians in Southern Syria between 1900 and the summer of 1902. Facing administrative reluctance and the death of Tawsultān in early 1902, more than half of the Chechen families followed the settlement policy, but a main core of Sufis and their relatives chose to request a decree from the sultan (*irāde*) by telegraph in August 1902. To justify his request, Tawsultān's disciple Ghirimsultān expressed the migrants' willingness to reach the province of Syria and pointed out the fact that Ottomans needed population growth there (BOA 2012). The Islamic Commission for Migrants endorsed the request and remarked that the migrant pathfinders had already found suitable land on their behalf in the district of ʿAjlūn, in Southern Syria (BOA 2012). Thereafter, the first wave of Chechens migrants successfully reached the prospected area in March 1903,[22] settling between Qaṣr Shabīb—an ancient fortress and pilgrimage halt—and al-Zarqāʾs railway station that had recently opened in 1902, under the supervision of a *Jandarma* officer (Rağā Al-Ḥammūd 1996: 139). The second wave of Chechen migrants arrived at al-Zarqāʾ in November 1903 thanks to the mediation of another of Tawsultān's disciples named Ēdilsultān Ēdilkirī, who actively requested the authorities' permission for their coming.[23] Other, sparse, waves came later, the last of which was in 1909, after another long administrative process[24] to represent at most a total of 200 families and approximately 10 percent of the Caucasian population in Ottoman Transjordan. Thus, the migration trajectory had, to a certain extent, thwarted Hamidian demographic engineering, which is a notable event in the migratory context of the late Ottoman era. This, however, does not imply that the authorities ostracized the migrants; they readily allotted them lands to form a constellation of Caucasian settlements around Amman. By 1905, Chechens were officially granted lands in al-Zarqāʾ and a dozen kilometers further north, close to the Sukhna spring.[25] In 1906, Chechens also founded Ṣuwayliḥ on the Amman–al-Salṭ road, where they were granted lands between 1909 and 1913 along with Circassians who came later (Ṭarīf 1994). Finally, the last Chechen village was founded in al-ʾAzraq between the late 1920s and 1934, during the Mandate era.

2. Patterns of a Territorial Rooting

Upon their arrival, Chechens had to guarantee the sustainability of their villages while being faced with plenty of environmental constraints. By the 1890s, Circassian villagers from Qunayṭra to Amman were represented by Mirzā Pasha, head commander of the *Jandarma*, who regularly confronted the Bedouin to uphold Ottoman law and

[21] The Armenophile French journal *Pro Armenia* issued several articles between 1901 and 1903 about the settlement of Chechens; see, for example, "Craintes de massacres," *Pro Armenia (1903)*: 67.

[22] *Mudhakkirāt Mirzā Ibn Sālmirzā Ibn Shaḥmirzā*, 1913, 7. Their presence in al-Zarqāʾ is testified in October 1904 and their settlement was said to exist for two years in Stoever and Norris (1930: 7). Also in Germer-Durand (1904: 26).

[23] Ēdilsultān to Ahmad al-Bayānī, 4/08/1321 (26/10/1903), Private Archives of Adnan Madhab.

[24] Khalīl Al-Hūrānī "Lajnat al-Muhājirīn," *Al Muqtabas*, October 24, 1910. Also cited in Rajā AL-Ḥammūd, *ʿAmmān wa Jiwāruhā*, 174.

[25] National Library of Jordan (NLA), Private Documents, 20/135/HM; Abujaber, *Pioneers Over Jordan*: 215.

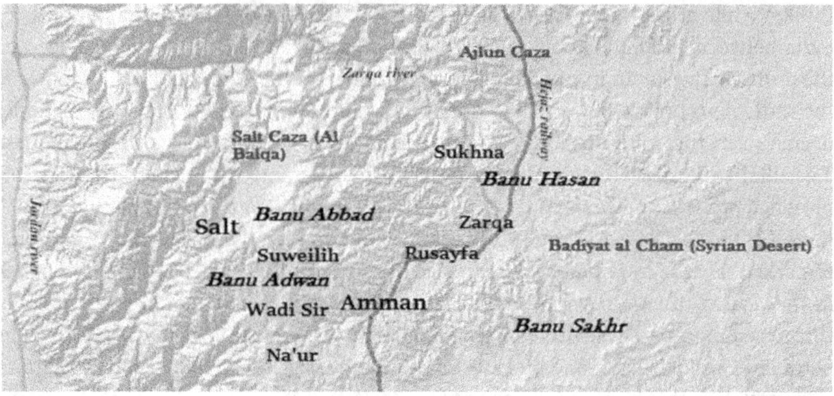

Figure 5.1 North-Central Transjordan: major settlements and tribes (1911–1918).

protected settlements (Rogan 1999: 67–8; Lewis 2000). In contrast, few Chechens in Southern Syria enrolled in the Ottoman army and the *Jandarma*, thus there was no permanent presence of soldiers in the villages. Moreover, al-Zarqā' and Sukhna were located far away from their district center of 'Irbid and formed the southern limit of the 'Ajlūn district, only Ṣuwayliḥ was in the al-Balqā' (Al-Jalūdī 1994: 163–70; Abū Sha'r 1995: 4). As a result, administrative remoteness fostered self-governance, but the settlers were also more exposed to land conflicts with the Bedouin, who represented the demographic majority. Chechen villages, like the other newly established settlements, were located on what the Bedouin considered their *dīrāt*, or tribal territories: the land allotments were also meant by the authorities to counterbalance these demographics and coerce the Bedouin to settle. During the 1900s, tensions over land ownership in the al-Balqā' heightened between the increasing Caucasian population and the Shawāyā or semi-nomad sheep-herding tribes, whose *dīrāt* formed their vital pasture lands, and they had less mobility than the Ruḥḥal or desert-based nomads.[26] The situation eventually led to a major confrontation, in 1907, between the Chechens of Ṣuwayliḥ and the Shawāyā of Banū 'Abbād.[27] Furthermore, land problems, especially in al-Zarqā' and Sukhna, were coupled with the climatic challenge of being located on the edge of the *bādiya*, the Syrian Desert, on the easternmost portion of the so-called *ma'mūra*, a North-South band of fertile land suitable for settlement.[28]

[26] Arab terminology used by the Bedouin is chosen. *Shawāyā* literally means the breeders while *Ruḥḥal* means the nomads. Actually the *Shawāyā* were also nomads and the *Ruḥḥal* also had livestock other than camels but the major difference was that the *Shawāyā* were concentrated in the *ma'mūram* fertile zone with more restricted territories, while the *Ruḥḥal* were desert-based with greater mobility.

[27] *Mudhakkirāt Mirzā Ibn Sālmirzā Ibn Shaḥmirzā*, 27. The event was echoed by a delegate of the al-Ṣalṭ district in the pan-Arab journal *Al-Ittiḥād al-'Uthmānī*, criticizing the official land allotments for Caucasian migrants on Bedouin lands; see Ḥashīmī (1908). As late as 1912, the Arab press still related conflicts between Caucasians and al-Balqā Bedouin over land ownership matters, see Rajā Al-Ḥammūd (1996 :141).

[28] Refer to studies dedicated to Ottoman/Mandate Syria which took a greater interest in the *ma'mūra/bādiya* evolving frontier in the semi-arid zones, as for instance in Metral (2006: 89–112).

Agriculture and land ownership were determining aspects of the socioeconomic dynamics which shaped the Chechen villages and their territorial integration. While Circassians engaged mostly in dry-farming of cereals, which best suited ambitions of intensive agriculture, Chechens were more interested in irrigated agriculture, as historian Raouf Abu Jaber noted in detail (Abujaber 1989). As a matter of fact, Chechens developed intensive small-scale agriculture with various and elaborated techniques but that depended on water resources. For instance, in 1914, the villagers of Sukhna improved irrigation of their gardens with the building of a water channel connected to the river.[29] Their woodworking skills also allowed them to produce cattle carts for the conveyance of water and harvests, and to develop milling activities.[30]

In terms of land ownership, Chechen villages illustrated the multitude of cases concerning the role of private (ott. *mafrūz*) and collective lands (ott. *mushā*ʿ). While the Land law of 1858 encouraged the increase of private ownership notably for better tax incomes, farmers still used the *mushā*ʿ tenure extensively in Ottoman Syria, and at the turn of the Mandate era, 82 percent of the villages in the ʿAjlūn district were characterized by this type of ownership; the Banū Ṣakhr of the al-Balqāʾ also largely resorted to this system (Fishbach 2000: 68). Tax avoidance was not the only reason for the existence of *mushā*ʿ and, as historian Martha Mundy noted, different types of ownerships could be explained by factors like climate and production management (Mundy 1996). The Sukhna agreement, signed in 1911 by the founders of the village, gives details of this distribution, with the settlers using Arabic words instead of Ottoman terminology.[31] The rotating system of cattle grazing (ar. *nawba*) and the harvest field (ar. *mazra*ʿ*a*) were organized under collective ownership with strict rules of conduct, while only the garden (ar. *bustān*) was private property (ar. *milk*). At the same time, Chechens relied extensively on these irrigated gardens, which were small, private agricultural plots (ott. *ḥawākīr*) that suited subsistence-oriented agriculture very well.[32] Larger collective land plots were most often located in the arid lands for grain cultivation supported by an early form of sedentary agropastoralism in the area.[33] Hence, it was the dryness and the small labor force which required collectivism. Cattle, in which Chechens were also distinctly interested, and were used for plowing the land and dairy production. In Ṣuwayliḥ, land distribution between Chechens and Circassians highlighted the different economic approaches to agriculture, with the

[29] Ḥājj Muḥammad, "Qad ittafaqnā ʿalā ḥafr al-nahr al-maʿlūm fīmā baynanā wa-l-Zarqāʾ . . . ," March 10, 1914, Private Archives of Dib Bashir.

[30] The milling activity of Sukhna is described in NLA, Government Documents, 25/4/2/10. Details of the various agricultural activities in the early decades of Sukhna's existence are to be found in the transcribed interview of the last Chechen migrant who passed away in the early 1990 (Ḥadīsa Bint Yūnus 1992). In "Min mudhakkirāt al-ḥājja Ḥadīsa," interviewed by Adnan Madhab on April 20, 1992, Unpublished, Private Archives of Adnan Madhhab.

[31] NLA, Private Documents, 1/13/HM.

[32] According to Khalīl al-Ḥūrānī in 1910, al-Zarqāʾ could have welcomed around 200 families with a balance between fertile and poor soils, while only around fifty families lived there. Chechens concentrated their agricultural activities in the fertile irrigated lands which probably explains why the settlers chose to form two other villages and soon chose to settle in al-ʾAzraq.

[33] The advent of agro-pastoral villages in Transjordan is thought to have been connected to the settlement of *Shawāyā* tribes, most notably as a consequence of the 1933 Land Settlement Law. See, for example, Rjoub and Mahmoud (2012: 231–43).

Figure 5.2 Fields, gardens and stables in Ṣuwayliḥ, 1922/1923 (Ṭarīf 1994).

Ethnic group	Families	Fields	Gardens	Stables
Chechens	98	46	61	67
Circassians	64	48	11	27

Chechens disposing of three times more gardens than the Circassians and the latter possessing twice as many large field plots, proportionate to the number of families.

However, such figures do not imply that the Chechen farmers were not engaged in commercially oriented agriculture. Yet, rather than joining into the regional trade network, they seem to have preferred the traditional economic relationship between villagers and direct neighbors based on the selling or bartering of modest agricultural surpluses.[34] For instance, some correspondence between an imam of Jarash and a Chechen Sufi leader of al-Zarqā' attested the existence of a barter market for spelled grain between al-Zarqā' and the Circassian settlements of Jarash and al-Ruṣayfa.[35] Thus, the Chechens set up an economic balance between subsistence-oriented agriculture, mostly produced in the private gardens, and grain farming partly used for trading and carried out on the collective land plots. Moreover, the *mushā'* system in al-Zarqā' was probably a way of renting property to Bedouin, whose presence and agricultural activity within the village domain was observed by Ottoman administrator Khalīl al-Ḥūrānī in 1910.[36] In this regard, Salmīrzā, Mīrzā explained that a formalized relationship between the villagers and the Bedouin came through the taxation of the latter by the Chechen Sufi leader, adopting a system close to that of the local *khāwwa* (brother right), reformulated by the author as *ṭalab al-'amān* (request for protection).[37] This fact on its own is noteworthy since the *khāwwa* was usually used by Ruḥḥal to tax settlers or Shawāyā but first and foremost it shows to what extent Transjordanians could self-manage land ownership according to "their own conceptualization of land" in the late Ottoman era, as debated by historian Michael Fishbach (Fischbach 2000).

Moreover, encounters with the Bedouin were an essential point in understanding the Chechens' territorial rooting in context. Alliances or oppositions between the Caucasians and the Bedouin indicate collusion or conflict of interests between them. For example, the Banū Ṣakhr are said to have mediated in favor of the Circassians during their confrontation with the Shawāyā for land ownership during the 1900s (Shamy 1996: 312–13). By the late nineteenth century, the Banū Ṣakhr were expanding toward the western fertile lands to create plantations and diversify their economy, while at the same time maintaining their nomadism and greater independence from the authorities. They eventually clashed with the *Shawāyā* of the area who, in reaction,

[34] This system prevailed in Southern Transjordan during the late Ottoman era and was seen as a lack of stability by the Ottomans; see Tell (2000).
[35] Imām 'Abd al-'Azīz to Shaykh 'Abdullāh, "Ilā al-'ālim al-rabbānī wa-l-ġawth al-ṣamdānī al-sayyid al-shaykh Ḥājjī 'Abdullāh Afandī," undated, Private Archives of Abdullah Junayd.
[36] K. Al-Ḥūrānī, "Lajnat al-muhājirīn," *Al Muqtabas*, October 24, 1910.
[37] *Mudhakkirāt Mirzā Ibn Sālmirzā Ibn Shaḥmirzā* (1913), 18–20.

formed the Balqāwiyya confederation, led by the Banū ʿAdwān (Meier and Tell 2015: 40; Tell 2013: 32). It seems that the Banū Ṣakhr strategically entered into good relations with the Caucasians after a while, just like they maintained alliances with some of the Shawāyā whose *dīrāt* were not threatened by their hegemony, thereby decreasing the power of the Balqāwiyya. Moreover, such relations allowed the Banū Ṣakhr to keep relying upon informal neighborly trade. In April 1912, the Chechens of al-Zarqāʾ and Ṣuwayliḥ, headed by Ēdilsultān "Shaykh ʿAbdullāh" Ēdilkirī, had a meeting with Ḥadītha al-Khuraysha, paramount shaykh of the Northern Banū Ṣakhr, in the desert fort of al-ʾAzraq to discuss the creation of a village close to the oases. Ḥadītha al-Khuraysha, as related by Salmīrzā Mīrzā, was disposed to help the Chechens because the village would provide grain harvests and thus make it unnecessary for the *Ruḥḥal*[38] to purchase staple food from the trade centers of the ʿAjlūn district and Amman.[39]

Interactions between Chechens and the Bedouin were also made possible by the Sufi elite which, in consequence, entrenched its leadership among the settlers by forming a cohesive and necessary framework. The first practical reason for it was the fact that the core group of Sufis were fluent Arabic speakers in contrast with much of the non-Arab settlers during the late Ottoman times who used Ottoman Turkish as the lingua franca and learned Arabic only after decades. It paved the way for the Chechen Sufi leadership to make of al-Zarqāʾ—with the other villages as satellites—a sort of settled shaykhdom, in a similar way to Ramthā in the ʿAjlūn district, which was self-ruled by the Sufi clan of al-Zuʿbī.[40]

Moreover, an Arabic-speaking Sufi culture and their rural anchoring impacted the Chechens' socio-political situation during the final years of Ottoman rule and its collapse marked by the Arab Revolt of 1916–1918 and the advent of Hashemite rule in Syria and then Transjordan (1920–1921). The historical memory of the Chechens concerning the Arab Revolt reveals different stances, with the majority adopting a wait-and-see approach, sharing with most of the Transjordanians the primary concern of starvation caused by the war (Tell 2000: 33–58). But the Sufi leadership was rather quick to support the new political trend fostered by the Anglo-French declaration of November 1918, nominally supporting Arab independence and led by the Hashemite monarch Fayṣal in Syria. In March 1919, Ēdilsultān "Shaykh ʿAbdullāh" Ēdilkirī signed, along with prominent Chechen figures of al-Zarqāʾ, a written agreement to support the independence of the "Arab nation." Notably, they requested the formation of an enlarged Arab state from Syria to Yemen, the withdrawal of foreign armies and the inclusion of "buffering communities" into the development of the Arab nation.[41] This declaration exemplified the situation of this rural, non-Arab population in the outcome of the opposition between Turkist Ottomanism and Arab localism in the post-Hamidian era.[42] Another example

38 According to the story, Ḥadītha al-Khuraysha was also representing the Banū Sirḥān and mediating for Shaykh Nūrī al-Shaʿlān of the powerful Banū Ruwalla.

39 *Mudhakkirāt Mirzā Ibn Sālmirzā Ibn Shaḥmirzā* (1913), 23.

40 Their social prestige was due to the fact that popular Sufi tombs were included in the area of their land ownership (Fischbach, 2000:13).

41 "Bismillāh alladhī tawaffaqnā fī istiqlāliyyat al-dawla al-ʿarabiyya...," March 23, 1919, Private Archives of ʿUthmān Dawlat.

42 The expression "Turkist Ottomanism" is borrowed from historian Frederick Answombe (Answombe 2014: 124). Even Turkist Ottomanism as conceptualized by the CUP did not exclude Arabs but it was

is the presence of a voluntary Chechen squad fighting with the Syrian independence fighters against the French at Maysalūn in July 1920. Despite the defeat of Hashemite rule in Damascus, the Chechens of al-Zarqā' had been connected to prominent figures advocating for Syrian independence and pan-Arabism, such as Nabīh al-'Aẓma and the Druze leader Sulṭān al-'Aṭrash, who rose against the French in 1925-1927.[43] This series of pivotal events eventually led to the gradual settling of a British administration in Transjordan by 1920 and the coming of the Hashemite monarch Abdullah to form the Emirate of Transjordan under British Mandate in 1921. With the partition of Ottoman Syria between British and French mandates, Abdullah succeeded in rapidly gaining a nominal allegiance from most of the powerful Bedouin shaykhs and urban notables, such as the Arab traders and Circassians particularly in Amman, partly because they were worried about maintaining their growing social and political importance in a new state entity. It could be stated that in the case of the Chechens, the Sufi leadership supported pan-Arabism before allegiance to Abdullah, proving that Caucasians were deeply influenced by their local environment, and were not, as they were often depicted, a transplanted community of colonists among Arabs. Because of their territorial rooting and also their cultural specificity, Chechens, quite logically, leaned toward Arab localism and then pan-Arabism, rather than being simply nominally co-opted since even during the early years of the Mandate era, Chechens remained absent in local administration and had very limited contacts with the embryonic emirate.[44]

Between 1921 and mid-1924, the administration of the young Emirate of Transjordan was geographically confined to areas that had previously been under Ottoman control, thus excluding large areas of desert and semi-desert. The most populated parts of Transjordan, including the numerous villages of the 'Ajlūn district, the domains of the Balqāwiyya tribes and the Circassian villages of the al-Balqā'—Amman being the new capital—were subject to heavier taxation while the nomads, especially the Banū Ṣakhr, were partly exempted from taxes in order to secure their all-important allegiance (Tell 2013: 67; Abu Nowar 2006: 95-6; Alon 2016: 56-7). At the same time, many of the Syrian independence-seekers forming the *istiqlālī* movement, once supporters of Fayṣal and the Hashemites, escaped from French repression to settle in Transjordan where they were overrepresented in the state apparel with the logical support of Fayṣal's brother Abdullah. The whole situation evolved into a major uprising against the nascent state in 1923, led by the Banū 'Adwān, and also nominally supported by townsmen including Circassians.[45] Throughout the 1920s, leaders of the Balqāwiyya Bedouin, Arab urban dwellers, and Circassians struggled to form the governing elite and counter the hegemony of newly settled Syrians in state institutions.[46]

notably the under-representation of Arabs in regional and local governing elites which progressively led to an "ethnolinguistic antagonism," refer to Kayali (1997) and Ahmad (2014: 112-39).

[43] "Nashkur al-qā'id al-mujāhid Ahmad Ramzī min al-Zarqā'...," November 18, 1920, Private Archives of 'Uthmān Dawlat.

[44] There were nevertheless few enrolled Chechens in the Arab Legion based in Amman by 1923, among whom were Aḥmad Ramzī and Hasan according to a picture found in the archives of Circassian leader Mirzā Waṣfī, NLA, Private Documents, 1/493.

[45] For a concise analysis of the event refer to Alon (2006: 7–42).

[46] Circassian lawyer Shams al-Dīn Sāmī of Amman was a good example of this complex situation. He was opposed to both French and British presence in Syria and Transjordan and was detained

Chechens were less impacted by the situation because al-Zarqā' and Sukhna were located on the eastern edges of state-controlled areas but mainly because of their different socioeconomic integration. Chechens, in fact, shared another major concern of the time with the Bedouin, which was trans-boundary movement between Transjordan and Syria.[47] For example, a private document mentioned that, in January 1922, Chechens of Sukhna organized for the resettlement of Chechens from Syria on their own plots of land for no compensation, showing that the villagers still had a great autonomy in ownership issues while at the same time being taxed by the authorities (Bashir 1922). In a letter dated February 1924, Chechens of Ra's al-'Ayn, Syria, thanked the new Sufi leader of the Transjordan Chechens, Shaykh Muṭī' Khān, for the sending of 'Uthmān Abū Bakr of Ṣuwayliḥ and financial support. Syrian Chechens were informed that Transjordan Chechens were deeply worried about their critical situation, probably referring to the French repression of Syrian independence movement (Shīshānī 1924). Thus, it also meant that Chechens were still active supporters of the independence movement, while the French authorities tried to co-opt ethnic "minorities" in Syria to decrease opposition, notably by forming Circassian or Druze squads.[48] Chechens shared with the Banū Ṣakhr and particularly the Northern clan sections represented by Ḥadītha al-Khuraysha, a common anti-French view mostly explained by the preoccupation with trans-boundary movement.[49] Major concerns of the Chechens also reflected the global situation of Transjordan during the years 1921 to 1924, with the political tolerance of Abdullah for tribal autonomy and the influential presence of Syria *'istiqlālī* movement. However, in August 1924, the British finally urged Abdullah to change his politics, notably because of the 1923 revolt and the diplomatic crisis between the French and the British over the *'istiqlālī* presence and uncontrolled cross-border raids (Dann 1976: 165–6; Mizrahi 2009: 83–90). The British then took a greater part in the conduct of Transjordanian affairs with the appointment of Henry Cox as the new British resident in Amman, who held this position until 1939 and supervised the progressive and effective state control over larger parts of rural and Bedouin areas.

3. Dealing with Expansion of Statehood

During the mid-to-late 1920s, the authority of the British Mandate gave an impetus to reforms to consolidate the state existence. In 1927, the Land Department was created—reformed as the Department of Lands and Survey (DLS) in 1929—in

following the 1923 revolt. As a government member, he militated to prevent non-Transjordanians from running for municipal elections in Amman while at the same time opposed the other members of the government who wanted to deliver Transjordan-based Syrian nationalists to the French and was thanked by the latter for this engagement. NLA, Private Documents, MKH /23/B/52; NLA, Private Documents, MKH/86/16, MKH/86/17.

47 For the Bedouins see Amadouny (1995: 533–49).

48 In 1930, Kurds, Circassians, Ismaelis, and Druze represented 63.4 percent of the squads forming the French *Troupes spéciales du Levant* while only representing 11 percent of the Syrian and Lebanese population, see Mizrahi (2002: 117). The first Circassian squad was formed in 1922; on the concept of minorities in the Mandate of Syria, see White (2011).

49 On Ḥadītha al-Khuraysha, Emir Istiqlālīs, see, for example, Alon (2007: 68–9).

order to improve land administration (Fiscbach 2000: 94–5), and then in 1928 the Organic Law or *al-Qānūn al-'Asāsī* was issued working as a national constitution. In 1929, the Legislative Council was formed, with sixteen members representing the most influential segments of the emerging nation, including two Circassian leaders (Guthorn 2015: 295-312). Evolution of the state administration led to the expansion of statehood in the previously remote rural areas. This was the case of al-Zarqā', which had already acquired the status of *nāḥiya* or municipality by the end of 1924, which means that a state administrator lived in the village (Zalūm 1994: 131; Abū Al-Sha'r 2009: 105-6). Al-Zarqā' was subsequently better connected to the centers of administration with its integration, along with Sukhna, into the newly created district of Amman[50] and the creation of a telegraph post in the village.[51] Al-Zarqā' was actually a very strategic place on which to bestow state presence in the eastern *ma'mūra*. In 1926, the headquarters of the Transjordan Frontier Force (TJFF) were relocated from Palestine to al-Zarqā',[52] east of the railway station, while the Arab Legion had been based in Amman since 1923. The main reason for a stronger military force in the area was the confrontation between Transjordan—both the British and Bedouin—and the Saudi Ikhwan,[53] to which was added the problematic presence of Druze in al-'Azraq, who were using the place as a fallback position during their 1925-1927 revolt against the French, causing further diplomatic trouble between the two Mandate powers.[54] al-Zarqā' became a stronghold for the Anglo-Hashemite state to structure and secure its borders. The presence of the TJFF headquarters also triggered new waves of immigration to al-Zarqā' with the settlement of people, the majority of whom were Arab traders and who were for the most part Syrians, Palestinians, and few Karakī Christians (Abū Al-Sha'r 2013: 111-12, 114–16), whose activities were eased by the rehabilitated Transjordan-Lebanon commercial trade route thanks to the Hejaz Railway.[55] Their quarter was built between the Chechen village and the Chechen *mushā'* lands that bordered the railway station and was known as Ḥārat al-Shwām (Syrian quarter).[56] On the north side of al-Zarqā' the Ḥārat al-'Arab (Arab quarter) gradually developed, with the settlement of Bedouin of Banū Ḥasan belonging to al-Zawāhira and al-Khalāyla sub-clans of al-Khawālida section (Wahīb 2012: 19), thanks to the 1933 Land Settlement Law and the granting of "immovable property" to Bedouin (Frantzman and Kark 2012: 492–3).

The social situation of the Chechens varied according to their location. In Sukhna, no demographic change was to be noticed until the late 1960s, while in Ṣuwayliḥ, several dozen Arab families from al-Salṭ and Palestine as well as a few Bedouin settled

[50] NLA, Official Journal, 81, 01/12/1924.
[51] NLA, Official Journal, 112, 01/09/1925.
[52] NLA, Official Journal, 135, 26/08/1926.
[53] An official agreement on borders between the Anglo-Hashemite state and the Saudis was signed in May 1927, see on the subject Gil-Har (1992).
[54] The situation is exposed in "En Syrie," *Les Annales coloniales*, 102, July 4, 1927, 2.
[55] NLA, Government Documents, 68/4/10/9.
[56] The construction of the first mosque of the Syrian quarter was self-financed by the local merchants in 1932, NLA, Government Documents, 16/4/6/19. The first church was founded around the same time by the Catholic White Fathers based in Sainte Anne, Jerusalem who created the diocese of Transjordan. Most of al-Zarqā' Christians were stationed soldiers at the time, see *Oeuvre d'Orient* 422 (1934): 178-9.

in the village in the early 1930s. It was attached to the district of Amman by 1933.[57] Agriculture remained the primary occupation for Chechens but it sometimes evolved into a more commercially oriented activity, notably in Ṣuwayliḥ with the success of grape cultivation (Fayḥrī and Al-Tall 1939: 19–20), that was helped by the fact that the village was a regional hub located on the two main commercial roads during the Mandate era: Amman-Jerusalem and Amman-ʾIrbid. However, in al-Zarqāʾ and Sukhna, like in the other peripheral semi-arid areas, agriculture suffered bad harvests between the late 1920s to early 1930s (Robins 2019: 40), to which can be added a major malaria epidemic, notably in al-Zarqāʾ, which occurred during the same years.[58] Thus, the socioeconomic and administrative situations in al-Zarqāʾ probably had a deep impact on the Chechens and their Sufi leadership.

In a document dated March 1927, Dawlat Tūbūlāt of al-Zarqāʾ[59] related the renewed allegiance of major Sufi figures representing the different clans of the "Chechen tribe" (ar. *ʿashīrat al-Jajāniyyūn* in the text) to the new Sufi leader, Shaykh Muṭīʿ Khān of al-Zarqāʾ.[60] There was a need expressed by Sufis to enhance group cohesion in order to promote a better social representation and to activate networking. When, in December 1928, the municipal council of al-Zarqāʾ was founded, all five members were Chechen Sufis and the long-tenured mayor, Bahāʾ al-Dīn, was the son of Shaykh ʿAbdullāh.[61] It was the same scheme in Sukhna, where the village representative or *mukhtār*, Yasaʿ Washī, a prominent farmer and local miller, had two assistants, all members of the Sufi order.[62] But an even better example of how the Chechen Sufis formalized their leadership was the creation of the Caucasian Club (ar. *al-Nādī al-Qawqāzī*) in Ṣuwayliḥ in 1932. The Caucasian Club was, at first sight, one of the many ethnic associations, like the Circassian Charity Association of Amman created the same year,[63] the existence of which was fostered by the 1928 Organic Law.[64] Actually, the Caucasian Club had two functions. First, it aimed to facilitate mutual understanding and cohesion between all Ṣuwayliḥ villagers speaking different languages by providing elementary education before the local government school was founded in 1934.[65] Second, the project was

57 NLA, Official Journal, 399, 02/09/1933.

58 On the malaria epidemic in Transjordan see Amadouny (1997: 453–84). Malaria in al-Zarqāʾ was imported by the soldiers of the TJFF who were mobilized in the malarial al-ʾAzraq oases in 1927, see Draper (1928: 135–7). Epidemics among the Chechens of al-Zarqāʾ are evoked in Robinson (1939: 14–15).

59 Tūbūlāt is cited by Mīrza Sālmirzā among the core group of Sufi Chechens during the migration and settlement periods.

60 Dawlat Tūbūlāt, "Faṣl fī bayān ma jarā min al-awwalīn wal-l-akhirīn," March 7, 1927, Private Archives of ʿUthmān Dawlat. Shaykh ʿAbdullāh died in 1923, which explains this succession, common to Sufi orders.

61 On the formation and projects taken over by the municipal council, see (Zalūm 1994: 69–72, 135–7). Municipal Archives of al-Zarqāʾ for the period 1928–1935 are also directly available in Abū Al-Shaʿr and Al ʿAssāf (2013).

62 Qāʾim Maqām Amman to Yassaʿ Ibn al-Ḥājj Wāshī, May 2, 1931; Muḥāfiẓ al-ʿĀṣima to Mukhtār Qaryat al-Sukhna, April 27, 1943, Private Archives of Dib Bashir.

63 NLA, Private Documents, 1/137; NLA, Private Documents, 1/138.

64 According to article 11, Transjordanians could found associations and according to the article 14, they were free to found private schools to "teach their own languages" (Shami, 1996: 317).

65 The first aim claimed by the founders in their 1932's document was to "perpetuate mutual understanding and good relationships between the different communities of the village" in "Al-Qānūn al-asāsī li-l-Nādī al-Qawqāzī," 1932, Private Archives of Abdullah Junayd. On the

sponsored by Shaykh Muṭīʿ Khān of al-Zarqāʾ[66] and financially supported by Chechen notables like Yasaʿ Washī (Junayd 1933).[67] Teachers were Chechen Sufis, such as ʿAbd al-Ḥamīd Qādiro, disciple of Muṭīʿ Khān, who was affected to the club's Sukhna branch.[68] Thus, there was a double opportunity for the Chechen Sufi leadership based in al-Zarqāʾ: to enhance social integration with an associative existence in the prosperous hub village of Ṣuwayliḥ, and to display local cultural leadership and strengthen intra-ethnic cohesion with Sufi networking. Moreover, Chechen Sufis interestingly chose education as a main means for social expression. The specific Arabic-speaking literary culture of the Chechens still played a great part in their local anchoring. When Ṣuwayliḥ government teachers surveyed the village in 1939, they noticed that Chechens had the best literacy rate of the village in written and spoken Arabic, almost twice that of the Circassians and three times better than that of al-Qaṭīshāt Arabs from al-Salṭ (Faḥrī and Al-Tall 1939: 25–6). As a consequence of greater state intervention, the Chechens then chose to stress cultural identity inherited from ethno-Sufism to display local and group leadership. In a similar cultural approach, Chechen Sufis reinforced their relations with figures of pan-Arabism in the years preceding the Arab Revolt of 1936-1939 in Palestine, marked by the rise of anti-Zionist sentiment among the Transjordanians. Shaykh Muṭīʿ Khān was, for example, in contact and in correspondence with the mufti of Jerusalem, Muḥammad ʾAmīn al-Ḥusaynī.[69]

Chechen encounters with the expanding state also produced new issues over land ownership. A good example of the consequences of land reforms instigated by the British is found in a court case between the Chechens of al-Zarqāʾ and the Land Department in 1929. Partition of lands by the villagers between individual and collective plots, the latter having being used for cattle grazing and cohabitation with the Banū Ḥasan for decades, was a system disregarded by the British. Mandate authority wanted to reduce and abolish the *mushāʿ* system in both Palestine and Transjordan for three main reasons, which are all involved in the present case. The first reason, widely debated by historians, was the misconception by the British of the system, that they considered inefficient and linked to the Ottoman past when the *mushāʿ* was tolerated and was allegedly a cause of weak economic competitiveness (Nadan 2003: 320-54). The second reason was the fact that an increase of individual ownership offered more precise registration and thus a better state control of land taxes. The third reason, which is also better studied in the case of Palestine, is that the British wanted to increase the state domain with the seizure of *mushāʿ* lands in order to undertake state projects by reinterpreting the inherited Ottoman division

provided teachings, details are to be found in "Barnāmaj al-ṣaff al-tamhīdī" and "Barnāmaj al-ṣaff al-khāmis" undated, Private Archives of Abdullah Junayd.

66 Shaykh Muṭīʿ Khān was pictured in the presence of Emir Abdullah, British officials and local Chechen and Arab figures for the official opening of the association. Copy of the original picture found in Private Archives of Abdullah Junayd.

67 Yassaʿ Washī to Al-Nadī al-Qawqāzī, January 1, 1933, Private Archives of Abdullah Junayd.

68 "Wāfaqat hayʾa al-idāra li-Nādī al-Qawqāzī," December 15, 1932, Private Archives of Abdullah Junayd.

69 Muḥammad ʾAmīn al-Ḥusaynī to Shaykh Muṭīʿ Khān, June 25, 1931, Private Archives of MuṭīʿShīshānī.

of land ownership.[70] In the court case concerned, the Land Department argued that the land tenures were not cultivated, had no named titles of property, and that they were by definition state lands or *ʾarāḍī ʾamīriyya*, from the Ottoman appellation *miri* lands. References were made to the Ottoman land law of 1858, which was reviewed 1913 and theoretically allowed the state to seize lands left uncultivated for three years, and to the fact that the *mushāʿ* lands fall into the category of *miri* lands. The Land Department feigned to ignore that *mushāʿ* could also be used for cattle grazing while taking advantage of the status of *miri* lands: the case report even used the term *maḥlūliyya* to mean land seizure, an interpretation of the Ottoman subcategory of *miri* lands called *maḥlūl*, which concerned land repossessed by the state.[71] The Chechens' lawyers replied that those concerned had intentionally left these lands under *mushāʿ* ownership for their important cattle grazing activity ever since their settlement and thus it could not be considered as an abandonment of agricultural land. They also asserted their status of settled migrants who had officially been granted these lands according to a 1905 land demarcation (ott. *ḥudūdnāme*) by the Ottomans. Interestingly, the Chechens' lawyers were ʿĀdil al-ʿAẓma and Shams al-Dīn Sāmī, two prominent figures of Transjordanian political life. Shams al-Dīn Sāmī was a Circassian leader of Amman and member of the first Legislative Council, while ʿĀdil al-ʿAẓma was a Syrian *ʾistiqlālī*, a member of the second Transjordan Legislative Council in 1931 and the brother of Nabīh al-ʿAẓma and nephew of Yūsuf al-ʿAẓma, with whom the Chechens were connected through their involvement at the battle of Maysalūn. Both were particularly active in opposing colonial rule and were among the first Transjordanians to oppose Zionism in the years preceding the first great Palestinian revolt in 1936 (Abu Nowar 2006: 26, 137). This court case was an illustration of the socioeconomic shock caused by British colonial land policies in rural areas and how the societal elite could endorse their role of counter-power in local affairs of land ownership. This situation, however, was significant for the period preceding the 1933 Land Settlement Law, which officially banned *mushāʿ* tenure. By that time, Chechen self-governance was strained by the expansion of statehood and land administration. In the case of al-Zarqāʾ, the lands concerned were actually meant to provide a larger area for the TJFF headquarters,[72] proving that the British used the old Ottoman terminology to seize lands in order to support well-defined colonial projects. ʿĀdil al-ʿAẓma defended the Chechens in a similar affair in Sukhna, between October 1932 and May 1933, when the Anglo-Iraqi Petroleum Company wanted to have free access to water resources for their production center in al-Mafraq.[73] The DLS defended the project, which was a major economic concern for oil conveyance from Iraq to Palestine, but ʿĀdil al-ʿAẓma succeeded in negotiating the renting of the land to the benefit of the Chechens.[74]

[70] On the British strategies to seize *miri* lands and ban collective ownership in the Middle East refer to Bunton (2007) and Nadan (2018).

[71] The British applied their strategic land administration as conceived in Palestine with the Mahlul Lands Ordinance of 1920, see Sait and Lim (2006: 69–70).

[72] NLA, Official Journal, 173, 15/12/1927.

[73] NLA, Government Documents, 26/2/4/25; 27/2/4/25.

[74] NLA, Government Documents, 67/2/4/25.

4. Founding al-ʾAzraq al-Shīshān in the 1930s

Another aspect of the relationship between the Anglo-Hashemite state and the Chechens are the circumstances of the founding of al-ʾAzraq at the beginning of the 1930s, a fourth village created by the Chechens, in the desert, 90 km east of al-Zarqāʾ. The area concerned was going through noticeable administrative change by April 1927 when Emir Abdullah decreed the creation of a desert district in the al-ʾAzraq area under military rule.[75] From then on, the British administration was expanding eastward through the determinant role of John Bagot Glubb, commander of the desert district and founder of the Desert Patrol in 1930.[76] Glubb drafted tribesmen of the powerful Banū Ḥuwayṭāt and Banū Ṣakhr into his Desert Patrol, notably to secure the Saudi-Transjordan borders, to end the *khāwwa* (bedouin taxation)[77] and the *ghazwa* (raid) and ensure their allegiance to the Anglo-Hashemite state. Most probably as a result of demographic and administrative change, a dozen Chechen families from al-Zarqāʾ and Ṣuwayliḥ chose to relocate, at first periodically, to the al-ʾAzraq oasis in the late 1920s. The fact that the Chechens had wanted to settle in al-ʾAzraq since 1912 but without success until then is certainly due to the insecure environment caused successively by the World War and Ikhwan raids from Saudi Arabia, which threatened the area between 1923-1924 and 1927-1930. They finally settled permanently between 1930 and 1932, when the presence of the TJFF and the Desert Patrol began to consolidate the eastern borders. The self-conducted resettlement project also illustrates the historical connection between the Chechen Sufi leadership and Ḥadītha al-Khurayshā, who remained the most prominent Bedouin figure and important land owner of the al-ʾAzraq area.[78] Before the arrival of the Chechens, the Bedouin had already allowed the Druze, led by Sulṭān al Aṭrāsh who led a revolt against the French, to form a refugee settlement in the north of the oasis of al-ʾAzraq in 1925, which became permanent by 1932 (Firro 1992: 298). With regard to the division of agricultural lands between the Chechens, the Druze and the Bedouin, a written document was produced in January 1934 and signed by Dawlat Tūbūlāt "on behalf of the Chechens":[79] a striking example of non-formal management of land ownership in the fringes of state-administered areas after the British land reforms.

The Chechen village was also an opportunity for the expanding state to rely upon a settlement in the heart of the desert. A very interesting affair occurred in 1932-1933 when the Anglo-Iraqi Petroleum Company wanted access to the great water resources of al-ʾAzraq. John Glubb personally opposed the project and exposed the situation to Frederick Peake, commander of the Arab Legion based in Amman who, in turn,

75 NLA, Official Journal, 161, 15/07/1927.

76 On the role of John Glubb in the building of the Anglo-Hashemite state refer to Massad 2001: 100-62; Bradshaw, 2016: 30-77; Fletcher, 2015 :133-237; Alon and Di Tonno 2010: 87-100.

77 As for 1927, the Banū Ṣakhr of al-ʾAzraq along with elements of the Banū Ḥuwayṭāt and Banū Sirḥān still imposed the *khāwwa* on Arab traders crossing the al-ʾAzraq area, NLA, Government Documents, 35/3/1/25.

78 He was even helped by John Glubb to increase his agricultural activities in the area (Alon 2007: 129).

79 "Qad jarā al-riḍā wa-l-ittifāq fīmā bayna al-fariqayn sākinay al-ʾAzraq," January 5, 1934, Private Archives of ʿUthmān Dawlat.

confronted the Department of Lands and Survey which, again, supported the company's interests.[80] Glubb referred to the Chechens to Peake in the following observation:

> There is, in the meantime, a noticeable increase of agriculture and demographics. Today, I have sent to you a request from some Chechens of al-ʾAzraq in order to build a new village in addition of the Druze village. This project would provide grain agriculture and an immovable settlement in the heart of the desert with all the expected benefits. It would be a shame if the company abruptly cause the depletion and the drying of water resources at this stage of things.[81]

As a matter of fact, John Glubb had a great interest in the foundation of the Chechen village. As early as 1933, he decided to found a school in the village, instructing the inhabitants to pay the teacher.[82] The project aimed, in the first instance, to provide literacy for the sons of the Banū Ṣakhr and Banū Sirḥān tribesmen in order to form a Bedouin martial elite with a basic education.[83] Al-ʾAzraq al-Shīshān progressively worked as a bridge for Glubb to maintain permanent contact with the Bedouin, notably with the creation of the al-ʾAzraq post of the Desert Patrol. Glubb, for example, shared the local leadership of his squadron with Barakāt al-Khurayshā of the al-ʾAzraq Banū Ṣakhr. Eventually, by August 1937, the Bedouin of the al-ʾAzraq post entrusted Chechen Sufi and village representative Dawlat Tūbūlāt to guard the patrol's horses,[84] showing the key local interconnections on which the sustainability of Glubb's armed force was based. Thus, there was a sort of continuity in the absorption of the Chechens and the desert tribes and notably the Banū Ṣakhr in the progressive eastward movement of state expansion. Al-ʾAzraq worked as the next station, after al-Zarqāʾ, that allowed the Anglo-Hashemite state to create and perpetuate its territorial reality east of the Hejaz Railway, which had been, until then, the very frontier of statehood.

Conclusion

Local scale studies often help to explain and detail the emergence of nascent nations of which Transjordan and Jordan offer a recent example. The case of the Transjordanian Chechens outlines the plurality of historical trajectories taken by the Caucasian *muhājirs* and the settled populations in the Middle East. It also portrays Transjordan's societal evolution in rural areas between the late Ottoman era and the 1930s, which was marked by administrative efforts to expand state rule by both the Ottomans and Anglo-Hashemites. The al-Zarqāʾ-al-ʾAzraq geo-administrative axis shows that the British strategy of state expansion was adopted in the logical continuity of the Ottoman administration. Just as the Circassian village of Amman enlarged

80 NLA, Government Documents, 34/2/4/25; 56/2/4/25; 57/2/4/25.
81 NLA, Government Documents, 38/2/4/25; 39/2/4/25.
82 John Bagot Glubb to Ahālī Qaṣr al-ʾAzraq, September 1, 1933, Private Archives of ʿUthmān Dawlat.
83 On Glubb's concern for education, see Fletcher (2015: 222–3).
84 ʿAbd al-Salām to Ḥājj Dawlat, 25/05/1356 (August 3, 1937), Private Archives of ʿUthmān Dawlat.

the area of state influence beyond al-Salṭ during the Hamidian period, al-Zarqā' and al-'Azraq had a very similar geographical importance during the Mandate era. Anglo-Hashemite state-building, thus, depended on the existence of these locally anchored villages and communities in order to settle statehood presence through the creation of infrastructures, even during the late administrative conquest of the desert. Socioeconomic characteristics of the Chechens also inform us about the complexity of the Transjordanian societal landscape, especially in the frontier zone of the *ma'mūra*. Chechens established durable relations with their neighbors and particularly the desert Bedouin to achieve a firm local anchoring without having much formal political importance, at least before 1928. Consequently, it is noteworthy that the late Ottoman era's localism also concerned Caucasian populations like the Chechens, who associated and maintained close links with major actors of pan-Arabism during the Mandate era. Their support of Fayṣal's pan-Arabism preceded and eased their allegiance to Abdullah and the Hashemites, who sought to become the cohesive referent entity in the process of nation-building. Local anchoring and the social integration of the Transjordanian Chechens was also deeply influenced by their ethno-Sufism, which had a determining role in spatial appropriation, socioeconomic patterns and public or political manifestation. Allowing a more nuanced picture of the Caucasians in the Ottoman and Mandate Middle East, the case study of the Chechens shows to what extent Transjordan, despite its demographically weak importance, represented a mosaic of human societies sharing different conditions, organizations, and aspirations.

Bibliography

Sources and archives

Başbakanlık Osmanlı Arşivi (BOA) (2012), "A. MKT. MHM, 520/8 in Uğur Ünal," *Osmanlı belgelerinde Kafkas göçleri, I*, Osmanlı Arşivi Daire Başkanlığı, 532–5.

Bashir, Dib (1922), "Naḥnu al-wāḍi'īn asmā'anā . . . ," 21/05/1340, January 20, Private Archives.

Dawlat, 'Uthmān (1919), "Bismillāh alladhī tawaffaqnā fī istiqlāliyyat al-dawla al-'arabiyya . . . ," March 23, Private Archives of 'Uthmān Dawlat.

Dawlat, 'Uthmān (1920), "Nashkur al-qā'id al-mujāhid Ahmad Ramzī min al-Zarqā' . . . ," November 18, Private Archives of 'Uthmān Dawlat.

Dawlat, 'Uthmān (1934), "Qad jarā al-riḍāwa-l-ittifāq fīmā bayna al-fariqayn sākinay al-'Azraq . . . ," January 5,Private Archives of 'Uthmān Dawlat.

Dawlat, 'Uthmān (1933), "John Bagot Glubb to Ahālī Qaṣr al-'Azraq," September 1, Private Archives of 'Uthmān Dawlat.

Dawlat, 'Uthmān (1937), "'Abd al-Salām to Ḥājj Dawlat, 25/05/1356", August 3, Private Archives of 'Uthmān Dawlat.

Dawlat Tūbūlāt (1927), "Faṣl fī bayān ma jarā min al-awwalīn wal-l-akhirīn," March 7, Private Archives of 'Uthmān Dawlat.

Ḥadīsa' bint Yūnus (1992), "Min mudhakkirāt al-ḥājja Ḥadīsa," interviewed by Adnan Madhhab on April 20, Unpublished, Private Archives of Adnan Madhhab.

Ḥājj Muḥammad (1914), "Qad ittafaqnā ʿalā ḥafr al-nahr al-maʿlūm fimābaynanā wa-l-Zarqā'...," March 10, Private Archives of Dib Bashir.
Ḥashīmī, Amīn (1908), "Al-Muhājirūn wa sukkān al-Bādiya," *Al Ittijirūn wa sukkān*, November 14.
(Al-)Ḥūrānī, Khalīl (1910), "Lajnat al-Muhājirīn," *Al Muqtabas*, October 24.
Ibn Sālmirzā Ibn Shaḥmirzā, Mirzā (1913), *Mudhakkirāt Mirzā Ibn Sālmirzā Ibn Shaḥmirzā*, 2 -4- 5, Private Archives of Layla Arslan.
Junayd, Abdullah (undated), "'Barnāmaj al-ṣaff al-tamhīdī' and 'Barnāmaj al-ṣaff al-khāmis," Private Archives of Abdullah Junayd.
Junayd, Abdullah (undated), "Imām ʿAbd al-ʿAzīz to Shaykh ʿAbdullāh, 'Ilā al-ʿālim al-rabbānī wa-l-ghawth al-ṣamdānī al-sayyid al-shaykh Ḥājjī ʿAbdullāh Afandī,'" Private Archives of Abdullah Junayd.
Junayd, Abdullah (1932a), "Al-Qānūn al-asāsī li-l-Nādī al-Qawqāzī," Private Archives of Abdullah Junayd.
Junayd, Abdullah (1932b), "Wāfaqat hayʾa al-idāra li-Nādī al-Qawqāzī," December 15, Private Archives of Abdullah Junayd.
Junayd, Abdullah (1933), "Yassaʿ Washī to Al-Nadī al-Qawqāzī," January 1, Private Archives of Abdullah Junayd.
Madhhab, Adnan (1903), "Ēdilsultān to Ahmad al-Bayānī," 4/08/1321, Private Archives of Adnan Madhhab.
National Library of Amman (NLA), Private Documents, 20/135/HM and 1/13/HM.
National Library of Amman (NLA), Official Gazette and Government Documents.
Nāshhū, Jawdat Ḥilmī (1995), *Tārīkh al-Sharkas (al-Adīgha) wa-l-Shīshān fī Liwāʾī al-rabbānī wa-l-ghawth -1920)*, Manshūrāt Lajnat Tārīkh al-ʾUrdun.
Shīshānī, Muṭīʿ (1924), Icepaste Aḥmad Dāghistānī to Muṭīkhān, 'Ḥaḍara al-ustādh al-shaykh Muṭīkhān al-muḥtaram . . . ," February 22, Private Archives of Muṭīʿ Shīshānī.
Shīshānī, Muṭīʿ (1931), "Muḥammad ʾAmīn al-Ḥusaynī to Shaykh Muṭīʿ Khān," June 25, Private Archives of Muṭīʿ Shīshānī.

References

Abū al-Shaʿr, Hind (1995), *ʾIrbid wa Jiwāruhā,1850–1928*, Amman: Al-Muʾassasa al-ʿArabiyya li-l-Dirāsāt wa-l-Nashr.
Abū al-Shaʿr, Hind, (2009), "Nashʾā Baladiyyat al-Zarqā (01/12/1928–19/05/1934)," *Al-Majalla al-ʾUrduniyya li-l-Tārīkh wa-l- Āthār*, 3 (2): 98–138.
Abū al-Shaʿr, Hind, and ʿAbdullah al-ʿAssāf (2013), *Al-Zarqā'. Al-Nashʾā wa-l-Taṭawwur (1903–1935)*, Amman: Wizārat al-Thaqāfa.
Abujaber, Raouf Saʿd (1989), *Pioneers Over Jordan: The Frontiers of Settlement in Transjordan, 1850–1914*, London: I.B. Tauris.
Abu Nowar, Maan (2006), *A History of the Hashemite Kingdom of Jordan: The Development of Transjordan, 1929–1939*, Oxford: Ithaca.
Ahmad, Feroz (2014), *The Young Turks and the Ottoman Nationalities*, Salt Lake City: The University of Utah Press.
Alon, Yoav (2006), "The Balqa Revolt: Tribes and Early State-Building in Transjordan," *Die Welt des Islams*, 46 (1): 7–42.
Alon, Yoav (2007), *The Making of Jordan: Tribes, Colonialism and the Modern State*, London: Tauris.

Alon, Yoav (2016), *The Shaykh of Shaykhs: Mithqal Al-Fayiz and Tribal Leadership in Modern Jordan*, Stanford: Stanford University Press.

Alon, Yoav, and Simone Di Tonno (2010), "Glubb Pacha (1930–1946) et le colonialisme britannique en Transjordanie," *Maghreb-Machrek*, 205 (3): 87–100.

Amadouny, Vartan (1995), "The Formation of the Syria-Transjordan Boundary, 1915–32," *Middle Eastern Studies*, 31 (3): 533–49.

Amadouny, Vartan (1997), "The Campaign Against Malaria in Transjordan, 1926–1946: Epidemiology, Geography and Politics," *Journal of the History of Medicine and Allied Sciences*, 52 (4): 453–84.

Anscombe, Frederick (2014), *State, Faith and Nation in Ottoman and Post-Ottoman Lands*, Cambridge: Cambridge University Press.

Aymes, Marc (2013), "Many a Standard at a Time: The Ottomans' Leverage with Imperial Studies," *Contributions to the History of Concepts*, 8 (1): 26–43.

Badaev, Said Emi (1998), *Vainakhskaya Diaspora v Turtsii, Iordanii i Sirii: Istori i Sovremennost*, PhD thesis in History, Russia: University of Makhachkala.

Banī Yūnus, Maʾmūn Aṣlān (2011), *Qāfilat al-ḥağğ al-Šāmī fī šarqay al-'Urdun fī-l-ʿahd al-ʿuṯmānī, 1516–1918*, Hammāda.

(Al-) Bashāyra, Rātib Mashāy (1999), *Al-Shīshāniyyūn al-'Urduniyyūn. Dirāsa Jughrāfiyya Bashariyya wa Iqtiṣādiyya*, 'Irbid: Dār al-Kindī li-l-Nashr wa-l-Tawzī.

Bīnū, Saʿīd (2007), *Al-Shīshān wa Hijratuhum ilā al-'Urdun*.

Bunton, Martin (2007), *Colonial Land Policies in Palestine, 1917–1936*, Oxford: Oxford University Press.

Bradshaw, Tancred (2016), *The Glubb Reports: Glubb Pasha and Britains's Empire Project in the Middle East, 1920–1956*, 30–77, London: Palgrave Macmillan.

Carroll, Lynda (2008), "Sowing the Seeds of Modernity on the Ottoman Frontier: Agricultural Investment and the Formation of Large Farms in Nineteenth Century Transjordan," *Archaeologies: Journal of the World Archaeological Congress*, 4 (2): 233–49.

Chatty, Dawn (2010), *Displacement and Dispossession in the Modern Middle East*, Cambridge: Cambridge University Press.

Chochiev, Georgy (2015), "Evolution of a North Caucasian Community in Late Ottoman and Republican Turkey: The Case of Anatolian Ossetes," in Anthony Gorman and Sossie Kasnarian (eds.), *Diasporas of the Modern Middle-East*, 103–37, Edinburgh: Edinburgh University Press.

Dann, Uriel (1976), "The Political Confrontation of Summer 1924 in Transjordan," *Middle Eastern Studies*, 12 (2): 165–6.

Dettmering, Christian (2005), "Reassessing Chechen and Ingush (Vainakh) Clan Structures in the 19th Century," *Central Asian Survey*, 24 (4): 469–89.

Draper, P. (1928), "Early Treatment of Malaria," *J.R Army Med Corps*, 5: 135–7.

Durkilī, Nadhīr (2004 [1935]), "Nuzhat al-adhhān fī tarājim ʿulamāʾ Dāghistān," in Michael Kemper and Amri Shixsaidov (eds.), *Muslim Culture in Russia and Central Asia. Vol. 4: Die Islamgelehrten Daghestans und ihre arabischen Werke*, 86, 98–9, Berlin: Klaus Schwarz Verlag.

Faḫrī Sāmī Ayyūb, and Al-Tall ʿAbduh Yūsuf (1939), *Dalīl Qarya Ṣuwayliḥ*, Amman: Maṭbaʿa al-'Urdun.

Firoo, Kais (1992), *A History of the Druzes, Volume 1*, Leiden: Brill.

Fishbach, Michael (2000), *State, Society and Land in Jordan*, Leiden: Brill.

Fisher, Alan (1987), "Emigration of Muslims from the Russian Empire in the Years After the Crimean War," *Jahrbücher für Geschichte Osteuropas*, 35 (3): 356–71.

Fletcher, Robert (2015), *British Imperialism and the 'Tribal Question'*, Oxford: Oxford University Press.
Frantzman, Seth, and Kark Ruth (2012), "Empire, State and the Bedouin of the Middle-East, Past and Present: A Comparative Study of Land and Settlement Policies," *Middle Eastern Studies*, 48 (4): 492–3.
Fratantuono, Ella (2019), "Producing Ottomans. Internal Colonization and Social Engineering in Ottoman Immigrant Settlement," *Journal of Genocide Research*, 21 (1): 1–24.
Germer-Durand (1904), "Rapport sur l'exploration archéologique en 1903 de la voie romaine entre Amman et Bostra," *Bulletin archéologique*, 26: 3–41.
Gil-Har, Yitzhak (1992), "Delimitation Boundaries: Trans-Jordan and Saudi Arabia," *Middle Eastern Studies*, 28 (2): 374–84.
Gingeras, Ryan (2011), "The Sons of Two Fatherlands: Turkey and the North Caucasian Diaspora, 1914–1923," *European Journal of Turkish Studies*. Available online: https://journals.openedition.org/ejts/4424.
Guthorn, Harrison (2015), "A Point of Order: A Battle for Autonomy in the First Legislative Council of Transjordan," in T. G. Fraser (ed.), *The First World War and its Aftermath*, 295–312, Chicago: University of Chicago Press.
Hamed-Troyansky, Vladimir (2017), "Circassian Refugees and the Making of Amman, 1878–1914," *International Journal of Middle East Studies*, 49: 605–23.
Ibragimova, Zul'fiā Hamzatovna (2006), *Čečenskij narod v Rossijskoj imperii. Adaptacionnyj period*, Moskow: Probel-2000.
Israilov, M. "Chechenskaya Diaspora v Stranah Blijnego Vostoka." Available online: https://pgu.ru/upload/iblock/e65/4.pdf.
(Al-)Jalūdī, Aliyyān (1994), *Qaḍā' 'Ajlūn. Dirāsa Tārīkhiyya (1863-1918)*, Amman: University of Jordan Press.
Jersild, Austin (2002), *Orientalism and Empire: North Caucasus Mountain Peoples and the Georgian Frontier, 1845–1917*, Montreal: McGill-Queen's University Press.
Kabbani, Muhammad, Nazim Adil Haqqani, and Seyyed Hossein Nasr (2004 [1995]), *Classical Islam and the Naqshbandi Sufi Tradition*, Wilmington: Islamic Supreme Council of America, 394, 425–7.
Kane, Eileen (2015), *Russian Hajj: Empire and the Pilgrimage Route to Mecca*, Ithaca: Cornell University Press.
Karpat, Kemal (1985), *Ottoman Population 1830–1914. Demographic and Social Characteristics*, Madison: The University of Wisconsin Press.
Karpat, Kemal (2002), "The Status of the Muslim Under European Rule: The Eviction and Settlement of the Çerkes," in *Studies on Ottoman Social and Political History. Selected Articles and Essays*, 7–27, Leiden: Brill.
Kayali, Hasan (1997), *Arabs and Young Turk:. Ottomanism, Arabism and the Ottoman Empire, 1908–1918*, Oakland: University of California Press.
Kemper, Michael (2002), "Khālidiyya Networks in Daghestan and the Question of Jihād," *Die Welt des Islams*, 42 (1): 41–71.
Lewis, Norman (1987), *Nomads and Settlers in Syria and Jordan, 1800–1980*, Cambridge: Cambridge University Press.
Lewis, Norman (2000), "The Syrian Steppe During the Last Century of Ottoman Rule: Hawran and the Palmyrena," in Martha Mundy and Basim Musallam (eds.), *The Transformation of Nomadic Society in the Near East*, 37–8, Cambridge: Cambridge University Press.

Massad, Joseph (2001), *Colonial Effects: The Making of National Identity in Jordan*, New York: Columbia University Press.
McCarthy (1955), *Death and Exile: The Ethnic Cleansing of Ottoman Muslims, 1821–1922*, Feltham: The Darwin Press.
Meier, Astrid, and Tariq Tell (2015), "The World the Bedouin Lived in: Climate, Migration and Politics in the Early Modern Arab East," *Journal of the Economic and Social History of the Orient*, 58 (1/2): 40.
Métral, France (2006), "Biens tribaux dans la steppe syrienne entre coutume et droit écrit," *Revue du monde musulman et de la Méditerranée*, 79/80: 89–112.
Mizrahi, Jean-David (2002), "Armée, Etat et Nation au Moyen-Orient. La naissance des troupes spéciales du Levant à l'époque du mandat français, Syrie, 1919–1930," *Guerres mondiales et conflits contemporains*, 207 (2): 117.
Mizrahi, Jean-David (2009), "De la région frontière à la ligne frontière: Les confins méridionaux de la Syrie de la fin de l'Empire ottoman au début des Mandats," *Vingtième siècle. Revue d'histoire*, 103: 83–90.
Mundy, Martha (1996), "La propriété dite mushāʿen Syrie. À propos des travaux de Ya'akov Firestone," *Revue du monde musulman et de la Méditerranée*, 79/80: 273–287.
Nadan, Amos (2003), "Colonial Misunderstanding of an Efficient Peasant Institution: Land Settlement and Mushāʿ Tenure in Mandate Palestine," *Journal of the Economic and Social History of the Orient*, 46 (3): 320–54.
Nadan, Amos (2018), "Revisiting the Anti-mushāʿ Reforms in the Levant: Origins, Scale and Outcomes," *British Journal of Middle Eastern Studies*. https://doi.org/10.1080/13530194.2018.1533451.
Nataev, Sajpudi (2010), *Čečenskij tajp: Suŝnost'ʾ, struktura i socialʾnaā dinamika*, Ph.D Thesis in History, Russia: University of Makhatchkala.
Nataev, S. A. (2015), "K voprosu ob institute tuhum/tohum/tuk"um/tukham u narodov Kavkaza," *Gumanitarnye, social'no-èkonomičeskie i obŝestvennye nauki*, 2: 265–9.
Nichols, Johanna (2004), "The Origin of the Chechen and the Ingush: A Study in Alpine Linguistic and Ethnic Geography," *Anthropological Linguistics*, 46 (2): 129–55.
Özyüksel, Murat (2014), *The Hejaz Railway and the Ottoman Empire. Modernity, Industrialisation and Ottoman Decline*, London: I.B. Tauris.
Peake, Frederick Gerard (1934 [1958]), *A History of Jordan and its Tribes*, Miami: University of Miami Press.
Rağā Al-Ḥammūd, Nawfān (1996), *ʿAmmān wa ğiwāruha ẖilāl al-fatra 1864-1921*, Beirut: Manšurāt Bank al-aʿmāl.
Rjoub, AbdelMajeed, and AbdelAziz Mahmoud (2012), "The Emergence of Agro-Pastoral Villages in Jordan: Hamamet al-Olaimat Village as a Case Study," *Journal of Human Ecology*, 38 (3): 231–43.
Robins, Philip (2019), *A History of Jordan*, Cambridge: Cambridge University Press.
Robinson, T. (1939), "Notes on a Case of Infantile Leishmaniasis in Transjordan," *J.R Army Med Corps*, 72: 14–15.
Rogan, Eugene (1999), *Frontiers of the State in the Late Ottoman Empire: Transjordan, 1850–1921*, Cambridge: Cambridge University Press.
Sait, Siraj, and Hilary Lim (2006), *Land, Law and Islam: Property and Human Rights in the Muslim World*, 69–70, London and New York: Zed Books.
Shami, Seteney (1996), "The Circassians of Amman: Historical Narratives, Urban Dwelling and the Construction of Identity," in Jean Hannoyer and Seteney Shami (eds.), *Amman, ville et société*, 312–13, Beirut: CERMOC.

Stoever, Edward Royal, and Frederick A. Norris (1930), "Section I: The Expedition of 1904–1905," in *Publications of the Princeton University Archeological Expeditions to Syria in 1904–1905 and 1909. Division I: Geography and Itinerary*, Leiden: Brill.
Ṭarīf, Jūrj (1994), *Al-Salṭ wa Jiwāruhā Khilāl al- Fatra 1864-1921*, Amman: Manshūrāt Bank al-Aʿmāl.
Tell, Tariq (2000), "Guns, Gold and Grain. War and Food Supply in the Making of Transjordan," in Steven Heydemann (ed.), *War, Institutions and Social Change in the Middle-East*, 38–9, Berkeley: University of California Press.
Tell, Tariq (2013), *The Social and Economic Origins of Monarchy in Jordan*, New York: Palgrave Macmillan.
Türesay, Özgür (2013), "The Ottoman Empire Seen Through the Lens of Postcolonial Studies: A Recent Historiographical Turn," *Revue d'histoire moderne et contemporaine*, 60 (2): 127–45.
Wahīb, Muhīb (2012), *Al-Ḥikāya al-Shaʿbiyya fi-l-'Urdun. Al-Zarqā*, Amman: Dār Yafā al-ʿilmiyya.
White, Benjamin (2011), *The Emergence of Minorities in the Middle East. The Politics of Community in French Mandate Syria*, Edinburgh: Edinburgh University Press.
Zalūm, Ḥ lūmLI (1994), *Al-Zarqā, Al-Madīna wa-l-Muḥāfaẓa, Māḍīhā wa Ḥāḍiruhā*, Amman: Al-Maktaba Al-Waīna waa.
Zelkina, Anna (2000), *In Quest for God and Freedom: The Sufi Response to the Russian Advance in the North Caucasus*, Bloomsbury: Hurst & Company.
Zelkina, Anna (1993), "Islam and Politics in the North Caucasus," *Religion, State and Society*, 21 (1): 115–24.

6

The Creation of Syrian Refugee Camps in Jordan

Contextual Factors

Ayham Dalal and Aline Fraikin

The word "context" refers to "the interrelated conditions in which something exists or occurs" (Merriam Webster 2020). It gives an example of how words might not be fully understood without the text which surrounds them. In that sense, the text is the context, in which word gains new meaning. Context is therefore complex and woven together. The same dictionary elaborates further, that "context" originates from the Latin word "*contexere*," which means "to weave or join together." In that sense, the context is both complex and important for understanding how a certain event or phenomenon occurs at certain moment in time, and the reasons behind the shape it takes.

In the field of refugee camp studies, context has never been addressed explicitly as such. While almost every paper has to present the context of the camp which it examines, some scholars pay more attention to the role of context than others. For instance, Adam Ramadan and Sara Fregonese (2017) explored the changes within the Palestinian refugee camps in Lebanon in the light of sovereignty. In particular, they "traced a genealogy of the state of exception" which showed how the shifting arrangements of these sovereignties in Lebanon shed their light on the camp as "hybrid spaces of political possibility" (ibid: 13). Along the same lines, Sari Hanafi (2008) addressed the role of the state in shaping the space of Palestinian camps in the Middle East. Through a comparative study, he noticed that when the state imposes its disciplinary power on a camp, they turn from "open camps" connected to the state urbanistically and socially, into isolated and "closed camps." While both papers focus on politics and sovereignty, another scholar has paid particular attention to economy and the labor market. By comparing two contexts, Jordan and Lebanon, Lewis Turner (2015) noticed that the encampment policies are heavily affected by the economic aspirations of both countries. In Lebanon, the need for low-wage workers from Syria enabled the refugees to be integrated into the Lebanese labor market, and thus, no camps were built. The encampment policy in Lebanon has been influenced by history as well, considering the involvement of Palestinian camps in the Lebanese Civil War. Meanwhile, Jordan recognized the economic impact of refugees—negatively through competition in the labor market and positively through attracting international funds, and therefore, encouraged the encampment of Syrians. All these papers shed light on important contextual factors regarding camp spatiality, but how did these factors affect the creation of camps in Jordan?

In this chapter we will address the way the context has shaped refugee camps for Syrians in Jordan. We will use the unique opportunity that the context of Jordan gives: within a small number of years, between 2011 and 2014, more than eight refugee camps were set up (Table 6.1). The nature, typology, size, location, management, layout, and population of these camps differed greatly, and thus, not all of them were built with economic logic in mind, as argued by some analysts (Turner 2015). Instead, we will argue that three main contextual factors influenced the establishment of Syrian camps in Jordan. These are: (1) the refugee-making process, which addresses the transitioning of Syrians from guests to refugees and its impact on camp production; (2) the shifting roles of actors, which will elaborate on how changes and shifts within the actors' scene produced shifts in camp typologies; (3) the restricted access to territory, which is the process by which Syrians were gradually distanced from urban areas and in which camps were transformed from "open" to "closed." Finally, the chapter sheds light on the importance of transitioning within the context and suggests that diversity of actors and shifts within one context are the reasons behind the diversity of camp typology within one territory, like Jordan, for instance.

The findings presented in this chapter are the result of an intensive archival analysis that took place between 2015 and 2016. The analysis included various resources such as reports, newspapers, and media articles. It was informed, in particular, by an in-depth analysis of the earliest UN reports that were produced in Jordan, in 2012, known as the "weekly updates." The initial findings were then triangulated with fieldwork investigations in Jordan between 2014 and 2018. Using a mixed method approach, the findings of the paper build on personal observations in al-Zaʿtarī, al-ʾAzraq, and the Emirati-Jordanian camps, and about twenty in-depth interviews with relief workers and actors in Jordan. This is in addition to many informal talks and discussions with experts, one interview with a Syrian refugee who was accommodated in al-Bashābisha camp, one interview with a volunteer in a Gulf aid institution, and over 30 interviews with Syrian refugees in al-Zaʿtarī, al-ʾAzraq, and the Emirati-Jordanian camp.[1]

The chapter is structured around the three main contextual factors found to be influential on the establishment of Syrian camps in Jordan. Each of these sections explains the meaning of the factor and the transitioning that occurred within it, and later, it reflects on how the transitioning impacted the production of camps. In order to facilitate the presentation of data, we will begin first by shedding light on Jordan as the

[1] The field work was on the one hand part of Ayham Dalal's former research (2014) and is on the other hand embedded in a 2018–2021 collaborative research project with Aline Fraikin at the Technical University of Berlin, called SFB 1265 "Re-Figuration of Spaces," which started in 2018 and deals with refugee camps in Berlin and in Jordan. We are grateful to the Deutsche Forschungsgemeinschaft (DFG, German Research Foundation), Project number 290045248—SFB 1265, for their financial support and for offering us an inspiring research environment at the Collaborative Research Center "Re-Figuration of Spaces."

Table 6.1 A List of the Syrian Refugee Camps Established in Jordan between 2011 and 2015, Showing Their Different Characteristics and Qualities (Source: Authors)

	Al-Bashābisha	**Cyber City**	**Stadium**	**Al-Za'tarī**	**King Abdullah Park (KAP)**	**Al-Rājihī Camp**	**Emirati-Jordanian Camp (EJC)**	**Al-'Azraq**	**Al-Rukbān**
Location	Al-Ramthā	Near al-Ramthā (Quality Industrial Zone)	Al-Ramthā (exact location unknown)	Near al-Za'tarī village (al-Mafraq region)	'Irbid	Exact location unknown	Al-'Azraq governorate	Al-'Azraq governorate	Syrian-Jordanian borders
Typology	Refurbished building	Refurbished building	Refurbished building	Humanitarian refugee camp	Refurbished Park	Military camp	Humanitarian refugee camp	Humanitarian refugee camp	Spontaneous camp
Type	Collecting center (Transitional)	Collecting center (Transitional)	Collecting center (Transitional)	Official camp	Collecting center (Transitional)	Collecting center (Transitional)	Official camp	Official camp	Spontaneous camp
Approximate Population size (2019)	3,000	380	140	80,000	350	2,000	7,000	35,000	75,000
Opening and closing date	April 2011–September 2012	May 2012–Sept 2016	April 2012 – April 2012	July 2012–now	June 2012–now	2013–unknown	April 2013–now	April 2014–now	Early 2015–now
Actors involved	Local actors, police, UNHCR, international NGOs	SRAD, Gendarmerie, UNRWA, UNHCR, ICRC, NGOs	UNHCR, international NGOs	JHCO, SRAD, UNHCR, military	Saudi National Campaign, UNHCR	SRAD and the Military	Government of UAE, the Emirati Red Crescent, SRAD	SRAD, UNHCR, MoPIC, Ministry of Housing	No direct actors, only occasional assistance

overarching context of this study, and particularly, on the many different camps that emerged in response to the Syrian influx.

1. Syrian Refugee Camps in Jordan

Since 2011 the influx of Syrian refugees to Jordan has set up a variety of refugee camps, some of which are less known due to their transitional role as collecting centers. According to UNHCR (2020), the number of Syrian refugees in Jordan amounts to around 650,000 refugees with less than a quarter living in three official refugee camps: al-Zaʿtarī, al-ʾAzraq, and the Emirati-Jordanian camp. Two other camps that had an important role at the beginning of the crisis and then started to slowly fade away are the King Abdullah Park in ʾIrbid and Cyber City near al-Ramthā. In addition to those, by tracing the earliest UN weekly reports and local news, it seems that other camps like Al-Bashābisha Complex, the Stadium, and al-Rājihī camp had an important but almost invisible role in the process of refugee accommodation in Jordan (Table 6.1).

Within a relatively short period of three years (between April 2011 and 2014), eight camps were set up, varying in size, typology, management, and locations. For the sake of clarity, we follow Michel Agier's suggestion (2011: 52) that the "official camps" are the "most standardized, planned and official form of encampments," and therefore, we consider that only al-Zaʿtarī, al-ʾAzraq, and the Emirati-Jordanian camps resemble this definition. The remaining five camps we consider as "transitional" and mostly used as "collection points" or "reception centers" as they are sometimes called in the reports.

The eight camps differ widely in both their architecture and layout. In a previous article, it was shown how the two largest camps, al-Zaʿtarī and al-ʾAzraq, differ in their planning (Dalal et al. 2018), with the former resembling an "informal settlement" while the latter resembles "mass housing" schemes, and both standing in contrast to the small, "five-star" camp managed by the Emirati Red Crescent known as the Emirati-Jordanian camp or EJC, which resembles a "gated community" (Dalal 2020).

The remaining five camps were much smaller in size and population counts. For instance, al-Bashābisha was a residential complex donated to the Jordanian police by a businessman called Nidal Al Bashabsheh in the border town of al-Ramthā (*The New York Times* 2012). As explained in a short documentary about the owner and his donations on YouTube (Mayyas, Zo'bi, and Shalhoub 2013), the camp consisted of seven identical buildings. Each building had three stories, and all were placed around an open yard. Another refurbished building was the Cyber City camp, which was located in the Quality Industrial Zone (QIZ) near ʾIrbid. The camp was formed around a six-story building with a total of 148 residential units (All of Jordan News 2015). These two camps, which were buildings, stand in contrast to another refurbished facility, namely a park near ʾIrbid, known as the King Abdullah Park (KAP). KAP is a small camp built within a fenced area that has shared toilets and eighty container units, each including two rooms, and each room expected to host ten refugees (UNHCR 2012a: 2). Information about the layout and structure of the other two remaining camps, the Stadium and al-Rājihī, is not available, due to the short duration of their use. However, it is assumed that the Stadium was a refurbished part of a Sport Stadium near al-Ramthā, as mentioned in the reports (UNHCR 2012b) and that the al-Rājihī camp was a refurbished building owned by the military, as hinted by information in the news (Jafra News 2012).

In addition to physical characteristics and typologies, these eight camps furthermore differ in their lifespan. For instance, while the three official camps and the KAP remain open until today, many of the other camps had a short lifespan. The Stadium camp is believed to have lasted only a few weeks: it was mentioned a few times in UN reports in 2012, and then was not mentioned anymore. Other camps, like al-Bashābisha and Cyber City, lasted a few years longer. According to the owner, a Jordanian businessman, al-Bashābisha camp started hosting Syrians in April 2011 and was eventually closed by September 2012 (Mayyas, Zo'bi, and Shalhoub 2013). Cyber City was opened in May 2012 but stayed in operation for a few years until it was closed in September 2016. Unfortunately, it is unclear when exactly al-Rājihī camp was opened, but news reports mention that it was opened early in 2013 (Jafra News 2012).

The population size of the camps differs widely as well. For instance, the population size of al-Zaʿtarī camp has varied a lot over the years. In fact, it increased steadily until reaching around 200,000 refugees in March 2013, and then has stabilized to around 75,000 since 2014. The second biggest camp population in Jordan is in al-ʾAzraq camp. Although it was prepared with the expectation of a "mass displacement" from 2013 onward, the camp hosts around only 35,000 refugees. The remaining camps are much smaller in size with the EJC hosting around 7,000 refugees and al-Bashābisha claiming to have hosted around 3,000 refugees at its peak. Cyber City and KAP hosted a population of about 350 each and the Stadium 140 refugees.

The profile of the population in the eight camps differed as well. For example, al-Rājihī camp was opened specifically for defectors from the Syrian army (Jafra News 2012); the Cyber City for Palestinian refugees from Syria and their relatives (Amnesty International 2013); the Stadium camp was opened for single travelers (UNHCR 2012b); al-Bashābisha, KAP, al-Zaʿtarī, and al-ʾAzraq camps, for Syrians arriving to Jordan without official papers; and finally, EJC for Syrians with additional vulnerabilities (IRIN 2013). The categorization of Syrians indeed confirms to us that the refugee camps are spatial mechanisms of separation, categorization, and containment (Agier 2011; Mcconnachie 2016). But which contextual factors played a role in the establishment of such a wide diversity of refugee camps within such a short period? In the following sections we explore three contextual factors that were identified as essential in shaping the process of establishing the eight Syrian refugee camps under discussion. These are the refugee-making process, the shifting of actors, and access to territory (work and mobility).

2. The Refugee-Making Process

According to the Geneva Convention (UNHCR 1951: 3), a refugee "is someone who is unable or unwilling to return to their country of origin owing to a well-founded fear of being persecuted for reasons of race, religion, nationality, membership of a particular social group, or political opinion." The application and implication of this "universal" definition varies widely from one country to another. For instance, not all countries were a signatory of this convention—including Jordan, and not all of them had the same "defense mechanism" against unwanted refugee movements. In signatory countries, the right to asylum was paralleled with what is known as the "*non-entrée*" regime that aims to protect stability, and in which the arrival of refugees is regulated by borders and visa procedures. Similar approaches might be missing in less non-signatory countries. This led to the suggestion that "while refugee law matters to developed states today for a variety of reasons, the most important is that it conscripts less developed countries to act in ways that provide a critical support to the developed world's migration control project" (Gammeltoft-Hansen and Hathaway 2015: 240). This results in a heterogeneous landscape of refugee definitions and procedures. Within the "*non-entrée*" regime of Europe, for instance, displaced populations, most of whom enter the territory illegally and under life-threatening circumstances, are obliged to register and apply for asylum in the state's respective institutions directly after their arrival (Schittenhelm 2019; Valenta et al. 2020). They then undergo the required asylum procedures (personal interview, examination, decision) before they are either granted asylum, i.e., as officially recognized refugees, and can legally stay—or rejected and therefore deported. In other parts of the world, displaced populations might not be immediately recognized as refugees, and therefore, strict procedures might not necessarily be applied. Instead, refugees endure what we called here, a "refugee-making process," i.e., the process by which displaced populations are gradually governed, shaped, and transformed politically into "refugees" according to the perspectives of the host country.

In a country like Turkey, the refugee-making process entailed a series of "ping-pong" politics with the objective of "reconstituting Syrians as objects of humanitarian assistance rather than political agents with rights" (Baban et al. 2017: 99). Similarly, Syrians in Jordan witnessed a series of arbitrary rules and regulations until they were transformed into "refugees." During this process, two phases played an important role in the creation of camps. The first phase is characterized by political ambiguity and the second by humanitarian legality.

2.1. Political Ambiguity

This phase is characterized by the absence of political will to categorize Syrians arriving to Jordan under any political classifications. This period stretched between 2011 and 2012, shortly before al-Zaʿtarī camp was opened. The conditions of this phase remain under-documented. Yet, it was experienced by the author upon his relocation from Syria to Jordan in 2011. Based on observation and data analysis, it seems that the Syrian populations arriving in Jordan were very heterogeneous. Large cities like Amman, ʾIrbid, and al-Zarqāʾ hosted skilled workers, businessmen, activists, and highly educated graduates, in contrast to the smaller villages and towns of the north, which hosted Syrians from rural areas affected by the war in Southern Syria. At that time, borders were open and Syrians were welcome as guests, which is a term that does not have any political implications (ILO 2015). In other words, there was no "refugee law" that had to be implemented upon the arrival of Syrians to Jordan. Likewise, most of the Syrians relocating to Jordan between 2011 and 2012 did not consider themselves as refugees (Pearlman 2018: 301–03).

During this phase, however, there was a particular group of arrivals that seems to have problematized the political conditions of Syrians in Jordan, namely the *sans-papier* or those fleeing under precarious conditions, crossing informal checkpoints at the border, and entering without official documents or passports. The increasing number of these "illegal" arrivals among the many Syrians fleeing the country might have pushed the Jordanian government to change its approach. This is in addition to perceiving refugees as a justifiable cause for attracting humanitarian aid, similar to the state's approach regarding other refugees (El-Abed 2014).

2.2. Humanitarian Legality

During 2012, the Jordanian government began to sense the increased pressure caused by Syrians on the decaying urban infrastructures and services in towns and villages. In many areas, finding adequate housing became an issue and influenced urbanization patterns in smaller towns like al-Mafraq (Alshadfan 2015; NRC 2015). Additionally, towns in the north, like al-Mafraq and 'Irbid, started to witness growing tensions between Syrians and the local community (Mercy Corps 2013). Under these conditions, the Jordanian government wanted, on the one hand, to hand the management of refugees over to the UNHCR and, on the other hand, to turn refugees, like in Turkey, into "humanitarian objects" (Baban et al. 2017). To do so, Syrians were gradually forced to register as refugees and obtain Asylum Seekers Certificates (ASC) from the UNHCR (Achilli 2015), otherwise, they would have "no free-of-charge access to the public health and education systems or eligibility for WFP food voucher and UNHCR cash assistance" (JRC and IFRC 2012: 6). Due to this process and the escalation of violence in Syria, the number of Syrians registered as refugees in Jordan jumped from a few hundred in 2012 to 70,000 in January 2013 to 570,000 in December of the same year (Figure 6.1). The Jordanian government followed up with other procedures in 2015, such as the issuing of a Ministry of Interior card (magnetic cards) and work permits. This process was automatically paralleled with a categorization process of the arrivals. For instance, not all arrivals were Syrians or members of the Syrian military but also included Palestinian refugees from Syria. Both, the registration of Syrians as refugees and the concomitant categorization process resulted in different types of camps.

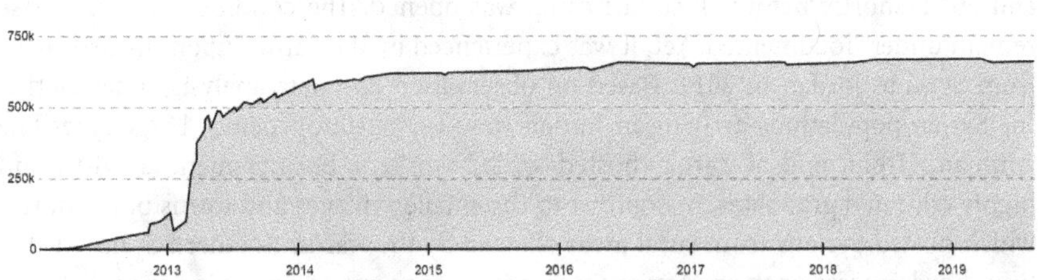

Figure 6.1 A diagram showing a staggering increase in the numbers of registered Syrians in Jordan in 2013 (Source: UNHCR 2019).

3. The Impact of Refugee-Making on Camps

The process of refugee-making was paralleled by the process of camp-making. On a macro level, the absence of a legal and humanitarian definition of the Syrian refugee in Jordan resulted in a series of small "experimental" camps that functioned as collecting points for those without official documents. These spaces included al-Bashābisha and the Stadium. The gradual transitioning of Syrians, from guests to refugees, produced camps like KAP and Cyber City that demonstrate this transitioning: they were initially built as collection centers but continued to function as camps for longer than planned. Additionally, the refugee-making process included a transition toward classifying the arrivals. This transformed Cyber City into a camp for Palestinians from Syria and later resulted in the creation of al-Rājihī camp, which was opened for military defectors who were separated from the other refugees in al-Zaʿtarī camp. Finally, when all Syrians in Jordan were forced to register as refugees, and therefore become humanitarian objects, this implied and justified the need to build official humanitarian camps. This explains why, although KAP and Cyber City were used before al-Zaʿtarī camp, the latter remains the first official camp for Syrian refugees in Jordan. The creation of these official camps, however, was also influenced by another contextual factor, namely, the actors.

3.1. Shifts within the Actors' Scene

The migration of displaced populations generally attracts an "influx management" system (Bulley 2014: 69), consisting of different actors and institutions. The presence of refugees in a host country, therefore, is automatically attached to a web of actors such as international organizations, donors, the host communities, governmental actors, and the military (Figure 6.2). Many scholars have pointed out the complex and often conflictual nature between these actors and how they affect governmentality in the camp and urban areas (Bariagaber 1999; Maestri 2017; Sandri 2017). Other scholars have examined the impact of different sovereignties in shaping the space of the camp in one context, like Lebanon, suggesting that due to a multiplicity of actors, sovereignty in a camp is rather hybrid and contested (Ramadan and Fregonese 2017). However, little attention has been given to the impact of actors on the creation of refugee camps.

A few studies have been dedicated to exploring the impact of actors on the Syrian refugee response in Jordan (Ababsa 2017; Achilli 2015; Burlin 2020; IRIN 2012). While these studies cover up different sides and aspects regarding the Syrian refugee response in Jordan, they all confirm the shifting nature of the actors' scene between 2011 and 2014. These shifts can be characterized by three phases.

3.2. Local Actors

The first phase, between 2011 and 2012, is dominated by a strong presence of local actors including private donors, philanthropists (like Nidal Al Bashabsheh), urban dwellers (neighbors and civil society organizations), and religious-based organizations (Ababsa 2017; IRIN 2012). These actors worked to assist Syrians in need, mainly in rural areas and small towns through personal relations and connections and with a strong

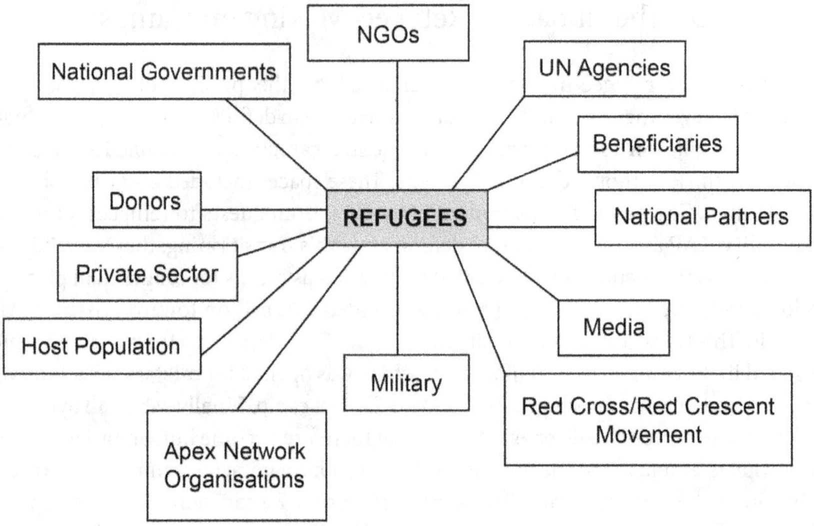

Figure 6.2 Actors typically involved in the refugee response (Source: UNHCR 2005: 11).

presence of Islamic organizations such as *al-Kitāb wa al-Sunna*. As suggested by Ababsa (2017), "the first assistance provided to Syrian refugees in 2011 and 2012 was channelled through the local Islamic charities present in every village" and mainly through zakat. The nature of this local response, however, remained hectic, ad hoc, and messy as suggested in reports (IRIN 2012). This triggered the actors' response in the following phase, which was characterized by an intensification of old and new international actors.

3.3. International Actors

The second phase, between 2012 and 2013, witnessed a proliferation of international actors on the scene. Most of these actors were attracted by the mounting number of Syrians in Jordan and the tone of the UN organization requiring an escalation of actions and refugee assistance "beyond Amman" (UNHCR 2012a: 2). In addition to well-known actors working inside Jordan, such as the UNHCR, UNICEF, and MSF, and royal NGOs such as the Jordanian Hashemite Charity Organization (JHCO), the crisis attracted a number of NGOs with a relatively new presence in Jordan, including "NRC (est. 2012), Acted (est. 2012), Medair (est. 2012), and Plan International (est. 2015)" (Burlin 2020: 124). The growth and multiplication of these actors did not only result in expanding their scope of work and staff numbers (UNHCR staff increased from 100 to 557 between 2012 and 2019) but also in overshadowing the local actors and projects that failed to grasp the context and make an efficient impact on beneficiaries, both Syrians and Jordanians (ibid: 125). This phase has also witnessed the rise of new international actors, namely Arab Gulf donors and charity organizations. In a compelling report, Ababsa (2017) suggests that: "the Syrian crisis has been a turning point in the history of humanitarian enterprise in terms of the increasing role assumed by Arab donors. Not only did Arab funding increase considerably, but the Gulf States have taken a leading role in organising fundraising events for the response." The report suggests that "in 2013, Gulf donor and Gulf NGO contributions to the Syrian crisis totalled US$ 910,3 million. A third of this amount was distributed in Jordan" (ibid). Some of the most active countries included Saudi Arabia, the Emirates, and Qatar. While the involvement of all these actors was meant to increase assistance to Syrians who become recognized officially as "refugees" in Jordan, and therefore, worthy of humanitarian interventions, the nature of these responses remained hectic, and therefore, provoked and justified the intervention of the Jordanian state.

3.4. State Actors

The third phase was characterized by the prevailing presence of governmental actors. Between 2011 and 2013, the Jordanian government was operating through different entities including the police, the military, the JHCO—which is a royal NGO connected to the government, and the Syrian Refugee Camps Directorate (SRCD). The SRCD was established in January 2013, substituting for the role of the police and the JHCO in managing refugee camps (UNHCR 2014). However, during mid-2013 and 2014, governmental actors started to take on a stronger role and, therefore, became more present on the scene. This includes the Syrian Refugee Affairs Directorate (SRAD), previously known as the SRCD, which expanded its scope of operation. It also witnessed the rise of other governmental actors, such as the Ministry of Planning and International Cooperation (MoPIC) and the Ministry of Interior (MoI). The former was responsible for coordinating the efforts of different humanitarian actors, while the latter became more involved in the process of refugee-making through the issuing of the MoI magnetic cards for all refugees. The increasing involvement of state actors in the Syrian refugee response in Jordan, however, was reported to be counterproductive. For instance, it was noticed that "humanitarian assistance is coming increasingly under the control of the Jordanian government with clear negative repercussions in terms of protection and services provision" (Achilli 2015: 7). The attempt to empower and centralize the role of state actors within the scene resulted in delays that hindered the delivery of humanitarian assistance and produced shifts in focus from the immediate needs of refugees toward developmental work based on attracting international funds (Burlin 2020). Moreover, the governmental actors became deliberately more involved in refugee management, which included strict policing, involuntary deportation, and closing the borders with Syria during that phase (Achilli 2015). All these aspects and shifts within the actors' scene affected the creation of refugee camps as well.

4. The Impact of Actors on Camps

Actors, and their transition in Jordan, had a clear impact on the process of camp creation. The involvement of some actors, such as Gulf donors and relief organizations, state organizations, local NGOs, and philanthropists contributed directly to the type of camp set up within each phase. For instance, al-Bashābisha camp emerged from the efforts of the local donor, Nidal Al Bashabsheh. Cyber City was suggested as a transitional camp to be refurbished by *al-Kitāb wa al-Sunna*, an Islamic charity with strong presence in the north of Jordan (Shamma 2012). KAP camp was opened with the donation of a Saudi campaign called Nulabbī al-Nidā' (Interview 2016), and EJC was opened and entirely run by the Emirati government through the Emirati Red Crescent. Only al-Rājihī camp was opened by the Jordanian government, to isolate military defectors.

On the one hand, there is clear evidence that the nature of the actors involved in a refugee response at a certain moment in time (local actors, NGOs, INGOs, state actors, etc.) can have a direct impact on the type of camp built. Local actors, for instance, seem to have favored accommodating refugees in refurbished buildings and facilities. This is in contrast to international and state actors that prefer to accommodate the growing number of refugees in official camps. Here, it is important to note that not all international actors are alike. In fact, the difference between the experience, principles, and ideologies of these international actors seems to have a direct impact on the nature of the camps built and their architecture. For instance, although EJC is an official camp, its principles of planning, layout, and management are derived from experiences in the Arab Gulf, and therefore, differ widely from those used in other camps managed by the UNHCR (for a detailed comparison see Dalal 2020). Moreover, the involvement of Arab Gulf organizations since 2012 contributed to a major change in the shelter policy in al-Zaʿtarī camp (namely replacing all tents with prefabs or caravans), which also had an impact on the design of other camps, like EJC, KAP, and al-ʾAzraq. Thus, their presence had influenced the spatiality of these camps. This shows that actors participate in shaping the spatiality and typologies of refugee camps in a very effective manner.

For instance, while al-Bashābisha camp was initially managed by the owner, Nidal, and the Jordanian police (Mayyas, Zo'bi, and Shalhoub 2013), its structure changed drastically after April 2012 when the UNHCR called for intensifying the role of INGOs in the north (UNHCR 2012a). Suddenly the camp became equipped with humanitarian flags and infrastructures, according to the weekly reports (see UNHCR 2012c: 1), turning from a locally managed collecting point to a transitional humanitarian camp. Similarly, the transition in managing al-Zaʿtarī camp from the JHCO and the police in 2012 to the UNHCR and SRCD in 2013 (UNHCR 2014) might have had an impact on weakening the management of the camp which allowed refugees to practice further control over the built environment. This is in contrast to al-ʾAzraq camp, which is officially managed and run by the UNHCR, yet, where state actors such as the SRAD, the police, the MoPIC, and the Ministry of Housing had a strong influence on the process of its creation. Due to this hybrid assemblage of actors, the resulting space of al-ʾAzraq camp resembled a mass housing project. This is because its planning involved various state actors such as the Ministry of Housing and local contractors to produce a settlement for "mass" displaced populations (see Dalal 2020). This means that the transitioning and diversification of actors does not only lead to the creation of different types of camps, but their shifting or competing roles within one camp can also affect how it is set up and, therefore, its use of space. In the following section we will explore the last contextual factor that has affected the creation of Syrian refugee camps in Jordan, which is the growing restriction on access to territory.

5. Restricted Access to Territory (Mobility and Work)

Restricting access to territory is nothing new in the context of refugees and forced migration. In fact, it is argued that the creation of camps is, largely, the result of the states attempting to isolate refugees in camps so that the relationship between the land, the nation, and the state is not disturbed (Agamben 1998; Agier 2011; Arendt 1951). Nonetheless, as the analysis above has shown, this restriction to accessing of land did not happen immediately for Syrian refugees in Jordan. It was developed hand in hand with the refugee-making process. Yet, the trajectories of both processes are not the same. For instance, Jordan has had open borders with Syria since 2001 and had a workforce agreement with Syria for over a decade (ILO 2015). This has allowed about 160,000 Syrians to work in Jordan through job contracts obtained by the employee (ibid). However, many Syrians who had exhausted their resources were unable to obtain such job contracts and were forced to find income through informal markets. Villages and small towns were claimed to have flourished and grown due to the influx (Freihat 2014), producing new economic urban dynamics and housing markets (Alshadfan 2015). This is on the one hand, while on the other, competition over resources and work opportunities fueled tensions between Syrians and Jordanians in host communities. These tensions were noted throughout 2012 in northern towns (see Mercy Corps 2013) and peaked in 2013.

According to a UN report, three out of four Jordanians considered it important to close the borders with Syria and confine refugees in camps (UN 2013). And in January 2013, the newly selected parliament called on the government to "restrict access to the territory" (ibid: 139). These escalations were in line with the general impression that Syrians were threatening Jordan's economy and overall stability (CSS 2013: 7). This feeds into the refugee-making process as well, where transforming Syrians in Jordan into refugees means that their access to the territory is conditional and generally limited. This led to the introduction of different laws and procedures to regulate the work of Syrians in Jordan, which were perceived as confusing and restricting (Lenner and Turner 2019). Finally, Jordan closed the border with Syria in 2014 (Achilli 2015) and reopened it later in 2018.

6. The Impact of Restricting Access to Territory on Camps

By gradually restricting access to territory, Syrian camps were transiting from "open camps" to "closed camps." The notion of open and closed camps was introduced by Sari Hanafi (2008) in his studies on urbanized Palestinian camps in the Middle East, where he suggested that a closed camp is zone that is spatially extraterritorialized, under the disciplinary power of the state, and socially segregated. This transitioning can be seen geographically by looking at a map (Figure 6.3). The earliest camps, like al-Bashābisha, Stadium, and KAP, were located in urban areas and facilities, therefore connected to their surroundings. al-Zaʿtarī camp and Cyber City were also built relatively close to urban areas, but shortly after they were set up, they were turned into closed camps. By contrast, camps like al-ʾAzraq and EJC were pushed further away from towns or urban areas, thereby severely isolating their populations, in places resembling a "lonely world stranded in a desert" (Agier 2010: 33). This means that, in an attempt to restrict the access of the refugee population to the territory, the creation of camps was relocated: from urban areas to isolated deserts.

A second means of implementing the transitioning, from open to closed camp, is by ending the interconnectedness between camps and urban areas, stabilizing camp' population, and transforming them into separate entities where disobedient and suspicious refugees can be disciplined. As interviews and reports show, the transitional camps were connected with each other, functioning as collecting centers until refugees are bailed out and sponsored to leave the camps through the so-called *kafāla* system. According to a male refugee who was bailed out from al-Bashābisha in 2012, "some people remained there for months and even were moved to other camps. I was lucky to have relatives who bailed me out after one week, but those who didn't know anyone in Jordan, where would they go?" (Interview 2017). Although the *kafāla* system was, in time, turned into a "class element" allowing the exploitation of Syrians (Aks Alser 2012; Turner 2015: 359), it was an official way out for those willing to leave camps and relocate to urban areas. The mobility of refugees between camps and urban areas was magnified in al-Zaʿtarī camp which functioned as a transitional space for those arriving illegally to Jordan during 2012 and 2013. According to a UN report, the camp registered over 190,000 Syrians in April 2013; yet "several tens of thousands or more have left the camp, either through the official channel of sponsorship by a Jordanian, spontaneous relocation, or returning to Syria with the assistance of Jordanian authorities" (UN 2013: 140). The boundaries of these camps were porous, allowing refugees to have access to the territory, to be mobile and even find jobs informally. This explains why, during 2011 and 2012, many Syrians preferred to have "the bail-out certificate more than the UNHCR certificate," because it made them "feel [. . .] safe" (Un Ponte Per 2012: 9).

The transitioning toward "closed camps" took place between 2013 and 2014. The Jordanian government stabilized the population of al-Zaʿtarī camp at around 80,000. Furthermore, it closed the border with Syria, leading to the creation of the al-Rukbān camp for Syrians who were stranded on the borders, and established al-ʾAzraq camp with the expectation of having to accommodate mass populations. The movement of Syrians between camps and urban areas became strictly regulated, and the camps turned into disciplinary places (Foucault 1979). Populations were fixed, hierarchies were created—such as Village 5 in al-ʾAzraq camp—and those who were found to work illegally in urban areas would be sent to al-ʾAzraq camp (Lenner and Turner 2019). In that sense, closed camps became the destination for the unwanted Syrians in Jordan. As a UN (2013: 139) report states:

> In view of the growing socio-economic impact of refugees, the Government has appealed for greater support from humanitarian agencies and the international

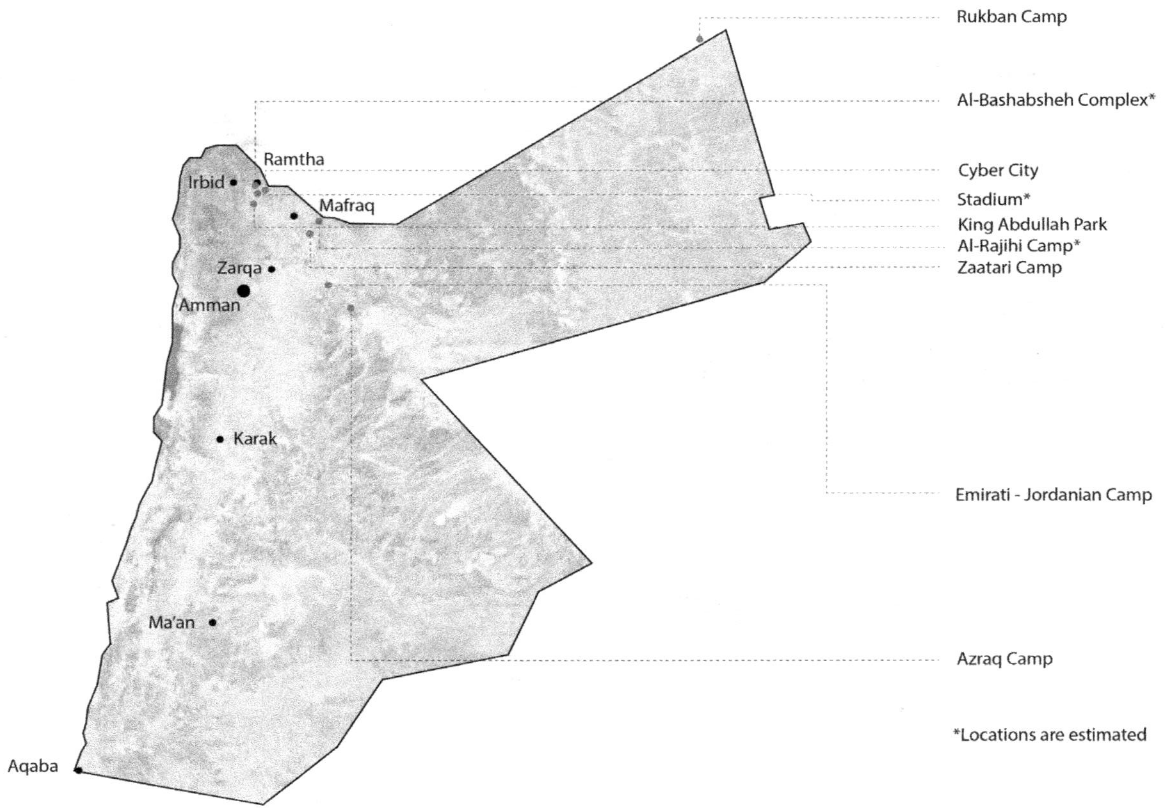

Figure 6.3 Locations of the different Syrian camps that emerged in Jordan between 2011 and 2017 (Source: Author's own 2017).

> community. Authorities have initiated efforts to limit the number of refugees working in the informal labor market and continue to direct all irregular new arrivals, most of whom arrive without any resources at all, to refugee camps in order to minimize competition on already scarce natural resources.

In other words, by attempting to restrict the access of Syrians to the Jordanian territory, the creation of camps experienced a transitioning: from being "open" (small, ephemeral, near to urban areas) to being "closed" (large, semi-permanent, and isolated from urban areas). But how are the contextual factors that have been discussed linked to each other? What lessons can be drawn in regard to the creation of refugee camps in general?

Between 2011 and 2014, eight different camps were set up in Jordan in order to accommodate Syrian refugees. The diversity of typologies, types, actors, and population profiles among them was the starting point for this research. What types of contextual factors played a role in creating these different camps? In this chapter, we answered this question by suggesting three main factors that played a role in the creation of Syrian camps in Jordan. These are the refugee-making process, the role of actors, and the restriction to territory. Each of these contextual factors had a particular impact on the creation of each of the camps and their spaces. For instance, the refugee-making process produced clear shifts in the type of camps offered to Syrians. The absence of a legal and humanitarian definition of the Syrian refugee in Jordan at the beginning of the influx resulted in a series of small "experimental" camps that functioned as collecting points for those without official documents. However, when Syrians were registered as refugees, they were turned into humanitarian objects, which justified the creation of official humanitarian camps. Al-Zaʿtarī camp was the first, followed by EJC and al-ʾAzraq camp. The refugee-making process was not the only contextual factor that impacted the space of the camp. One of the major findings of this research is the ability of the actors to exert significant influence on the process of camp creation. For instance, local actors produced camps which had a rather local character, such as a residential housing and refurbished hangars. This is in contrast to international humanitarian actors that preferred to construct official camps with a clear layout and standardized shelters. The mounting role of Gulf actors had its impact on the creation of camps as well. EJC was built reflecting "Gulf" standards, which were compared to "five stars" services (IRIN 2013), while the donation of caravans changed the structures of a camp like al-Zaʿtarī completely (Dalal 2014). This process, however, was not as linear as it may seem. In fact, the rising role of state actors such as the SRAD, MoI, MoPIC, and Ministry of Housing, in collaboration with the UNHCR, produced a camp with different characteristics, similar to a mass housing project (Dalal 2020). Finally, the attempt to restrict the access of Syrians to the Jordanian territory, also through regulating mobility and work, crystallized the shape of these camps. What was initially deemed as an interconnected network of small "open" camps built within and around towns and villages in the north was gradually transformed into "closed" camps. Many of the earliest camps, such as al-Bashābisha, the Stadium, and Cyber City, disappeared and only official camps remained, with fixed population size, and an imposed disciplinary role on their spaces to which disobedient refugees are moved. In other words, restricting access to territory reshaped the boundaries of these camps and turned them from spaces of human flow into dried swamps with stable populations.

While few scholars have paid attention to the role of contextual factors on the creation of camps, such as politics (Al-Qutub 1989; Hanafi 2008), sovereignty (Ramadan and Fregonese 2017), and economy (Turner 2015), the case in Jordan has provided us with a special setting to examine the role of context. Within a relatively short period of time (2011–14), eight camps in Jordan were created to accommodate Syrian refugees. The diversity of types, actors, and typologies of these camps presented a stimulating background against which to understand the role of context on the diversity of these camps. Clearly, the transitioning and shifting of the different contextual factors resulted in the creation of different types of camps (Figure 6.4). Each camp is unique and has different characteristics from the others (see also Dalal 2020). The contextual factors are interwoven into each other and sometimes difficult to separate. Yet, with this research, we have contributed to the emerging debate on the role of context on the creation of camps by highlighting the impact of actors and the diversity of dynamics (such as the refugee-making process and restricting access to territory) which can sometimes be grouped together under more general terms like hegemony, sovereignty, or politics. Having said that, this chapter not only helps us understand the complexity of the contextual factors affecting the creation of Syrian refugee camps in Jordan, but it also suggests that there is a benefit and a need to address these factors in other regions, countries, and territories where camps are and will be produced.

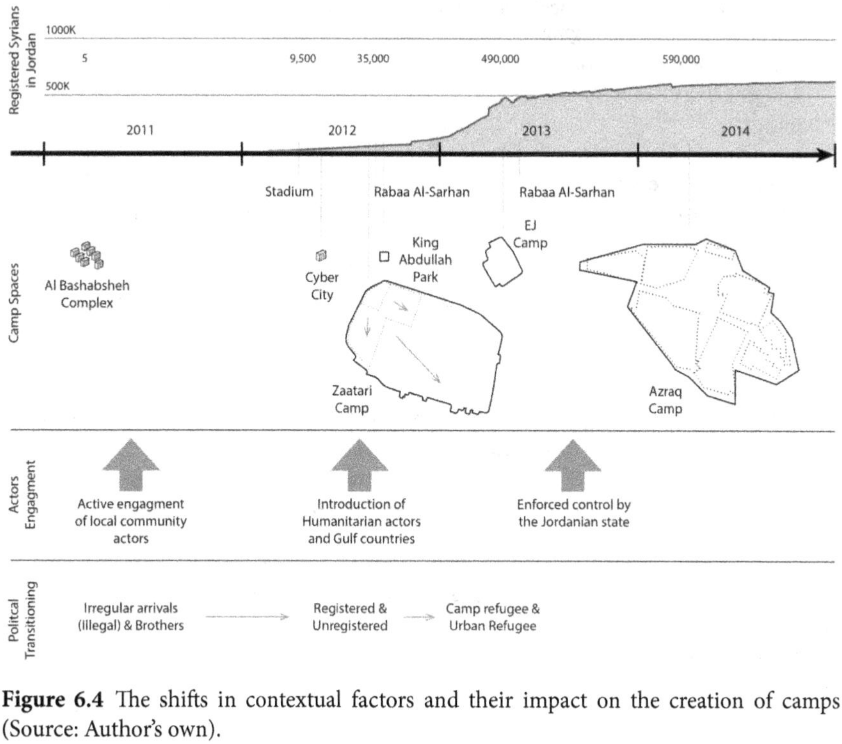

Figure 6.4 The shifts in contextual factors and their impact on the creation of camps (Source: Author's own).

Bibliography

Ababsa, Myriam (2017), "Islamic NGOs Assistance to Syrian Refugees in Jordan and Gulf Donors Support," Conflits et migrations. Réflexions sur les catégories et la généalogie des migrations au Moyen-Orient. Available online: https://lajeh.hypotheses.org/723 (accessed October 13, 2020).

Achilli, Luigi (2015), "Syrian Refugees in Jordan: A Reality Check," *Migration Policy Centre*, European University Institute. Available online: https://cadmus.eui.eu/handle/1814/34904.

Agamben, Giorgio (1998), *Homo Sacer: Sovereign Power and Bare Life*, Standford: Stanford University Press.

Agier, Michel (2010), "Humanity as an Identity and its Political Effects (A Note on Camps and Humanitarian Government)," *Humanity: An International Journal of Human Rights, Humanitarianism, and Development*, 1: 29–45.

Agier, Michel (2011), *Managing the Undesirables: Refugee Camps and Humanitarian Government*, Cambridge: Polity Press.

Aks Alser (2012), "Syrian Refugees in Jordan are Facing Manipulation Due to Harsh Living Circumstances [Arabic]." Available online: https://www.aksalser.com/?page=view_articles&id=9ac5f019e07e4c4e2c0497809887e065 (accessed July 19, 2017).

All of Jordan News (2015), "Mā qālahu al-Majālī wa al-Badārīn ʿan Mukhayyam Saybir Sitī lil-lājiʾīn al-Falasṭīniyīn min Sūriyā." Available online: http://www.allofjo.net/index.php?page=article&id=90116 (accessed July 22, 2017).

Al-Qutub, Ishaq Y. (1989), "Refugee Camp Cities in the Middle East: A Challenge for Urban Development Policies," *International Sociology*, 4: 91–108. Available online: https://doi.org/10.1177/026858089004001006

Alshadfan, Razan (2015), *The Trends of Housing Transformation in Border Cities Hosting Refugees: The Case of Mafraq City*. MA diss., University of Ain Shams and University of Stuttgart.

Amnesty International (2013), "A Dog Has More Freedom," – Palestinians at Cyber City Camp for Refugees from Syria.

Arendt, Hannah (1951), *The Origins of Totalitarianism*, San Diego: Harvest Book - Harcourt, Inc.

Baban, Feyzi, Suzan Ilcan, and Kim Rygiel (2017), "Playing Border Politics with Urban Syrian Refugees: Legal Ambiguities, Insecurities, and Humanitarian Assistance in Turkey," *Movements. Journal for Critical Migration and Border Regime Studies*, 3 (2): 81–102.

Bariagaber, Assefaw (1999), "States, International Organisations and the Refugee: Reflections on the Complexity of Managing the Refugee Crisis in the Horn of Africa," *The Journal of Modern African Studies*, 37 (4): 597–619.

Bulley, Dan (2014), "Inside the Tent: Community and Government in Refugee Camps," *Security Dialogue*, 45: 63–80. Available online: https://doi.org/10.1177/0967010613514788.

Burlin, Alexander (2020), "Theorizing Development Challenges in the Syrian Refugee Response in Jordan: Interests, Management, and Accountability," *Journal of Identity and Migration Studies*, 14 (1): 117–33.

Center for Strategic Studies (2013), *Public Opinion Survey: Some Current Issues in Jordan 2013*, Amman: Center for Strategic Studies.

Dalal, Ayham (2014), "Camp Cities Between Planning and Practice: Mapping the Urbanisation of Zaatari Camp," MA diss, Ain Shams University and Stuttgart University.

Dalal, Ayham (2020), "The Refugee Camp as Urban Housing," *Housing Studies*, 1–23. Available online: https://doi.org/10.1080/02673037.2020.1782850.

Dalal, Ayham, Amer Darweesh, Philipp Misselwitz, and Anna Steigemann (2018), "Planning the Ideal Refugee Camp? A Critical Interrogation of Recent Planning Innovations in Jordan and Germany," *Urban Planning*, 3: 64–78.

El-Abed, Oroub (2014), "The Discourse of Guesthood: Forced Migrants in Jordan," in Anita Fábos and Riina Isotalo (eds.), *Managing Muslim Mobilities: Between Spiritual Geographies and the Global Security Regime*, 81–100, New York: Palgrave Macmillan.

Foucault, Michel (1979), *Discipline and Punish: The Birth of the Prison*, New York: Vintage Books.

Freihat, Moath (2014), "Syrian Refugees in Jordan: Economic Risks and Opportunities," *Arab Reporters for Investigative Journalism (ARIJ)*. Available online: https://en.arij.net/investigation/syrian-refugees-in-jordan-economic-risks-and-opportunities/ (accessed December 20, 2020).

Gammeltoft-Hansen, Thomas, and James C. Hathaway (2015), "Non-Refoulement in a World of Cooperative Deterrence," *Columbia Journal of Transnational Law*, 53: 235–84.

Hanafi, Sari (2008), "Palestinian Refugee Camps: Disciplinary Space and Territory of Exception." [Migration Policy Centre], [CARIM-South], CARIM Analytic and Synthetic Notes, 2008/44, Retrieved from Cadmus, European University Institute Research Repository. Available online: http://hdl.handle.net/1814/8631.

ILO (2015), *Access to Work for Syrian Refugees in Jordan: A Discussion Paper on Labour and Refugee Laws and Policies*, Beirut: ILO.

IRIN (2012), "Civil Society at Heart of Syrian Refugee Response." Available online: https://www.irinnews.org/fr/node/251895 (accessed July 22, 2017).

IRIN (2013), "Serving Up Five-star Service for Refugees the UAE Way."Available online: http://www.irinnews.org/report/99019/serving-five-star-service-refugees-uae-way (accessed July 22, 2017).

Jafra News (2012), "Transferring Defectors with High Ranks to Rajhhi [Arabic]." Available online: http://www.jfranews.com.jo/more-41317-1-%7Bclean_title%7D (accessed May 10, 2016).

JRC and IFRC (2012), "Syrian Refugees Living in the Community in Jordan. Assessment Report," Amman. Available online: lien https://reliefweb.int/report/jordan/syrian-refugees-living-community-jordan-assessment-report.

Lenner, Katharina, and Lewis Turner (2019), "Making Refugees Work? The Politics of Integrating Syrian Refugees into the Labor Market in Jordan," *Middle East Critique*, 28: 65–95. Available online: https://doi.org/10.1080/19436149.2018.1462601.

Maestri, Gaja (2017), "The Contentious Sovereignties of the Camp: Political Contention Among State and Non-state Actors in Italian Roma Camps," *Political Geography*, 60: 213–22. Available online: https://doi.org/10.1016/j.polgeo.2017.08.002.

Mayyas, Mourad, Fawwaz Zo'bi, and Anas Shalhoub (2013), "The Initiative of a Man, Mr. Nidal Al-Bashabsheh with Syrian Refugees." Available online: https://www.youtube.com/watch?v=q71U0E1mu-k&t=15s (accessed May 10, 2016).

Mcconnachie, Kirsten (2016), "Camps of Containment: A Genealogy of the Refugee Camp," *An International Journal of Human Rights, Humanitarianism, and Development Humanity*, 7: 397–412.

Mercy Corps (2013), "Mapping of Host Community-Refugee Tensions in Mafraq and Ramtha, Jordan." Available online: https://data2.unhcr.org/en/documents/details/38301.

Merriam Webster (2020), "Context." Available online: https://www.merriam-webster.com/dictionary/context (accessed December 29, 2020).

Norwegian Refugee Council (2015), *In Search of a Home: Access to Adequate Housing in Jordan*, Amman: NRC.

Pearlman, Wendy (2018), "Becoming a Refugee: Reflections on Self-Understandings of Displacement from the Syrian Case," *Review of Middle East Studies*, 52 (2): 299–309. Available online: https://doi.org/10.1017/rms.2018.93.

Ramadan, Adam, and Sara Fregonese (2017), "Hybrid Sovereignty and the State of Exception in the Palestinian Refugee Camps in Lebanon," *Annals of the American Association of Geographers*, 107 (4): 949–63.

Sandri, Elisa (2017), "Volunteer Humanitarianism: Volunteers and Humanitarian Aid in the Jungle Refugee Camp of Calais," *Journal of Ethnic and Migration Studies*, 44 (1): 65–80. Available online: https://doi.org/10.1080/1369183X.2017.1352467.

Schittenhelm, Karin (2019), "Implementing and Rethinking the European Union's Asylum Legislation: The Asylum Procedures Directive," *International Migration*, 57: 229–44. Available online: https://doi.org/10.1111/imig.12533.

Shamma, Muhammad (2012), "Settling in the North is Hindering Syrian Refugees and Relief Organizations [Arabic]." Available online: http://ar.ammannet.net/documentary/news/1026/ (accessed February 2, 2015).

The New York Times (2012), "Jordanian Donors Privatize Relief." Available online: https://www.nytimes.com/2012/05/03/world/middleeast/jordanian-donors-privatize-relief.html (accessed February 2, 2016).

Turner, Lewis (2015), "Explaining the (Non-)Encampment of Syrian Refugees: Security, Class and the Labour Market in Lebanon and Jordan." *Mediterranean Politics*, 20: 386–404. Available online: https://doi.org/10.1080/13629395.2015.1078125.

UNHCR (2013), *Syria Regional Response Plan: Jordan*, https://www.unhcr.org/publications/syria-regional-response-plan-january-december-2013

UNHCR (1951), *Convention and Protocol Relating to The Status of Refugees*,

UNHCR (2005), *Reach Out Training Materials*, Geneva: United Nations Higher Commissioner for Refugees. Available online: https://www.unhcr.org/media/convention-and-protocol-relating-status-refugees.

UNHCR (2012a), *Update No. 2 Syria Regional Refugee Response*. Available online: https://data2.unhcr.org/en/documents/details/37002.

UNHCR (2012b), *Syrians in Jordan: Situation Report April 24–30 2012*. Available online: https://reliefweb.int/report/jordan/syrians-jordan-situation-report-april-24-30-2012.

UNHCR (2012c), *Syria Regional Refugee Response*, July 12, 2012. Available online: https://reliefweb.int/map/syrian-arab-republic/syria-regional-refugee-response-jordan-lebanon-iraq-turkey-12-july-2012.

UNHCR (2014), Za'atari *Refugee Camp: 2013 Safety and Security Report*. Available online: https://data2.unhcr.org/en/documents/details/39914.

UNHCR (2020), *Jordan: Statistics for Registered Syrian Refugees (as of 29 February 2020)*. Available online: https://data2.unhcr.org/en/documents/details/74320.

Un Ponte Per (2012), "Comprehensive Assessment on Syrian Refugees Residing in the Community in Northern Jordan," Available online: https://reliefweb.int/report/

jordan/comprehensive-assessment-syrian-refugees-residing-community-northern-jordan.

Valenta, Marko, Jo Jakobsen, Drago Župarić-Iljić, and Hariz Halilovich (2020), "Syrian Refugee Migration, Transitions in Migrant Statuses and Future Scenarios of Syrian Mobility," *Refugee Survey Quarterly*, 39 (2): 153–76. Available online: https://doi.org/10.1093/rsq/hdaa002.

7

Social Cohesion through the Housing of Syrian Refugees within Jordanian Homes

NRC Shelter Program in the ʾIrbid Governorate (2013–2015)

Myriam Ababsa

As Jordan entered the fourth year of the Syrian refugee crisis, the government shifted from humanitarian to long-term sustainable developmental approaches in order to "build social cohesion and resilience," according to the UN 2015–2016 Regional Refugee and Resilience Plan (UNHCR 2016). Following discussions with its main donors, Jordan decided to grant the Syrian refugees access to its formal labor market against increased international economic support. Social inclusion became the emerging theme supporting employment policies in order to reduce tensions between Jordanians and Syrian refugees. Northern municipalities benefited from World Bank support as part of the Jordan Emergency Services and Social Resilience Project (JESSRP), in order to "enforce community resilience and social cohesion." In sociological terms, resilience is the capacity of a social group to withstand and recover from shocks and crises.

Social cohesion is one of the means of building a functioning and harmonious society. It results from functioning vertical relations between communities and their institutions, based on transparency and accountability, and horizontal relations between different social groups, based on economic interdependencies and complementarities at a local level (including relations between neighbors). Horizontal relations are key to enhancing solidarity, trust, and personal well-being (Norton et al. 2012 in Kuhnt et al. 2017). However, vertical relations tend to favor citizens, and few countries develop accountability mechanisms. Jordan is an exception as, since its independence in 1946 it has integrated several waves of refugees from Palestine into its society and into the very social fabric of its main cities. This social integration has been facilitated by the fact that refugees from Palestine were granted full citizenship in 1952, thus facilitating vertical social cohesion. Citizens of Palestinian origin contributed to the modernization of the economy and were a decisive component of Jordan nation building.

The ten refugee camps created by UNRWA[1] arround cities have been progressively integrated into the urban fabric, to a point that it is now difficult to recognize, for instance, the boundaries between the Jabal al-Ḥusayn and the al-Waḥdāt Palestinian camps and the rest of the city of Amman. In comparison, the integration of Syrian refugees into Jordanian society and within its urban fabric has been more challenging, as they have been perceived as a threat to stability and to the economy. Jordan hosted more than 800,000 Syrian refugees[2] between 2011 and 2014 of which 650,000 hold a UNHCR (United Nations High Commissioner for Refugees) asylum seeker card. They had to register with their local district police to obtain a Ministry of Interior card. They were given access to schools and hospitals but were not granted the right to work until 2016. The majority of Syrian refugees live in the large cities of Amman, al-Zarqāʾ, and ʾIrbid. In 2020, the three Syrian refugee camps of al-Zaʿtarī, al-ʾAzraq, and Marājīb al-Fuhūd, located in the desert 10 kilometers from al-Mafraq and al-ʾAzraq were hosting only 19 percent of the refugees.[3] Tensions have been increasing between poor Jordanians and Syrian refugees, who are blamed for the rises in rents and unemployment. The 2008–2013 Jordanian housing program *Decent Housing for a Decent Living Program* produced only 8,448 units, and no alternative program was created for low-income citizens. Few humanitarian programs deal with housing per se, other than by giving cash for rent. UNHCR shelter policies focus on the refugee camps and not on the urban settings (UNHCR 2015). The UNHCR only began working on refugees within urban settings in 2009 (Darling 2016).

In this context of tension over access to housing, the Norwegian Refugee Council (NRC)[4] conducted an innovative shelter program in northern Jordan, between July 2013 and February 2015. A thousand Jordanian landlords received financial support to build extra housing units. In exchange, they had to provide twelve to eighteen months of free accommodation to vulnerable Syrian families. The aim of the program was to solve part of the housing crisis by providing affordable formal units to Jordanian families in the long term, while resolving immediate housing issues for Syrian families, to give them time to pay back their debts and settle. It also formalized social interactions between the host communities and the refugees through the signature of formal rental contracts. The project was suspended in February 2015 after the assassination by ISIS of the pilot Muʿādh al-Kasāsiba in Syria. Syrians were then once again asked to register

1 UNRWA (The United Nations Relief and Works Agency for Palestine Refugees) is the UN agency created in 1949 for the refugees from Palestine. It directs ten camps in Jordan: three in Greater Amman municipality (Amman New Camp, or Al-Waḥdāt, Jabal al-Ḥusayn and Mārkā), Talbiyya south of Amman, al-Zarqāʾ, al-Baqaʿa on the road to Jarash, Jarash camp, Sūf, al-Ḥuṣn, and ʾIrbid camp. They host 390,000 Palestinian refugees. https://www.unrwa.org/where-we-work/jordan

2 The 2015 Population and Housing Census states that Jordan hosts 1.3 million Syrian refugees, but the figure is greatly overestimated. The Fafo (a Norwegian research foundation) mission in 2019 did not find the number of refugees counted by the Census in the several localities of the al-Mafraq and ʾIrbid governorates.

3 There are 123,000 Syrian refugees in two UNHCR camps (Ababsa 2018) and in the Emirati camp, https://www.unrwa.org/where-we-work/jordan; https://data2.unhcr.org/en/situations/syria/location/36

4 Created in 1946, under the name of Europahjelpen (Aid to Europe) to give humanitarian assistance to people subjected to forced migration, the Norwegian Refugee Council is one of the largest International NGOs, with 15,000 employees in thirty-two countries. Its role expanded in the 1980s with the rise of Norwegian oil and gas exports.

with the Ministry of Interior and renew all their service cards in a security check. The NRC shelter project resumed in 2016 but with a new concept. Instead of moving refugees to match them with renovated housing units according to their family size, it was decided to help Syrians renovate the dwellings they were already renting.

This chapter assesses the impact of this housing program on social cohesion, seen as interdependency and trust, in the ʾIrbid governorate. It fills a gap in the academic literature on the Syrian crisis, as most papers focus on the housing conditions in the camps (Alhawarin et al 2018), or on integration in European countries. However, few deal with refugee housing within urban settings (Fawaz 2014). This chapter is based on fieldwork conducted in the ʾIrbid governorate between November 2014 and January 2015 as a consultant for the report *In Search of a Home* (NRC 2015). Using part of the NRC shelter project database of 4,584 cases applying to receive free housing (between July 2013 and December 2014), it presents original data about Syrian refugee family composition during the time of refuge, and the necessity of sharing apartments with relatives (married children, but also married siblings and in-laws). I also met fifteen beneficiary families, Jordanians and Syrians, and mayors. The chapter first presents the housing conditions of the refugees, how families share housing units, and then the impact of the NRC shelter project on social cohesion in northern Jordan.

1. Syrian Refugee (under) Housing in Jordan

The integration of refugees in urban settings is a security challenge for the state, as it is a source of social tensions. It is also a challenge in terms of planning, as it takes the form of informal urban sprawl, puts pressure on infrastructures, and widens social disparities within the cities. Jordan copes with the crisis with international financial support, but with few housing-specific policies (Hamilton et al 2018).

The rapid influx of Syrian refugees into northern Jordan during 2013 had a strong impact on the housing market: rental prices went up and thousands of Jordanian families were expelled in order to host Syrian families paying higher rents.[5] Apartments built for students near the JUST university in ʾIrbid were rented to Syrians at a higher rate, leaving the students to find other accommodation. In 2014, the border was closed and conditions in Syria limited the possibility of returning. At this moment, Jordanian landlords started to prefer hosting Syrian refugees, forced to rent (and share) apartments at high prices. Mayors reported hundreds of Jordanian evictions by their landlords, in favor of Syrian tenants.

1.1. Family Ties on Both Sides of the Border

At the begining of the crisis, Syrian refugees relied on Jordanian hospitality, especially in the northern governorates of al-Mafraq and ʾIrbid. As half the migrants were coming from the Darʿā governorate, they were welcomed in al-Ramthā and north al-Mafraq.

[5] UN Habitat presentation during an NRC UNHCR shelter working group, attended by the author on February 26, 2014.

Before the creation of Jordan and Syria at the fall of the Ottoman Empire, this region formed the Ḥawrān plains (Sahl Ḥawrān). As several mayors of the ʾIrbid governorate municipalities recalled at a meeting in 2014, this region, on both sides of the border, shares a common history, language, and tradition. Major tribes and families, such as the al-Sharayda, al-Zuʿbī, al-Rifāʿī, al-Jaradāt, ʿAlwāna, al-Ṭībāwī, Muqdād, Ṣmayd, and al-Zarayqāt, are present in both countries and were separated only in 1921 by the creation of the Emirate of Transjordan under British Mandate, and Syria under French Mandate.[6] No study has yet tackled the question of marital ties between Syrians and Jordanians in north Jordan during the twentieth century, within or outside of the same tribe. There is a tradition in the ʾIrbid governorate towns and villages for men to marry rural Syrian brides, mainly from the region of Darʿā, on the border. This was confirmed by the mayors of al-Ṭayyiba, Kufr Yūbā (West ʾIrbid), and al-Ḥuṣn, at a meeting in December 2014. Several reasons were mentioned for this tradition: young Syrian girls are supposed to be "softly spoken," and "prettier." Another reason for this trend is that the dowry is three to five times cheaper in Syria than in Jordan, even before the crisis, at around 1000 JD to 2000 JD, compared to around 5,000–10,000 JD in northern Jordan.[7] According to Central Bank statistics, there were 291,000 Syrians working in Jordan in 2001 (Al Khouri 2004). The consequence is that, from 2011 to 2014, some Syrian refugees managed to settle in the ʾIrbid governorate thanks to direct and indirect family ties (Ababsa 2021; Peaucelle 2020). Some statistics point to this fact. According to a 2015 UNHCR Home Visit Report, 34.6 percent of Syrian refugee families in Jordan were female-headed. This is a very high number compared to the former ratio in Syria with only 8 percent of female-headed households. In the ʾIrbid governorate, this ratio reaches a record of 40.6 percent (UNHCR 2015). Particularly in the ʾIrbid governorate, which is only 30 km from Darʿā and 90 km from Damascus, this can be explained by the fact that some families split so that the women could obtain support.[8] The men would remain in Syria to fight or to work. But this also points to the existence of family networks prior to the crisis through Jordano-Syrian marriages, and as a consequence, the existence of relatives to protect single mothers. These relatives could be Syrians but also Jordanian in-laws. The NRC, however, gauged that only 23 percent of cases were female-headed in the ʾIrbid governorate, which is half the estimate made by the UNHCR. The NRC did not consider a family to be a female-headed household if an adult male came regularly from Syria to support them.[9] In July 2019, some 83 percent

6 Interviews with ʾIrbid governorate mayors and members of several municipal councils were held on December 16 and 17, 2014: with the director of al-Wasṭiyya district (mutaṣarrif), with al-Ṭayyiba Municipality (raʾīs dīwān baladiyya), and with member of Kufr Yūbā municipal council (West ʾIrbid Municipality) and of al-Ḥuṣn (Bānī ʿUbayd district), on December 16, 2014. Appointments with Greater ʾIrbid Municipality members; with al-Kūrā district director, with al-Ṭayyiba district director, and with a Syrian mukhtar in al-Ṭayyiba, on December 17, 2014. Interviews conducted with Mrs. R.B, ʾIrbid NRC employee.

7 Some Jordanian mayors added that Syrian brides can "enjoy the kindness of Jordanian men." But the other reason is that having fewer relatives to visit than possible Jordanian brides, they have to stay at home, which is much less expensive.

8 The UNHCR tends to support female-headed households, even if some of them are not the most vulnerable.

9 NRC officers would enter the houses and check the presence and number of male shoes at the entrance.

of the 662,000 registered Syrian refugees in Jordan were living outside formal camps in host communities; 530,000 of them were renting apartments and substandard housing units in the northern part of the country. Much of the Syrian refugee population outside of formal camps had settled in already impoverished rural and urban areas in the north of Jordan such as parts of the ʾIrbid and al-Mafraq governorates. During the field visits to the ʾIrbid governorate, I met a single mother, Ens., who was living with her children and parents in a tent on the roof of the (rented) "building of some relatives" in Dayr Abī Saʿīd. There were fourteen people sharing one tent. Her husband was in jail in Syria.

In 2015, the majority of Syrian refugees were located in the Amman–al-Ruṣayfa–al-Zarqāʾ area and around ʾIrbid and al-Mafraq (Figure 7.1). Relative to the local population, according to the 2015 census, their presence was most visible in the governorate of al-Mafraq, where 37.8 percent of the population was composed of Syrian refugees (207,923 out of 549,948 individuals), and ʾIrbid with 19.3 percent of Syrian refugees (343,207 out of 1.77 million inhabitants). This spatial distribution can be explained by the existence of job opportunities in the major cities (in construction and services) and by the existence of familial and work networks that were established long before the crisis.

In the search for work opportunities and proper schooling for children, Syrian refugees settled in the northern part of Jordan, within 100 kilometers of the border. Syrians formed more than half the population in some rural neighborhoods south of ʾIrbid, in al-Ramthā, and in the area north of al-Mafraq. They are also represented in the east of al-Zarqāʾ, where the Emirati camp is located (Figure 7.2).

1.2 Competition for Rents

The arrival of Syrian refugees exacerbated Jordan's existing housing crisis, especially in large cities. The 2015 housing and population census revealed a housing crisis, manifested by a high vacancy rate (18 percent), combined with the fact that 10 percent of housing units were overcrowded. Fifteen percent of the total number of households (or 298,890 households) were sharing conventional dwellings between two and three families in 2015. Twenty-seven percent (81,218) were Jordanian families, mainly young married sons living with their parents, while 73 percent (217,672) were foreign families, mainly Syrian refugees and Egyptian workers.[10] The influx of Syrian refugees increased the demand on rented housing units. Syrian refugees have been employed in the construction sector, replacing Egyptian workers (Ajluni and Kawar 2014). In the ʾIrbid governorate, 183,799 new housing units were built between 2004 and 2015. Of these, 43,486 were built formally, with a prior construction permit (*rukhṣat al-bināʾ*) (24 percent) mainly to be rented; 83,660 were regularized after completion, most of them were constructed by owner-builders. The remaining units were not registered: 56,653 (31 percent, informal) (Hamilton et al. 2018).

Of these new housing units in the ʾIrbid governorate, 84,000 were rented—most of them to non-Jordanians (76,553). These rents created a good source of income in the governorate: I estimate at 187 million JD the rents that were paid every year in the ʾIrbid governorate. This constituted a major form of support to the local economy, and

[10] DOS 2015, table 2.7 by citizenship (Jordanian, non-Jordanian).

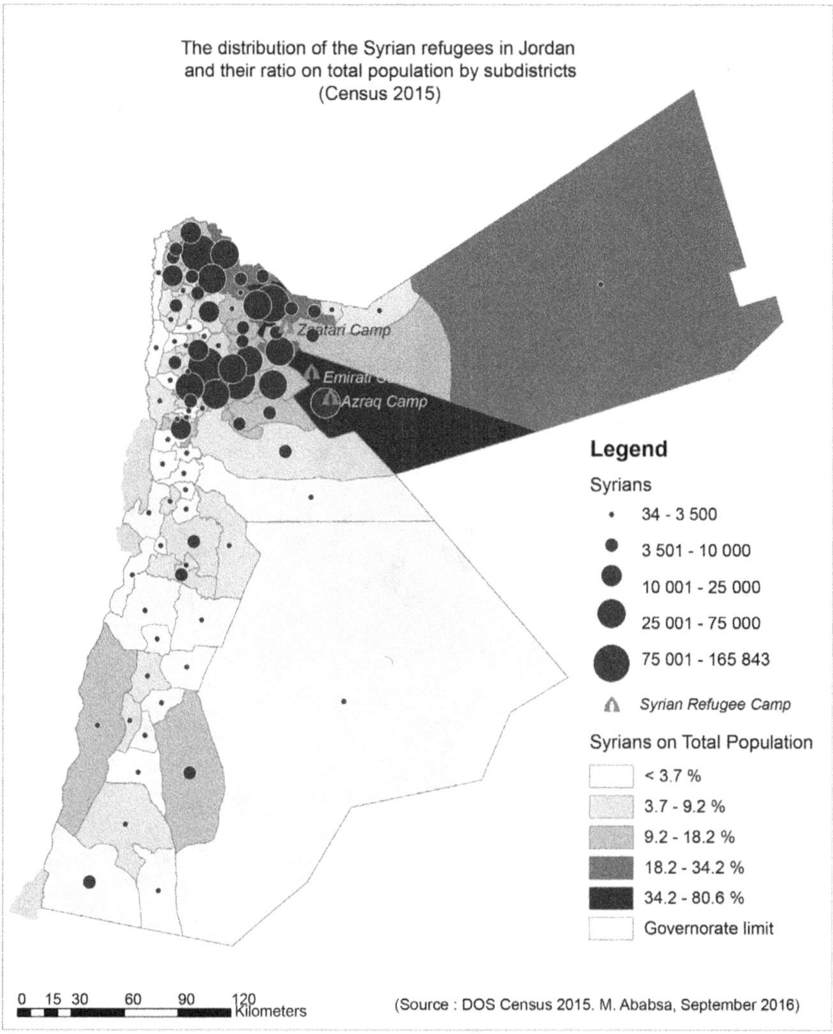

Figure 7.1 Distribution of Syrian refugees in Jordan in 2015 (Population Census 2015).

also the basis for contractual links between host communities and refugees.[11] Eighty percent of the rents were more than 100 JD per month in 2015 in 'Irbid, whereas 80 percent of the rents were under 100 JD in 2004. In 2015, half of the rents were over 150 JD per month in 'Irbid, which is high compared to the median monthly household income of 625 JD at the time (Figure 7.3).[12]

[11] Calculated from JPHC 2015 table 2.10, by multiplying each rental unit by its maximum monthly rent.

[12] Estimated from HEIS 2017 table 2.3. 57.6 percent of Jordan households bring in less than 833 JD per month in 2015.

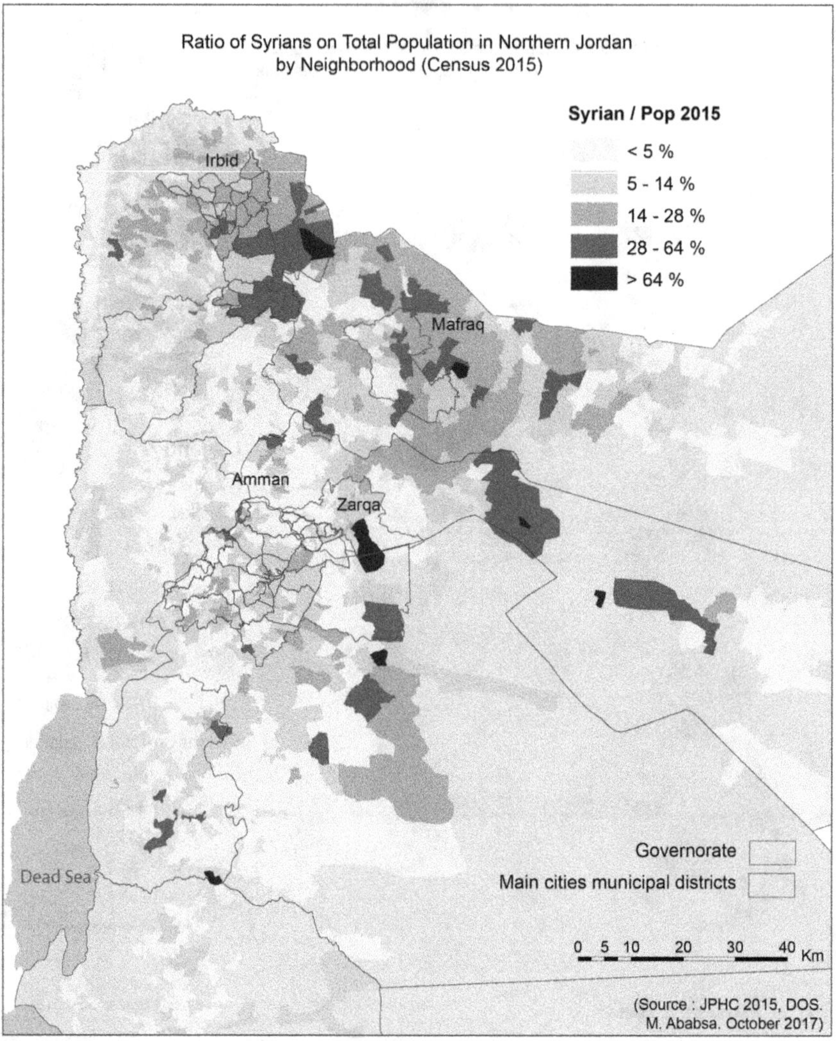

Figure 7.2 Ratio of Syrian refugees to total population in northern Jordan in 2015.

The increase in rents particularly affected young Jordanians, who had to delay their wedding, as they could not find any apartment to rent for 100–150 JD, which they could do before 2011.[13] In low-income Jordanian families in the 'Irbid governorate, marriages were delayed due to the unavailability of housing, or married sons live in their parents' home. The other reason for the delay in getting married is the high unemployment rate, at 42 percent for young people (IMF 2020). In the 'Irbid governorate, in 2014, 80 percent of the Syrian refugees were living in apartments, 15 percent in cement houses, and 1.3 percent in tents (UNHCR 2014). A significant proportion (48 percent) of them

[13] Fieldwork in the 'Irbid governorate, December 2014. Confirmed by the census 2015.

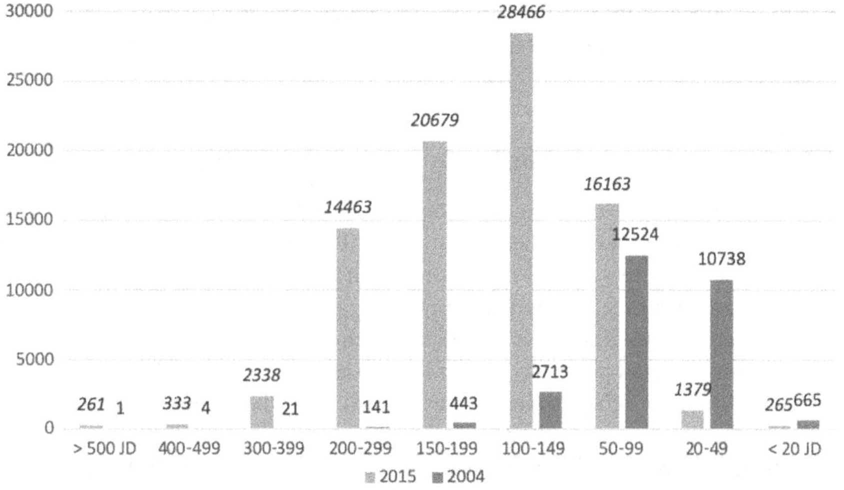

Figure 7.3 Number of rented apartments by rent amount in JD in the 'Irbid governorate (2004 and 2015). Source: DOS, *Population and Housing Census* 2004 and 2015, table 2.10.

lived in accommodation affected by damp or mold (NRC 2015). Many reported facing significant problems with septic tanks and sewage systems, with the bad odors that come with it. Furthermore, 18 percent of the rented accommodation did not provide basic shelter from the weather, with roofs leaking rainwater or plastic sheets in place of windows. Most Syrian refugees were suffering from lack of thermal comfort inside their shelter because of poor insulation, humidity, and poor heating facilities. One-third of households had no access to any sort of heating and had very poor clothing and an insufficient number of blankets. For the others, the most common type of heating was gas, followed by kerosene and wood. Such conditions are detrimental to health (UNHCR, UNICEF, WFP 2014).

The NRC assessment of housing conditions of applicants revealed that vulnerable Syrian families were resorting to renting substandard accommodation, often at inflated prices. Forty-two percent of the refugees had to pay between 100 and 200 JD a month for apartments that had been rented at half the price before the crisis (UNHCR 2014).[14] This was half their income. In January 2014, Syrian refugees outside of the camps were living in rudimentary shelters or tents, abandoned or partially constructed buildings, or in overcrowded and poorly maintained flats (UNHCR 2015). In search of affordable housing and assistance, Syrian refugees were experimenting with multiple displacements. In the 'Irbid governorate, a third of Syrian refugees moved once, and the other two-thirds moved more than twice (24 percent two times and 25 percent three times) (Care 2014). These multiple displacements impacted the ability of Syrian refugees to access basic services like health and education (NRC 2015). This

[14] In November 2014, an apartment in one of villages around 'Irbid was rented at 70 JD to Jordanians, but 150 JD to Syrian refugees. Interview in the 'Irbid governorate with a Jordanian beneficiary of the NRC shelter program.

also badly impacted the possibility of children attending a full school year. Changing schools during the term results in the loss of the semester, according to the Ministry of Education law.

1.3. Competition for Housing as a Source of Tension

Eighty-three percent of Jordanians and 77 percent of Syrians identified access to housing as a cause of tension within their community (REACH 2014). In 2014, the UNDP (United Nations Development Programme) published a survey of household income and expenditure in the ʾIrbid and al-Mafraq governorates, conducted in collaboration with the Department of Statistics (DOS). It was only posted online for two months, as the questions were not politically acceptable, and as it included mistakes. It accredited the idea that Syrian refugees were the main reason for the increase in rental prices and that their presence created additional intercommunal tension: 98.2 percent of the Jordanians surveyed noted an increase in general prices since 2010;[15] 91.9 percent said that this was due to the presence of Syrian refugees; and 55.2 percent added that their income had decreased because of the Syrian refugees. This denoted a major concern among inhabitants in the northern governorates over the Syrian presence.

In May 2015, an assessment of the social cohesion in host communities in northern Jordan was published by the NGO REACH, based on a survey of the perception of delivery of municipal services in sixteen municipalities[16] (governorates of ʾIrbid, al-Mafraq, and al-Zarqāʾ). The panel consisted of 6,166 people (83 percent Jordanians, 15 percent Syrians, and 2 percent of other nationalities). It found that "the arrival of Syrian refugees has led to further strain on already overburdened municipal services." The challenges to social cohesion emerged on two levels: tensions between Jordanians and Syrians about rental prices, job opportunities, and public hygiene (reduction of water delivery, increase in pests), and poor communication between citizens and local government. This last point had become a major issue since the beginning of the crisis. According to this survey, the most prominent changes in their communities since the influx of refugees were water shortages (38 percent), rising cost of living (29 percent), waste accumulation (12 percent), and increased competition over jobs (8 percent). More than 72 percent of Jordanian respondents stated that these issues led to tensions in the area where they live (REACH 2015). The main drivers for social tension included structural causes that predated the Syrian crisis (high levels of poverty, resource scarcity), socioeconomic causes (cultural and social norms between Syrian villagers and urban Jordanian dwellers), and proximate causes (decreasing access to affordable quality housing, access to jobs, and the perception of the international aid is mainly targeted at Syrians) (WVI 2015).

[15] UNDP, DOS 2014, "Household Expenditure and Income Survey in the governorates of ʾIrbid and al-Mafraq," in Arabic. The report suffered from methodological issues and was available online for only one month.

[16] Nine "treatment" municipalities: al-Ramthā al-Jadīda, al-Sarḥān, al-Shuʿla, al-Zaʿtarī and al-Manshiyya, Balaʿamā al-Jadīda, Gharb ʾIrbid, ʾIrbid al-Kubrā, al-Mafraq al-Kubrā, and Sahl Hawrān) and seven "control" municipalities: al-Kfarāt, al-Mazār al-Jadīda, al-Yarmūk al-Jadīda, al-Zarqāʾ, Ḥūshā al-Jadīda, Riḥāb al-Jadīda, Sabḥā, and al-Dafyāna.

1.4. Vulnerability and Isolation

In 2014, 74 percent of Syrian refugees in host communities were classified as "extremely vulnerable" or under the abject poverty line (which is to be able to afford only to buy food, or 336 JD per year per capita in 2010) with only 26 percent classified as being a moderate or low level of vulnerability,[17] or around the Jordanian poverty line of 68 JD per capita per month (WFP 2014). Refugees living in Jordan mainly relied on diminishing savings and cash assistance to meet their basic needs. Two-thirds of refugees reported an income of less than 200 JD a month, and half of those most vulnerable had an income of less than 100 JD a month. This income derived, most of the time, from informal employment at 10 JD a day, once or twice a week. According to the NRC shelter database 2014, 60 percent of Syrian refugees living in host communities managed to pay their rent with income from work; 12 percent of Syrian refugees had a permenant job, even though it was prohibited. Two-thirds had casual jobs, in agriculture (olive picking in the fall, work in greenhouses), in construction, and in services (waiters in restaurants, etc.). The percentage of Syrian refugees who declared that they had no job was 26.1 percent. After nearly four years, only 10 percent of refugees still had enough savings to pay the rent. Twelve percent were receiving assistance from community-based organizations (mainly Islamic charities) or local individuals. But 13.5 percent of those who were most vulnerable were unable to pay their rent and had to rely on donations from the UNHCR (NRC 2015). A third of refugees were in debt to their landlord, and some landlords preferred to evict them and to replace them with other Syrian tenants (Care 2014). A typical case is illustrated by Basma (46 years old), who used to live in a small apartment rented for 100 JD a month. She lived there along with her husband, children, and her elderly mother. This made a total of nine people sharing a room. The house suffered from a leaking roof, which led to visible mold problems on the ceiling and walls. Basma's nineteen-year-old son was working, for less than 100 JD a month.

A consequence of impoverishment and perceived tensions was isolation at home. Isolation is a frequent negative coping mechanism for forced migrants, that affects women and men, forcing them to keep children out of school for fear of aggression (in the street). In host communities, children and women can become isolated at home, with one-third "rarely" or "never" leaving their homes for fear of harassment (UNHCR, UNICEF, WFP 2014). In July 2013, the International Medical Corps depicted the disastrous state of the Syrian refugees' mental health in Jordan (EMPHNET, WHO, IMC 2013). Such traumas impact the Syrian refugees' capacity to integrate into the local community in Jordan.

The Syrian refugees hosted within the ʾIrbid governorate's towns and villages were, for the most part, under the poverty line. Although some had family ties prior to the

[17] In 2014, UNHCR started assessing the vulnerability through a common grid, the Vulnerability Assessment Framework (VAF), based on the welfare (difference between income and expenditure), dependency ratio, health, food security, and shelter. The poverty thresholds are based on the Jordan poverty line of 68 JD per person per month drawn in 2010. People who are under this poverty line are considered as highly vulnerable by the VAF, and people under the abject poverty line are severely vulnerable (UNHCR 2019).

war, most had to rent small, expensive apartments and share them with close relatives as a coping strategy.

2. Overcrowding and Family Composition in Time of Refuge

In a context of rental price inflation and resource depletion, half of Syrian refugee families had to share their homes with relatives.

2.1. Sharing a Home

The 2015 Population and Housing Census provides an insight into the housing conditions of non-Jordanians in Jordan. Half the non-Jordanian households were sharing housing units as the rent had become too expensive (51 percent). This was true for Syrians, as well as for Egyptian and Asian workers. In detail, 21 percent of non-Jordanian households lived in apartments shared between two families and 19 percent between three families. A total of 217,672 non-Jordanian households were sharing their housing units (Table 7.1). According to the census, a household was defined as being relatives sharing the same meal under the same roof. An unmarried adult fed by the head of household was not counted as a separate household, a married one was.

Within the ʾIrbid governorate, 38 percent of non-Jordanian households (or 29,771 households, mainly Syrian refugees) were sharing their housing unit between three families. This was exceptionally high, and it created internal tensions, particularly in the kitchen and the bathrooms. Twenty-four percent of non-Jordanian households were sharing with one other family (18,825 households), and 27,957 non-Jordanian households were living by themselves, without sharing their unit (Table 7.1). Sharing apartments helps reduce renting costs but has bad consequences on child protection, with lack of intimacy for women. Having to share the kitchen and bathrooms with another woman (sister, sister-in-law, or mother-in-law) created frequent tensions.[18]

Most of the shared occupied housing units were located south of ʾIrbid, in al-Ḥuṣn and in the southeastern part of the ʾIrbid governorate, in rural areas (al-Naʿīma), and throughout the city of Amman (Figure 7.4).

According to the NRC shelter project database, an average of 1.7 families were sharing apartments. The average apartment size was 91 m^2 in the ʾIrbid governorate. An apartment counts an average number of 2.8 rooms closed by a door (which is how NRC defines a "housing unit" in its shelter project). A third of refugees were living with more than ten people per apartment, reducing the minimal vital space required. This means that an average of 3.4 people were sharing bedrooms, which defines overcrowding, with adults, adolescents, and children of both sexes in the same room.[19]

[18] Interviews December 2014, ʾIrbid governorate.

[19] Using Sphere standards to estimate sufficient living space is not appropriate for urban settings as most Syrian households met the standard of 3.5 m^2 per person, but were, nevertheless, suffering from insufficient living space (UNHCR, UNICEF, WFP 2014).

Table 7.1 Number of Non-Jordanian Households (HH) Sharing Housing Units (HU) by Type and by Governorate in 2015

	One Non-Jordanian HH per HU		**Two Non-Jordanian HH per HU**		**Three Non-Jordanian HH per HU**	
Governorate	Conventional HU	*Non-Conventional HU (tents, etc.)*	Conventional	*Non-Conventional*	Conventional	*Non-Conventional*
Amman	151,526	*1,310*	68,813	*330*	49,261	*214*
al-Balqāʾ	10,580	*1,011*	1,293	*52*	2,854	*72*
al-Zarqāʾ	34,621	*3,999*	18,008	*3,504*	14,565	*4,515*
Māʾdabā	4,206	*71*	463	*0*	430	*0*
ʾIrbid	27,957	*535*	18,825	*234*	29,771	*298*
al-Mafraq	18,101	*23,308*	1,022	*878*	481	*457*
Jarash	8,385	*418*	3,339	*176*	250	*3*
ʿAjlūn	2,540	*69*	138	*0*	91	*0*
al-Karak	4,184	*23*	1,326	*4*	2,147	*12*
al-Ṭafīla	843	*10*	2	*2*	0	*0*
Maʿān	1,597	*16*	528	*0*	832	*0*
al-ʿAqaba	5,612	*370*	829	*10*	2,404	*21*
Kingdom	270,152	*31,140*	114,586	*5,190*	103,086	*5,592*

Source: DOS, Population and Housing Census 2015, table 2.7 by citizenship.

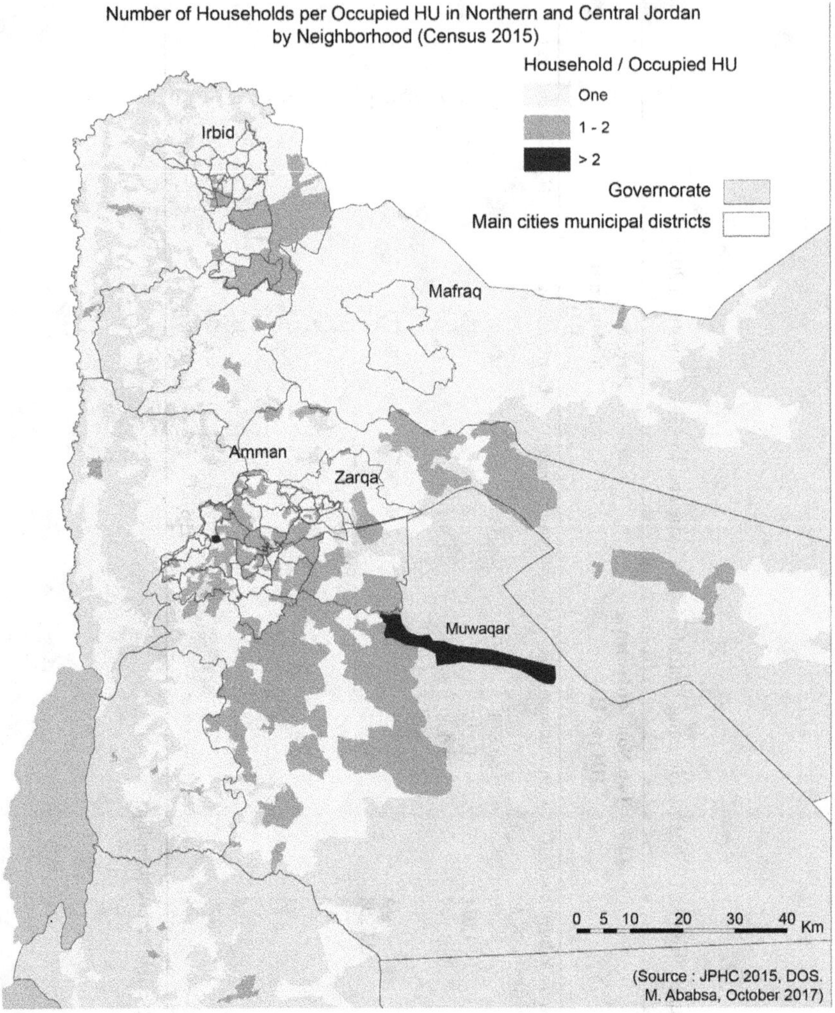

Figure 7.4 Number of households per occupied Housing unit (HU) in Northern and Central Jordan by neighborhood. Source: DOS, *Population and Housing Census* 2015.

2.2. Family Composition in Time of Refuge

The NRC shelter program database offers an exceptional insight into the family composition of refugees in exile. By the end of December 2014, out of 4,584 Syrian refugee families applying to receive free accommodation from the NRC project, 48 percent were composed of an immediate nuclear household of one or two parents and children. A third of families included two nuclear households (32.9 percent), 14.2 percent included three households, and 5 percent four or more households (Table 7.2). Two-thirds of the most vulnerable Syrian refugees (70.7 percent) lived in extended families.

Table 7.2 Number of Syrian Households Sharing the Same Dwelling, in Northern Jordan, December 2014

	Number of Syrian households sharing the same dwelling					
Governorate and District	**1**	**2**	**3**	**4**	**5 +**	**Total**
ʾIRBID Governorate						
Banī Kināna	17	7	7	1		32
Banī ʿUbayd	413	287	114	44	1	859
East ʾIrbid	195	133	50	16		394
ʾIrbid City	233	223	108	30		594
al-Kūrā	318	194	75	32		619
al-Mazār	148	87	50	21	2	308
North ʾIrbid	103	78	34	4		219
al-Ramthā	15	10	6	5		36
al- Ṭayyiba	121	96	46	14		277
al-Wasṭiyya	152	85	21	8		266
West ʾIrbid	201	134	66	21		422
Total ʾIrbid Governorate	*1,916*	*1,334*	*577*	*196*	3	*4,026*
ʿAJLŪN Governorate						
ʿAjlūn	56	29	11	9		
al-ʿUyūn	36	15	7	1		
al-Shafā	1					
al-Jnayd	8	5	1			
Total ʿAjlūn Governorate	*101*	*49*	*19*	*10*		*179*
AL-MAFRAQ Governorate						
al-Mafraq	3	6	3			
al-Ruwayshīd		1	2			
Total al-Mafraq Governorate	*3*	*7*	*5*			*15*
JARASH Governorate						
Jarash	196	120	38	9		363
AMMAN Governorate						
Amman				1		1
TOTAL	**2,216**	**1,510**	**639**	**216**	**3**	**4,584**

Source: Author calculation from NRC Shelter Database, July 2013–Dec 2014.

Prior to the war, Syrians were not sharing housing units at this level, even in the rural southern regions of Darʿā. According to the 2004 Syrian Population and Housing Census, only 4.7 percent households had to share their dwelling with relatives (Table 7.3). However, it was common practice in the Damascus and Darʿā governorates, with 9 percent of households without their own dwelling, according to the census. This was a very high figure, pointing to the lack of affordable housing in these governorates. In Jordan, in the same year, almost no Jordanian family had to share housing units.[20]

As a result of the coexistence of several generations and of relatives, the average number of individuals per family was very high among Syrian refugee families in ʾIrbid, about 8.4, while in Syria it was only 5 (Courbage 2007) and 5.4 in Jordan. In some of the most vulnerable cases, more than ten people were living under the same roof. The

20 I have compared the number of inhabited housing units to the number of households by governorate. With 941,155 inhabited housing units for 941,467 households (DOS, Population and Housing Census 2004).

Table 7.3 Number of Households Sharing Their Housing Units in Syria, in 2004

	Population 2004	Household number	Inhabited housing units	Households sharing HU	Percent of HH sharing HU
Damascus	1,552,161	340,864	310,284	30,580	*9.0*
Rif Damascus	2,273,074	426,228	404,957	21,271	*5.0*
Darʿā	843,478	132,843	120,752	12,091	*9.1*
al-Suwaydāʾ	313,231	64,135	61,901	2,234	*3.5*
al-Qunayṭra	66,627	10,624	10,274	350	*3.3*
Ḥalab	4,045,166	706,498	674,239	32,259	*4.6*
Ḥamā	1,384,953	233,563	220,612	12,951	*5.5*
Ḥumṣ	1,529,402	271,500	258,679	12,821	*4.7*
ʾIdlib	1,258,427	201,685	194,796	6,889	*3.4*
Ṭarṭūs	701,395	143,051	141,045	2,006	*1.4*
al-Ḥassaka	1,275,118	181,195	179,083	2,112	*1.2*
al-Raqqa	793,514	120,163	114,065	6,098	*5.1*
Dayr al-Zūr	1,004,747	132,874	130,163	2,711	*2.0*
Total	**17,920,844**	**3,150,358**	**3,003,073**	**147,285**	***4.7***

Source: Author calculation from the 2004 Syrian Population and Housing Census.

Table 7.4 Syrian Refugee Family Composition by Family Members (NRC 2014)

	Female HH	Male HH	Total	*Percent*
Parents and children	233	1,822	2,056	*44.9*
Father and relatives	24	753	777	*17.0*
Mother and children	293	261	554	*12.1*
Siblings with/without children	63	432	495	*10.8*
In-laws	98	313	411	*9*
Man and two wives		24	24	*0.5*
Other	141	124	267	*5.8*
Grand total	852	3,729	4,584	*100*

Source: Author calculation, NRC database, Shelter project, 4 584 cases, 31-12-2014.

average family size of the beneficiaries of the NRC shelter project was of 9.6 persons.[21] In order to attribute them a proper dwelling in terms of size and number of rooms, the NRC recorded the family composition within the dwelling of the applicants. It constitutes a unique source for describing the composition of Syrian families in refuge (Table 7.4).

Of 4,584 cases, half the families living under the same roof were composed of parents with their children, including some grandparents. This is similar to the situation in Syria prior to the war. Seventeen percent were households headed by a father, with children (and married sons); 12 percent of the families were composed of mothers and children without fathers.

Much more interestingly, 11 percent of families sharing the same dwelling were composed of siblings: brothers and their wives and children, or married sisters living

[21] NRC Beneficiaries Database, Jordan, 966 moved in cases, December 31, 2014.

together with their children. This was an unusual situation in Syria prior to the war and so was an adaptation to the context of exile and refuge.[22] However, it confirms anthropologists' theories on the importance of siblings in the Middle East, much more than the patriarchal models: brothers have to look after their sisters, protect them (Conte 2011). In Syria, as in the entire Middle East, marriage with a first or second cousin is the norm in order to "protect honor," as both the girl and the boy are well known from childhood, and to reduce the dowry. This was the case in 35 percent of the marriages in 2009, with variations from 22.1 percent in the urban coastal region of al-Lādhiqiyya to 67.5 percent in the more tribal and rural eastern governorate of al-Raqqa (Othman, Saadat 2009). To this, one must add marriage by exchange (*badal*), between two brothers and two sisters not from the same family. This type of marriage avoids dowry payments and is said to prevent domestic violence against women, as the brother would be worried about the fate of his sister (Conte 2011).

Domestic tensions arose around the use of the bathrooms and of the kitchen in a context of water shortages. Those tensions increased with a mother-in-law sharing the same kitchen and bathroom as her daughter-in-law, at the time of cooking and for personal care. Offering a new housing unit was a way to solve part of the "mother-in-law issue" within most of the beneficiary families.[23] Among the NRC shelter program beneficiaries, I met Aziza, a 55-year-old widow, when she moved to the apartment provided for her family in Kufr ʾAsad. A member of the Bashayra tribe, she had lost a total of fourteen members of her extended family during the war in Syria. She recalled her family dignity, when, during the 1967 War, her father sheltered Jordanian fighters arriving from al-Qunayṭra. A mother of five girls and four boys, she lost a daughter during the hostilities in Syria, in their village of al- Ḥirāk, near Darʿā, in 2014. One of her sons managed to find work in construction, but he did not bring home more than 10 JD per day, on the days he was able to work. One of her daughters' husbands was also working. He regretted that he had not moved to Turkey.[24]

Despite the strong solidarity between family members, and the several coping strategies adopted, most of the Syrian refugees were in dire need of assistance for housing in 2014, when their meager savings had been depleted after one year of migration. The NRC shelter project came as a relief for nearly 5,000 Syrian households and 1,000 Jordanian landlords. It was also a very innovative way of enhancing social cohesion through bridging[25] between Jordanians and the Syrian refugees.

3. The Norwegian Refugee Council Host Communities Shelter Program

The NRC Urban Shelter project started in August 2013 in the ʾIrbid governorate, with the agreement of the Ministry of Planning and International Cooperation. The NRC

22 There was the case, for instance, of Rania, a 31-year-old refugee who used to live with her family and widowed sister in the town of Zūbya, in al-Mazār, ʾIrbid. Her son was sick and needed constant treatment, which UNHCR cash assistance made possible.

23 E. J., head of NRC shelter programs, intervention during a Ifpo seminar, May 16, 2019.

24 Interview in Kufr ʾAsad, December 1, 2014.

25 Refers to links across social groups (Altaï 2020).

Table 7.5 NRC Fund Amount to Landlords in JD by Contract Length

Number of housing units	*12-month contract*	*18-month contract*
1	1,000	1,400
2	2,000	2,800
3	3,000	4,200
4	4,000	5,600

Source: NRC flyer about the Shelter program, 2015.

announced in the press that it would give financial support to any Jordanian landlord currently engaged in the building of additional rooms or housing units within the 'Irbid governorate, in exchange for hosting refugees.

3.1. NRC support to Jordanian landlords

In mid-2013, flyers and posters in Arabic were distributed in each 'Irbid governorate municipality and in the NRC drop-in centers. They encouraged any Jordanian house-owner, with property deeds, wishing to renovate his home or add an additional floor to apply to the NRC shelter program. The conditions given were that the landlord should have valid ownership documents (*tapu* or *gūshān*)[26] and that the property should not be situated more than 2 kilometers away from the nearest public services. The NRC did not put any income conditions for the applicants, with the mistaken preconception that most of them, as Jordanians, had reduced incomes. The NRC offered to cover only up to 80 percent of the construction or renovation costs. The payment was based on 1,000 JD per housing unit if it was inhabited by a Syrian refugee family for over 12 months, and 1,400 JD if over 18 months. A housing unit was defined as a room closed by a door. An apartment could then include between one and three housing units, plus one bathroom and one kitchen. The maximum amount of 5,600 JD was then given to the landlords in three installments over a period of three months to create new housing units (Table 7.5).

The amounts provided by the NRC were high compared to governmental support to vulnerable groups for their housing needs. As a comparison, the governmental housing schemes from 2008 to 2013 offered 547 plots of land in site and services projects across the kingdom. The beneficiaries received 5,000 JD to build their homes within the framework of the King's Initiative for the Poor. In order to finish new housing units, half of Jordanians had contracted loans with the Housing Bank and Islamic banks and were borrowing from relatives.[27] According to the 2014 Department of Statistics Household Expenditure and Income Survey for 'Irbid and al-Mafraq, half of these loans were for more than 5,000 JD.[28] Of these loans, 27.2 percent were for building a residence and 16.6 percent for property maintenance.

[26] *Tapu* is the Ottoman word for title deed and *gūshān* the Arabic colloquial one.
[27] Interviews, Jordan 2014.
[28] By removing half of the HH who have no loan. We did not include the category "don't know" in order to have a sample close to 100 percent. Household Expenditure and Income Survey, 'Irbid and al-Mafraq governorates, Department of Statistics, UNDP, December 2014.

In 2013-2014, the NRC gave an average of 3,900 JD but could give up to 5,600 JD by applicant, which would cover a third to a quarter of total construction costs (15,000 to 20,000 JD to build a second floor). As a consequence, 70 percent of landlords made improvements to their apartment, with the idea of giving it to their children later on. The NRC estimated that the construction of 4,000 units injected more than 7 million JD into the Jordanian economy (1,750 JD per housing unit on average), through construction materials, labor costs, and other income generating opportunities. According to the Jordanian Housing and Urban Development Corporation, NRC shelters had a positive impact as they allowed for the construction of high standard apartments, increasing the value of the properties and giving job opportunities to Jordanian companies.

Out of 966 contracts signed and delivered, 936 were in the 'Irbid Governorate. It was a direct contribution of 936 new apartments to the housing stock, or a fifth of the housing units built formally by the private market (5,529 in 2013, Housing and Urban Development Corporation statistics) (Figure 7.5).

3.2. Syrian Beneficiaries' Acceptance of NRC Shelter

Syrians who wanted to apply for the free accommodation were directed to the NRC by partners such as the UNHCR, Save the Children, Care, and local NGOs. A lot were also self-registered in the NRC office in the center of 'Irbid. Seventy-five percent of the Syrian refugees who applied to the NRC shelter program had spent time within the UNCHR camps. Faced with the high demand for free accommodation, the NRC developed its own tool to estimate the vulnerability of Syrian applicants for its various assistance projects. It involved a scoring system based on the level of vulnerability.[29] By the end of December 2014, the NRC shelter project database included 4,964 cases—head of household and relatives—totaling 42,000 individuals. Forty percent of the applicants, although poor, were declared ineligible (1,938), as they had an acceptable level of income and support (from family members or NGOs). A quarter of the cases were accepted, matched to a property and moved into apartments, or were soon to be moved (20 percent were moved in, and 6.3 percent were matched to a property). A quarter of the applicants were on waiting lists. Around 10 percent of vulnerable Syrian refugees declined apartments offered to them, mainly because of their remote location in villages, far from relatives and job opportunities. From the very start, the main criticism of the NRC shelter program was that it forced Syrians to move to remote rural locations. And indeed, an internal non-acceptance analysis showed that moving beneficiaries from rural to urban areas resulted in 67 percent acceptance versus 17 percent non-acceptance, whereas moving them from urban to rural areas had the opposite effect—12 percent acceptance versus 71 percent non-acceptance.[30]

[29] To become eligible to the NRC shelter program, a Syrian family had to total 30 points. It gave priority to young, female, and elderly headed households and to a number of disabilities (ranging from 5 to 15 points, according to the presence of male adults). It also considers health conditions (ranging from 2 to 4 points); living conditions (taking in overcrowding and insalubrity, ranging from 7 to 11 points); economic conditions (and whether external assistance is given or not, ranging from 5 to 10 points); and the security of tenure (including risk of eviction, ranging from 6 to 10 points). Comments are added to flag vulnerable cases that could not reach the 30 points score.

[30] NRC, 2014, Non Acceptance Analysis. Jordan office. February 2014—unpublished report.

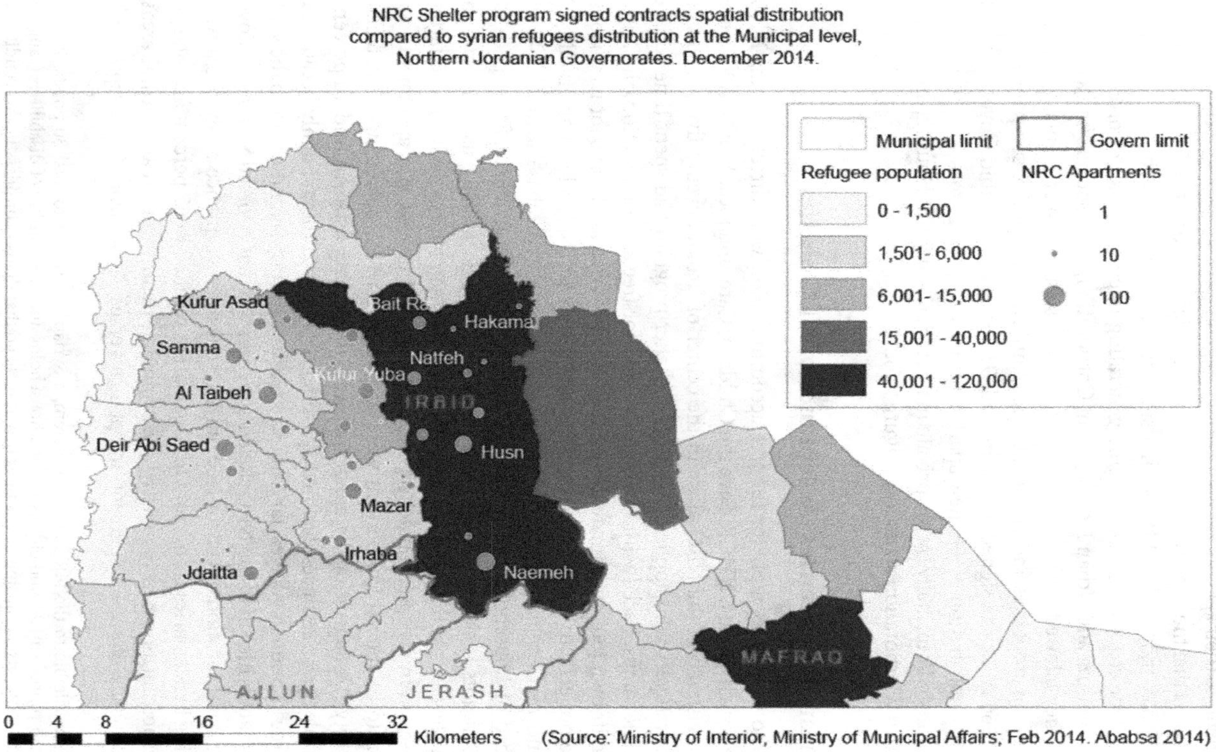
NRC Shelter program signed contracts spatial distribution
compared to syrian refugees distribution at the Municipal level,
Northern Jordanian Governorates. December 2014.
Municipal limit
Govern limit
Refugee population
NRC Apartments
0 - 1,500
1,501- 6,000
6,001- 15,000
15,001 - 40,000
40,001 - 120,000
1
10
100
Kufur Asad
Samma
Al Taibeh
Deir Abi Saed
Bait Ra
Hakama
Natfeh
Kufur Yuba
IRBID
Husn
Mazar
Irhaba
Jdaitta
Naemeh
MAFRAQ
AJLUN
JERASH
0
4
8
16
24
32
Kilometers
(Source: Ministry of Interior, Ministry of Municipal Affairs; Feb 2014. Ababsa 2014)

Figure 7.5 NRC shelter program spatial distribution.

Figure 7.6 NRC shelter program Syrian beneficiary receiving his new apartment, Jdaytā, ʾIrbid governorate. December 2, 2014 (photo Ababsa).

Once a Syrian family had been matched to a Jordanian property, three rental contracts were signed: one in order to protect the owners from degradation, another to protect the refugees from eviction, and one with the NRC. If a landlord had applied to host several families, he had to sign separate contracts with each one. The NRC counseling department followed each step of the program, mediating between the refugees and the Jordanian landlords. At the start of the program, some landlords tried to obtain additional payment from the refugees, for water and electricity (50 JD per month, whereas a normal bill was between 30 to 40 JD). The NRC had stipulated that independent electricity and water meters would be set in each apartment, but the installation costs were high (250 JD for an electricity meter), and some landlords did not want to comply.

Between 2013 and 2015, a total of 960 Jordanian families benefited from the NRC Host Communities Shelter program. In the ʾIrbid, ʿAjlūn, and Jarash governorates, 5,586 housing units were renovated, in 142 locations, hosting 20,000 Syrian refugees.[31] It was considered by the NRC and the government as a successful program. The main issue was that NRC "matched" Jordanian housing units only with the size of households, not with the district of residence. In half the cases, the housing units were in rural areas and small towns, thus increasing transportation costs to markets and jobs. Settling in a remote village in search of cheaper rent has the consequence of being cut off from the refugee community and from job opportunities. Moving also affected

[31] http://en.ammonnews.net/article.aspx?articleno=32904#.XUZ_KZMzY_U

Figure 7.7 NRC shelter program in a remote village, ʾIrbid governorate. December 2, 2014 (photo Ababsa).

families legally, caused extended families to be separated, and broke community support bonds (Wagner 2017). These refugees had already moved a lot in search of better job opportunities and cheaper rents.

As the majority of beneficiaries moved from one area to another within the NRC program, it affected their access to health services negatively as they were linked by their Ministry of Interior registration card to hospitals within their district of registration. For instance, Bashar, a 48-year-old Syrian refugee, married with five children, received from the NRC a basement apartment in al-Ṭayyiba—a town of 20,000 inhabitants located 13 kilometer west of ʾIrbid (Figure 7.7). As the apartment was in a remote location, far from any markets, clinics or schools, he had to pay 40 JD a month for transportation to drive his children to school in al-Ṭayyiba. The landlord had offered them the apartment, after the NRC contract, for a monthly rent of 75 JD, which was affordable but relatively high for a rural area.[32]

3.3. Relations between Landlords and Syrian Refugees at the End of the Rental Contract

At the end of their shelter contract with the NRC, less than half (46 percent) of the beneficiaries stayed in the district in which the NRC had given them a shelter. The

[32] Interview in al-Ṭayyiba, December 2014, for the preparation of NRC report, *In Search of a Home*.

other half went back to the district where their Ministry of Interior card had been issued. Out of the beneficiaries whose contract had ended, less than a third remained in the same property. In two-thirds of the cases, the Jordanian landlord offered the Syrians the option to stay in the apartment, but half of the landlords asked for a higher rent. Some landlords had wrongly considered NRC support as rent compensation. As a consequence, at the end of the contract, they asked for an average rent of 170 JD, twice the former price.

The Syrian refugees who managed to stay were paying an average rent of 108 JD a month in 2015. This was much less than they had been paying prior to joining the NRC shelter program. According to the NRC, the reduction in rent was explained by the fact that the program had provided more units on the market.

At the end of their contract, the majority of the beneficiaries of the NRC shelter program tried to join relatives in order to share the rent costs. Two-thirds were worried about finding next month's rent. At the end of her contract with the NRC, Ens. and her family moved to al-Ramthā. They rented an apartment for 130 JD, plus 20 JD for water and electricity. She was receiving 180 JD a month in cash assistance from the UNHCR Iris eye scan system "basmat al-ʿayn" (cash assistance for the most vulnerable, mainly women). From time to time, she worked as a maid for Jordanian families. Nevertheless, in January 2015, her parents were planning to go back to Syria, and she was afraid of such a prospect.

4. The Impact of NRC Shelter Program on Social Cohesion

4.1. Improved Living Conditions and Social Relations

The NRC project improved housing security for Syrian refugees. Previously, 24 percent of participants had been under threat of eviction. This percentage dropped significantly after joining the project in 2015, and 35 percent of participants expressed an improvement in their sense of security after joining the program. Only 7 percent mentioned feeling insecure for reasons related to the uncertainty of their situation after finishing the contract. In regard to housing, most of the beneficiaries appreciated having a place to live outside the camps because they had more privacy and more stability. However, during the focus groups, they mentioned several downsides to their housing units, including location and utilities (NRC 2015).

After six months, refugees had managed to send their children to school, and most important of all, child labor had been reduced by four (from 21 percent to 5 percent of cases according to the 2015 NRC survey). Along with psychological relief, the reduction in child labor is the major benefit of rent-free accommodation. As rent was secured, Syrian refugees had more money to spend on medication and food. While benefiting from free shelter over a period of one year to eighteen months, a third of the Syrian beneficiaries said they felt more secure, two-thirds of them managed to pay back their debts.

The NRC shelter program helped Syrian refugees to build temporary resilience in the large towns and cities in which it was implemented. But the project failed in

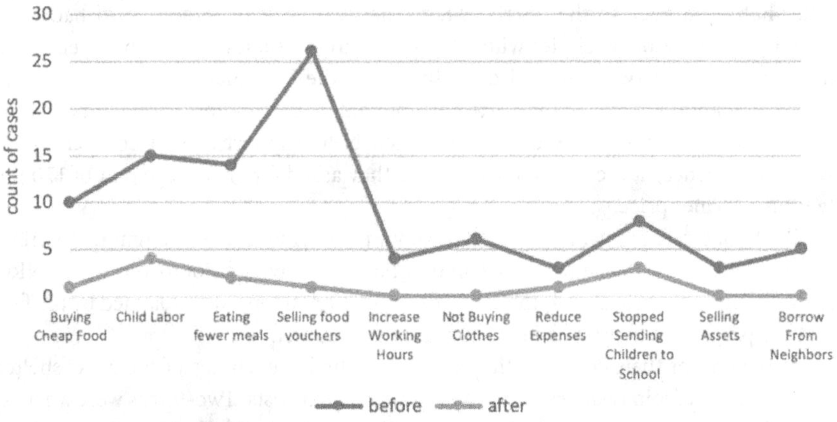

Figure 7.8 NRC shelter program Syrian beneficiaries changes in coping mechanisms. Source: NRC 2014. Sample size 90.

villages, where refugees were cut off from job opportunities. Some said that they felt unwelcome by closed communities and that integration was easiest in the cities. This might be linked to the general poverty of villagers and to the misperception that Syrians were receiving more support than they were. Sociological research proves that socioeconomic deprivation erodes community social cohesion much more than ethnic diversity (Oliver and Mandelberg 2000 in Kuhnt 2017). On the other hand, Jordanian towns and cities were perceived as more open as they include a wider range of civil society organizations, with more active women who develop stronger links with refugees. In addition, large Jordanian towns and cities include Palestinian refugees: Jordanians there have had more experience in integration, and Palestinian refugees themselves were keen to welcome the Syrian refugees (as proved by several Palestinian women's associations providing health services to Syrian women).

This project was a major step from emergency responses toward developmental interventions. Jordanian landlords felt this impact was hugely positive, as they received large sums of money to refurbish old apartments (an average of 3,900 JD), that they could use as they wished at the end of the program. This amount was seen as an additional gift (*hiba*), leading to the possibility of planning a future wedding for their son, or a new source of rental income at the end of the program.[33]

On a social level, most beneficiaries stated that Jordanians were friendly. However, beneficiaries that were located in rural areas inhabited by members of the same family and constituted closed tribal communities, sometimes felt unwelcome. In 60 percent of the cases, refugees considered that they had good relations with their neighbors. Only 20 percent had formal relations, 7 percent hardly talked with them, and 10 percent had no connection at all (Figure 7.9). The contractual relationship through the NRC shelter program resulted in close and good relations (from 30 to 34 percent).

[33] Interviews with mayors and heads of districts, 'Irbid governorate, December 2014.

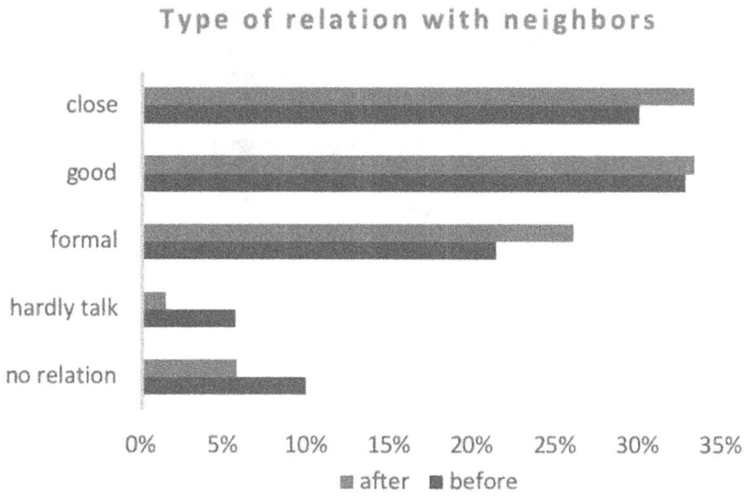

Figure 7.9 Evolution of relations with neighbors before and after the shelter project. Source: NRC 2014. Sample size 90.

A Care survey of the social inclusion of refugees in Jordan gave the same estimates of "six in ten Syrian refugees reported they felt either an 'extremely close' or 'very close' connection to Jordanian society" (Care 2020).

Relations with landlords were much improved within the NRC program: considered as close in one third of the cases, and good in another third. The contract, of course, reduced the "no relation" category from 9 percent to 2 percent (Figure 7.10).

The survey finally checked the impact of the program on Syrian beneficiaries' relations with relatives. In 84 percent of cases, the project had no impact, and the relations stayed the same. In 9 percent of cases, they improved, and in 7 percent declined (NRC 2014). In 39 percent of cases, Syrians had close relations with their relatives, 39 percent were good. Only 5 percent had formal relationships, 6 percent hardly talk, and 11 percent had no relationships (Figure 7.11).

4.2. NRC New Shelter Concept

The NRC shelter project was suspended in 2015, with a total of 5,586 housing units renovated in 142 locations in the 'Irbid, 'Ajlūn, and Jarash governorates, hosting 20,000 Syrian refugees.[34] But as resilience became the motto of the developmental policies for Jordan, mixed shelter programs that benefit both to Jordanians and Syrians were now welcomed.

The project resumed at the end of 2016 but with a new concept. Instead of moving refugees to match them with renovated housing units, it was decided to help Syrians renovate the dwelling they were renting. This also benefited the Jordanian landlords as windows, doors, and insulation were renovated. But the amount of money engaged in

[34] http://en.ammonnews.net/article.aspx?articleno=32904#.XUZ_KZMzY_U

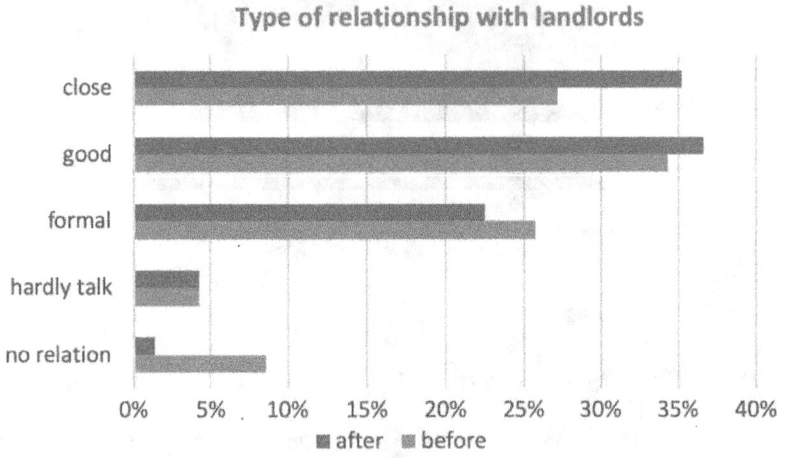

Figure 7.10 Evolution of relations with landlords before and after the shelter project. Source: NRC 2014. Sample size 90.

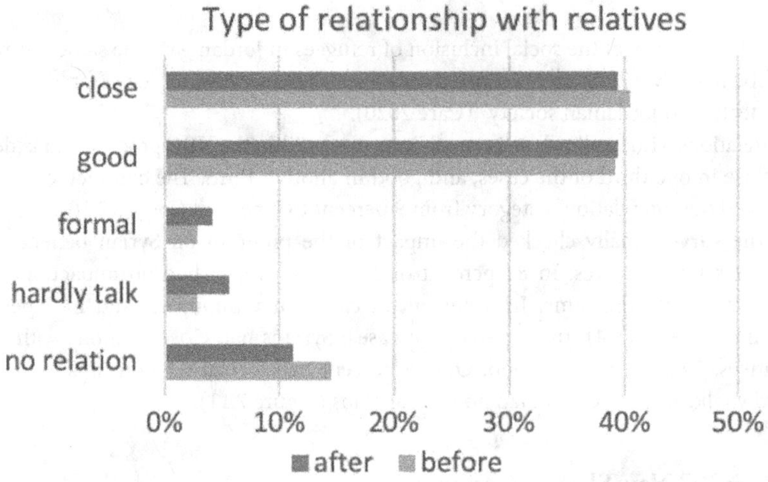

Figure 7.11 Evolution of relations with relatives before and after the shelter project. Source: NRC 2014. Sample size 90.

each project was reduced, at less than 1,500 JD per case. During 2017, 792 shelters were repaired, benefiting 8,390 Syrians (NRC 2018). The main repairs concerned window insulation and solar panel installation.

NRC is moving to a neighborhood upgrading approach, which also benefits poor Jordanians and other refugee groups (Sudanese, Yemenis, etc.). Smaller amounts are provided to the landlords to repair their houses, but rental contracts are signed and community infrastructure renovated (social services, stairs, gardens). The refugee crisis has been transformed into an opportunity to transfer participatory best practices from the international humanitarian experiences to long-term urban planning.

Conclusion

The Norwegian Refugee Council's initial Shelter Program developed in Jordan (2013-2015) represents a successful experience in terms of direct housing production (more than 1,000 apartments were renovated and 5,000 rooms created), but much more so in terms of social cohesion. It reduced tensions on housing in the ʾIrbid governorate by reducing the deficit, targeting Jordanians and reinforcing social relations between the host communities and the refugees (bridging) but also between owners and tenants (bonding). The program aimed at providing housing for all, while facilitating coexistence between the host and Syrian communities, as they became neighbors and had a contractual relationship.

It constitutes an interesting case of affordable and participative housing policies that benefited middle-class Jordanians in the long term and Syrian refugees in the short term. It constituted an alternative to the neoliberal housing policies directed by the market and meant to house upper-class segments. Most interestingly, it forced the communities to live together and served as a genuine tool to social cohesion, even over a short period of time. Such social cohesion was based on regular interactions between the landlords and the refugees, as they were close neighbors. However, this shelter program was very costly and required a lot of counselling dimensions to establish and supervise repair and rental contracts. The NRC shelter program has contributed to the provision of locally adequate housing, as defined by the High Commission for Human Rights, which does not simply consist of a roof and four walls but also the right to live in security, peace, and dignity.

Bibliography

Ababsa, Myriam (2018), "An Urbanizing Camp? Zaatari Syrian Refugee Camp in Jordan," *Conflits et migrations. Réflexions sur les catégories et la généalogie des migrations au Moyen-Orient*. Available online: https://lajeh.hypotheses.org/1076.

Ababsa, Myriam (2021), "Diwans and Madafas at the Heart of Irbid Social Life (Jordan)," SIAS Working Paper Series, n°32, 125–37. Sophia University Center for Islamic Area Studies, Tokyo.

Ajluni, Salem, and Mary Kawar (2014), *The Impact of the Syrian Refugee Crisis on the Labour Market in Jordan: Preliminary Analysis*, Beirut: ILO.

Alhawarin, Ibrahim, Ragui Assaad, and Ahmed Elsayed (2018), "Migration Shocks and Housing: Evidence from the Syrian Refugee Crisis in Jordan," *Economic Research Forum*, Working Paper 1213.

Al Khouri, Riad (2004), "Arab Migration Patterns: The Mashreq," in IOM (ed.), *Arab Migration in a Globalized World*, 21–34, Geneva: International Organization for Migration.

Altaï (2020), "Learning Module 1. Social Cohesion. Monitoring, Evaluation, Capitalisation of Minka Middle East Initiative," Report for Agence Française du Développement.

Care (2014), "Lives Unseen: Urban Syrian Refugees and Jordanian Host Communities Three Years into the Syrian Crisis," Care Jordan.

Care (2020), "9 Years into Exile: Building Hope and Durable Solutions. Searching for the Future: Analyzing Perceptions of Refugees and Jordanian Host Communities, Nine Years into the Syria Crisis," Care Jordan, 2019 Annual Urban Assessment Summary Report.

Conte, Édouard (2011), "Elles seront des sœurs pour nous. Le mariage par permutation au Proche-Orient," *Études rurales*, 187 (1): 157–99.

Courbage, Youssef (2007), "La population de la Syrie: des réticences à la transition (démographique)," in Baudouin Dupret and Youssef Courbage (eds.), *La Syrie au présent. Reflets d'une société*, 177–213, Arles: Actes Sud, Sindbad.

Darling Jonathan (2016), "Forced Migration and the City: Irregularity, Informality, and the Politics of Presence," *Progress in Human Geography*. Available online: https://doi.org/10.1177/0309132516629004 (accessed February 19, 2020).

DOS (Department of Statistics) (2015), "Population and Housing Census." Available online: http://dosweb.dos.gov.jo/censuses/population_housing/census2015/.

EMPHNET, WHO, IMC (2013), "Assessment of Mental Health and Psychosocial Support Needs of Displaced Syrians in Jordan." Available online: https://data2.unhcr.org/en/documents/details/41640.

Fawaz, Mona (2014), "Housing, Land and Property Issues in Lebanon. Implications of the Syrian Refugee Crisis," UNHCR, UN-Habitat.

Hamilton, Ellen, Victor Mints, Jose Luis Acero Vergel, Myriam Ababsa, Tammaa Waad, Yuan Xiao, Aris Molfetas-Lygkiaris, and John Raymond Wille (2018), *Jordan - Housing Sector Assessment - Housing Sector Review (English)*, Washington, DC: World Bank Group. Available online: http://documents.worldbank.org/curated/en/855101555960778525/Jordan-Housing-Sector-Assessment-Housing-Sector-Review (accessed February 19, 2020).

Housing and Urban Development Corporation (2014), *Population Indicators*, Jordan: Housing Policy Department, Directorate of Policies, Data Section.

IMF (2020), "Jordan: 2020 Article IV Consultation and Request for an Extended Arrangement."

Kuhnt, Jana, Ramona Rischke, Anda David, and Tobias Lechtenfeld (2017), "Social Cohesion in Times of Forced Displacement – The Case of Young People in Jordan," Göttingen, Georg-August-Universität, Discussion Papers.

MOPIC, HCSP (Host Community Support Platform) (2013), "Needs Assessment Review of the Impact of the Syrian Crisis on Jordan." Available online: https://www.alnap.org/help-library/needs-assessment-review-of-the-impact-of-the-syrian-crisis-on-jordan.

Norton, Andrew, and Arjan de Haan (2012), "Social Cohesion: Theoretical Debates and Practical Applications with Respect to Jobs," Background paper for the World Development Report. Available online: https://openknowledge.worldbank.org/handle/10986/12147.

Norwegian Refugee Council (NRC) (2014), "Evaluating the Socio-economic Effects of the Urban Shelter Project on Syrian Beneficiaries Living in ʾIrbid Governorate," October 22, 2014.

Norwegian Refugee Council (NRC) (2015), "In Search of a Home. Access to Adequate Housing in Jordan." Available online: https://data2.unhcr.org/en/documents/details/45405.

Norwegian Refugee Council (NRC) (2011), "From Shelter to Housing: Security of Tenure and Integration in Protracted Displacement Settings." Available online: https://www.nrc.no/resources/reports/from-shelter-to-housing-security-of-tenure-and-integration-in-protracted-displacement-settings/.

Norwegian Refugee Council (NRC) (2018), "Urban Shelter Fact Sheet 2018. Jordan." Available online: https://reliefweb.int/report/jordan/unhcr-jordan-factsheet-june-2018.

Othman, Hasan, and Mostafa Saadat (2009), "The Prevalence of Consanguineous Marriages in Syria," *Journal of Biosocial Science*, 41 (5): 685–92.

Oliver, J. Eric, and Tali Mendelberg (2000), "Reconsidering the Environmental Determinants of White Racial Attitudes," *American Journal of Political Science*, 44: 574–89.

Peaucelle, Héloïse (2020), "La présence syrienne à Irbid (1). Une ville jordanienne tournée vers la Syrie," *Les Carnets de l'Ifpo*. La recherche en train de se faire à l'Institut français du Proche-Orient. Available online: https://ifpo.hypotheses.org/10786, le 31 août 2020.

REACH (2014), "Evaluating the Effect of the Syrian Refugee Crisis on Stability and Resilience in Jordanian Host Communities." Available online: https://reliefweb.int/report/jordan/evaluating-effect-syrian-refugee-crisis-stability-and-resilience-jordanian-host.

REACH (2015), "Social Cohesion in Host Communities in Northern Jordan. Assessment Report," May 2015. Available online: https://reliefweb.int/report/jordan/social-cohesion-host-communities-northern-jordan.

UNHCR (2014), "A Year in Review. UNHCR Jordan." Available online: https://www.unhcr.org/protection/operations/555359396/unhcr-jordan-year-review-2014.html.

UNHCR (2015), "Living in the Shadows – Jordan Home Visits Report 2014," January 2015. Available online: https://www.unhcr.org/protection/operations/54b685079/living-shadows-jordan-home-visits-report-2014.html.

UNHCR (2016), "3RP. Regional Refugee Resilience Plan 2015–2016 in Response to the Syria Crisis," 2015 Available online: https://reliefweb.int/report/syrian-arab-republic/3rp-regional-refugee-and-resilience-plan-2015-2016-response-syria-crisis.

UNHCR, Action Against Hunger, ILO (2019), "Vulnerability Assessment Framework. Population Study 2019." Available online: https://reliefweb.int/sites/reliefweb.int/files/resources/68856.pdf.

UNHCR, UNICEF and WFP (2014), "Joint Assessment Review of the Syrian Refugee Response in Jordan," UN High Commission for the Human Rights (UN OHCR) (2014), "The Right to Adequate Housing," Fact Sheet 21, May 2014. Available online: https://data2.unhcr.org/en/documents/details/39484.

Wagner, Ann-Christin (2017), "Frantic Waiting: NGO Anti-Politics and 'Timepass' for Young Syrian Refugees in Jordan," *Middle East - Topics & Arguments*, 9 (December): 107–21.

WFP (2014), "Comprehensive Food Security Monitoring Exercise." Available online: https://www.wfp.org/publications/jordan-comprehensive-food-security-monitoring-exercise-registered-syrian-refugees-2016.

WVI (World Vision International) (2015), "Social Cohesion Between Syrian Refugees and Urban Host Communities in Lebanon and Jordan." Available online: https://reliefweb.int/sites/reliefweb.int/files/resources/World%20Vision%20International%20DM2020%20Social%20Cohesion%20Report.pdf.

8

Syrian Refugee Settlement in ʾIrbid and Urban Fragmentation

A Case Study of Ḥayy al-Afrāḥ and Its Surroundings

Héloïse Peaucelle

The waves of forced migrations that have affected the Middle East since the second half of the twentieth century have been the impetus for urban transformation, driving socio-spatial dynamics and spurring new urban development logics (Agier 2015; Doraï 2016; Fawaz et al. 2018; Kaedbey 2021).

ʾIrbid, the second largest city in Jordan in terms of metropolitan area, is a case in point (Tawālbeh 1982; Abū al-Shaʿr 2009; Abū Ghanima 2014).[1] Three successive waves of migration, each involving the settlement of significant numbers of refugees, have deeply affected the urbanization of ʾIrbid (Shunnaq and Schwab 2000; Aldeek and Mistarihi 2020). Firstly, following the first Arab-Israeli conflict of 1948, 15,000 Palestinian refugees settled in ʾIrbid (Koumach 1987), which at the time was inhabited by a mere 7,000 indigenous inhabitants (al-Taʿany 2007). About one-fifth of them, the most vulnerable who could not sustain their livelihoods, were housed in the ʾIrbid refugee camp initially established by the League of the Red Cross Societies in 1950 and later expanded by the United Nations Relief and Works Agency for Palestine Refugees (UNRWA)[2] in an unsettled area in the northern part of the city. The camp was located in a marginal area, separated from the center by the ʾIrbid cemetery and located below the ʾIrbid hill, which produced a spatial fragmentation between the city and the camp. In the following years, refugees from the camp who had managed to integrate themselves into the local job market and become self-sufficient moved out of the camp to re-establish themselves in its vicinity, thus generating urban growth in that area

1 Considering that the ʾIrbid metropolitan area consists of Liwas Qasabat ʾIrbid and Banī ʿUbayd (which includes the municipalities of Greater ʾIrbid and West ʾIrbid), the population of this area was estimated to be 1,068,060 in 2020, according to the Statistics Department of the Ministry of Planning and International Cooperation.
The total population of the governorate was estimated at 2,003,800 in 2020.
http://dosweb.dos.gov.jo/DataBank/Population_Estimares/PopulationEstimatesbyLocality.pdf

2 https://www.unrwa.org/where-we-work/jordan/irbid-camp

(al-Ta'any 2007). Secondly, in the aftermath of the 1967 Six-Day War, 17,000 additional Palestinians from the West Bank found refuge in 'Irbid, who then represented around 40 percent of the population of 'Irbid.[3] Their arrival along with the strong rural exodus that was taking place at the time opened a new era of urban expansion. Again, as in 1948–1950, the most vulnerable 1967 displaced persons were settled by UNRWA in the 'Azmī al-Muftī Camp (also known as al-Ḥuṣn Camp), located in a rural area 10 kilometer south of 'Irbid: in time, some of them began to settle in the city, mostly in and around the first 'Irbid Camp.

The third wave of refugees that swept 'Irbid city is composed of Syrian refugees following the outbreak of the Syrian conflict in 2011. It should be noted here that migration from Syria to 'Irbid is nothing new (Koumach 1987; Abū Ghanima 2014; Peaucelle 2020) and that on the eve of the Syrian conflict, the city was already hosting more than 4,000 Syrians (Department of Statistic 2004)[4] who were integrated into the economic and social fabric of the city. In 2021, in 'Irbid governorate, about 136,000 Syrian refugees are registered with the United Nations High Commissioner for Refugees (UNHCR):[5] the majority of them came from the border Syrian governorate of Dar'ā, between 2011 and 2014, when Jordan closed its borders with Syria, and they reside, as "urban refugees," in 'Irbid city, sometimes following a stay in the al-Za'tarī refugee camp (in the al-Mafraq governorate) or other early retention centers where they were initially registered.[6]

While the Palestinian refugee camp, now fully integrated into 'Irbid's urban fabric as a city neighborhood (Doraï 2020), continues to maintain an actual and/or symbolic centrality for Palestinian refugees, is there a similar locale for Syrians? What is the place of these refugee-populated spaces in the city? The geographical mapping of the Syrian presence in 'Irbid shows that Syrians are disseminated throughout the city with, however, strong concentrations in certain neighborhoods (Figure 8.1). One of these is Ḥayy al-Afrāḥ. The neighborhood has welcomed more than 27,000 Syrian inhabitants, thus becoming the neighborhood with the highest share of Syrians in 'Irbid and, after the Palestinian refugee camp, the second most densely populated neighborhood. Today, it represents a place of convergence for refugees that is identified by all residents as a "Syrian hub" for Syrian immigrants.

Beginning with a look at Ḥayy al-Afrāḥ, this chapter proposes to study the dynamics of the settlement of Syrian refugees in 'Irbid and the ensuing spatial and social rearrangements of a host neighborhood. To what extent does the presence of

3 In 1961, the population of 'Irbid was 44,685. It reached 113,548 in the 1979 census (Department of Statistic, several tables, in al-Khaṭyb, 1988).

4 http://dosweb.dos.gov.jo/censuses/population_housing/census2004/census2004_tables/

5 According to data from the UN High Commissioner for Refugees Agency. http://data2.unhcr.org/en/situations/syria/location/36 The number of Syrians in the governorate is, however, disputed by the Jordanian Ministry of Interior, which, based on the 2015 census, estimates that at least 343,552 Syrians live in 'Irbid.

6 Three official Syrian refugee camps (al-Za'tarī, al-'Imārātī, and al-'Azraq) currently host less than 20 percent of the total number of refugees, but none of them are located in the 'Irbid governorate. Therefore, the 'Irbid governorate and city only host "urban" or "rural" refugees. https://data2.unhcr.org/en/situations/syria/location/36. However, the 'Irbid governorate has a retention facility in the municipality of Ramtha, north of 'Irbid: the King Abdullah Park that had 600 persons in 2021, mostly Palestinians from Syria who are not allowed to enter Jordan.

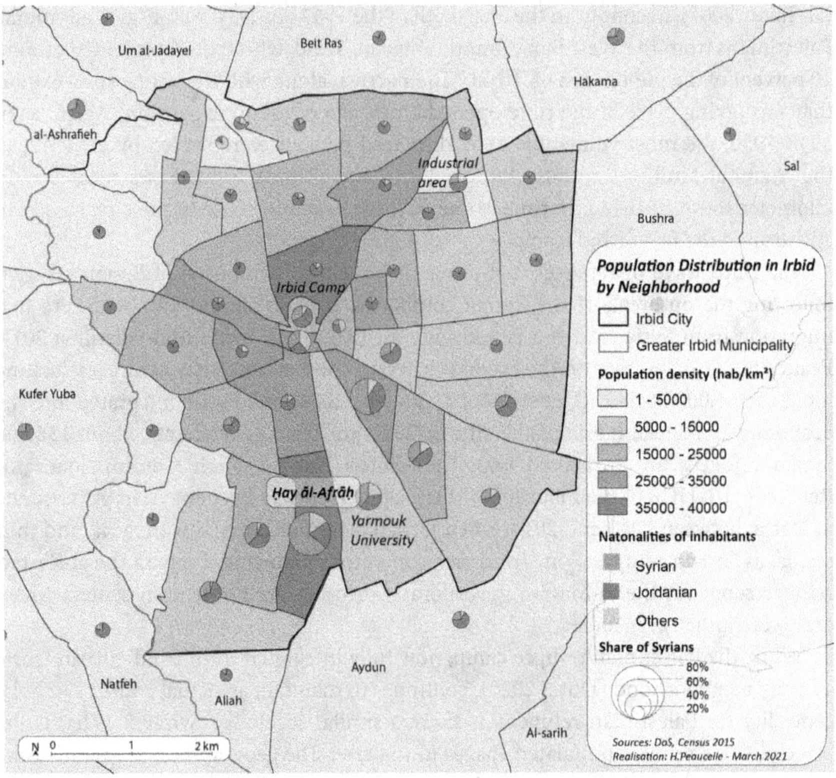

Figure 8.1 Distribution of Syrians in the city of ʾIrbid. Sources: Department of Statistics, the 2015 housing and population census.

Syrian refugees contribute to redefining specific spaces and the surrounding areas with regard to their relations with other population groups and nationally defined spatial planning? Taking up one of the major contributions initiated by the Chicago School to describe the "spatial configuration of the city" (Grafmeyer and Joseph 1979), the focus is on the mechanisms of extension, succession, and concentration of population (Levy 1998).

This chapter will endeavor to show that despite the absence of camps or specific centralities developed for Syrians in ʾIrbid, which is the opposite of what was the case for Palestinian refugees, spaces of gathering have been created and turned into centralities by the Syrian refugees. Subsequently, such spaces are redefined by urban and metropolitan functions, thus affecting the city's settlement dynamics. These urban transformations are part of processes that include other neighborhoods and participate in urban sprawl (Battegay 2003).

The data used for this chapter draw from an ethnographic survey conducted in ʾIrbid in 2019 and 2020, as part of a PhD thesis in geography. Interviews were conducted, mainly with Syrians or Jordanians of Syrian origin living in ʾIrbid. In addition, semi-structured interviews, as well as numerous informal interviews, were carried out with inhabitants, students, and shopkeepers of different origins. The ethnographic material used for this contribution also consists of a set of direct observations in the spaces frequented by Syrians in 'Irbid during this period, particularly in the districts or spaces mentioned in the chapter. The set of data collected in the field thus favors a dialogue between a global approach to land-use planning, a point of view of the respondents from which representations emanate, and direct observations.

This chapter is organized in two parts. The first part focuses on the spatial reconfigurations within Ḥayy al-Afrāḥ, starting with the historical development of the neighborhood, pinpointing the dynamics of its urbanization, urban functions, and social standing before and after the arrival of the Syrian refugees in 2011/2012. These mobilities suggest a reconfiguration of the social mosaic in the neighborhood and beyond (Brun and Lévy 2000).

The second part is concerned with the causes and consequences of these reconfigurations beyond the neighborhood of Ḥayy al-Afrāḥ, namely in the surrounding neighborhoods and, further, the new urban development dynamics in the eastern part of the city, which are greatly influenced by urban changes in Ḥayy al-Afrāḥ. Mention will then be made of the role of political patronage and the *laissez-faire* attitude of the authorities, which facilitate these rapid and unregulated urban and social transformations.

1. Urban Reconfigurations in Ḥayy al-Afrāḥ: From Student Centrality to Refugee Neighborhood

1.1. Urban Construction of Ḥayy al-Afrāḥ

Ḥayy al-Afrāḥ is a residential neighborhood located 1.5 kilometer from the historical center of 'Irbid. It flanks the west side of Yarmouk University, the second university to be established in the kingdom after Jordan University in Amman, which was initially opened in 1976 on agricultural land south of the center of 'Irbid (al-Ta'any 2007). Ḥayy al-Afrāḥ's social and urban development has therefore been largely determined by student migration, the students' social inclusion and ensuing movements within 'Irbid, and the urban planning vision of the authorities.

Starting in 1978, a study on the integrated regional development of northern Jordan, carried out by the Japan International Cooperation Agency at Jordan's request,[7] established a regional urban structure with the intention of making the governorate of 'Irbid an industrial and educational center at the regional and global scale. However, actual urban planning plans were only developed later, following a turbulent decade of student protests over both internal university matters and Jordan's pro-Western policies that reached a peak in the spring of 1986 when the

[7] Since 1975, the Japanese cooperation has been active in Jordan. On a request from the King, the JICA, in cooperation with the Engineering Consulting Firms Association Japan and the International Development Center of Japan, submitted a report on the "integrated Regional Development of Northern Jordan survey" in 1978.

government resorted to military means to crush the student movement (Satloff 1986). In the event, Yarmouk University, which was initially to be relocated 15 kilometer from the city center on a larger student campus, was in fact integrated within ʾIrbid's municipal boundaries in order to exercise increased governmental control over the students. The presence of students has brought economic benefits to the city, especially to the neighborhood of Ḥayy al-Afrāḥ, but it also created a significant division within the city.

Ḥayy al-Afrāḥ belongs to the part of ʾIrbid that developed together with the expansion of the university population. In the 1980s, this is where some of the first collective housing in the city was built: building blocks with five floors provided small flats, studios, and some larger family apartments. The high concentration of students in this neighborhood has been increased by the establishment of another university, the Jordan University of Sciences and Technology (JUST), in 1986. Until today considered as an "elite educational centre in the Middle East,"[8] JUST competes for the top position in the rankings of the best universities in the country and in the Arab World.[9] The reputation of this academic institution has thus become a growing attraction for Arab students. Although JUST is located about 15 kilometer outside ʾIrbid and Ḥayy al-Afrāḥ, most students at ʾIrbid University and JUST, including Jordanians from other regions, the Gulf States, and Palestine, chose to settle within Ḥayy al-Afrāḥ, ʾIrbid's lively student neighborhood. By settling in this neighborhood, they triggered an abundance of commercial and service activities.

Investments in the local economy increased when about 25,000[10] ʾIrbidī expatriates were expelled from Kuwait during and following the Gulf War of 1990–1991 and came back to ʾIrbid with their savings (Department of Statistics (DoS) 1994, in al-Taʿany 2007). While the wealthiest of them settled in the western districts of the Jordanian capital, a new local upper middle class emerged in ʾIrbid, mainly in the southern suburb of ʾAydūn, which is directly south of Ḥayy al-Afrāḥ, and started new businesses in Ḥayy al-Afrāḥ. From 1990 to 2010, ʾIrbid expanded only moderately, but it became vertically denser and commercially increasingly active, especially in both ʾAydūn and Ḥayy al-Afrāḥ, where businesses and services mainly oriented toward fulfilling student needs mushroomed: restaurants, stationers, bookshops, internet cafés, etc. Emblematic of this commercial boom is Shafīq ʿIrshaydāt Street, known as "University Street," which runs alongside the university campus and binds it to Ḥayy al-Afrāḥ, and which became a commercial hub not only for university students but also for the local inhabitants of ʾIrbid. As an anecdotal indicator of this commercial abundance, in the 2002 Guinness Book of Records it was rated as the street with the most internet cafés per capita in the world.[11]

8 https://www.just.edu.jo/Units_and_offices/Offices/IRO/Pages/About-Irbid-Read-More.aspx

9 In 2021, JUST was ranked as the 13th best university in the Arab World: https://www.qschina.cn/en/university-rankings/arab-region-university-rankings/2021

10 Including a majority of Jordanians of Palestinian origin.

11 https://www.albawaba.com/loop/six-random-times-jordan-broke-guinness-world-record-699672

1.2. The Segregation Processes in Ḥayy al-Afrāḥ since 2011

Since 2011, the dynamics of residential and commercial settlement has been disrupted by the arrival of Syrian refugees, leading to the marginalization of University Street and the Ḥayy al-Afrāḥ neighborhood.

Residential settlement dynamics

As mentioned above, until 2011, Ḥayy al-Afrāḥ was mainly inhabited by students. By the end of the 2012 academic year, some of those who left their dwellings to go back home were replaced first by young single Syrian refugees attracted by the neighborhood's commercial activity and adequate public transport and services.

As Yaser, a Syrian refugee in his 20s, put it, their settlement there was a strategy of "invisibility" and possible integration into the city: "As young men we couldn't rent flats anywhere in the city, because some landlords refused to deal with us, so moving into student accommodation was an opportunity to blend in with our peers" (Yaser, Syrian refugee, 27 years old, April 2020). Some Syrian families did not hesitate to crowd into the small flats initially intended for students, considering this as a temporary situation pending a forthcoming return to Syria.

The arrival of the Syrian refugees had mixed effects on the neighborhood. Initially, the rents increased, peaking at the end of 2013 and 2014, at the time when the largest waves of Syrian refugees hit ʾIrbid. Then, they gradually decreased, first for the smallest flats, and then for the entire housing stock in the neighborhood. This decrease was actually the result of students seeking housing in other parts of ʾIrbid, in particular in the neighborhood of Aydun and toward the east in the residential areas that had recently been established on either side of the main bus station. Many of them did not want to stay in Ḥayy al-Afrāḥ and complained about the sudden worsened living conditions in the neighborhood due to overcrowding,[12] noise and difficulties in adapting to the presence of the refugees, and a "noisy" and "dirty" population that often found itself in conflict with their landlords. Moreover, the neighborhood became identified as a "Syrian refugee area" or, more specifically, "Little Darʿā" because most of the inhabitants came from the Syrian province of Darʿā.[13] This evolution created the stigma of a poor refugee neighborhood, and it affected how the population of ʾIrbid at large viewed it.

In 2015, the closure of the border augured a long-term settlement in exile. Some families relocated to the neighborhood on a more permanent basis, seeking larger flats, while others, among them the more affluent, moved out to the new residential housing parks. From this period onward, there is a progressive decline in demand in Ḥayy al-Afrāḥ, and therefore a corresponding decline in the rents for the smallest flats, while the pressure increased on flats of more than three rooms. The closure of the border

12 A report by a Shelter Working Group (SWG), constituted by UNHCR and the NGO Norwegian Refugee Council, stated that 50 percent of the apartments hosting Syrians in ʾIrbid were overcrowded in 2017. According to the SWG, an overcrowded shelter either has more than four individuals per room or more than one household per room (Welsh and Jourdi 2018). However, the case of Ḥayy al-Afrāḥ can be considered as being well above the average for the governorate because it represents the highest density of this geographical space.

13 According to UNHCR data, more than 70 percent of Syrians in ʾIrbid came from Darʿā.

Figure 8.2 A residential street in Ḥayy al-Afrāḥ. May 2021. Source: H. Peaucelle.

then allowed the gradual stabilization of rents, which until then had been constantly rising in the face of demographic pressure in the neighborhood.

Commercial resettlement dynamics

The movement of people away from Ḥayy al-Afrāḥ also gradually involved small entrepreneurs such as shopkeepers, barbers, and owners of coffee shops and restaurants, whose products and services did not match the refugees' needs and purchasing power. Ahmad, a barber who had owned and managed a salon on University Street since the mid-2000s, was one of those who left in 2019, relocating his business in a new neighborhood east of 'Irbid city, where his traditional student customers have also moved.

> In the beginning it was a godsend: the first Syrians who arrived in Ḥayy al-Afrāḥ in late 2011 to 2012 were quite wealthy people who integrated well into the local economy; but they were followed (and replaced) by much poorer population dependent on charity. [. . .] Since 2013, there has been a big problem of prostitution in the neighbourhood. It started with Syrian women, but it then also involved Jordanian and Asian women. Because of that, we have had a new clientele at the salon, among them mainly young Jordanian soldiers on temporary leave who like to visit these places of prostitution, and visitors from the Gulf. The problem of this new clientele is that they are not regulars, while the expatriate students used to come at least every week to be shaved or to have a haircut. (Ahmad, Jordanian barber, 32 years old, June 2020)

Figure 8.3 Some closed shops, hotels, and coffee shops on University Street ʾIrbid. May 2021. Source: H. Peaucelle.

Beyond stigmatizing references to Syrian refugees, Ahmad's discourse, which echoes the narratives of many former entrepreneurs based on University Street, also reveals differences and similarities between the Syrian refugees and the indigenous population in their use of space and facilities. Be that as it may, the departure of the students and ensuing closure of many commercial ventures have contributed to the socioeconomic marginalization of the Ḥayy al-Afrāḥ neighborhood.

To better grasp the Ḥayy al-Afrāḥ segregation process, the filtering process theory developed by the Chicago School, based on several indicators such as the rental value of housing and social and demographic indicators related to housing occupation, allows us to capture the chain of residential and commercial mobility sequences and analyze housing redistribution (Bourne 1981; Levy 1998).

More precisely, the "active filtering" theory is applied, based on physical residential mobility of both university students and Syrian refugees due to changes in the living environment and the housing market.[14]

The outcome of the research, as illustrated in the diagram, shows how the introduction of new dwellings to the market, together with changes in rent and housing variations, has led to the redistribution of dwelling occupancy in Ḥayy al-Afrāḥ. The diagram also shows how the relocation of shops fits into the chain of residential movements and housing prices.

[14] The indicators used come from qualitative data collected through interviews with residents and former residents of Ḥayy al-Afrāḥ.

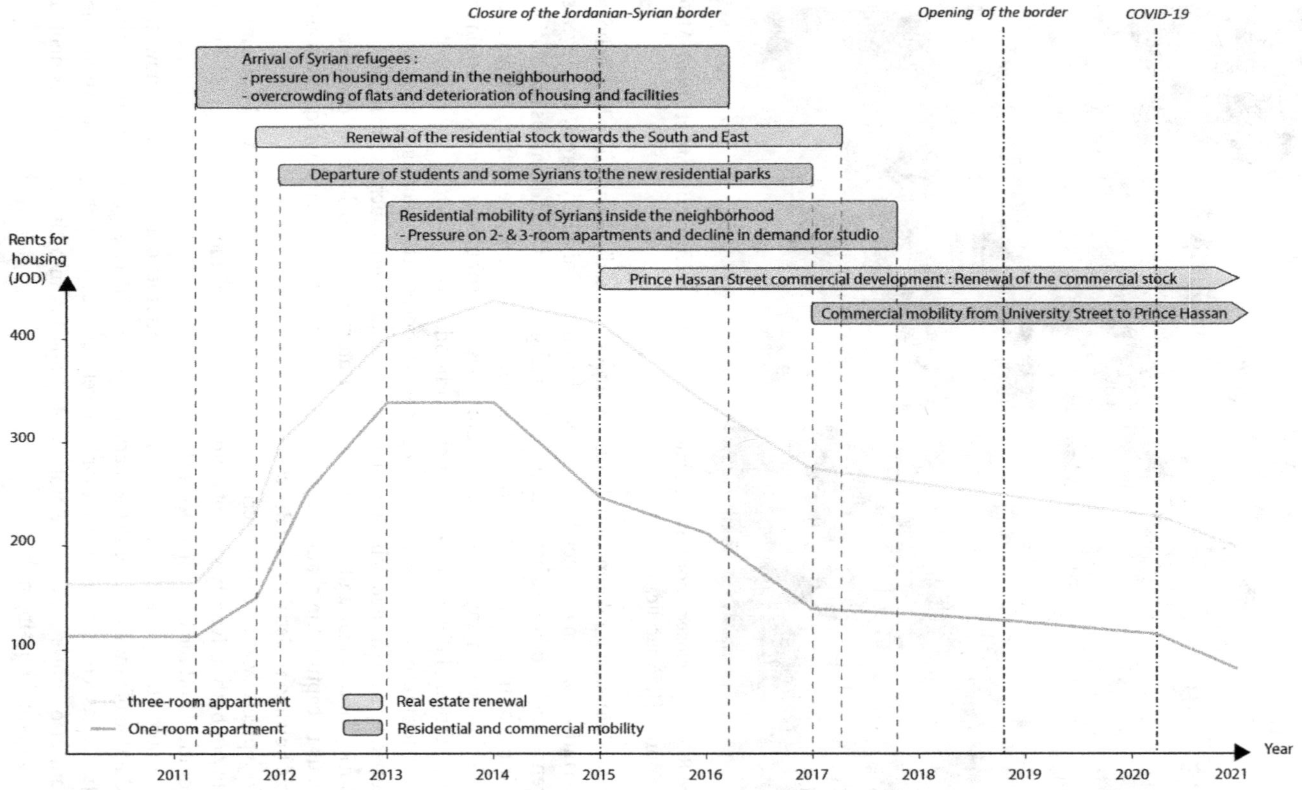

Figure 8.4 Variation of residential and market rents, and movements in Ḥayy al-Afrāḥ. Sources: Estimates based on interviews conducted in Ḥayy al-Afrāḥ and online with residents and former residents of the neighborhood, 2020 and 2021.

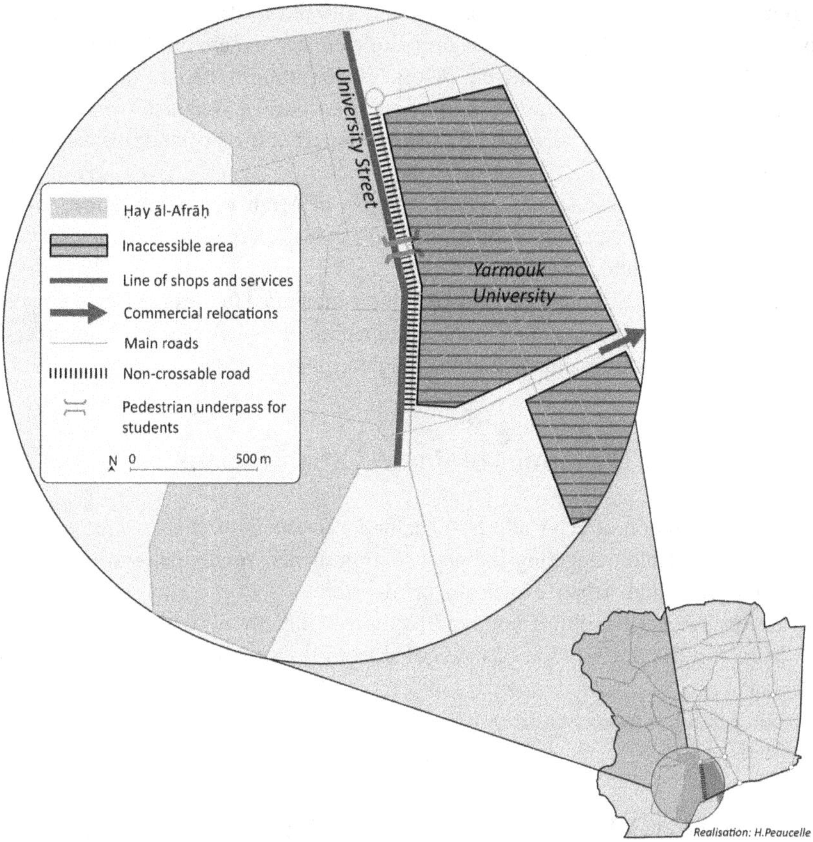

Figure 8.5 Accessibility for Syrians to the eastern side of the city from Ḥayy al-Afrāḥ.

Urban morphology and marginalization

The dynamics of settlement and movement into and out of the neighborhood that have been reviewed above, together with the study of the evolution of the urban morphology, point to spatial fragmentation. Until 2011, University Street acted as a link between the university compound and Ḥayy al-Afrāḥ's attractive residential neighborhood for foreign students. Following the settlement of the Syrian refugees, the ensuing deterioration of living conditions in the neighborhood, and the closure of many businesses, University Street has been symbolically turned into a border with the university. The two spaces that once complemented each other have become a juxtaposition of quasi-hermetic spaces, separated by an expressway coming from the south (from al-Ḥuṣn and Amman). The only physical link between them is an underground tunnel allowing pedestrians to cross the University Street (see Figure 8.5). While students and staff can use the tree-lined campus streets to reach the east of the city, the university's 70-hectare enclosed space is an obstacle in the heart of the city for Syrian refugees. This distancing from the eastern districts of the city is reinforced by the fact that Syrians are not allowed to drive or own a vehicle in Jordan (Peaucelle 2021). To get around the campus is therefore only possible by walking or using ʾIrbid's relatively disorganized public transport network. These difficulties of accessibility and mobility do not encourage Syrians to venture out of the neighborhood, especially toward the eastern part of the city, and this contributes to its isolation.

The physical and social separation of Ḥayy al-Afrāḥ was compounded by the fact that few Syrian refugees could afford the expensive access to the university and therefore to the campus grounds.

The physical separation of the two areas has contributed to the ongoing segregation of Ḥayy al-Afrāḥ, a process involving a combination of mobility factors influenced by adverse subjective representations of the neighborhood.

2. Dynamics of Rapid Urban Expansion

The marginalization of Ḥayy al-Afrāḥ has had a tremendous effect on the evolution of the city of ʾIrbid, triggering the construction of new residential and commercial neighborhoods and urban expansion on the east side of the city. This process of expansion has been induced both indirectly and directly by the arrival of Syrians in ʾIrbid. On the one hand, it has stemmed from the search for relocation of shops seeking to get closer to the students, whose frequented spaces have been displaced. On the other hand, it has arisen from the arrival of new Syrian investors and consumers in ʾIrbid.

2.1. Commercial Expansion in the City: The Lure of the East

From 2013 onward, ʾIrbid has witnessed the economic development of a new axis, Prince Hassan Street. Linking the South Gate of Yarmouk University with the eastern route out of the city, it has absorbed some of the market activity previously in Ḥayy al-Afrāḥ.

Formerly, this area had barely been urbanized and was known as the location of the city's main bus station, which connected it with sixty destinations, including the major cities in the north of the kingdom (Amman, ʿAjlūn, al-Mafraq, and Jarash). In the 2010s, three important commercial ventures were established along Prince Hassan Street, which have since led to its urbanization and boosted its commercial appeal. The first is a fancy three-floor restaurant, al-Dūmarī, that was opened in 2013 by a Syrian investor based in Kuwait. It became a meeting place for Syrians connected with the Gulf countries as well as the Jordanian middle classes and soon became one of the most frequented restaurants in the city.

In the same year, two malls were opened at opposite ends of the street: the Sameh Mall and the ʾIrbid City Centre Mall. The Sameh Mall is located in an unsightly building at the eastern edge of the city on the strategic crossroads of Waṣfī al-Tall Street with Prince al-Hassan Street (Figure 8.6), which exposes it to a large clientele. The shopping center was initially crowded with villagers from the governorates of ʾIrbid,

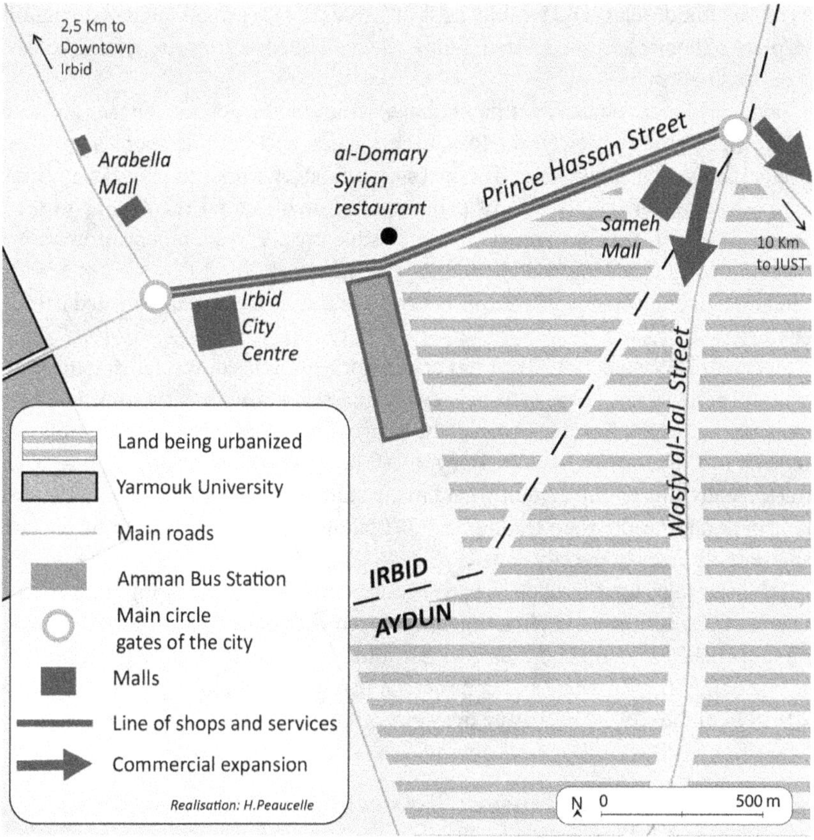

Figure 8.6 Prince Hassan Street, a neighborhood undergoing urban and commercial expansion—photo Google Earth, April 2021.

'Ajlūn, and Jarash. A few months after its opening, the Sameh Mall won a UNHCR tender and became the first Jordanian supermarket to accept digital food vouchers distributed to Syrian refugees.[15] Today, the Sameh Mall remains identified as a mall for Syrian refugees, for whom special offers are made. In addition, checkouts earmarked for Syrian refugee customers have been set up in order not to delay local customers.

In contrast, the 'Irbid City Centre Mall is located in a fancy building and hosts western brands such as *H&M*, *Starbucks*, and the *Carrefour Hypermarket.*[16] It obviously

[15] In Jordan, eligible Syrian refugees, designated through a vulnerability assessment framework, receive a monthly cash or food voucher from the UN World Food Programme, which enables them to purchase food items in partner shops throughout the country. By distributing cash and food vouchers instead of traditional rations, the UN World Food Programme aimed to support the country's economy. [https://www.wfpusa.org]

[16] The hypermarket is the second of the French chain to open in 'Irbid. A shop had opened previously, in 2012, in the historic town center, but had to close a few months later because local customers preferred the souks of the center, and traffic issues in the center did not allow it to attract a new clientele. [Interview with Carrefour Direction, 'Irbid, June 2020.]

targets the middle class and wealthy class of ʾIrbid. In order to maintain its reputation as a place of family leisure and tranquillity, the mall filters entries and refuses access to young or single men.

Since 2015, real estate investments have abounded in this neighborhood, which has grown up in just a few years. Restaurants, cafés, and clothing shops have sprung up along this new urban axis. The investors, most of whom are Jordanian,[17] have taken advantage of the absence of planning and architectural regulations to set up their buildings in this new, open, and accessible area. The alignment of new shops and restaurants following the opening of the imposing ʾIrbid City Centre Mall has therefore led to the emergence in this district of a multiplicity of unregulated uses and activities.

Since 2015, Waṣfī al-Tall Street has also become urbanized, specializing in student cafes and restaurants. Some of these new businesses moved directly from University Street, their owners having followed the process of relocating businesses following the arrival of Syrian refugees in Ḥayy al-Afrāḥ, as mentioned above. Waṣfī al-Tall Street, ideally situated in ʾAydūn where many students now reside, 2 kilometers from al-Yarmūk and on the road leading to JUST, allows businesses there to better target expatriate students in the city.

This seemingly uncontrolled or barely controlled urbanization brings into question the role of institutional and planning actors faced with contrasting factors: the arrival of impoverished refugees and their concentration in certain student neighborhoods on the one hand; the real estate and commercial investment boom implying a very rapid expansion of the city led by private investors on the other.

2.2. Urbanization in Tension: Between Planning Attempts and Unregulated Development

In 2010, the Greater ʾIrbid Urban Growth Plan (GIUGP) was developed by the Ministry of Municipal Affairs, the Amman Institute, Planning Alliance,[18] and the Municipality of Greater ʾIrbid, in consultation with the population through public participatory meetings. Although the plan was never officially adopted, it put forward urban planning and policy recommendations for the next two decades, addressing different scales of intervention and spawning three sub-plans: the *Growth Plan*, which considered the regional scale; the *Area Plan*, which addressed the level of the Greater ʾIrbid Municipality; and the *Community Plan* that targeted downtown ʾIrbid more specifically. However, the population model on which the GIUGP was based anticipated a natural increase of 2,74 percent for the 2009–2030 period, including a zero-immigration rate (ʾIrbid Situation Report 2010).[19] The arrival of massive numbers of Syrian refugees obviously upset these demographic forecasts, resulting in unplanned

[17] More than 130 Syrian merchants have invested in ʾIrbid since 2011, but most of them set up their businesses around the center of town, taking less of a commercial risk in those traditional areas or relying on old networks of Syrian merchants established there. Some of them also settled in Ḥayy al-Afrāḥ, but most of these buisnesses are informal.

[18] A Canadian private urban planning office.

[19] Demographic trends were provided by the Department of Statistics in 2004.

radical urban transformation, also associated with other urban development trends: one of these unexpected developments concerned Ḥayy al-Afrāḥ, the neighborhood being one of the areas in the plan regarding the urban development and economic investment corridor; its transformation into a predominantly residential area has contradicted the predictions. Also, whereas the ʾIrbid 2030 growth plan envisaged the promotion of increased residential density around the bus station and on Prince Hassan Street, the commercial development of the street has derailed these objectives. This evolution can be explained by nepotism and corruption. For example, the acquisition by a Ramathawi parliamentarian of the land where the ʾIrbid City Center Mall was built was highly controversial because of the suspicion of corruption regarding the acquisition of the land, which distorted the land use foreseen in the planning for ʾIrbid.

Through its deregulated development led by private politicians/investors, Prince Hassan Street bears witness to the neoliberal logic of the city's construction. The proposed urban system is characterized by a tendency toward privatization, sometimes benefiting foreign investors, and deregulation, particularly through urban planning that allows derogations to a few, most often connected with the political class (Harvey 2011). Conceived as investment products, the various private developments contribute to the process of socio-spatial marginalization. On the one hand, along Prince Hassan Street, the spaces reserved for certain categories of poor inhabitants, like the Sameh Mall and second-hand shops, contribute to the stigmatization of the poorest population groups, the same groups that are relegated to marginalized areas such as the Ḥayy al-Afrāḥ neighborhood. On the other hand, places such as the ʾIrbid City Centre Mall or al-Dūmarī restaurant have become the most fancy and posh places in the city. They have attracted most of the commercial ventures formerly located on University Street, thus also contributing to the marginalization process of the Ḥayy al-Afrāḥ neighborhood.

Conclusion

The urban transformations resulting from the arrival of Syrians in the city of ʾIrbid are expressed at different levels on the scale of the Ḥayy al-Afrāḥ neighborhood, the residential settlement dynamics evolved, and thus the concentration of Syrians in the neighborhood succeeded that of a student population. The differences in lifestyles and the problems of cohabitation between these groups led to the segregation of the neighborhood. This marginalization was reinforced by the separation of the different elements that make up the area. Moreover, beyond the neighborhood, at the city scale, the shops that moved away from Ḥayy al-Afrāḥ were relocated on Prince Hassan Street, which developed partly as a result of the flight of those shops from Ḥayy al-Afrāḥ. The abundance of new signs along Prince Hassan Street, an axis in permanent construction, has formed an anarchic commercial centrality. The malls and shops that it hosts specialize in adapting to the demands of consumers, the various inhabitants of ʾIrbid: the Syrian refugees, the expatriate students, and the Jordanian middle classes. The diversity of uses of the place and the mechanisms of specialization, privatization, and exclusion contribute to segmenting the space of this commercial axis. Therefore, it is by looking at these dynamics together with urban planning trends that urban transformations should be considered.

This marginalization of the spaces where a population composed of Syrian refugees is concentrated echoes that of the Palestinian neighborhoods of the city, in particular 'Irbid Camp. Their conception is, however, dissimilar: while the camps are spaces established by UNRWA and the local authorities, the neighborhood of Ḥayy al-Afrāḥ received the Syrian refugees spontaneously. The marginalization of the neighborhood is thus a matter of *laissez-faire* by the municipality. It also reveals the neoliberal urbanism at work in 'Irbid (Semmoud et al. 2014). Through the commodification of the city (Dikec 2002; Harvey 2007) and unregulated urban growth, 'Irbid is part of this type of development, one that is widely known in Arab towns (Barthel and Planel 2010; Verdeil and Souami 2006; Daher 2013; Semmoud and Alaime 2012). In this process, the poorest, including refugee populations, are relegated to the urban margins (Fawaz 2010; Doraï and Puig 2012). These rapid transformations in different spaces of the city thus characterize the constant instability of the urban topography that neoliberal functioning qualifies (Peck, Theodore, Brenner 2009).

Bibliography

Abū Ghanima, Zyad (2014) *'Irbidī yatadhakkar. Nubdhat tārīkhiyya . . . maḥaṭṭāt fī syratīn zātya*, Vol. I & Vol. II, Amman: Rawand Graphics.

Aldeek, Zaid, and Mahmoud Mistarihi (2020), "Towards a Modern Design of Undeveloped City Using a Spatial Modelling Analysis; A Case Study of Irbid City in Jordan," *International Journal of Sustainable Development and Planning*, 15 (4): 547–57.

Agier, Michel (2015), *Anthropologie de la ville*, Paris: Presses Universitaires de France.

Barthel, Pierre-Arnaud, and Sabine Planel (2010), "Tanger-Med and Casa-Marina, Prestige Projects in Morocco: New Capitalist Frameworks and Local Context," *Built Environment*, 36 (2): 176–91. Available online: https://doi.org/10.2148/benv.36.2.176.

Battegay, Alain (2003), "Les recompositions d'une centralité commerçante immigrée: la place du pont à Lyon," *Revue européenne des migrations internationales*, 19 (2): 9–22.

Bourne, Larry Stuart (1981), *The Geography of Housing*, Silver Spring, London, New York: V. H. Winston.

Brun, Jaques, and Jean-Pierre Lévy (2000), "De l'extension au renouvellement métropolitain: mosaïque sociale et mobilité," in Françoise Dureau et al., *Métropoles en mouvement*, 229–46, Paris: Anthropos.

Daher, Rami Farouk (2013), "Neoliberal Urban Transformations in the Arab City," *Environnement Urbain / Urban Environment*. Available online: http://journals.openedition.org/eue/411.

Dikec, Mustafa (2002), "Police, Politics, and the Right to the City," *GeoJournal*, 58: 91–8.

Doraï, Kamel (2016), "La Jordanie et les réfugiés syriens," *La Vie des Idées*. Available online: http://www.laviedesidees.fr/La-Jordanie-et-les-refugies-syriens.html.

Doraï, Kamel (2020), "Lire la ville à partir d'une figure informelle: camps, urbanisation et migrations forcées au Moyen-Orient," in Félix Adisson, Sabine Barles, Nathalie Blanc,

Olivier Coutard, and Leïla Frouillou (eds.), *Pour la recherche urbaine*, 197–201, Paris: CNRS Editions.

Doraï, Kamel, and Nicolas Puig (2012), *L'urbanité des marges, migrants et réfugiés dans les villes du Proche-Orient*, Paris: Téraèdre.

Fawaz, Mona (2010), "Neoliberal Urbanity and the Right to the City: A View from Beirut's Periphery," *Development and Change*, 827–52.

Fawaz, Mona, Ahmad Gharbieh, Mona Harb, and Dounia Salamé (2018), *Refugees as City Makers*. Available online: https://www.aub.edu.lb/ifi/Documents/publications/research_reports/2018-2019/20180910_refugees_as_city_makers.pdf.

Ghassān Abū al-Sha'r, Hind (2009), *'Irbid wa Jiwāruhā, 1850-1928*, Amman: Publications of the Ministry of Culture.

Grafmeyer, Yves (1994), "Regards sociologiques sur la ségrégation," in Jacques Brun and Catherine Rhein (eds.), *La ségrégation dans la ville: concepts et mesures*, 85–118, Paris: L'Harmattan.

Grafmeyer, Yves, and Isaac Joseph (1979), *l'école de Chicago. Naissance de l'écologie urbaine*, Paris: Flammarion.

Greater Irbid Municipality, The Ministry of Municipal Affairs, Amman Institute for Urban Development & Planning Alliance (May 2010), *Irbid 2030: Regional Growth Plan*.

Harvey, David (2007), "Neoliberalism as Creative Destruction," *The Annals of the American Academy of Political and Social Science*, 610 (21): 22–44.

Harvey, David (2011), *Le capitalisme contre le droit à la ville. Néolibéralisme, urbanisation, résistances*, Paris: Amsterdam Editions.

Japan International Cooperation Agency and The Hashemite Kingdom of Jordan (1978), *Integrated Regional Development Study of Northern Jordan*.

Kaedbey, Rouba (2021), "Stratégies locatives et ascension sociale des propriétaires-bailleurs à Horch el-Qatil, banlieue sud de Beyrouth," *Cybergeo: European Journal of Geography, Space, Society, Territory*. Available online: https://doi.org/10.4000/cybergeo.36264.

Koumach, Faycal (1987), *La ville d'Irbid, études sur les migrations et l'urbanisation dans le Nord de la Jordanie*, thèse de doctorat de géographie, Université de Tours.

Levy, Jeann-Pierre (1998), "Dynamique du parc immobilier et mobilité résidentielle," in Marion Segaud, Catherine Bonvalet and Jacques Brun (eds.), *Logement et habitat, l'état des savoirs*, 36–44, Paris: La Documentation Française.

Ministry of Municipal Affairs (2010), *Irbid Plan: Situation Analysis Report*.

Peaucelle, Héloïse (2020), "La présence syrienne à Irbid (1). Une ville jordanienne tournée vers la Syrie," *Les carnets de l'Ifpo. La recherche en train de se faire à l'Institut français du Proche-Orient*. Available online: https://ifpo.hypotheses.org/10786.

Peaucelle, Héloïse (2021), "Mobilités contraintes, pratiques différenciées. Tactiques de déplacement et d'installation des Syriens à Irbid (Jordanie)," *Espace populations sociétés*. Available online: https://doi.org/10.4000/eps.12062.

Peck, Jamie, Nik Theodore, and Neil Brenner (2009), "Neoliberal Urbanism: Models, Moments, Mutations," *SAIS Review*, 29 (1): 49–66.

Shunnaq, Suleiman, and William Schwab (2000), "Continuity and Change in a Middle Eastern City: The Social Ecology of Irbid City, Jordan," *Urban Anthropology and Studies of Cultural Systems and World Economic Development*, 29 (1): 69–96.

Semmoud, Nora, and Alaime Matthieu (2012), "Urbanisme dans le Monde arabe: entre ancrage à l'économie-monde et processus de marginalisations socio-spatiales. Le cas d'Aqaba en Jordanie," *Architecture symbolique et renouveau des espaces marginalisés* (conferenceproceedings): 221–32.

Semmoud, Nora, Bénédicte Florin, Olivier Legros, and Florence Troin (2014), *Marges urbaines et néolibéralisme en Méditerranée*, Tours: Presses universitaires François-Rabelais.

Souami, Taoufik, and Eric Verdeil (2006), *Concevoir et gérer les villes - Milieux d'urbanistes du sud de la Méditerranée*, Paris: Economica, Anthropos.

Satloff, Robert (1986), "They Cannot Stop Our Tongues: Islamic Activism in Jordan," *The Washington Institute for Near East Policy*. Available online: washingtoninstitute.org/media/3683.

Al-Ta'ani, Mohammad (2007), *An Empirical Study of Central City. Planning and Urban Design of the City of Irbid*, Amman, Jordan: Publications of the Ministry of Culture.

Tawālbeh, Mohammad (1982), *Irbid City. A Study in the Geography of Cities*, Irbid: Yarmouk University.

UNHCR, online (March 2020). Available online: https://data2.unhcr.org/en/situations/syria/location/36.

Welsh, Cassandra, and Elias Jourdi (January 2018), *Assessment of the Jordanian Marketplace. Basic Needs and Shelter Working Groups - Jordan Multi-Market Assessment*, UNHCR & NRC. Available online: https://data.unhcr.org/en/documents/details/61728..

Part 3

Social Reconfigurations: Solidarity Networks and Humanitarianism

9

Displacing Female Labor

A Gendered Perspective on Transnational Families during the Syrian Conflict

Ann-Christin Zuntz

Conventional cartography of Syrian displacement in the Middle East tells a story of linear flight and stuckness in exile. Maps on the website of the UNHCR Syria Regional Refugee Response depict refugee communities in Syria's neighboring countries as blobs of different sizes or as areas colored in darker shades, often alarmingly red (UNHCR 2020). However, the static gaze that the UNHCR, the international community, and host states direct at Syrians' presence fails to capture the intricate ways in which the latter relate to sites of origin and refuge. These representations of displacement make forced migration look like a one-way ticket, obscuring older circular mobilities in which current flight trajectories are inscribed. They also replicate a state-centric view of Syrians' movement that draws attention to official frontiers and acts of border crossing (Malkki 1992). For many Syrians, however, borders in the Levant only became relevant relatively recently: when they were closed during the Syrian conflict. In this chapter, I tell an alternative story of refugee movements between Syria and Jordan. I foreground mobilities that bind places together and create zones of exchange and habitation which are not identical with countries on the map. By retracing the footsteps of Habiba and her five sisters between the outskirts of Ḥalab and al-Mafraq, a provincial town in northern Jordan, I aim to capture the affective and economic dimensions of family life during displacement. Over the last two decades, the sisters have moved back and forth between the two countries for various reasons: to work in agriculture, to get married, and to flee conflict. In this chapter, I look at their movements through a transnational lens. Since the early 1990s, the concept of "transnationalism" has caused important conceptual shifts in the ways we think about migration (for an overview, see Glick Schiller et al. 1992; Bauböck and Faist 2010; Faist et al. 2013): mobile people often simultaneously live and contribute to communities of origin and host communities, and some bypass assimilation altogether (Portes et al. 2017). The "transnational practices" (Faist 2010: 20) of migrants and those left may combine material and virtual, sentimental, and monetary gestures, including mutual visits, remittance-sending, and the exchange of messages, gifts, and even spouses. They are facilitated by new and more accessible forms of transportation and communication technologies. In this chapter, I make two claims: First, displacement does not merely disrupt transnational families like Habiba's. Rather, it reconfigures, and sometimes expands, cross-border kinship-based ties. A richer understanding of how the Syrian refugee crisis unfolds in a landscape already shaped by the low-skilled migration of men, but also entire families, explains *where* in the Middle East displaced Syrians choose to seek refuge and jobs and *how* populations with few assets survive in exile: through their embeddedness into transnational support networks that they can capitalize on in times of conflict. Second, this chapter adds a much-needed gendered perspective to the study of Syrian migrations and displacements in the Middle East. I contend that women's roles in transnational families may shift in times of displacement. In the context of the Syrian humanitarian response, the growing number of female-headed refugee households has attracted the attention of aid agencies (e.g., CARE 2016). However, following Chant (2014), I would like to redirect the discussion from poor women's increased financial contribution to household income, to the diversification of their labor, only some of which is remunerated.[1] Making a group of sisters from rural Ḥalab the protagonists of this chapter allows me to highlight the richness of their lives, as well as the ways in which they care for each other and their loved ones. In al-Mafraq, Habiba and her sisters provide a substantial part of the family income through work in agriculture, marriages with more affluent partners, and as preferred beneficiaries of humanitarian assistance—but they are rarely in control of financial resources. While Syrian men have stopped being their families' main breadwinners, husbands, fathers, and brothers retain the upper hand when it comes to deciding how resources are distributed: money, employment opportunities, and even a girl's hand in marriage.

In media and fundraising campaigns, the passive suffering of "women and children" (Enloe 1990) is often represented as emblematic of refugeehood (Hyndman and Giles 2011; Johnson 2011). In the context of the Syria humanitarian response, Turner (2019) finds that "doing gender" often equals "helping women." However, the goal of this chapter is not to treat Syrian refugee women as an undifferentiated mass. Before 2011, Syrian women's experiences varied greatly, depending on their class, region of origin, religious and ethnic affiliation, educational status, and location in rural or urban areas (Chatty 2013; Kastrinou 2016; Rabo 2008; Rugh 1996; Salamandra 2004). Through the propaganda and institutions of the Syrian state, females were also exposed to ideals of "modern" working women, although real women often found it hard to reconcile the demands of their job and family lives (Lei Sparre 2008; Rabo 1996). During the 2011 revolution, a substantial number of working-class women played an important role in organizing peaceful resistance at the grassroots level but have also been targeted by gender-based violence by the Syrian regime and other parties to the conflict (Alsaba and Kapilashrami 2016). To avoid painting Habiba and her sisters as mere victims of displacement and the patriarchy, this chapter follows Hilhorst, Porter, and Gordon (2018) in adopting a relational notion of "gender": it brings to the fore

1 In this chapter, I adopt a broader understanding of "labor," taking guidance from scholars like Sylvia Chant who consider women's caring responsibilities a form of unpaid, and often unacknowledged, labor.

the various networks that female refugees find themselves in, shifting the focus on structural power relations that open up specific subject positions to displaced women as mothers, farm workers, and, sometimes, volunteers and students. A focus on refugee relationality implies that to understand female employment strategies, we should not look at mobile women as atomized individuals but also need to concern ourselves with how they access resources through family members and marriage (cf. Joseph 1994, 2004). Extended Syrian families often function as profitable economic units, with different household members taking on paid or unpaid tasks (e.g., Rabo 2008; Rugh 1996). Ultimately, the chapter disentangles how different forms of work—waged and (unpaid) reproductive labor—are organized within one family and stretched across different locations in Syria and Jordan.

The first two sections of this chapter discuss the role of Syrians in agriculture in al-Mafraq before and after 2011. Before the conflict, the landless poor like Habiba's family made a living through circular migrations within Syria and beyond its frontiers. The sisters' working experience in northern Jordan is symptomatic of the segmentation of Arab labor markets and the increased share of migrants and women in the agricultural workforce. After 2011, former migrants-turned-refugees often found jobs with the same Jordanian employers, but they also experienced a severe drop in social status and a new legal limbo. The third section looks at the other, unpaid, work that female refugees *also* do: reproductive labor that holds transnational families together. As the gradual hardening of the Syrian-Jordanian border disrupts customary mobility circuits and disperses families across different sites in the Levant, Habiba and her sisters find themselves at the heart of marital politics that aim to strengthen old ties and facilitate access to new resources. Syrian brides' loss of value on transnational marriage markets also reflects changed relationships with the host community.

The chapter draws on fourteen months of ethnographic fieldwork with displaced Syrians in northern Jordan in 2016/17, as part of my doctoral thesis (Wagner 2019b). At the time of my study, al-Mafraq was home to around 100,000 locals and similar numbers of Syrians (mayor of al-Mafraq, personal communication, 2016). I befriended Habiba and her sisters through volunteering with a small European organization; in this capacity, I first acted as an interpreter between the sisters and aid workers during house visits and NGO training. Approaching one's research subjects with the help of humanitarian actors raises methodological and ethical concerns. Refugees in the Middle East have been disproportionately targeted by academic research, usually with little improvements to their living conditions (Nayel 2013). In a volatile region, Jordan stands out because of its political stability and lenient visa regime, making it an attractive destination for academics. During the time of my fieldwork, volunteering with refugees was certainly the established mode of making contact with potential informants for fellow PhD researchers and more senior academics from the Global North (Pascucci 2018). In al-Mafraq, I met Syrian refugees who had been registered, assisted, questioned, and trained repeatedly by big aid agencies like the UNHCR and Save the Children, grassroots organizations, domestic authorities, and Jordanian and foreign scholars. In this regard, humanitarian actors were more than simple gate-keepers that regulated access to study informants. Syrians' ample experience with the aid sector and academics shaped the very stories they told me—or chose to withhold—because they did not want to compromise access to further humanitarian assistance. During first encounters, my interlocutors often provided standardized refugee narratives about flight and suffering in exile that obscured alternative forms of economic agency and more complicated histories of belonging; they also concealed livelihood strategies deemed unacceptable to aid workers and scholars from the Global North, for example, early marriage and child labor. I tried to address this "humanitarian bias" through repeated follow-up visits without company. Being treated like a private "guest," not like an NGO worker, facilitated different discussions about family life and relationships. At Habiba's family home, I often took part in meals and sleep-overs. Over time, I held their newborn babies and paid my respects at wakes for relatives who had been killed in Ḥalab. Through accompanying Habiba on trips to the souq and her older siblings' homes in al-Manshiyya, outside al-Mafraq, I got a better sense of the places that the sisters inhabited, if only fleetingly, and the fault lines between refugees and the host community, as well as gendered barriers in public space. Still, my relationship with the family remained ambivalent. While Habiba's parents referred to me as a "daughter," they also asked me for money and gifts, wishes I found difficult to fulfill as a PhD student on a tight budget. Once, Habiba's father tried to talk me into a sham marriage with a Syrian friend who planned to migrate to Germany and open a shop there. These contradictions are far from exceptional. Anthropologists often struggle with the transactional dimension of relationships with interlocutors whom they befriend in the field. While fieldwork pays off in the form of doctoral theses, publications, and promotions, at least for researchers, the latter often remain attached to Western notions of friendship as "voluntary and void of calculation and interest" (De Regt 2019: 102). Over time, I began to understand that Habiba's family saw our interactions not merely as instrumental. Rather, their demands indicated that I had been incorporated into their transnational support networks—and thus become the recipient, but also provider, of affection and material resources.

1. Agricultural Labor—Migrants

"When my mother married my father, she didn't know anything about sheep and milk, she had to learn everything!" (Rufida, Habiba's 18-year-old sister) The first section of this chapter explores the pre-war lives and travels of Habiba's family. Before 2012, the year the family permanently relocated to al-Mafraq, they mostly lived in the northern suburbs of Ḥalab, close to Al Kindi Hospital, one of Syria's most modern medical facilities. At that time, the family consisted of Habiba, her five sisters, and three brothers—in 2016 ranging in age from their late twenties to only five—as well as their parents, Abu and Um Mohammed. As Rufida explained to me one day, her mother came from a poor urban family and got married early to a Bedouin man. What Rufida meant by "Bedouin" was more than lineage; it also referred to the lifestyle of livestock herders. As Chatty (2013 [1986]) famously argued, various Arab states implemented sedentarization politics after World War II, but this did not lead to the disappearance of mobile livelihoods. Rather, Bedouins made use of modern technologies, including trucks, to expand their pastoralist activities over the entire Middle East. They also diversified their sources of income, finding employment in agriculture, trade, and transport. The travels of labor migrants like Abu Mohammed, now in his early fifties, remain rooted in these older forms of mobility. At the time of his wedding more than thirty years ago, some of his relatives still lived in tents. While he and his wife have always inhabited houses—mostly cement block homes—they initially engaged in traditional Bedouin activities, making and selling cheese. When they had children, they switched to working on farms. For most of Habiba's childhood, the family resided on the grounds of a chicken factory outside Ḥalab. Parents and children also regularly found jobs during the olive harvest in rural Ḥalab. One of the rare pictures of Habiba's childhood shows a fifteen-year-old smiling shyly while hiding behind olive trees. Hard labor from an early age made up most of her life even before 2011. Like many poor Syrians, Habiba and her older sisters dropped out of school after grade 9, when compulsory education ended. Although Habiba's family spent a lifetime on the doorstep of Syria's largest urban center, they were not city-dwellers. Rather, their lives were lived on sites of agricultural production and according to agricultural rhythms. Besides, they were also too poor to enjoy urban leisure activities or Ḥalab's historical treasures. As Abeer, Habiba's 28-year-old sister, explained: "We always worked." On the outskirts of Ḥalab, the girls' freedom of movement was limited. Habiba and her sisters only went out when accompanied by their parents and brothers. Years later, in mid-sized al-Mafraq, a much smaller city, Habiba was still too afraid to take taxis on her own.

During the lifetime of Abu Mohammed, the struggles of Syria's rural poor tell a story of unfulfilled promises. Since the 1960s, the Baathist state expanded infrastructure and public services to the countryside and co-opted rural populations through career opportunities in state bureaucracies and the military, but the poorest segment of the rural population failed to benefit from these measures (Batatu 1999; Hinnebusch et al. 2013). In the 1990s, Syria transitioned from socialist experiments to crony capitalism and witnessed the emergence of an excess workforce: the rural (and urban) poor. While educational reforms had increased literacy rates and created a young population not interested in the traditional agricultural profession, they were still outside the regime's clientelist networks that would have granted them access to white-collar jobs (Imady 2014). Baathist rule had entrenched a new form of poverty, one less characterized by threats to poor people's immediate survival but by the absence of opportunities for upscaling existing livelihoods. Habiba's family was among the worst off because they did not own land. In the early 1980s, it was estimated that between 20 and 35 percent of agricultural households in the Middle East were landless, although this number seems to have grown in Syria since then (Forni 2003). Their survival strategies were symptomatic of two wider trends in Middle Eastern agriculture in the twentieth century: the increasing contribution of women and migrants to farming.

On the one hand, women's share of agricultural labor in the Middle East has increased dramatically over the last forty years. In 2010, more than 60 percent of the economically active population on Jordanian and Syrian fields was female (FAO 2011). While women have always worked as unpaid labor on their families' farms, the modernization of farming and changes to the structure of the workforce led to the appearance of female wage labor groups and even female labor contractors. Abdelali-Martini and Dey de Pryck (2015) describe the consequences of Syria's agricultural intensification program that started in 1975. While new technologies entailed the mechanization of male tasks, menial labor for women, e.g., weeding, harvesting, and dealing with small livestock, remained. Young men also left the agricultural sector because of better employment prospects in construction and trade. However, waged labor did not increase female economic independence, as women needed their fathers' and husbands' approval and did not dispose of their salary individually. Lower social status, wage differentials, and the added burden of domestic duties cemented gender inequalities. During Habiba's childhood and in 2016 al-Mafraq, her family followed a similar pattern. While Abu Mohammed accompanied his unmarried daughters to work, their wages were paid to him.

On the other hand, high levels of poverty in the most productive agricultural regions in northern and eastern Syria triggered circular migrations to rural and urban destinations within the country and beyond its frontiers. It is quite likely that Abu Mohammed was an internal migrant before he first came to Jordan. In al-Mafraq, he proudly told me about his experience with Syrian Kurds and even taught me some Kurdish words. Like many farm workers in northern Syria, he probably worked in the olive harvest in Syria's Kurdish territories (cf. Wessels 2008). In 2009, a relative mentioned that there were jobs in al-Mafraq. For the next three years, the family and their unmarried children shuttled back and forth between Ḥalab and northern Jordan. That Abu Mohammed switched from internal to international migration in the late 2000s might not be arbitrary. After 2000, the privatization of state farms and worsening water scarcity, due to decades of intensive irrigation, put many farmers out of work, resulting in a 33 percent decrease of agricultural labor (Aïta 2009). Around 2008/2009, the compounded effects of a severe drought and the cut of diesel and fuel subsidies worsened employment opportunities in northern Syria, leading to a mass exodus of hundreds of thousands of farm workers (Fröhlich 2016; Selby, Dahy, Fröhlich and Hulme 2017).

Compared to other Syrian labor migrants who later returned to al-Mafraq as refugees, the family's migration had been limited in scope. In 2016, I also encountered numerous former small-scale farmers from rural Ḥalab and Homs who had complemented income from agriculture with regular migrations inside Syria, to destinations further away, including Lebanon, Jordan, and the Gulf. Their movements occupied distinct roles in the household life cycle. At various moments in their lives, men, but also women, went abroad to prepare for a wedding, pay for their children's education and care for the elderly, and to make savings for their old age (Khalaf and Alkobaisi 1999; Proudfoot 2015; Rabo 2008, 2010; Wagner 2019b; Wessels 2008). Work was usually organized along kinship lines and by men, and women did not have to negotiate with labor contractors and transport companies. Hence, organizational knowledge was highly gendered. Many refugee women whom I met in al-Mafraq in 2016 came from similar rural backgrounds and had worked abroad alongside their parents and husbands. Still, they often struggled to recall the names of specific villages or areas. This does not mean that migrant women's perspective is not important; rather, it indicates that men and women may experience mobile livelihoods differently. In al-Mafraq, most of my research was conducted with female refugees, and their sketchy memories made it difficult for me to retrace their pre-war travels. However, the fact that Syrian labor migrations remained invisible was also encouraged by host states before 2011. Quite tellingly, seasonal workers like Abu Mohammed were absent from migration statistics in neighboring countries like Jordan (MPC 2013b) and Lebanon (MPC 2013a), where the Syrian workforce was estimated at 300,000–500,000 before the onset of the Syrian conflict (Mehchy and Doko 2011). From the perspective of labor-receiving countries, Syrian migration provided a cheap and exploitable workforce that hardly used any public services at their destination. While transnational labor migration achieved de facto regional integration from below, the lack of institutional frameworks and restrictive national immigration policies produced a deeply fragmented "pan-Arab labour market" (Thiollet 2017: 30) that prevented migrant settlement in host societies. In Jordan, for example, remittances from white-collar workers in the Gulf had led to upward social mobility and a decrease in domestic manual labor, especially in agriculture and construction. However, many Jordanians returned home during the oil crisis in the Gulf countries in the 1980s, and the mass-scale repatriation of Jordanian-Palestinians after the Second Gulf War caused soaring unemployment rates of up to 30 percent in the early 1990s. Structural adjustment policies and the shrinking of the public sector put additional strain on Jordan's labor market, provoking the tightening of immigration policies and attempts at indigenizing labor. As early as 1984, Egyptian workers were thus required to obtain work permits. A decade later, migrant labor was restricted to certain low-skilled sectors. Jordan prevented migrants from overstaying their welcome by keeping them in legal limbo, irregularizing huge segments of foreign labor, issuing employer-bound visas, and excluding them from the trade unions. Similar restrictive policies were implemented in Lebanon (Chalcraft 2007) and the Gulf (Thiollet 2017). Even before 2011, Habiba's family never obtained work permits—like many other Syrian migrants, they flew under the radar.

However, Habiba's family was not simply wandering around. Like other former Syrian migrants that I spoke with in 2016, they coped with insecure livelihoods through a combination of mobility and retaining fixed points. Before the Syrian conflict, the migrations of various household members kept families together and allowed them to accumulate resources, as long as they remained firmly centered in places of origin. Habiba's family, too, had such a fixed point: a house close to Al Kindi Hospital that they had started building in the 2000s, that had absorbed all their revenues from farm work, and where Abu Mohammed and his wife had planned to spend their old age, surrounded by their children. When the house was destroyed in 2012, the family decided to seek refuge in al-Mafraq, where I met them four years later. Even in autumn 2016, their lost home was never far away, as the second half of my fieldwork coincided with the final days of the siege of Ḥalab. Together with one of his sons-in-law, Abu Mohammed constantly watched the news on opposition channels like Orient News and Ḥalab al-Yawm. In between, they switched to Turkish and Kurdish television. Without understanding what was said, the men were transfixed by images of destruction. Al Kindi Hospital, the site of their former dream house, had become an icon of the struggle between regime and opposition forces. In October 2016, it was completely destroyed (Elwazer, Kourdi and Yan 2016; Sky News 2016), like most of the surrounding neighborhoods (UNITAR 2016). In al-Mafraq, like before the war, the family lived in rented accommodation. They shared a damp three-bedroom apartment with broken windows and leaking drains, sparsely furnished with carpets, cushions-, and an old TV that an NGO had given them. In the girls' room, long dresses that belonged to Habiba, Abeer, and their two teenage sisters, were neatly piled up in one corner because they shared a single wardrobe. At night, the girls slept on thin mattresses. Most months, Abu Mohammed struggled to pay the 200 Jordanian dinar (USD 282) rent. With dreams of ownership shattered and former homes altered beyond recognition, Abeer experienced a strong sense of alienation. On social media, she referred to herself as "a flower in salty soil."

2. Agricultural Labor—Refugees

The second part of this chapter looks at the family's return, as refugees, to al-Mafraq and its agricultural economy. For Abu Mohammed, relocating to al-Mafraq because of the conflict was the obvious choice: the town was already part of the family's customary migration circuit in the Levant, and he had good relationships with local employers. Besides, one of Habiba's older sisters had recently married a Jordanian from a nearby village. Abu Mohammed's reasoning reflects wider spatial trends in the flight routes of Syrian refugees. After 2011, evidence from Jordan (Lagarde and Doraï 2017; Wagner 2019b; Zuntz 2021), Lebanon (Vignal 2018), and Iraqi Kurdistan (De Gonzague and Dessi 2014) suggests that entire communities from rural Syria managed to capitalize on older connections with foreign employers to seek refuge and jobs in neighboring countries. Diverse reasons motivated some of them to return to al-Mafraq, and not to other places where they had lived and worked in the past. There is anecdotal evidence that some Jordanian employers proactively reached out to former Syrian farm workers, inviting them back on their lands. Rumors, relayed to me by a local pastor, have it that a al-Mafraq resident organized buses to bring rural populations from Homs governorate during the Syrian army's Homs offensive in spring 2012, going as far as helping them to obtain identity documents before their departure. Positive personal working experience and knowledge of transport routes equally affected Syrians' decision to seek refuge in northern Jordan. Many of my interlocutors also highlighted the importance of a shared language and a conservative form of Sunni Islam. Linguistic and cultural differences made it less attractive to them to flee to multi-ethnic, liberal Lebanon or non-Arabic-speaking Turkey.

In 2016, the family's pre-war knowledge of al-Mafraq translated into an intimate grasp of the town's winding street market and its public transport options, as well as interactions with local residents. Abeer, the most daring of the sisters, once invited me into a crammed shop in the mechanics' area of the souq, to sip lemonade with a Jordanian blacksmith that her father had befriended years earlier. When I visited the family, Abu Mohammed's local friends were often gathered in the living room. Unlike refugees who were newcomers, the sisters also noticed changes in the cityscape. On a trip to the countryside, Habiba pointed out new buildings on the outskirts of al-Mafraq which had not existed seven years earlier—a sign of the recent real estate boom caused by the influx of refugees. More importantly, the family's familiarity with al-Mafraq's local labor market meant that Abu Mohammed and his unmarried daughters could find jobs even when other refugees did not.[2] Even when the harvest was particularly poor, Habiba's elderly father managed to procure jobs for himself and three unmarried daughters throughout the entire season, alternating between different employers. While many Syrians complained about the scarcity of jobs, he relied on widespread professional networks. But work was no fun. Every morning at 4:00 a.m., he and his daughters joined a mass of female and underage workers. A bus picked them up from home and took them to a greenhouse in Jordan's Eastern Desert—Habiba never found out its exact location. The buses full of Syrian women, children, and the elderly did not return until the late afternoon. These Syrians were particularly cheap to employ. In 2016, Habiba and her sisters each earned five Jordanian dinars (USD 7) a day, some of which went to the owner of the bus, a Jordanian woman. The strenuous work—gathering fruits and sorting products into pallets, rudely pushed forward by Egyptian foremen—frequently made Rufida, Habiba's teenage sister, faint. They usually worked six days a week, even during Ramadan, when hard labor was compounded by fasting. Thick black face veils were meant to protect the girls not only from the blazing sun but also unwanted glances, as sexual harassment against Syrian women was common. Habiba's entire family had to stop working when Abu Mohammed, their only male company, broke his hand. Some months later, only she and her father went back to work in the olive harvest in al-Manshiyya, a nearby village—Rufida and Abeer were too sick to join.

As the family's working experience indicates, refugees have re-entered highly segmented labor markets in Syria's neighboring countries. According to an op-ed in the English-language *Jordan Times*, only 3–4 percent of workers in agriculture are Jordanians (Anani 2017). Despite their familiarity with al-Mafraq and its surroundings, as refugees, Syrians experienced a severe drop in social status (El Miri and Mercier 2018). Such social degradation is felt in more exploitative working conditions, including greater dependency on Jordanian employers and middlemen, lower salaries, and sexual harassment. While Habiba and her sisters experienced it in the fields, other Syrian workers were exposed to similar treatment in al-Mafraq's restaurants, supermarkets, construction sites, and quarries. As before 2011, Syrian women and children are often recruited along lineage lines. However, the massive influx of refugees led to a surplus of foreign labor, heightening the competition among Syrians and other migrants—in al-Mafraq, mostly Egyptians—and decreasing Syrians' bargaining power. Jordanian employers aptly play out the different labor forces against each other by introducing wage differentials and working hierarchies among migrants. While the arrival of Syrian refugees willing to accept lower wages pushed other low-skilled migrant workers with equally shady legal status further into the informal economy (Hartnett 2019), many Syrians earn less than established Egyptians. In 2015, the average monthly income of Syrian workers was below the Jordanian minimum wage (Yahya, Kassir, and El-Hariri 2018). Syrian women, in

2 For a long time, I unsuccessfully tried to gain access to the farms. Once Habiba fell out with the Jordanian owner of the bus that transported the sisters to the fields. Another time, a Jordanian farm owner had promised me access to his greenhouses but pulled out at the very last moment. Clearly, refugee labor was a sensitive topic, and none of the Jordanian employers and their middlemen felt comfortable with having foreign observers around. Thus, I had to rely on the recollections of Habiba and other Syrian women to get an idea of their working conditions in agriculture.

particular, found themselves at the bottom of the migrant hierarchy, subject to the orders of foreign foremen. In the greenhouses, Habiba spent a lot of time sorting vegetables—often tomatoes—into pallets. This is not uncommon since Jordan is one of the biggest tomato exporters in the world, and 18 percent of its tomato-cultivated area is located in al-Mafraq governorate (ILO 2014). However, much of the agricultural production around al-Mafraq, "traditional and low-tech" (ILO 2014: 15), is a losing game. Cheap, rightless, and abundantly available refugee labor of women like Habiba keeps afloat otherwise unsustainable agricultural production in northern Jordan.

Besides the gendered nature of low-skilled farm work and their cheap salaries, there is another reason why Jordanian employers prefer Syrian women: although they do not hold work permits, they are not likely to get deported. Since 2011, Jordan's new refugee-reception policies have reshaped Syrians' transnational labor regimes. Former seasonal migrants who used to go under the radar of the host state and the humanitarian system are now subjected to stricter documentation schemes. In July 2014, the Jordanian authorities forbade the UNHCR from providing documentation to Syrians outside the camps without proper sponsorship. In 2015, the Jordanian Ministry of Interior began to register Syrian refugees outside camps and issued its own "identity cards" (Achilli 2015). Habiba and her family were eager to obtain and update UNHCR and Jordanian forms of documentation because they guaranteed their access to aid, limited public services, and freedom of movement in urban areas. One type of document they never applied for, however, were work permits, although the 2016 Jordan Compact had granted Syrians in Jordan 200,000 work permits in exchange for advantageous loans and preferential access to EU markets (Barbelet, Hagen-Zanker, and Mansour-Ille 2018). Sadly, employment programs seemed badly matched with Jordan's largely informal and casual economy (Lenner and Turner 2018). For someone like Habiba, who changed employers frequently and according to agricultural seasons, more permanent, employer-bound work permits were of little interest. And local businesses had little incentive to regularize foreign staff: Employers of informal workers usually had to pay a fine if caught, but did not pay social security for their hidden staff and disposed of Syrians quickly (Bellamy et al. 2017). In the meantime, thousands of male workers caught without a permit were deported to camps and to Syria (Human Rights Watch 2017). In al-Mafraq as in other Jordanian cities, labor patrol checks were a frequent scare to male Syrians—but they mostly happened inside towns, in restaurants, and shops, which employed Syrian men. By way of contrast, Habiba's jobs were out of sight, in greenhouses in the Eastern Desert and olive groves west of al-Mafraq. The remoteness of her workplaces protected her against unfair persecution by the Jordanian state but also exposed her to exploitation at the hands of her employers and co-workers. But Habiba's efforts did not stop here. Much of her work took place inside her own home.

3. Reproductive Labor

The final section of this chapter makes visible Syrian women's unpaid domestic work that plays a big role in reproducing the transnational family. Habiba's and her sisters' lives were an endless cycle of cooking, cleaning, and childrearing; even unmarried girls were already involved in bringing up younger siblings and their older sisters' offspring. One night, I stayed over in the girls' room, and we chatted until sunrise. After the morning prayer, Habiba, Abeer, and Rufida got up and began tidying up the family apartment. It was only 5:00 a.m., and this was the first in a seemingly endless list of domestic tasks. Married women like Salma, their older sister, were also expected to have quick and multiple pregnancies and to produce male offspring. When Salma, after giving birth to three daughters, fell pregnant again, her mother excitedly told me: "I can tell from the shape of her belly. It's like Layan's belly, and she also delivered a boy!" Like work in farming, reproductive labor is reconfigured by conflict and displacement, to the extent that Salma came to associate her children's birth with the chronology of the war: "Nour was born before the war. When Shinan was born, there was only war in Darʿā. One week after Iman's birth, we had to flee Ḥalab." On a more mundane level, mobility also shaped the sisters' everyday lives in Jordan, where the family had been split between al-Mafraq and nearby al-Manshiyya, a village surrounded by olive groves. Layan and Salma, the two oldest sisters, had moved to al-Manshiyya with their husbands and children (as did their older brother and his Syrian wife). Despite strong restrictions on their freedom of movement inside al-Mafraq, the unmarried girls were allowed to visit their siblings to assist with household chores. After Layan gave birth to her second son, Habiba stayed with her in al-Manshiyya. Some weeks later, it was Rufida's turn to wait on Salma after she had returned from the hospital with her newborn son in her arms.

In al-Mafraq, Syrians maintain not only pre-war ties with Jordanian employers and labor brokers but also with loved ones back home and in other sites of refuge. Like Syrians' embeddedness in local economies, kinship-based transnational networks are far from new, replicating older cross-border connections and travel routes. Abu Mohammed's sister had married in Maʿān, a city in the south of Jordan, twenty years before the war, and Habiba and her siblings visited her frequently. In Syria, Salma had married her paternal cousin. When she finally gave birth to a son in al-Mafraq, he was named after his father's father who had remained in Ḥalab. Family members on both sides of the border stayed in touch on social media. When Abu Mohammed's nephew was killed in Ḥalab, he held a wake in his honor in their living room in al-Mafraq. The family was too poor to send financial support to relatives in Syria, but many other refugees did. Access to aid money in exile allowed refugees to replicate pre-war remittance patterns, albeit on a much smaller scale. Many felt a moral obligation to support family members left behind, but also that this was expected of them. "When we go home, they will ask: What did you bring?" The fact that Abu Mohammed's family did not send or receive remittances testifies to their deprivation, and to the poverty of those close to them. While other refugees received support from Germany, where a new Syrian diaspora had emerged, or from relatives in the GCC countries, none of his close relatives seemed to have succeeded in making a living abroad.

However, scarce resources put a strain even on tight-knit families, and young unmarried women with little education were a liability. While I lived in al-Mafraq, I witnessed a seemingly endless stream of potential suitors, often uninvited, pass through the family's living room. They had come to wed Habiba and Abeer. Abu Mohammed rejected a handsome suitor whom Habiba had fallen in love with because he was a poor Jordanian school teacher and unable to pay the requested dowry. However, since the beginning of the war, the girls' marriage prospects had worsened. The sisters found it difficult to find suitable spouses within their own kinship networks as extended families had been dispersed across countries. Unlike Salma, Habiba and Abeer had no cousins within reach whom they could marry. For Syrians in al-Mafraq, marrying among one's kinfolk was another way of strengthening their social networks and a core element of the normative life course in the countryside. In many cases, marital arrangements were made even when one party was still in Syria or had been displaced to another country. But problems arose when parents had to accept suitors from outside the family, as in the case of Habiba's first wedding. In fact, the problem for young Syrians consisted less in finding marriage candidates—after all, entire villages had fled to al-Mafraq together—but rather in the elevated risk of divorce. Some years before I met her, Habiba's first marriage had ended during her honeymoon when her Syrian husband beat her so severely that she fled to her parents' house, leaving her dowry behind. It took her two years to finalize the divorce papers, and she never retrieved her belongings. While kinship networks still exerted social control over their members in exile, obliging them to redistribute resources and job opportunities with Jordanian farmers and NGOs, there is no denying that it was diminished in al-Mafraq's greater anonymity. Family ties were also eroded through strong competition over jobs and frequent movement within al-Mafraq and to other places in Jordan and abroad (cf. Lokot 2018; Stevens 2016).

Even Habiba's sisters who did not experience divorce had to come to terms with absent husbands. For the spouses of former migrants, long-distance relationships were nothing new. But border and humanitarian regimes had entrenched more permanent forms of living apart, while preventing Syrian men from providing for their families. Whereas Salma lived in al-Manshiyya, her Syrian husband stayed in al-Zaʿtarī Camp and had to apply for exit permits every fortnight to visit his family. In her everyday life, Salma, newly pregnant, was on her own. Unable to work with four young children, she struggled to find NGOs that would pay her rent. I often found her in her parent's living room, surrounded by her doting sisters. Even Layan, whose husband was Jordanian, found it hard to get by. As a low-ranked soldier, he served with the Jordanian army in the desert, usually for weeks at a time. In the village, she and her two children inhabited the ground floor of a house owned by her Jordanian in-laws. While not destitute, she was far from well-off and the apartment was scarcely furnished. Whereas the sisters endured loneliness and financial strain, their spouses retained decision-making power over where to live, how many children they should have, and even their wives' dress codes. While female refugees' responsibilities toward their families often grew in exile, their rights and entitlements did not (cf. Chant 2014).

Syrian-Jordanian marriages, which had been common in al-Mafraq and al-Manshiyya before the war, seemed to have ceased. As Layan explained to me, "suddenly, Jordanian men could find Syrian women everywhere, so they stopped marrying them." That refugee women stopped being suitable (first) wives even for poorer Jordanians was yet another sign of the social degradation that returning Syrians were experiencing in the host country. However, unmarried Syrian women in al-Mafraq found another way to capitalize on the rupture in their social circles and life plans, becoming the *second* wives of older Jordanian men instead. This was far from being an individualistic escape—rather, marrying "out" usually benefited the bride's entire family. For weeks, Abeer received visits from a 50-year-old Jordanian from ʾIrbid city, who was already married but had only one daughter. While she had taken an instant dislike to him and refused him repeatedly, he kept returning, promising her a house of her own. The bride-against-her-will complained to me: "My family is expecting me to get married because he promised to help us." Eventually, the sisters became the second wives of two Syrian brothers from al-Raqqa. Like Habiba's family, the grooms had worked in Maʿān before 2011,not in farming, but as truck drivers in the phosphate industry. The war had separated them from their wives and children in Syria, and after years of waiting, they had decided to start new families. When Habiba and Abeer finally got married, their wedding dresses were brought from al-Zaʿtarī camp where the rent was cheaper. While her sister's white dress cost fifty Jordanian dinars (USD 71), Habiba's new husband could only afford to rent a cheaper, greenish dress for her. The last I heard from the sisters in 2018 was that they had both moved to Maʿān and had both had a son.

Conclusion: Work That Works for (These) Female Refugees

This chapter looked at how the complex spatialities and household economies of a transnational Syrian family have been reshaped by war and displacement. It told the story of a group of Syrian sisters from the outskirts of Ḥalab who came to know remote places in northern Jordan intimately, and it contrasted different types of labor that young female refugees engage in: farming, childrearing, and household chores. In all cases, women's hard work does not only benefit themselves but contribute to the survival of their tight-knit family, now stretched across various locations in the Middle East. The chapter acknowledged movement and mobility-based coping strategies as an ambivalent lifeline for disenfranchised populations. Being mobile shapes where and as what marginalized Syrians work and whom they marry, although my female protagonists seem to have little control over their movements even in times of peace. Hence, my research adds to an emerging body of literature on interlinkages between economic and forced migration in the Middle East (Chatelard 2010; Lagarde and Doraï 2017; Wagner 2019a, 2019b; Zuntz 2021) and elsewhere in the Global South (Horst 2006; Monsutti 2008). Looking at Syrian displacement through a transnational lens helps us understand how, at a time when neighboring countries closed their borders, places, and people inside and outside Syria remained closely connected.

A few caveats are warranted. First, I do not aim to romanticize refugees' transnational connectivities. Since 2011, restrictive border and humanitarian regimes have curtailed Syrians' movements in and beyond Jordan. The closure of Jordan's northern border interrupted Habiba's family's migratory circuits in the Levant, cutting them off from the place that they used to consider home: Ḥalab. Inside the host country, some family members, like Salma's husband who resides in al-Zaʿtarī Camp, are affected more directly by Jordan's recent containment strategies. Refugees' socioeconomic status further limits the extent to which they can pursue transnational practices.

The material resources, but also the social connections that mobile people bring, determine how far they can travel in times of peace and war (Van Hear 2014). Even before 2011, disenfranchised farm workers like Habiba's family never made it further than the Jordanian borderlands. In 2016, Abu Mohammed used social media to stay in touch with relatives trapped elsewhere. Unlike most refugees in al-Mafraq, however, the family was too poor to send remittances back home. At least for now, it seems impossible that they could accumulate savings and, eventually, acquire a material home, as they had done in pre-war Syria. Second, Habiba's experiences are far from being representative of all Syrian women in Jordan, but rather of those of a specific low-income, rural segment of the refugee population. Age and marital status further shape displaced women's responsibilities and rights. Unmarried (and newly wed) females like Habiba and her sisters find themselves at the bottom of employment, but also family, hierarchies: on the fields, they are subjected to badly paid and exploitative labor. At home, they do the lion's share of domestic work but are also expected to accept marital unions arranged for them by older family members.

Distinct female positions within multigenerational patriarchal families—mothers, mothers-in-law, daughters, etc.—are impacted differently by displacement and the contact with humanitarian action, much of which focuses on "female empowerment" (cf. Turner 2019, Zuntz and al. 2021). Habiba's and Abeer's encounters with the NGO world were fleeting. In 2016, both enrolled in numerous short NGO trainings, ranging from English classes to hairdressing and making jewelry, run by local churches, aid agencies, and UN organizations. One day, Habiba asked me to accompany her to a course on removing landmines. At home, she spread out the newly obtained certificates on the carpet in her parents' living room, proudly handing me one after the other. Her enthusiasm was moving. It reminded me of the earnest look on the school girl's face in her childhood picture. Habiba, who had never worked outside her family, suddenly dreamed of working for an NGO and contributing to Syria's reconstruction after the war. In reality, none of these trainings ever led to any form of waged labor. Their lack of formal qualifications made it impossible for the sisters to find more permanent employment, even with NGOs. Before they got married, Habiba and Abeer periodically returned to working in agriculture. But as I write this chapter, Habiba's youngest sister, now sixteen years old, is still in school. As she is fluent in English, she often translates during NGO house visits, an activity her parents grudgingly accept. Unlike her older sisters, her education has turned into a resource, saving her from menial labor and early marriage. Generational differences, it seems, play a part in determining whether refugee girls from rural backgrounds get access to new lifestyles in Jordan. At least some young women, like Habiba's youngest sister, were able to take advantage of the education available to her in Jordan because they entered the host country at a young age. For others, like Habiba, displacement to Jordan came at a time when she had already dropped out of school in Syria. By contrast, middle-aged women, like Um Mohammed, seem to carve out greater freedoms in al-Mafraq. Less subject to restrictive gender norms, they freely attend vocational trainings and wait in the queue outside NGO offices for assistance. While greater contact with aid agencies does not usually translate into real jobs, it brings with it new opportunities for socializing with females outside one's own family. Jobs, volunteering positions, and even potential spouses for one's children are all circulated through these emerging female networks in al-Mafraq.

An ethnographic understanding of the sisters' labors in exile reveals the blind spots of current female empowerment programs aimed at including displaced women into Middle Eastern workforces. The lack of a coordinated aid response at the regional level and dwindling international funds have turned Middle Eastern countries into a laboratory for humanitarian programs that foster urban refugees' economic self-reliance. However, preliminary results from NGO and academic studies suggest that enhancing refugee livelihoods in the Middle East and elsewhere has had limited success (Carpi 2017; Easton-Calabria et al. 2017). Aid agencies' attempts at increasing refugees' self-reliance often fail because they overlook weak host economies and displaced populations' lack of rights (Easton-Calabria and Omata 2018). As I argued in this chapter, refugees' informal and exploitative labor also keeps Jordan's struggling agricultural sector afloat, while perpetuating the country's historically hostile immigration policies. Acknowledging that poor Syrians have long coped with precarious lives through transnational support networks has important consequences for economic empowerment programs which target individuals, instead of families, and do not take into consideration refugees' social obligations toward their next of kin (Easton-Calabria et al. 2017). Before their weddings, Habiba and Abeer had to drop out of an NGO-led teaching scheme because they could not reconcile it with their household chores. As married women in Maʿān, they are not allowed to leave their husbands' homes on their own. Would they even want to work outside the house? When I conducted follow-up interviews in northern Jordan in 2019, many women dreamed of being able to afford *not* to work. Married women from rural backgrounds, who had few income opportunities besides hard work on farms, interpreted the paid labor that was available to them as a symptom of poverty and their husbands' inability to provide for their families. Back in 2016, Habiba and Abeer covered their faces with black veils when they went to the fields. They felt ashamed that someone might tell from their suntan that they were forced to toil in the company of foreign men. Unsurprisingly, the perspectives and aspirations of the displaced are so far largely absent from the design of livelihood programs (Barbelet and Wake 2017). A differentiated view of Syrian livelihoods furthers our understanding of how transnational families are remolded by displacement. It is also needed to ensure that humanitarian project design remains sensitive to complex power dynamics, including gender, but also rural-urban divides, class and generational differences, and ultimately women's own ideas about what constitutes a good life.

Bibliography

Abdelali-Martini, Malika, and Jennie Dey De Pryck (2015), "Does the Feminisation of Agricultural Labour Empower Women? Insights from Female Labour Contractors and Workers in Northwest Syria," *Journal of International Development*, 27: 898–916.

Achilli, Luigi (2015), "Syrian Refugees in Jordan: A Reality Check," *Policy Brief*, European University Institute. Available online: http://cadmus.eui.eu/bitstream/handle/1814/34904/MPC_2015-02_PB.pdf?sequence=1.

Aïta, Samir (2009), "Labour Markets Performance and Migration Flows in Syria," *National Background Paper*, Florence: European University Institute, Robert Schuman Centre for Advanced Studies. Available online: http://www.economistes-arabes.org/Cercle_des_economistes_arabes/Samir_Aita_files/LMM%20Syria-%20Final%20version.pdf.

Alsaba, Khuloud, and Anuj Kapilashrami (2016), "Understanding Women's Experience of Violence and the Political Economy of Gender in Conflict: The Case of Syria," *Reproductive Health Matters*, 24 (47): 5–17.

Anani, Jawad (2017), "A New Approach to Agriculture," *Jordan Times*, May 1. Available online: http://jordantimes.com/opinion/jawad-anani/new-approach-agriculture.

Barbelet, Veronique, Jessica Hagen-Zanker, and Dina Mansour-Ille (2018), "The Jordan Compact: Lessons Learnt and Implications for Future Refugee Compacts," *Overseas Development Institute*. Available online: https://www.odi.org/sites/odi.org.uk/files/resource-documents/12058.pdf.

Barbelet, Veronique, and Caitlin Wake (2017), "Livelihoods in Displacement: From Refugee Perspectives to Aid Agency Response," *Overseas Development Institute*. Available online: https://www.odi.org/sites/odi.org.uk/files/resource-documents/11729.pdf.

Batatu, Hanna (1999), *Syria's Peasantry, the Descendants of Its Lesser Rural Notables, and Their Politics*, Princeton: Princeton University Press.

Bauböck, Rainer, and Thomas Faist (eds.) (2010), *Diaspora and Transnationalism: Concepts, Theories and Methods*, Amsterdam: Amsterdam University Press.

Bellamy, Catherine, Simone Haysom, Caitlin Wake, and Veronique Barbelet (2017), "The Lives and Livelihoods of Syrian Refugees," *HPG Commissioned Report*, Overseas Development Institute, London. Available online: https://www.odi.org/publications/10736-lives-and-livelihoods-syrian-refugees.

CARE (2016), "On Her Own: How Women Forced to Flee from Syria Are Shouldering Increased Responsibility as They Struggle to Survive," CARE. Available online: https://www.care.org/sites/default/files/documents/care_on-her-own_refugee-media-report_sept-2016.pdf.

Carpi, Estella (2017), "Learning and Earning in Constrained Labour Markets: The Politics of Livelihoods in Lebanon's Halba," in Juliano Fiori and Andrea Rigon (eds.), *Making Lives: Refugee Self-Reliance and Humanitarian Action in Cities*, 11–36, London: Save the Children.

Chalcraft, John (2007), "Labour in the Levant," *New Left Review*, 45: 27–47.

Chant, Sylvia (2014), "Exploring the 'Feminisation of Poverty' in Relation to Women's Work and Home-based Enterprise in Slums of the Global South," *International Journal of Gender and Entrepreneurship*, 6 (3): 296–316.

Chatelard, Géraldine (2010), "What Visibility Conceals: Re-Embedding Refugee Migration from Iraq," in Dawn Chatty and Bill Finlayson (eds.), *Dispossession and Displacement: Forced Migration in the Middle East and North Africa*, 17–44, London: British Academy.

Chatty, Dawn (2013 [1986]), *From Camel to Truck: The Bedouin in the Modern World*, Cambridge: The White Horse Press.

Crawley, Heaven, and Dimitris Skleparis (2017), "Refugees, Migrants, Neither, Both: Categorical Fetishism and the Politics of Bounding in Europe's 'Migration Crisis,'"

Journal of Ethnic and Migration Studies, 44 (1): 48–64. https://doi.org/10.1080/1369183X.2017.1348224.
De Gonzague, Justin, and Federico Dessi (eds.) (2014), *Two Countries, One Exile*, unpublished.
De Regt, Marina (2019), "In Friendship One Does Not Count Such Things," *Etnofoor*, 31 (1): 99–112.
Easton-Calabria, Evan, Ulrike Krause, Jessica Field, Anubhav Tiwari, Yamini Mookherjee, Caitlin Wake, Veronique Barbelet, Estella Carpi, Amy Slaughter, and Kellie Leeson (2017), "Research in Brief: Refugee Self-Reliance: Moving Beyond the Marketplace," *RSC Research in Brief 7*, University of Oxford. Available online: https://www.rsc.ox.ac.uk/publications/refugee-self-reliance-moving-beyond-the-marketplace.
Easton-Calabria, Evan, and Naohiko Omata (2018), "Panacea for the Refugee Crisis? Rethinking the Promotion of 'Self-reliance' for Refugees," *Third World Quarterly*, 39 (8): 1458–74.
El Miri, Mustafa, and Delphine Mercier (2018), "'L'encampement' des réfugiés syriens au Moyen-Orient: Déborder les frontières de la vulnérabilité par le travail," *Paper presented to Les réfugiés syriens au Moyen Orient - Encampement, vulnérabilités et travail*, LEST – CNRS/Aix-Marseille University, February 13.
Elwazer, Schams, Eyad Kourdi, and Holly Yan (2016), "Syria: Hospital Attacked as Regime Makes Gains in Aleppo," *CNN*, October 2. Available online: https://edition.cnn.com/2016/10/02/middleeast/syria-aleppo/index.html.
Enloe, Cynthia (1990), "Women and Children: Making Feminist Sense of the Persian Gulf Crisis," *The Village Voice*, September 25.
Faist, Thomas (2010), "Towards Transnational Studies: World Theories, Transnationalisation and Changing Institutions," *Journal of Ethnic and Migration Studies*, 36 (10): 1665–87.
Faist, Thomas, Margit Fauser, and Eveline Reisenauer (eds.) (2013), *Transnational Migration*, Cambridge: Polity Press.
FAO (2011), *The State of Food and Agriculture 2010–2011: Women in Agriculture: Closing the Gender Gap for Development*, Rome: FAO.
Forni, Nadia (2003), "Chapter 12: Land Tenure and Labour Relations," in Ciro Fiorillo and Jacques Vercueil (eds.), *Syrian Agriculture at the Crossroads*, FAO Agricultural Policy and Economic Development Series No. 8, FAO. Available online: http://www.fao.org/docrep/006/y4890e/y4890e0t.htm.
Fröhlich, Christiane (2016), "Climate Migrants as Protestors? Dispelling Misconceptions About Global Environmental Change in Pre-revolutionary Syria," *Contemporary Levant*, 1 (1): 38–50.
Glick Schiller, Nina, Linda Basch, and Cristina Blanc-Szanton (1992), "Transnationalism: A New Analytic Framework for Understanding Migration," *Annals of the New York Academy of Sciences*, 645 (1): 1–24.
Hartnett, Allison Spencer (2019), "The Effect of Refugee Integration on Migrant Labor in Jordan," *Review of Middle East Studies*, 52 (2): 263–82.
Hilhorst, Dorothea, Holly Porter, and Rachel Gordon (2018), "Gender, Sexuality, and Violence in Humanitarian Crises," *Disasters*, 42 (S1): S3–S16.
Hinnebusch, Raymond, Atieh El Hindi, Munzer Khaddam, and Myriam Ababsa (2013), *Agriculture and Reform in Syria*, St Andrews: University of St Andrews, Centre for Syrian Studies.
Horst, Cindy (2006), *Transnational Nomads. How Somalis Cope with Refugee Life in the Dadaab Camps of Kenya*, New York: Berghahn Books.

Human Rights Watch (2017), "'I Have No Idea Why They Sent Us Back'. Jordanian Deportations and Expulsions of Syrian Refugees," *Human Rights Watch*, October 2. Available online: https://www.hrw.org/report/2017/10/02/i-have-no-idea-why-they-sent-us-back/jordanian-deportations-and-expulsions-syrian.

Hyndman, Jennifer, and Wenona Giles (2011), "Waiting for What? The Feminization of Asylum in Protracted Situations," *Gender, Place & Culture*, 18 (3): 361–79.

ILO (2014), "Market Study and Marketing Strategy of Tomato Sector in Mafraq," *ILO*, August 10. Available online: https://www.ilo.org/wcmsp5/groups/public/@arabstates/@ro-beirut/documents/genericdocument/wcms_319818.pdf.

Imady, Omar (2014), "How a Microfinance Network Could Have Preempted the Syrian Uprising," *Syria Studies*, 6 (1): 81–122.

Johnson, Heather L (2011), "Click to Donate: Visual Images, Constructing Victims and Imagining the Female Refugee," *Third World Quarterly*, 32 (6): 1015–37.

Joseph, Suad (1994), "Problematizing Gender and Relational Rights: Experiences from Lebanon," *Social Politics*, 1 (3): 271–85.

Joseph, Suad (2004), "Conceiving Family Relationships in Post-war Lebanon," *Journal of Comparative Family Studies*, 35 (2): 271–93.

Kastrinou, A., and A. Maria (2016), *Power, sect and state in Syria. The Politics of Marriage and Identity amongst the Druze*, London: I. B. Tauris.

Khalaf, Sulayman, and Saad Alkobaisi (1999), "Migrants' Strategies of Coping and Patterns of Accommodation in the Oil-Rich Gulf Societies: Evidence from the UAE," *British Journal of Middle Eastern Studies*, 26 (2): 271–98.

Lagarde, David, and Kamel Doraï (2017), "De la campagne syrienne aux villes jordaniennes. Un réseau marchand transfrontalier à l'épreuve du conflit syrien," *Espace Populations Sociétés*, Centre National de la Recherche Scientifique. Available online: https://halshs.archives-ouvertes.fr/halshs-01654034.

Lei Sparre, Sara (2008), "Educated Women in Syria: Servants of the State, or Nurturers of the Family?," *Critique: Critical Middle Eastern Studies*, 17 (1): 3–20.

Lenner, Katharina, and Lewis Turner (2018), "Making Refugees Work? The Politics of Integrating Syrian Refugees into the Labor Market in Jordan," *Middle East Critique*. https://doi.org/10.1080/19436149.2018.1462601.

Lokot, Michelle (2018), "'Blood Doesn't Become Water'? Syrian Social Relations During Displacement," *Journal of Refugee Studies*, December 7, 2018. Available online: https://doi.org/10.1093/jrs/fey059.

Long, Katy, and Jeff Crisp (2010), "Migration, Mobility and Solutions: An Evolving Perspective," *Forced Migration Review*, 35: 56–7.

Malkki, Liisa (1992), "National Geographic: The Rooting of Peoples and the Territorialization of National Identity among Scholars and Refugees," *Cultural Anthropology*, 7 (1): 24–44.

Mehchy, Zaki, and Amer Mahdi Doko (2011), "General Overview of Migration Into, Through and from Syria," *CARIM Analytic and Synthetic Notes 2011/41*, European University Institute. Available online: http://cadmus.eui.eu/bitstream/handle/1814/17794/CARIM_ASN_2011_41.pdf?sequence=1&isAllowed=y.

Monsutti, Alessandro (2008), "Afghan Migratory Strategies and the Three Solutions to the Refugee Problem," *Refugee Survey Quarterly*, 27 (1): 58–73.

MPC (2013a), "Lebanon," *MPC Migration Profile*, European University Institute. Available online: http://www.migrationpolicycentre.eu/docs/migration_profiles/Lebanon.pdf.

MPC (2013b), "Syria," *MPC Migration Profile*, European University Institute. Available online: http://www.migrationpolicycentre.eu/docs/migration_profiles/Syria.pdf.

Nayel, Moe Ali (2013), "Palestinian Refugees Are Not at Your Service," *The Electronic Intifada*, May 17. Available online: https://electronicintifada.net/content/palestinian-refugees-are-not-your-service/12464.

OEC (2017), "Jordan - Exports," *Observatory of Economic Complexity*. Available online: https://atlas.media.mit.edu/en/profile/country/jor/.

OECD and UNHCR (2018), "Safe Pathways for Refugees. OECD-UNHCR Study on Third Country Solutions for refugees: Family Reunification, Study Programmes and Labour Mobility," *UNHCR*. Available online: https://www.unhcr.org/uk/5c07a2c84.

Pascucci, Elisa (2018), "The Local Labour Building the International Community: Precarious Work within Humanitarian Spaces," *Environment and Planning A: Economy and Space*, 51 (3): 1–18.

Portes, Alejandro, Luis Eduardo Guarnizo, and Patricia Landolt (2017), "Commentary on the Study of Transnationalism: Pitfalls and Promise of an Emergent Research Field," *Ethnic and Racial Studies*, 40 (9): 1486–91.

Proudfoot, Philip (2015), "Red Chinos, Resistance, and Masculinities in Crisis," *Muftah*, October 28. Available online: http://muftah.org/red-chinos-resistance-masculinities-in-crisis/#.WCCyxPmLTb0.

Rabo, Annika (1996), "Gender, State and Civil Society in Jordan and Syria," in C. Hann and E. Dunn (eds.), *Civil Society Challenging Western Models*, 153–74, London and New York: Routledge.

Rabo, Annika (2008), "'Doing Family': Two Cases in Contemporary Syria," *Hawwa*, 6 (2): 129–53.

Rabo, Annika (2010), "To Roam or to be Rooted? Movement, Mobility and Settlement in Northeast Syria," in Nefissa Naguib and Bert de Vries (eds.), *Movement of People in Time and Space: Heureux qui comme Ulysse a fait un beau voyage*, 49–67, Bergen: Uni Global University of Bergen.

Rugh, Andrea (1996), *Within the Circle: Parents and Children in an Arab Village*, New York: Columbia University Press.

Salamandra, Christa (2004), *New Old Damascus: Authenticity and Distinction in Urban Syria*, Bloomington: Indiana University Press.

Selby, Jan, Omar S. Dahi, Christiane Fröhlich, and Mike Hulme (2017), "Climate Change and the Syrian Civil War Revisited," *Political Geography*, 60: 232–44.

Sky News (2016), "Aleppo's Largest Hospital in Rebel-Held Area Is 'Destroyed,'" *Sky News*, October 3. Available online: https://news.sky.com/story/russian-planes-destroy-syrias-cave-hospital-10604281.

Stevens, Matthew R. (2016), "The Collapse of Social Networks among Syrian Refugees in Urban Jordan," *Contemporary Levant*, 1 (1): 51–63.

Thiollet, Hélène (2017), "Managing Transnational Labour in the Arab Gulf: External and Internal Dynamics of Migration Politics since the 1950s," in Leila Vignal (ed.), *The Transnational Middle East*, 21–43, London: Routledge.

Turner, Lewis (2019), "Syrian Refugee Men as Objects of Humanitarian Care," *International Feminist Journal of Politics*, 21 (4): 595–616.

UNHCR (2020), "Syria Regional Refugee Response," *UNHCR*, February 27. Available online: https://data2.unhcr.org/en/situations/syria.

UNITAR (2016), "Syria Aleppo City / Jebel Saman District / Aleppo Province," *UNITAR*, December 19. Available online: http://unosat-maps.web.cern.ch/unosat-maps/SY/CE20130604SYR/UNOSAT_A3_Aleppo_DamagePercentageNeighborhood_20160918opt.pdf.

Van Hear, Nicholas (2014), "Reconsidering Migration and Class," *International Migration Review*, 48 (1): S100–21.
Vignal, Leila (2018), "A Transformed Syria in its Transforming Transnational Environment," *Keynote Lecture Given at 2018 CCS Conference*, University of St Andrews, August 2.
Wagner (now Zuntz), Ann-Christin (2019a), "Acts of 'Homing' in the Eastern Desert – How Syrian Refugees Make Temporary Homes in a Village Outside Zaatari Camp, Jordan," in Johannes Lenhard and Farhan Samanani (eds.), *Home - Ethnographic Encounters*, 175–88, London: Bloomsbury Academic.
Wagner (now Zuntz), Ann-Christin (2019b), "Transnational Mobilities during the Syrian War – An Ethnography of Rural Refugees and Evangelical humanitarians in Mafraq, Jordan," Doctoral thesis, University of Edinburgh.
Wessels, Joshka (2008), *To Cooperate or Not to Cooperate? Collective Action for Rehabilitation of Traditional Water Tunnel Systems (Qanats) in Syria*, Amsterdam: Amsterdam University Press.
Yahya, Maha (2018), "Syrian Refugees: The People Who Want Four Things Before They Go Home," *BBC*, April 6. Available online: https://www.bbc.com/news/world-43578469.
Yahya, Maha, Jean Kassir, and Khalil El-Hariri (2018), *Unheard Voices. What Syrian Refugees Need to Return Home*, Beirut: Carnegie Middle East Center.
Zetter, Roger (2007), "More Labels, Fewer Refugees: Remaking the Refugee Label in an Era of Globalization," *Journal of Refugee Studies*, 20 (2): 172–92.
Zuntz, Ann-Christin, Palattiyil, George, Amawi, Abla, Al Akash, Ruba, Nashwan, Ayat, Al Majali, Areej, and Harish Nair. 2021. "Early marriage and displacement – a conversation: How Syrian daughters, mothers and mothers-in-law in Jordan understand marital decision-making." *Journal of the British Academy* 9: 179-212.

10

Hosting Syrian Refugees in Jordan

Refugee-Led Humanitarianism and National Response

Valentina Napolitano

Since the start of the protests in Syria in March 2011 and the violent conflict that ensued, Jordan has welcomed nearly 665,000 refugees.[1] While at the beginning family/tribal and charitable networks were involved in the reception of refugees, the institutional response was not long in coming and was organized in 2013 around the Jordan Response Plan for the Syrian Crisis (JRPSC). This became the main means of coordination between the Jordanian authorities (Ministry of Planning and International Cooperation, Ministry of the Interior, and Ministry of Labour), UN agencies (in particular the United Nations High Commissioner for Refugees), governmental and non-governmental organizations, and donors. The JRPSC addressed all aspects related to the Syrian presence in Jordan (access to public services, housing, education, health, social protection, and justice) and subsequently integrated a development plan intended to mitigate the effects of the crisis on host communities through the improvement of infrastructure and public services.

In addition to this institutional reception policy, other forms of solidarity and mobilization for the benefit of refugees were organized at the local level, notably within the Syrian community that has been long established in Jordan. Before the conflict, some 40,000 Syrians lived in the country:[2] mainly seasonal workers in agriculture, construction, and trade (cf. Zuntz in this volume); political opponents who arrived in the 1980s;[3] Syrian entrepreneurs[4] and students established in Jordan and the Gulf

1 Publicly available information, on the United Nations High Commissioner for Refugees (UNHCR) *Syrian Refugee Regional Response* webpage.

2 Based on the 2004 national census (De Bel-Air 2016).

3 Following clashes led by a branch of the Muslim Brotherhood (MB) in northern Syria, which suffered a bloody repression by Hafez al-Assad's regime, several thousand Syrians from Hama and Aleppo found refuge in Jordan, notably thanks to the policy of support for the MB in the kingdom at that time. Currently there is no official estimate as to the exact number of Syrians who came to Jordan at the time.

4 From 2005 onward, following the retreat of the Syrian army from Lebanon, many Syrian entrepreneurs who were established in Lebanon moved their businesses to Jordan (De Bel-Air

States.[5] Following the outbreak of violence in Syria, these Syrian migrants[6] played a role in receiving relatives and getting aid and basic necessities. They then created associations in order to provide services to refugees in various spheres (education, health, employment). These initiatives contributed to the emergence of "refugee-refugee humanitarianism" (Fiddian-Qasmyie 2016) which, without claiming to rival the imposing machine of international aid, offers local assistance adapted to the needs of the most deprived Syrian families, while creating spaces for socialization, commitment, and reconfiguration of Syrian society in exile. Research has shown the conversion of Syrian political activists from anti-regime mobilization into humanitarian field in Lebanon and Turkey (Ruiz 2018; Fourn 2018) and the way pre-existing political networks favored the organization of aid in response to the Syrian humanitarian crisis (Napolitano 2018). By adopting a long-time approach of Syrian migration, this chapter focuses on forms of migrant-led humanitarianism in Jordan, placing them more broadly in the context of the Jordanian response and the transformation of the humanitarian field engendered by the Syrian conflict on a regional scale. It sheds light on new forms of reception and hospitality that are organized on the periphery of and/or in contention with state policies (Agier 2018; Vandevoordt 2019), while showing that refugees are not only recipients of assistance but also demonstrate a capacity for action and organization, even becoming providers of aid to other migrants and refugees (Fiddian-Qasmiyeh 2015, 2016; Sharif 2018; Pincock et al. 2020). To do so, this chapter uses a theoretical approach that draws on both the sociology of migration and the sociology of collective action, two disciplinary fields that have so far had little interaction (Siméant 1994).

Initially, I show that the succession of several migratory waves can become a resource for the organization of collective action among migrants, in a context constrained by more or less restrictive reception policies. Syrian migrants who arrived in Jordan before the start of the war had several resources at their disposal: financial capital, knowledge of the way Jordanian institutions operate, as well as a foothold in different areas of society. These resources enabled them to avoid or circumvent obstacles they may encounter in the financing, assembling, and registering of independent organizations. The Jordanian authorities operated strict surveillance of refugee mobilizations and prohibit forms of association.[7] I will then show how humanitarian action crystallizes forms of civic engagement among migrants and refugees that are guided by different motivations. These commitments end up being professionalized in the context of the difficulty of access to the labor market for Syrians in Jordan.

2016). This phenomenon increased after the start of the conflict in 2011, with the relocation of Syrian businesses in the north of Jordan, particularly in the agricultural sector.

5 According to the available information, close to 500,000 Syrians lived in Saudi Arabia in 2010 and about 70,000 lived in other Gulf countries, notably in Kuwait (Valenta et al. 2020). Many of the Syrian students from families which had migrated to the Gulf used to complete their university studies in Syria. Since 2011, they have mostly turned toward Jordan.

6 Despite the rigidity of the migrant/refugee categories in this study, I use the term "migrant" to refer to Syrians who arrived in Jordan before 2011, regardless of how their legal status may have changed after this date. The term "refugee" is used in reference to Syrians who arrived after 2011 and who are registered with the UNHCR.

7 Information from the founder of the *Bareeq* organization. On the restrictions adopted regarding the right of association in Jordan, see also: Human Rights Watch 2016; Wiktorowicz 2000.

This chapter is based on novel empirical data that were collected during a field survey conducted in the capital, Amman, and in ʾIrbid, in the north, between 2018 and 2020, with seven Syrian charities and humanitarian associations.[8] These associations are among the most active and high profile in the public arena and are characterized by being non-denominational, even if religious faith is one of the reasons for the investment of their members. They are still little known compared to denominational humanitarian actors, particularly Islamic ones which, having received funding from the Gulf States, have enjoyed greater visibility in the field (Hasselbarth 2014; Ababsa 2014). My methodology consisted of interviews conducted with the founders and members (volunteers and employees) of the associations,[9] as well as informal conversations with Syrian refugees who are beneficiaries of their programs. These were complemented by observations during collective activities (training courses, aid distributions, festivals, and children's activities).

1. From Informal Reception to Institutional Response

Between March 2011 and the beginning of 2012, Syrians entering Jordan did not need a visa because of a bilateral accord signed between these two countries in 1994. Moreover, many families from Southern Syria, particularly the governorates of Darʿā and Ḥumṣ, were linked by tribal or matrimonial ties to the towns of northern Jordan (al-Ramthā, ʾIrbid, and al-Mafraq, among others). It was primarily through these pre-existing family/tribal and professional networks that the first Syrian refugees sought to secure their subsistence, including accommodation, food, and basic commodities (see Zunt in this volume). Many of the Syrian refugees I met had stayed with relatives for a few months before being able to rent a flat. However, this mutual family aid has diminished over time in the face of the growing economic pressures faced by both Syrian and host populations in the context of a tense labor market (Stevens 2016) and rising prices caused by the arrival of refugees (see Ababsa in this volume). These early private aid networks were supplemented by local initiatives of solidarity: food collections were organized, between April 2011 and September 2012, a wealthy Jordanian family (al-Bashābisha) from the border town of al-Ramthā provided a residential complex that could accommodate up to 600 refugees (see Dalal and Frankin in this volume). In parallel to such spontaneous support, religiously based humanitarian interventions were also emerging. On the one hand, there were local *al-Zakāt* committees financed by private alms and linked to the Ministry of Religious Affairs, and on the other hand were the more visible old Islamist social organizations whose scope of action extends over all the territories concerned. These include the Islamic Charity Social Centre (*Jamʿiyyat al-Markaz al-ʾIslāmiyya al-Khayriyya*), affiliated with the Muslim

[8] *This Is My Life*, *Souriyat Across Borders*, the *Group of Syrian Students in Jordan*, *Bareeq for Education and Development*, *Molham Volunteering Team*, the *House of Donation* in Amman, and the *Ahed Voluntary Group* group in ʾIrbid.

[9] In order to maintain the anonymity of my interviewees, their names have been changed. The names of organizations cited are real.

Brotherhood, and *The Book and the Sunna* (*Al-Kitāb wa al-Sunna*), a Salafist (quietist) organization, which receives private funds from the Gulf countries in order to provide for the basic needs of refugees (El Nakib and Ager 2015; Ababsa 2014).

At an institutional level, the Jordanian government, which initially based its official discourse on notions of "Bedouin hospitality," "Islamic solidarity," or "pan-Arab solidarity" (El-Abed 2014), acted in concert with the UNHCR in order to control the flow of arrivals. Starting in April 2012, temporary transit centers were set up near the Syrian border (cf. Fraikin and Dalal in this volume). They received refugees crossing the border without papers and/or illegally (i.e., not through official border posts). During 2013, the number of refugees registered with the UNHCR increased from 120,000 to 576,0001,[10] which led Jordan to establish three proper refugee camps in the north of the country. Two of them are managed by the UNHCR and various UN and non-governmental organizations in terms of educational, medical, and social services and by the Jordanian authorities in terms of administration, security, and logistics. These are the al-Zaʿtarī camp, set up in July 2012 near the town of al-Mafraq, where the number of residents rose to 150,000 refugees in 2013 and now stands at around 79,000;[11] and the al-ʾAzraq camp, opened in April 2014, which currently hosts some 40,000 refugees.[12] A third camp, funded and operated autonomously by the United Arab Emirates (UAE) Red Crescent at Marājīb al-Fuhūd in the al-Zarqāʾ governorate, in 2015, hosts around 6,500 refugees (Ababsa 2015). Since their establishment, these refugee camps have become a showcase for humanitarian assistance and a symbol of Jordan's hospitality toward Syrian refugees. In these camps, every aspect of daily life is taken in charge by the humanitarian actors (housing, water, electricity, access to school and health), a reason that has encouraged the poorest refugees to remain there in spite of the hard-living conditions and the limited possibility of mobility outside the camps. Therefore, it is in urban areas, where nearly 82 percent of the refugees live and where international humanitarian actors are less present, that other forms of support are being structured thanks to local initiatives driven by the Syrian migrant community that relies on its international roots to provide aid to refugees.

2. International Resources Used by Syrian Entrepreneurs for Civic Engagement

Alongside the hospitality provided by relatives, Jordanian society, and government assistance, mobilizations emerged first through the work of Syrian entrepreneurs and liberals. *This Is My Life* (*Hāḏihi ḥayātī*) is a charity that was established before the start of the Syrian conflict, in 2010, by Mehdi, a Syrian entrepreneur in his forties from the ʾIdlib region who came to Jordan in 2003 to complete his business studies. This organization assists orphaned and cancer-stricken children through recreational

10 See the UNHCR web page *Syria Regional Response*, September 2021.
11 See the UNHCR's Zaatari Camp Fact Sheet, August 2021.
12 See the UNHCR's Azraq Camp Fact Sheet, July 2020.

activities. In 2012, with the arrival of refugees in Jordan, the organization reoriented its actions to include help to Syrian refugee children and families. Registered in Switzerland in 2016, it then extended its activities to Turkey and northern Syria, relying on a network of relatives and trusted persons living in those regions. The organization is funded through online kitty campaigns, as well as by mobilizing Syrian migrants settled in Qatar, where Mehdi moved in 2015 for professional reasons. In Jordan, the charity is mainly involved in distributing aid in the form of monthly sponsorship of orphans, recreational activities, and psychological support, while in Syria it has built housing to accommodate displaced families.

Another organization, *Bareeq for Education and Development*, was founded in 2015 on the initiative of Syrian entrepreneurs. Based in the district of al-Nazzāl in south Amman, this organization offers tutoring for school children, and courses in literacy and vocational training (e.g., sewing, hairdressing, make-up, IT) mainly aimed at women. *Bareeq* was created thanks to Rim, a Syrian-American woman in her fifties based in Dubai who, after the start of the war in Syria, became involved in humanitarian work first in the north of the country, then in the al-Zaʿtarī camp in Jordan, when access to Syrian territory became more complicated following the presence of the Islamic State group. This project was born from a meeting between Rim and Ossama, a businessman from a wealthy Syrian family established in Jordan since 1970, during an event to collect donations organized in Amman. It runs mainly on donations from Ossama, as well as from Syrian relatives and donors that Rim manages to mobilize in the UAE. *Bareeq* additionally seeks to increase its budget with one-off grants from UNHCR, foreign embassies, and international NGOs, such as the Union of Medical Care and Relief Organizations (UOSSM).

As entrepreneurs and liberals, the founders of these two organizations, based between Jordan and the Gulf States, have international links that facilitate fundraising and the foreign registration of their organization. There are common motives behind the founders' choice to invest in helping refugees. First of all, they mentioned the moral duty to help people in need and to work for the transformation of the Syrian society. Added to this is the sense of identification they feel with their fellow citizens and the injustices they have suffered in Syria. Mehdi, for example, recounts that he had never been able to be active in the social field due to surveillance by the Syrian regime and that his presence in Jordan, after the popular uprising and the conflict in Syria started, was a unique opportunity for him to make himself socially useful. For Ossama, showing solidarity with the refugees is equivalent to an act of condemnation of the abuses committed by the Damascus regime. Moral, social, and political motives are thus articulated to explain the choice of these men and women to invest themselves in charitable actions. Their previous experience in this field, their knowledge of the Jordanian context, and their rooting in multiple family and/or professional networks at the local and international level make these actions possible. While Syrians, who have a certain amount of social and economic capital, are on the front line in organizing aid to refugees, forms of mobilization are also being structured in the university environment among students from different waves of migration.

3. Humanitarian Action as a Meeting Point for Syrian Students

Despite the restrictions put in place in the 1970s to limit the creation and scope of action of student clubs in Jordan (Hussainy 2012), universities were still places for socializing that, with the onset of the Syrian conflict, firstly organized protests and then humanitarian aid. The Syrian students, around 3,000,[13] are from families who arrived in the 1980s, families who settled in the Gulf countries and who, due to the high cost of schooling there, started sending their children to study in Jordan, as well as students with refugee status.

One of the first student groups was created in 2012 at Yarmouk University, in ʾIrbid, in the Faculty of Science and Technology: five students, from families that had left Syria in the 1980s for political reasons, founded the *Ahed Voluntary Group* (*Majmūʿat ʿAhd al-ṭawʿiyya*). Among them, Zayn and Yazen, students at the Faculty of Engineering, were from Syrian families who have been in the UAE since the 1980s. Faced with the extreme precariousness in which refugee families found themselves when they arrived in ʾIrbid, the students organized collections of donations in the form of food baskets and clothing. According to Yazen, the city of ʾIrbid was neglected by international actors who mainly addressed either people in the capital or those in the refugee camps established in other governorates (al-ʾAzraq and al-Mafraq). Little by little, the group of students began to systematize the distribution of aid. Visits to the homes of families, which were identified through networking, were organized to establish their needs. The students then approached their relatives and friends in the UAE to raise funds. For Zayn and Yazen, these actions to help refugees in Jordan represent a concrete way of helping their fellow citizens; it is also a way to prove their solidarity with their country of origin even though they were born and raised in the UAE. Moreover, as they came from families that previously suffered persecution by the Damascus regime, these two students identify with the current victims of the Syrian regime's violence, hence the need to take action.

A second student association appeared in 2014 at the University of Jordan in Amman, the *Group of Syrian Students in Jordan* (*Tajammuʿ al-ṭalaba al-sūriyyīn fī al-ʾUrdun*). Among the founders is 23-year-old Aḥmad, born in Amman to a family of traders from Aleppo who arrived in the country in 1982. A graduate in journalism, Ahmad says that in its early days, the students' association was formed to coordinate rallies organized in front of the Syrian Embassy at every significant episode in the conflict. Then, following the ban on demonstrations imposed on Syrian nationals by the Jordanian authorities in 2015, the *Student Group* decided to change its orientation, "to stop meddling in politics" and instead devote itself to "social service" (*khidma ʾijtimaʿiyya*), meaning a way to improve the daily living conditions of Syrians in need. For Ahmad, humanitarian investment is thus a direct extension of his support for the Syrian uprising. In his case, as in the case of many political activists who participated in the protests in Syria and found refuge in neighboring countries, humanitarian action

[13] According to estimates provided by the representative of the Syrian Students' Association in Jordan, in 2019.

becomes an alternative field of action in the face of the increasing militarization of the conflict and the remoteness of any possibility of overthrowing the regime, on the one hand, and the need to alleviate the suffering experienced by the population in exile, on the other (Fourn 2018, Ruiz de Elvira 2018). In addition to organizing orientation and aid campaigns for Syrian students in Jordan, the *Student Group* takes on the task of organizing charity events for the neediest families. Home visits are arranged in poor neighborhoods in East Amman, as well as in refugee camps and informal camps in the north of the country. Targeted aid is distributed at the beginning of winter and during the month of Ramadan. On several occasions, the organization coordinates campaigns to distribute food aid, clothes, and school supplies in the form of competitions between groups of students from different universities who have to develop their own action project. The winning team is symbolically recognized at a collective ceremony. The initiative has become an important means of connecting Syrian students in addition to the social actions themselves.

While the *Syrian Student Group* has no official status, meetings are held informally in Ahmad's office, where he is self-employed in the field of audio-visual communication. Moreover, to get around the lack of official registration with the Jordanian authorities, the association calls on local charities that give it legal cover during aid distribution campaigns. This strategy is adopted by Ahmad in order to get around the impossibility of registering his association and is made possible thanks to the networks of contacts that Ahmad has in Jordan. Thus, during one of these activities organized in the informal camps in the border region around al-Mafraq,[14] the students relied on a Jordanian charity, the *Mount Zamzam Association (Jamʿiyyat Jabal Zamzam al-khayriyya)*, created in 2015 in order to assist refugees and the most vulnerable members of the host communities, which in exchange for a small fee, agrees to make its premises available for organizing a day of activities for the children of the region (Figure 10.1). While Ahmad regrets that aid to Syrian refugees is being clawed back by organizations who wish to profit from it, albeit for small sums, he nonetheless deals with them in order to bypass administrative constraints and pursue his goal of helping Syrian families.

Among the other students who collaborate with the association on an ad hoc basis, there are students from older migrations, as well as a smaller number of refugees who, in addition to their studies, work to provide for their families. Maryam, originally from Darʿā, is twenty-three years old and lives with her family in the al-Zaʿtarī camp. In addition to her pharmaceutical studies, she participates in the "charity" competitions organized by the association. These activities represent an opportunity to help people around her in a concrete way, and it is thanks to her that the *Student Group* manages to organize aid distributions in the al-Zaʿtarī camp, to which access is still subject to long administrative procedures. She also got in touch with one of the organizations the *Student Group* works with and was able to find a job before getting a grant in one of the EU-funded programs.

[14] These are groups of mainly rural Syrians who have settled in tents in the countryside surrounding the towns and are helped very little by UNHCR humanitarian aid.

Figure 10.1 Distribution of aid by Syrian students in informal Syrian refugee settlements, north of Jordan.

In view of these experiences, it appears that the university environment is a space that is conducive to linking Syrian students from different migratory waves and that humanitarian action since 2012 has brought them together. These are the same students who, faced with the impossibility of accessing the job market, find job opportunities in humanitarian action.

4. The Professionalization of Aid among Syrians

Over the years, these initiatives, originally conceived as forms of commitment by Syrians to help other Syrians, have undergone a process of professionalization through the adoption of the objectives and modes of action of international NGOs and the increasing number of salaried members. Although the convergence of activist and professional careers within humanitarian organizations is not a new phenomenon (Dauvin and Siméant 2002), in the context of the Syrian crisis, salaried employment in humanitarian initiatives is propelled by the restricted access to the labor market in refugee-hosting countries. The volunteer status that is attributed to staff from beneficiary communities within international and local humanitarian bodies allows these restrictions to be circumvented, even if it contributes to creating a form of invisible and subordinated labor (Driff 2018).

In Jordan, following the signing of the *Jordan Compact* with the European Union, Syrian refugees were granted work permits in the sectors open to migrant workers (mainly agriculture, construction, tourism, and manufacturing).[15] The professions have, however, remained inaccessible, leading to the departure of many of the most

[15] Jordan pledged to formalize the status of 200,000 Syrian workers in exchange for development aid and tax relief for exports of its products to the European Union (Lenner and Turner, 2018).

educated Syrians to third countries. Those who were unable to leave the country saw the possibility of professional training within the humanitarian organizations.

Among Syrians in Jordan, those who were established long ago find it easier to go abroad. Syrian traders and students who have residence permits in the Gulf States frequently go back and forth, or return there permanently. Syrians who arrived after 2011 cannot move abroad because of their refugee status. For this reason we observe a work division in Syrian humanitarian organizations, with earlier Syrian migrants in charge of coordination and funding, and Syrians arrived after 2011 who ensure the continuation of local initiatives. Following Mehdi's departure to Qatar, the *This Is My Life* organization relies on three former volunteers who have now become employees: two Syrian refugees who arrived in 2012 and a Jordanian of Palestinian origin. Among them, Lina, originally from Damascus, arrived in Amman in 2012, at the age of eighteen. She started working with the organization as a volunteer during the summer and then became the activities coordinator after finishing her studies in human resources management. She notes that if she had not found this job, she would have sought to leave the country, as do most university graduates. Apart from Ahmad, who works in the audio-visual sector, the *Syrian Student Group* has a constant turnover of volunteers, with students completing their university courses and either returning to the Gulf countries or seeking scholarships to emigrate abroad. In *Bareeq*, too, it is the Syrian teachers who arrived after 2011 and did not continue their activities in the public sector and a young graduate in English who are coordinating local teaching activities. Thus, a kind of internal division of labor is taking place with the older migrants providing the sometimes remote leadership of the activities, fundraising and communication work, and the refugees being responsible for the implementation of the activities at the local level.

In parallel to these internal reconfigurations, we also notice that the collective actions of Syrians in Jordan are part of the reconfigurations of the humanitarian world on a wider scale. Several of the organizations in which Syrian migrants and refugees are involved are the offshoots of organizations whose main headquarters are in Turkey, where the Syrian opposition is based.[16] The latter initially enjoyed the support of the Jordanian state even though they are not allowed to establish an official headquarters in the country (Al Husseini 2013). It is therefore through humanitarian action that they seek to establish a foothold among the Syrian population in Jordan. Among the organizations that maintain links with opposition actors is the *Molham Volunteering Team*, which has its main headquarters in Turkey and, in addition to its Jordanian base, is also active in Lebanon and northern Syria. The Amman headquarters, located near the University of Jordan, was created, like other organizations mentioned in this chapter, through the action of a group of Syrian students. The organization takes its name from Molham, a young Syrian from the Ghouta, near Damascus, who was involved in humanitarian aid and died at the beginning of the conflict. The head

[16] I am referring to the groups that formed the Syrian National Council established in Istanbul in August 2011 as the main platform for coordination between the opposition groups. These include the Muslim Brotherhood, the Local Coordination Committees, the Damascus Declaration, the National Bloc, the Kurdish Bloc, the Assyrian Democratic Organization, independent figures, and tribal leaders.

of the Jordanian branch, Khaled, was a friend of Molham's. Originally from Mīdān in Damascus, Khaled was in his second year of pharmacy when the conflict began, forcing him to suspend his studies. He then traveled to Jordan to visit his sister, who was married to a Jordanian, and stayed there in the face of rising violence. After a year in Jordan, Khaled gave up his studies and became involved full-time in collecting food and clothing for the refugees in the al-Zaʿtarī camp, first as a volunteer, working with other students, and then as an employee recruited to work for *Molham*. Basel was put in charge of opening a branch of the organization in Jordan in 2012. Dealing primarily in medical assistance, the organization is mainly financed by groups close to the Muslim Brotherhood. This has earned it criticism from other students who have decided instead to maintain an independent status. Registered as a non-profit organization in Germany, *Molham* can work without any particular obstacles in Jordan. As in other Syrian organizations, those working in *Molham* have a variety of profiles, including recent Syrian arrivals such as Khaled and Fatima, 23, from Ḥalab, and Abdullah, 28, from a family from Hama that arrived in 1982. They all met at university where they participated in rallies in support of Syria. During a group meeting, Khaled explained to me that his involvement in humanitarian action was a way for him to pay tribute to his friend Molham and to the other victims of the conflict. For Fatima, the organization represented a key place of sociability around which she was able to recompose her life in exile. For Abdullah, it was an opportunity to be useful and to renew his link with Syria, even though he was born and raised in Jordan. Despite the diversity of their motives for investing in *Molham*, which overlap with those of other students involved in humanitarian activities, it represents an opportunity to find a job, to socialize, and to open up to other countries such as Turkey, where on several occasions these young people went for training in the organization's headquarters. After several years, Khaled and Abdullah chose to migrate to Turkey in 2020, where Syrian political opponents have more freedom of action, which shows that humanitarian activities have also generated new migratory movements on a regional scale.

Another organization, founded in 2015, that fits into this Syrian associative landscape that has grown out of opposition groups is the *House of Donation (Dār al-ʿAṭāʾ)*, a home for widows based in the al-Nāṣir neighborhood in the north of Amman, which houses around thirty women with their children. This organization was formed by the larger body, the *Homs League Abroad* (*Rābiṭat Humṣ fī al-mahjar*), an NGO founded on the initiative of a group of Syrian opponent businessmen from the city of Ḥumṣ and currently based in Germany and Turkey. It has several shelters for women in Amman, Jordan, Gaziantep and Antakya, Turkey, and Tripoli, Lebanon, as well as cultural and training centers in all three countries. In addition to providing the families with accommodation, the organization promotes their involvement in entrepreneurial projects (in the field of sewing and catering) that aim to provide these women with an income. In Jordan, the coordination of the activities is handled by 25-year-old Taym, also from Homs. He arrived with his family in 2013 and was recruited through mutual acquaintances who put him in touch with the founders of the *League*. Alongside Taym, a team of three refugee women residing in the home coordinates educational and professional activities. *Molham* and the *House of Donation* are distinguished by the fact that their members are salaried and that their work is organized in coordination with the main office in Turkey, as well as by their links with political activists, who constitute their main source of funding.

While militant, professional, and political logics intersect within the Syrian association network in Jordan, we can also see that the evolution of Syrian-led humanitarianism in Jordan is also linked with the changes in host-country reception policy more generally. The latter is marked by a shift from an emergency humanitarian response to a longer-term perspective, which also affects the programs and objectives pursued by Syrian humanitarian actors.

5. From Emergency Care to Long-Term Development

Since 2014, Jordan's assistance policy has integrated refugee relief programs with activities more focused on the development of Jordan. The "refugee response," which aims to improve humanitarian services (food aid, housing, health, education, justice, and social protection), is combined with the "resilience response," which is aimed more specifically at "vulnerable" Jordanians, through community and environmental projects designed to reduce tensions between refugees and host communities. This includes combining emergency humanitarian assistance with programs to develop Jordanian infrastructure, services, and the economy (Al Husseini and Napolitano 2019). The JRPSC for 2020–2022 builds on this approach of combining refugee assistance (referred to as the Global Compact on Refugees) with a sustainable development plan (the Jordan National Plans)[17] that incorporates the goals set by the United Nations and aims to leverage international assistance in order to continue the country's developmental journey. The direction taken by Jordan's reception policy must be understood not only in the context of the continuation of the Syrian presence but also in the context of a general decrease in international aid. It aims to remind donors that not only are refugees still in need of assistance but also that the Jordanian people, in a situation of increased socioeconomic insecurity, need to be supported so that Jordan can maintain its role as a guarantor of regional stability and participate in mechanisms to curb migratory flows toward Western countries (Knudsen and Berg 2023).

It is in this broader context that the changes in the Syrian associative fabric are also taking place. On the one hand, we note the development of activities that take into account the sustainable settlement of Syrians with the adoption of a language and repertoire of actions that aim to meet the expectations of donors. In 2019, several years after the beginning of their involvement in solidarity with Syrian refugees, it could be seen that campaigns for the distribution of food aid and basic necessities were still being carried out by several of the organizations mentioned earlier, but were limited to particular key periods, such as the beginning of winter when the *Syrian Student Group* distributed blankets, mats, and stoves, as well as the period of Ramadan, during

[17] See the Jordan Response Plan to the Syrian Crisis 2020–2022, published on the webpage of the Ministry of Planning and International Cooperation: http://www.jrp.gov.jo/Files/JRP%202020-2022%20web.pdf

which collective meals are organized for families in need. At the same time, however, the issue of education and vocational training become increasingly important in the activities promoted by the associations. The *Syrian Student Group*, in addition to actively seeking scholarships, establishes collaborations with vocational training centers and international actors (such as UNESCO) and puts these institutions in contact with Syrian students who wish to participate in the training courses offered. For other organizations, the education and training of Syrian children and women have become a central objective. This is the case for *Souriyat across borders (*Sūriyyāt *ʿabra al-ḥudūd)*, founded in 2012 by a group of Syrian women (entrepreneurs and doctors) living in Jordan, the Gulf States (Saudi Arabia and the United Arab Emirates), and the UK, which aims to provide medical assistance to the war-wounded, specializing in the provision of prostheses, rehabilitation, and reintegration of the disabled. With the closure of the Syrian-Jordanian borders in 2015, the organization shifted its focus to teaching foreign languages, tutoring, and art classes, as well as orientation courses for students wishing to apply for scholarships abroad. *Bareeq*, which also focuses on women, is developing a real capacity to use the language of international actors in order to respond to calls for proposals by donors. In its educational programs, several of its projects, for example, promote the empowerment of women. We also note that most Syrian organizations are beginning to include Jordanians among their beneficiaries, a way of promoting forms of socialization between refugees and the host communities on a long-term perspective.

Conclusion

By tracing the evolution of forms of solidarity between different waves of Syrian migrants and Jordanian reception policy more generally, this contribution shows first of all that circulation provides migrants with a way into networks (family, social, and economic) as well as multiple geographical spaces that prove to be carriers of indispensable resources for the organization of mobilizations in contexts constrained by the restrictions that host countries impose on migrant populations. While the Jordanian authorities exercise strict surveillance on refugee activism and hinder any form of association, the existence of a well-established Syrian community in the country, with branches in Europe and the Gulf States, has made possible the emergence of an associative fabric involved in welcoming refugees who have been fleeing the war since 2011/2012. By reactivating family, friends, and professional networks, it has facilitated the financing and registration abroad of charitable organizations or the maintenance of their activities under an unofficial status. The fact that Syrians are anchored in different spaces also makes them particularly receptive to changes in the humanitarian landscape and to seizing opportunities that arise. They adapt to the expectations of donors but also to changes in state reception policy and in some cases offer themselves as intermediaries between international organizations and refugees. They are also involved in and contribute to the emergence of new polarities linked to the management of the humanitarian crisis caused by the Syrian conflict, which has led to new movements of people, of know-how, and of resources between Syria, Jordan, and Turkey, and also between these countries, the Gulf countries and Europe.

Finally, migrant-led humanitarianism also constitutes an observatory for the new social interactions at work among Syrians in exile. In particular, it provides an opportunity for earlier migrants to reconnect with their country and to express their sense of identification with the victims of the conflict. For refugees, arrived after 2011, it has opened up opportunities to rebuild a social network in exile and also to find a professional occupation while prolonging forms of engagement that are impossible in the political arenas both in Syria and Jordan.

Bibliography

Ababsa, Myriam (2014), "Gulf Donors and NGOs Assistance to Syrian Refugees in Jordan," UNHCR Gulf Report. Available online: https://reliefweb.int/sites/reliefweb.int/files/resources/GULFreportdesign14.pdf.

Ababsa, Myriam (2015), "De la crise humanitaire à la crise sécuritaire. Les dispositifs de contrôle des réfugiés syriens en Jordanie (2011–2015)," *Revue européenne des migrations internationals*, 31 (3): 73–101.

Agier, Michel (2018), *L'étranger qui vient: repenser l'hospitalité*, Paris: Seuil.

Al Husseini, Jalal (2013), "La Jordanie face à la crise syrienne," in François Burgat (ed.), *Pas de printemps pour la Syrie*, 282–8, Paris: La Découverte.

Al Husseini, Jalal, and Valentina Napolitano (2019), "La politique jordanienne à l'égard des réfugiés syriens: entre hospitalité et protection des intérêts nationaux," *Confluences Méditerranée*, 110 (3): 127–42.

Dauvin, Pascal, and Johanna Siméant-Germanos (2002), "Chapitre 2. Carrières militantes et professionnelles dans l'humanitaire," in Pascal Dauvin and Johanna Siméant-Germanos (eds.), *Le travail humanitaire. Les acteurs des ONG, du siège au terrain*, 59–103, Paris: Presses de Sciences Po.

De Bel-Air, Françoise (2016), "Migration Profile: Jordan," *Migration Policy Centre*, 6. Available online: https://cadmus.eui.eu/bitstream/handle/1814/44065/MPC_PB_201606.pdf.

Driff, Leila (2018), "Être réfugié et 'volontaire' : les travailleurs invisibles des dispositifs d'aide internationale," *Critique internationale*, 81 (4): 21–42.

El-Abed, Oroub (2014), "The Discourse of Guesthood: Forced Migrants in Jordan," in Anita Fabos and Riina Osotalon (eds.), *Managing Muslim Mobilities*, 81–100, London: Palgrave Macmillan.

El Nakib, Shatha, and Alastair Ager (2015), "Local Faith Community and Related Civil Society Engagement in Humanitarian Response with Syrian Refugees in Irbid," *Jordan Report to the Henry Luce Foundation*. Available online: https://jliflc.com/wp-content/uploads/2015/06/El-Nakib-Ager-Local-faith-communities-and-humanitarian-response-in-Irbid-.pdf.

Fiddian-Qasmiyeh, Elena (2015), "Refugees Helping Refugees: How a Palestinian Refugee Camp in Lebanon is Welcoming Syrians," *The Conversation*. Available online: https://theconversation.com/refugees-helping-refugees-how-a-palestinian-camp-in-lebanon-is-welcoming-syrians-48056.

Fiddian-Qasmiyeh, Elena (2016), "Refugees Hosting Refugees. Local Communities: First and Last Providers of Protection", *Forced Migration Review*, 53: 25–7.
Fourn, Léo (2018), "De la révolution au travail humanitaire. Reconversions de militants syriens exilés au Liban," *Revue internationale de politique compare*, 25 (1): 63–81.
Hasselbarth, Sarah (2014), *Islamic Charities in the Syrian Context in Jordan and Lebanon*, Beirut: Friedrich-Ebert-Stiftung. Available online: http://library.fes.de/pdf-files/bueros/beirut/10620.pdf.
Hussainy, Mohammed (2012), "Increasing Democratic Political Engagement Among University Students in Jordan," *Policy Paper Friedrich-Ebert-Stiftung*. Available online: https://library.fes.de/pdf-files/bueros/amman/09593.pdf.
Human Rights Watch (2016), *Statement on Proposed Amendments to Jordan's 2008 Law on Associations*. Available online: https://www.hrw.org/news/2016/08/07/human-rights-watch-statement-proposed-amendments-jordans-2008-law-associations.
Knudsen, A. J. and K. G. Berg (2023), *Continental Encampment: Genealogies of Humanitarian Containment in the Middle East and Europe*, London: Berghahn Books.
Lenner, Katharina, and Lewis Turner (2018), "Making Refugees Work? The Politics of Integrating Syrian Refugees into the Labor Market in Jordan," *Middle East Critique*. Available online: https://doi.org/10.1080/19436149.2018.1462601.
Napolitano, Valentina (2018), "Circulations transnationales et transformations de l'engagement. Les militants palestiniens dans l'espace syro-libanais," *Revue internationale de politique comparée*, 25 (1–2): 105–128.
Pincock, Kate, Alexander Betts, and Evan Easton-Calabria (eds.) (2020), *The Global Governed? Refugees as Providers of Protection and Assistance*, Cambridge: Cambridge University Press.
Ruiz de Elvira, Laura (2018), "From Local Revolutionary Action to Exiled Humanitarian Work: Activism in Local Social Networks and Communities' Formation in the Syrian Post-2011 Context," *Social Movement Studies*, 18 (1): 36–55.
Sharif, Hind (2018), "Refugee-Led Humanitarianism in Lebanon's Shatila Camp," *Forced Migration Review*, 57: 10–12.
Siméant, Johanna (1994), "Immigration et action collective. L'exemple des mobilisations d'étrangers en situation irrégulière," *Sociétés contemporaines*, 20: 39–62.
Stevens, Matthew (2016), "The Collapse of Social Networks Among Syrian Refugees in Urban Jordan," *Contemporary Levant*, 1(1): 51–63.
Valenta, Marko, Jo Jakobsen, Drago Župarić-Iljić, and Hariz Halilovich (2020), "Syrian Refugee Migration, Transitions in Migrant Statuses and Future Scenarios of Syrian Mobility," *Refugee Survey Quarterly*, 39 (2): 153–76.
Vandevoordt, Robin (2019), "Subversive Humanitarianism: Rethinking Refugee Solidarity Through Grass-roots Initiatives," *Refugee Survey Quarterly*, 38 (3): 245–65.
Wiktorowicz, Quintan (2000), "Civil Society as Social Control: State Power in Jordan," *Comparative Politics*, 33 (1): 43–61.

11

Post-2014 Christian Iraqi Refugees

Reconfiguration of Faith-Based Assistance in Jordan

Norig Neveu

In June 2014, when the fighters of the "Islamic State in Iraq and the Levant" swept across northern Iraq, King Abdullah II of Jordan made statements stressing the need to protect Middle Eastern Christians and to guarantee their presence in the region. He encouraged them to seek refuge in his country, guaranteeing a simplified procedure for visas and offering them the chance to travel with Royal Jordanian Airlines. In doing so, his speech was in line with a long-term policy of the Jordanian monarchy in defending religious tolerance and interfaith dialogue formalized by the Amman message (Neveu 2010, Robbins and Rubin 2013).[1] This speech echoed a rhetoric that was increasingly widespread in the Middle East, particularly among Christian ecclesiastic authorities, presenting the Christian presence as a bulwark against the development of Islamism or "radicalization" in the region. King Abdullah II's statements were widely publicized both in Jordan and internationally.[2]

Following this call, since 2014, hundreds of Christian families settled in Jordan. Churches and faith-based NGOs—Caritas in particular—were the main actors mobilized for the reception policies and welcoming features for these migrants. In 2015, around 10,000 Iraqi Christians belonging to different churches had settled in Jordan out of a total of around 50,000 Iraqi refugees according to UNHCR.[3] The number of Iraqi refugees increased progressively after 2014 (UNHCR 2018, 2020).

[1] The Amman message was delivered on November 9, 2004, by Sheikh Izz Eddine Al Khatib Al Tamimi, at the initiative of the Āl al-Bayt Foundation. It takes up the two central points of the official Jordanian discourse, the need for intra- and inter-religious dialogue. The address insists on the need for tolerance between the different religious components of Jordanian society and more generally between the different faiths. See http://www.ammanmessage.com/.

[2] See, for instance, the New York Times: https://www.nytimes.com/2014/10/27/world/middleeast/for-mosuls-christians-a-shelter-in-jordan.html; Al Jazeera: https://www.aljazeera.com/gallery/2015/9/18/life-on-hold-for-iraqi-christian-refugees-in-jordan, etc.

[3] The question of the number of Iraqi refugees in Jordan is a sensitive one. In 2007, a Fafo report estimated their number at 161,000, a figure that was heavily debated by the Jordanian government, which obtained a re-evaluation of their number at around 500,000 (Bakewell 1999; Chatelard 2009: 18). This number was again discussed and re-evaluated later (around 150,000).

Most of them settled in Amman and are registered with UNHCR under the status of "asylum seekers," which meant they could not access formal work and children could not be registered in Jordanian public schools. They settled in Jordan in a context of both the confessionalization of political dynamics in the region (Hashemi and Postel 2017) and the arrival of thousands of Syrian refugees in the country raising major challenges in terms of reception policy for the state (see Achilli 2015; Zuntz and Napolitano in this volume). In 2014, the arrival of Iraqi refugees was not a new phenomenon in Jordan, since thousands of Iraqis had been leaving their country from the 1990s onward and after the First Gulf War. Many arrived after 2006 and the sectarian violence that followed the fall of Saddam Hussein's regime. In most cases, Jordan was a transit country for these migrants before their resettlement in the United States, Canada, Australia, or Europe (Chatelard 2002; Fattah 2007; Marfleet 2007; Sasoon 2008).

The issue of Iraqi refugees in the Middle East has been analyzed from different perspectives. Beyond the analysis of transit strategies or the political and economic issues related to the recognition of their number in the welcoming countries (Chatelard 2008), their case study raised new questions concerning the use and mobilization of solidarity networks by refugees (Gurak and Caces, 1992), both in transit countries such as Jordan (Chatelard 2004), Turkey (Danıs 2004a) or Syria (Doraï 2011; Ali 2011), and in relocation countries such as the United States and Great Britain (Rahe 2002). In a context of the sectarianization (Ismael and Fuller, 2008) of the political dynamics in Iraq, especially after 2003, the religious or confessional data has gradually become a key element in the management of migration policies, particularly for Iraqis.

The denominational issue has come to the forefront in various respects. The question of the reshaping of modes of belonging in exile, particularly the religious one, has been the subject of several publications, based for instance on the case studies in Michigan (Shoeb, Weinstein, and Halpern 2007) or of the Chaldean Iraqis in London (Al-Rasheed 1998) and in Sarcelles, France (Veillard-Baron 2013). As the migration from Iraq developed, the prominent place of the diaspora in political and economic life and within religious institutions in Iraq has been highlighted, as well as the role of the clergy and faith-based NGOs in the management of assistance to migrants (Fiddian-Qasmiyeh 2011a). Finally, researchers took into account the imposition of the confessional data as an actual category in the framework of reception policies (state and international organizations). For instance, in 2005, two attacks took place in Amman and were attributed to Iraqis. Following these attacks, the entry of Iraqis into Jordan was restricted, particularly for young Shiite men. After 2006, the number of Iraqi migrants entering Jordan decreased considerably and they were mainly middle-class Sunnis (Chatelard and Doraï 2009). The increasing use of religious data within the strategies of reception policies (identification system of international organizations such as the UNHCR, the border control or visa policies, etc.) needs to be more broadly addressed.

After 2011, with the arrival of thousands of Syrian refugees fleeing the conflicts in their country and the development of Islamic humanitarianism (El Nakib and Ager 2015), the need to articulate the religious fact and the migratory phenomenon became apparent within research work (Borchgrevink and Erdal 2017; Ozkan 2011; Petersen 2012). In keeping with this research, this chapter tackles the notion of "religious migrants" by investigating how churches and faith-based charities welcomed Christian Iraqis mainly coming from Qaraqosh, Mosul, or Baghdad in Jordan after 2014. Those migrants fleeing the persecution of ISIS tended to be assimilated to the first Christian martyrs by the clergy. Within the political debates, they were presented first as Christian and then as Iraqis and were somehow detached from their national group of belonging. Most of those migrants were or are waiting to be resettled in the United States, Canada, or Australia and vehemently expressed the impossibility—from their perspective—of going back to live in Iraq.

The religious "genealogy" of humanitarianism calls into question the dichotomy commonly established between faith-based NGOs and secular NGOs (Duriez and Roussel 2007; Prud'homme 2007; Ferris 2011; Furniss and Meier 2012; Ruiz de Elvira and Saeidnia 2020). Sectarian violence, in parallel with the rising sectarian divisions of the post-2003 Iraqi social and political spheres, has contributed to the increasing role of faith-based networks as a key resource for migrants. In this way, the migration issue crossed the religious field and entered the debates of the churches and the faith-based charities. For instance, while the Vatican insists on maintaining the Christian presence in the Middle East, this does not fit the expectations of the Iraqi migrants. This has led to contradictory policies, which this chapter aims to decipher.

This chapter investigates the policies developed by Christian charities, such as Caritas, and members of the Christian clergy toward Christian Iraqi refugees in Jordan post-2014. It is based on fieldwork I conducted in Amman between 2017 and 2021 and focuses on the case study of the Mārkā parish, Mary Mother of the Church, locally known as Dayr al-lātīn. Since 2015, Father Khalil Jaʿar, the priest in charge of the parish, has welcomed Iraqi families, opened an informal school for Christian Iraqi children, developed craft projects and opened a clinic. During the fieldwork I interviewed religious authorities, volunteers, and beneficiaries of Christian assistance in the neighborhood of the parish of Mārkā, in the northeast of Amman. Tracing the debates, networks, and competitions existing between Christian humanitarian actors, I carried out a series of interviews with Caritas and Melkite or Latin Catholic clerics (such as Father Mario Cornioli), who developed initiatives for Christian Iraqi refugees in Amman.

How did the issue of migration come to the forefront of the Catholic church's debates? How have faith-based charities and Christian clergy influenced denominational policies, modes of belonging, as well as the migration path and policies? How did migrants reinvigorate local religious institutions in Jordan? How have religious humanitarian actors established themselves as key actors within the humanitarian field? What strategies for adapting to the realities of the field and humanitarian careers have been developed over the last ten years? To tackle these issues, this chapter will first detail the protocols and reception mechanisms developed by Caritas and the Catholic church in Amman and highlight the sectarian or denominational logics in humanitarian policies. Then, the case study of the Christian school of Mārkā and the initiative of Fr. Khalil Jaʿar retraces an unofficial response of reception and assistance policies for these refugees. This response has been the subject of debates and discussions within the church and between the faith-based charities of the region.

1. Welcoming the Iraqi Christian Refugees in Jordan after 2014: Institutions and Policies

Religious or denominational criteria become a key relational capital for these "religious migrants." How does it reflect in the geography of humanitarian assistance in Amman and on their appropriation of the host city? My approach takes up the criticisms leveled toward certain readings of sectarian dynamics, which object both to the invisibility of the complex modes of belonging of the refugees and to the tendency to individualize categories of a set of problems that concern a group of migrants in a more general way. The issue here is to tackle how, in the case of Christian Iraqis, the processes of political confessionalization have had major consequences both in terms of reception policies and mobilized networks, an observation that can be formalized more broadly for post-2011 migrations to and from the Middle East.

1.1. Organization of the Assistance

As mentioned earlier, the presence of Iraqi refugees in Jordan is part of the genealogy of migration dynamics that has faced the country since its independence, despite a certain lack of research interest on this case study (Fattah 2007). From the 1990s, the Gulf Wars, the fall of Saddam Hussein's regime in April 2003 (Graham-Brown 1999), and, above all, the sectarian violence that struck Iraq after 2006 (Ismael and Fuller 2008) have generated major flows of migration toward Syria and Jordan, as well as a renewed academic interest. For Jordan, as for other countries in the region, the peak of the refugee movement corresponds to the post-2006 period of sectarian violence.

According to Chatelard and Doraï, between 1990 and the fall of the Baathist regime in 2003, Jordan was the only country bordering Iraq that offered easy movement conditions to the Iraqi population. Three types of migrants were involved: an economic elite seeking service, a middle class whose mobility was linked to work opportunities, and more vulnerable refugees fleeing the local situation. By the end of 2002, there was a reported population of 300,000 Iraqis in Jordan (Chatelard and Doraï 2009). According to the UNHCR, the country had between 450,000 and 500,000 refugees in 2008 (Chatelard 2008), with the Jordanian state claiming a higher number.

The mobilization of confessional data has also been imposed on reception policies in several respects. In Jordan, the implementation of these restrictive reception policies echoed the king's political stance from 2004 onward. He was the first representative of the region to use the term "Shiite crescent" to refer to what he defined as the emergence of a Shiite axis that would have Iran at its center and extend to the Middle East as far as Lebanon and would represent a threat for the region.

In a context of the sectarianization of political dynamics, the organization of assistance to refugees, historically rooted in religious dynamics, focused in some contexts on faith-based organizations. The history of Christian charities in Jordan coincides strongly with the chronology of migrations, particularly the arrival of Palestinian refugees, as does the development of the churches' humanitarian activities in favor of migrants. In the case of the Iraqis, since 2003, local churches structured the coordination of assistance to Christian Iraqis through their national, regional, and international networks. The Middle East Council of Churches, an ecumenical structure founded in 1949, organized meetings with church leaders in Jordan to discuss how to organize assistance to Christian Iraqis who left their country. After several meetings, they decided to administer programs through the churches. In this framework, the distribution of assistance to refugees was entrusted to different churches. For instance, the Latin Catholic Bishopric of Jordan relied on its institutional links with its counterparts in Iraq and selected 225 families to which food and medical assistance was provided. The Melkite church, in charge of the Baghdad congregation, cared for seventy-six families who settled in Jordan in 2003 by providing assistance for paying the rent, education, health, etc. The Syriac church not only took care of Syriac Iraqis but also Assyrian, Armenian, and Chaldean families as some of these churches did not have proper representatives or churches in Jordan at this time. It is on the basis of this operating and distribution model that the development of post-2014 assistance must be understood. Caritas provided assistance to all Iraqi refugees but a specific action coordinated by the churches was dedicated to Iraqi Christians.

1.2. Are Iraqi Christian Refugees Like Any Others?

Sectarian violence, alongside the rise of sectarian divisions in the social and political spheres of post-2003 Iraq, has contributed to the expression of an exceptionality of the situation of Iraqi Christians both by humanitarian actors and by political representatives. This led to several narratives: their representation as warrant of religious coexistence and inter-religious dialogue in the region. This discourse was shared by political representatives and by the clergy, notably the Catholic one and especially the Vatican. For the latter, this observation led to a political conclusion: the necessity to keep a Christian presence in the Middle East and therefore to avoid the resettlement of Christian Iraqi refugees out of the region.

During the same period, the question of the status of Middle Eastern Christians or "minorities" in the Middle East was the subject of a political appropriation, particularly by conservative parties, both in Europe and in North America, taking up the same elements of argumentation. In addition to the increasing visibility of their situation in the media and in political discourse, new Christian charities have emerged to provide aid to these Christians, notably the French association SOS Chrétiens d'Orient. These structures represent a major evolution within Catholic humanitarian aid, which, in order to avoid any form of proselytism, had until then been careful not to address a mainly Christian public. While organizations such as Caritas continued to carry out projects for all Iraqi refugees, the exceptionality of King Abdullah II's speech in 2014 led to the development of specific assistance programs for Christian Iraqi refugees at different levels: reception, schooling, and accommodation. A 2015 Caritas report stated:

Figure 11.1 Covering picture of the activity report "Displaced Iraqis . . . One year of exodus," Caritas 2015.

> Caritas Jordan with the support of the Government of Jordan Hashemite charity organization (JHCO) has provided critical relief to the Iraqi refugees who have arrived in Jordan since the ISIS takeover of northern Iraq. Caritas Jordan on behalf of the Catholic Church and in collaboration with local faith-based organizations and parishes, have conducted a needs assessment and registered 8123 of the newly arrived refugees. They have opened 16 churches[4] to approximately 1,000 of the most vulnerable refugees to ensure they have temporally shelter and that their immediate needs are met. (Caritas activity report "Displaced Iraqis . . . One year of exodus," June 2015)

In 2014, Caritas organized, in coordination with the government, the reception of around a thousand Christian Iraqis. Most of them were welcomed in Catholic parishes, receiving medical care, daily meals, and basic necessities. This solution of reception in parishes was widely publicized at the time, notably on the website of Fr. Rifaat Badr: abouna.org promoting Christian activities in Jordan. In this context, for instance, Fr. Rifaat Badr welcomed seven Iraqi families in his parish in Nāʿūr, southwest of Amman. They lived in the main hall near the church and stayed in the town for three years before their resettlement. He insisted on the involvement of these families in the daily life of his parish. Women took care of the maintenance of the church but also cooked for religious ceremonies (this recalls Danıs' observation in Istanbul, Danıs 2004b). After a year, they moved to apartments with the rent covered by the Red Crescent. Most of them left Jordan between 2015 and 2017 to settle in Australia.[5] The priest pointed out the precariousness of these reception conditions as well as the resilience of the families facing this situation.

These Iraqi refugees had the status of "invited guests" in Jordan—which means that unlike the Palestinian refugees of 1948 and 1967, they did not have uncontested

4 These included the churches of al-Zarqāʾ, al-Salṭ, Fuhays, Mādabā, Mārkā, al-'Ashrafiyya, Marj al-Hamām, Tlaʿ al-ʿAlī, Nāʿūr, al-Hāshimī, and Jabal al-Ḥusayn.

5 Interview with Rifaat Badr, 2018.

residence in the territory—and most of them were registered as asylum seekers with the UNHCR which prevented them from having access to work and schooling for their children. Over the years, the defense of the rights of these refugees by humanitarian actors, particularly Caritas and Christian church leaders, led these confessional humanitarian actors to integrate them into the category of "non-Syrian" refugees (see in this volume by Solenn Al Majali) to stress the lack of means they had access to.

When I began my fieldwork in 2017, most Christian Iraqi refugees were living in three working-class neighborhoods of Amman: Mārkā, al-Hāshimī al-Shamālī, and Jabal al-Ḥusayn. Most of the refugees I interviewed said that they had settled there because they already had relatives there. This settlement logic is similar to that of the Iraqi refugees who had settled in Jordan after 2006. The settlement logics of humanitarian organizations adapted to these dynamics, and vice versa. For example, the Caritas clinic in al-Hāshimī al-Shamālī was opened in 2009. In addition to kinship networks, it is access to assistance that has encouraged the concentration of settlement around these three districts. Some families first settled by their own means in other neighborhoods but had to move once they could not provide for their needs. Z., an Iraqi woman from Qaraqosh I interviewed in 2018, mentioned settling first in the neighborhood of the University of Jordan before she had to move to Mārkā to benefit from the assistance of the church.

Access to assistance was a decisive criterion in their choice of location within the urban area: access to schools for their children, health and housing mainly, but also religious spiritual life. In Jabal al-Ḥusayn, some migrants centered their social life and cultural activities around the Jesuit centre[6] and the De La Salle College, where masses were organized. In al-Hāshimī al-Shamālī, the Caritas clinic as well as the Melkite and Latin churches were central within the organization of the migrants' daily life, some of them also visiting Mārkā, the neighboring district. In 2019, the Caritas clinic in al-Hāshimī welcomed around 60 to 100 people per day.[7] In Mārkā, assistance to refugees was structured around the Latin parish and some evangelical churches. Other churches played a major role in assistance to migrants, in particular the Syriac Orthodox Church of al-Suwayfiyya when it was under the authority of Fr. Emmanuel Banna. It used to welcome tens of refugees every day until Fr. Banna's death in 2017. The same goes for the priests of the Melkite Church of Marj al-Hammām and Fuhayṣ, for instance.

Beyond the lived experience of the refugees, the clergy itself had to adapt to the reality of this urban geography. As mentioned earlier, some of the churches to which the refugees belonged, notably the Chaldean and Assyrian churches, had no representation in Amman. Priests were therefore sent to Amman to meet the religious needs of the migrants, on a permanent basis in the case of the Chaldean priest, or on an ad hoc basis. Fr. Zayd, the Chaldean priest, was sent from Iraq to Amman after 2014 for liturgical and spiritual guidance. He organized Chaldean masses in the Latin churches of the three above-mentioned neighborhoods: on Sunday morning in Mārkā,

6 The Jesuit center had a refugee service for urban refugees in Amman and is located near the library of the Pontifical mission.

7 Interview with Gaby Daw, 2019.

Sunday afternoon in Jabal al-Ḥusayn, and Friday morning in al-Hāshimī. He was also in charge of the Chaldean Youth movement in Jordan. In 2018, an Assyrian priest was coming every two weeks from Iraq to give masses in the Latin church of Mārkā.

The reception of Iraqi Christian refugees in Jordan was thus underpinned by confessional dynamics in several respects: firstly, the categorization by politics, church, and faith-based representatives of the migrants as "religious migrants." This tended to separate them from the Muslim Iraqi refugee situation. Secondly, this reflected in the communication strategies aimed at donors, depicting them as an incarnation of contemporary martyrdom. Thirdly, this partly conditioned the dynamics of urban settlement of the migrants based on solidarity and faith-based assistance networks. It is the setting up and articulation of these networks that the case study of Mārkā allows us to decipher.

1.3. Assistance Policy: Structuring the Faith-Based Network

Our investigation concerning the assistance policies toward Iraqi Christian refugees in Jordan focused on the case of the Mārkā parish. Here is the account by Fr. Khalil Ja'ar, priest of the parish, of the migrants' arrival in Mārkā, heavily imbued with the martyrological references mentioned earlier:

> I was a parish priest in al-Suwayfiyya from 2004 to 2013 and then I was sent to Mārkā. The parish at that time was doing badly; there was only one mass a week attended by about 15 women. This was a crisis for me as a priest. Six months later, Caritas called me and asked me if I could take in refugees. I took in 150 people in 2014. I first gave them the possibility to live with me in the parish premises and then little by little we rented flats next to the church in order to preserve their dignity. I always say, I share my life with 21st century saints. I am even ashamed sometimes of my condition compared to them. (Interview, 7/11/2017, Mārkā)

Kinship and religious networks played an important role in the experience of the refugees in Mārkā. After 2011, within the academic approach, the question of hospitality as constitutive of Muslim societies has been raised (Shryock 2008; Mason 2011; Zaman 2016). These studies tackled the need to go beyond a perception of religious matters as a potential dividing factor in humanitarian contexts instead of highlighting the positive role potential faith-based organizations and local faith communities can play in displacement situations (Fiddian-Qasmiyeh 2011a; Løland 2021). It is in this perspective that this chapter considers the organization of the daily life of these refugees in Mārkā but also the structure of faith-based assistance initiatives by Fr. Khalil.

The case study of Mārkā shows the importance of the priests' initiatives to anchor the issue of the refugees in local and also transnational networks of assistance and humanitarianism (Shami 1996). As shown in other contexts and periods, in Mārkā the Christian Iraqis consider Jordan as a transit country before being resettled in Canada, the United States, or Australia, depending on their networks and where their relatives have already settled. This transit situation has been prolonged for a large proportion of these refugees, first because of the coincidence of their arrival in Jordan with the one of thousands of Syrian refugees sharing the same aspirations to leave and then because of the Covid-19 sanitary crisis and the subsequent border closures. In this context, in Mārkā, Fr. Khalil Jaʿar's activity was of central importance for their inclusion in transnational solidarity networks. First of all, he relied on the previous waves of migration and the reception policies already developed by the church from the 1990s onward. He set up a sponsorship system: Iraqis who settled in Australia or in the United States and especially in San Diego would provide from 100 to 200 US$ every month to refugees recently arrived in Amman. This system was based, according to the priest, not only on his knowledge of former migrants but also on tours he made abroad to churches attended by Iraqi refugees in the United States and UK. Each of these sponsorships represents examples of refugee-refugee assistance (Fiddian-Qasmiyeh 2016) and was carefully documented by the priest in records he kept in his offices. In addition, he carefully kept a copy of the UNHCR registration certificates of each refugee as he also played a privileged role of intermediary with the UNHCR to advocate in favor of the Christian Iraqi need for assistance.

According to Fr. Jaʿar, he based his choice of helping a particular family on the assessment of their situation. To do so, he relied heavily on the advice of the Chaldean priest, Fr. Zayd, who would recommend beneficiaries to the Mārkā parish. This cooperation within the assistance policy took different forms as Fr. Jaʿar mentioned that when the Aramaic father had the opportunity to resettle in Australia, he gave him all the documents concerning the members of his church before leaving. He entrusted him with the spiritual and material assistance of his community until the appointment of a new Aramaic priest. Moreover, within this system of cooperation, the three fathers mentioned earlier emphasized their assistance policy as a refugee-refugee one. The Iraqi priests insisted on their own status as refugees and the precariousness of their situation. In the case of Fr. Khalil Jaʿar, he would introduce himself as being from a Palestinian refugee background, which would partly explain his particular attention to the situation of refugees.

Beyond these networks of men of religion, it is through associations that Fr. Jaʿar developed projects and raised funds. He could count on the support of traditional Christian charities such as l'Œuvre d'Orient or the Pontifical Mission. In addition, he was the representative of an international institution: Messenger of Peace. Thanks to it, he could carry out projects outside the umbrella of the church, with international logistic and financial support. This independence from ecclesiastical structures and hierarchy contributed to the priest's capacity for action and to his mode of mobilization, which was widely publicized on a national and even international scale and generated some debates within the church.

Yet, the arrival of hundreds of Iraqi refugees in Mārkā revitalized the parish: several masses were said every week by different churches' representatives (Chaldean, Aramaic) as Latin masses multiplied. In Mārkā, as well as in other parishes of the city, various Christian groups were created, such as the Chaldeans. The arrival of these migrants allowed some priests to realize spiritual and social projects recalling the

Christian ideal of the holy mission, including educational projects such as an informal school for Iraqi children in Mārkā.

2. A School for Iraqi Children: Preparing Resettlement

The arrival of Iraqi refugees in Jordan also raises the question of the nationalization of assistance in a migratory context. As in the case of the Yemenis and Sudanese (see Al Majali in this volume), the argument most often used by church leaders and faith-based charities alike was to compare the situation of Iraqi refugees in Jordan with that of Syrian refugees. In this context, starting in 2015, Fr. Khalil Ja'ar opened an informal school in Mārkā for Iraqi children with a curriculum designed to prepare them for relocation to North America or Australia. By opening this informal school, he was taking a stand in an internal church debate in which the official Vatican position was to encourage Iraqi Christians to stay in the Middle East or return to Iraq. It was the Father's involvement in both associative and international networks that enabled him to develop this informal school and a series of initiatives in support of migrants in Mārkā.

2.1. Informal Education to Prepare for Migration

The issue of education for refugee children became central to the social debate in Jordan after 2011 and the arrival of Syrian refugees. The state faced an unprecedented situation, whereas the primary education of Palestinian refugees had been taken care of by UNRWA schools, no equivalent institution could guarantee the education of Syrian children in the camps or in the cities where the majority of them had settled. A two-shift system was introduced, with Syrian children attending school in the afternoon to follow the Jordanian curriculum. For Iraqi children, in the absence of refugee status, access to public education was not guaranteed and, as already mentioned, since their parents could only work informally, access to private education, often very expensive, was impossible.

In this context, in February 2015, Fr. Khalil Ja'ar put in place an informal school program for 350 children called the "Mārkā School for Iraqi Children." In fact, the parish complex in Mārkā included a school of the Latin Patriarchate of Jerusalem that had been opened in the early 1960s and had expanded considerably in 1968 with the arrival of the Rosary Sisters, a female Catholic congregation of Palestinian origin, as educational staff but also with the settlement of Palestinian refugees in the area. The Patriarchate school today records around 500 pupils, both Christian and Muslim. Using this infrastructure, Fr. Ja'ar decided to open an informal afternoon school for Iraqi Christian children.

A second shift in the afternoon for the Christian Iraqi refugee children was inaugurated in 2015. In an interview with the former headmistress of the school, she insisted on the notion of "rights to education" but also the unexpected success of the school when it opened. In November 2014, the school team planned to welcome

Figure 11.2 Worshipers wearing a "Jordanian Chaldean parish" scarf during a mass in Mārkā, 2018 (photo: N. Neveu).

a maximum of fifty children. The pedagogical team quickly had to adapt the school project to welcome around 350 pupils, coming from the neighborhoods of Mārkā, al-Maḥaṭṭa, and al-Hāshimī. The opening of this school was made possible financially through the fundraising organized by the Latin Patriarchate, the solidarity of parishes frequented by Iraqi refugees, in the UK mainly, and the support of the "Messenger of Peace," the association directed by Fr. Khalil Ja'ar. This enabled the teaching team to pay not only for the teachers' pension but also for the children's transportation from their homes by buses chartered by the school (especially for the children living in al-Hāshimī and al-Maḥaṭṭa). Thanks to international solidarity networks, the school also covered the cost of the children's uniforms—burgundy with a logo representing Tiber and

Euphrates—the books, and snacks. Raising funds through international networks, while guaranteeing the opening of the school, also placed the initiative in a form of dependence and precariousness with regard to the sustainability of these funds. For example, in 2018, the financial support of the French Embassy for this initiative, around 140,000 euros per year, was granted for a period of only two years. This informal school developed thanks to the associative and solidarity networks mobilized, shaped, and framed by Fr. Khalil Jaʿar and his team, calling for constant remobilization of aid and assistance from different partners. The precariousness of the funding has led to changes in the school schedule. In 2015, children had class five days a week, but in 2018 they were attending school only three days a week, from 12:30 to 4:00 p.m. due to financial issues.

In terms of curriculum, the children received lessons in English and Arabic, Mathematics and Science, and Religious Education, all provided in English. The curriculum of the school did not correspond to the official Jordanian curriculum, although the latter was applied during the morning shift in the same school (Latin Patriarchate School). It was primarily the importance of teaching in English that was emphasized, taking the PSHE (personal, social, health, and economic) method from the British curriculum. The educational team in charge of setting up this program had in mind to prepare the children for resettlement in an English-speaking country thanks to education. No classes in history were provided as the idea was to help them adapt to the educational system of an unknown host country they were preparing to migrate to. In 2018, the head of the school stressed: "I talked with people in Australia, they were saying to Iraqis in Jordan, don't send your kids to public schools in Jordan but to the Dayr al-lātīn [Mārkā] one, they will pass all the tests in Australia." For the very well-structured team of the Dayr al-lātīn, one of the priorities of the school was to teach children an English curriculum, to prepare their migration.

2.2. Training Good Christians?

Religious education was also central to the educational project of the Mārkā school, and, as part of the curriculum, it was provided by the Rosary Sisters, who gave Bible classes. During an interview in 2019, one of the Rosary Sisters pointed out that one of the Iraqi children in the school had won the competition of Bible recitation in Jordan in 2018. In addition, religious education classes were provided by Fr. Zayd, the Chaldean priest, every Friday. The Catholic scouts were also involved in the training of the children. They organized awareness campaigns on child protection (regarding psychological and sexual abuse). The Christian identity of these children was at the heart of the school's educational project, with times of prayer, particularly in Aramaic, planned during the gatherings in the schoolyard. The preparation of religious celebrations was also a concern for the teaching team. In 2017, I attended the parish's Christmas show for children. Taking place in the large hall of the parish, the show brought together about a hundred people, and the troupe of young amateurs staged Biblical episodes, advocating the values of love and tolerance. The pedagogical function of theater in the context of religious education made it possible to highlight exemplary Christian figures (as shown in different historical context by Verdeil 2016).

At the same ceremony, a Christmas gift-giving event was organized with another partner institution, the Lion's Club of Amman. The following year's Easter celebrations were coordinated in partnership with Jordanian Christian schools, while the parish church was used during Easter week to host masses from different churches to which the Iraqi Christians belonged.

Finally, beyond school time, during the holidays, the teaching team set up summer camps to extend disciplinary and pedagogical supervision. This involved educational and recreational activities or visits to places of worship or piety that are central to Jordanian Christianity (the Baptism Site, Mount Nebo, Mādabā). The spiritual guidance work was organized in collaboration with other priests, in particular Fr. Zayd, who was in charge of the Chaldean Youth movement, structured around the Jesuit center in Jabal al-Ḥusayn.

Beyond the activities strictly reserved for children, the parish space was a place to highlight the importance of family ties, particularly in the context of conflict and migration when these populations faced major reconfigurations within the kinship structures, due to deaths or changes in status and lack of access to work. For example, a meal containing meat was organized twice a week for children and their families. The idea was both to ensure that all family members had a minimum amount of protein in their diet and to put the family structure back at the heart of the parish project.

In many ways, through its educational function, its insistence on family structure and the formation of good Christians, the assistance policy and the project developed by Fr. Khalil Ja'ar in Mārkā recalls the missionary model as it underlies the organization of a complex social world for Iraqi children and their families. In addition, a classic Christian church social activity was taken on: health care. The children and their families could, in fact, also visit the parish clinic. The latter was run in partnership with Caritas, whose nurse was employed on site. The dispensary was intended to ensure the medical follow-up of the children and to provide first aid while paying specific attention to medical problems widespread in the Middle East: high blood pressure and diabetes. Thus, beyond the pedagogical project, it was a response to the migratory situation of Iraqi refugees and the structuring of a social world around the church that Fr. Khalil Ja'ar developed through his school project, not without generating debates within the church and among Christian humanitarian actors, as we shall see below. The development of assistance and hospitality corresponded in his case to a strong engagement in the debates concerning migration and reception policies in Jordan and more generally in the region.

2.3. From School Staff to Workshops: Offering Job Opportunities to Iraqis

The school project included several components, firstly for children, but also for young people, since beyond access to the first school cycles, access to education was also complex for young Iraqis, as were university or diploma courses. In January 2017, a computer lab was opened with training for an international diploma for teenagers and young adults. The idea here was to promote professionalization and diploma training for young adults, again with the idea of preparing them for integration into professions in the host countries. This project has developed over the years, notably with the accreditation of the Messengers of Peace association to be an examination center to deliver the international ICDL (International *Certificate* of Digital Literacy) diploma on digital skills. This international diploma would be of value wherever young people settle.

This issue of access to employment for Iraqi refugees came up repeatedly during interviews with members of the Mārkā parish team, particularly those involved in the school project. The headmistress of the school until 2019, a British-Iraqi, graduated from the UK, indicated during an interview that she had moved to Jordan at the request of Fr. Khalil Ja'ar to take charge of and develop the school project, which explains the influence of the British model for the curriculum. Until 2019, she was a central element of what Fr. Ja'ar called the "government" of the parish. She was in charge of several projects, including the recruitment of teachers for the school. The twenty to twenty-five qualified teachers providing education to the children were, themselves, Iraqis. Most of them began their relationship with the school when coming to register their children for classes or through the church. Their involvement in the school's pedagogical project responded to an injunction mentioned earlier: to guarantee respect for the background and experience of the pupils as well as the specificity of their modes of belonging. As many teachers pointed out, the school welcomed pupils who had been severely traumatized by what they had had to flee, hence the importance of having staff who were trained in, or above all aware and sensitive to, these issues. In addition, this structure made it possible to involve adult refugees in the project. Although they could not be salaried, because of their status, the teachers were compensated for the lessons they gave: their rent was covered by the parish administration.

Indeed, in the church-world that Fr. Khalil had established, it was important to give the children an idea of life afterward, when the transit period in Jordan would be over, while ensuring their Christian education. The involvement of the adults in the parish was thus highly valued, since they could not work officially. In this context, various projects were set up in the premises that had initially served as a place of refuge and accommodation for these refugees. On the first floor, a nursery for children of Syrian refugees—Muslim and Christian—was opened in 2018. The second floor was initially set up as a café for fathers of families and more generally for male refugees. A space was also used as a hairdressing salon for men and women. These activities reveal two dynamics: firstly, the desire to structure places of sociability for people, particularly men, who were idle and potentially weakened by the experience of migration and the violence encountered in Iraq. In the café, men played cards or dominoes and could meet without fear of money issues. The desire to structure the community around the parish went with the idea of working on the self-esteem of the members of this group, hence the body treatments offered through the hairdressing services.

Gradually, these social spaces were replaced by workshops, with the development of several programs to promote the professional integration of refugees. In 2019, according to Fr. Ja'ar, the sewing center in the al-Za'atarī refugee camp for Syrian refugees (see Dalal and Fraikin in this volume) closed and he bought the equipment to open a workshop. The women involved in this project were responsible for sewing children's school uniforms, but above all for making cloth nappies to be used by refugee families and sold during charity events. In many respects, it is within a traditional Christian-gendered social order that the places of work and socialization were developed within Fr. Ja'ar's parish. From there, the priest made a point of making weekly visits to the homes of some of the refugees living in the neighborhood, particularly the more precarious ones, bringing them food vouchers according to their needs (distributions were also organized every week on the parish premises). The parish became a central space for organizing the migrants' daily life and a space with a vocation—while responding to the imperatives of the waiting situation imposed by transit—both to guarantee social order within the group of migrants and to prepare for their migration, particularly for the youngest. This is very similar to the control on the dimension and activities of social life through faith-based activities studied in the case of one of Mafraq's Evangelical Churches by Ann-Christin Wagner (now Zuntz 2018b). From 2015 onward, members of the parish have carefully built up a local audience and social order from Christian humanitarian assistance and the establishment of a welcoming and local hosting policy.

3. Competing Migratory Projects: Caritas, the Church, and the Migrants

Fr. Ja'ar's initiatives were met with a variety of reactions from both church authorities and Christian humanitarian actors, the latter evolving over the years as the migration situation changed. First, while the church showed its support for his initiative, its official policy was to encourage the return of refugees to Iraq, or at least to ensure that they settled in Jordan and remained in the Middle East. The Iraqi churches were advocating the same objectives, calling for the return of their members to their country of origin. It is with this in mind that some of the charitable and humanitarian work was developed, in contrast to the projects set up in the parish of Mārkā. The tension between the desire of the Iraqi Christian believers to leave, the official policy of the church and clerics, and the implementation of alternative projects by the clergy, is not unique to Jordan. It points to the church as a growing actor of reception policies in the context of post-2014 migration, with both the implementation of migration policies, to be negotiated with local and state institutions, and the deployment of mechanisms on the ground to adapt to the migrants' situation.

3.1. The Caritas Schooling Project and Preparing Them to Go Back

As mentioned before, Caritas teams and volunteers were and still are central actors in the field for the reception of Iraqi migrants in Jordan. As Caritas is a humanitarian actor acting specifically outside refugee camps to help refugees, migrants, and vulnerable people, its presence in Amman has been widely developed since 2011 and the arrival of thousands of Syrian refugees in the capital. The action of the faith-based charity focuses primarily on health care, through cooperation with hospitals such as the Italian Hospital in al-ʾAshrafiyya or the Luzmilla Hospital in Jabal al-Luwaybda, both Christian hospitals with which, sometimes with the support of the UNHCR, partnerships have been set up for the care of both Iraqi and Syrian refugees. Several Caritas clinics have opened in Amman over the last fifteen years, including the aforementioned al-Hāshimī and Mārkā ones.

In the case of assistance to Iraqis, Caritas representatives in Jordan regularly pointed out both the complexity of the Iraqis' situation and the limited resources available to them compared to Syrian refugees. However, as mentioned earlier, Caritas was entrusted, in 2014, in coordination with the Royal Palace, with the reception and assistance of Iraqi Christian refugees who responded to King Abdullah II's appeal, with the provision of accommodation and emergency care, the payment of some rents, etc. The reception of this wave of refugees was part of the assistance policy that has been developed by Caritas since the 1990s for Iraqi refugees in the country.

In this context, Caritas was also concerned with the education of young Iraqis, but by deploying an alternative response to the one set up in Mārkā. In 2018, during an interview with Omar Abawi, the head of the Caritas program for Iraqi refugees, he stressed that Caritas embodied the official narrative of the Latin church against the resettlement of the refugees in Australia or North America. Thus, Caritas developed a different policy in terms of schooling by encouraging Iraqi children to follow the Jordanian curriculum in about twenty Latin schools in Amman and its region. Most of the schools they selected were Catholic (Melkite or Latin) private schools, which formed an educational network. Caritas covered the inscription fees. During an interview, the headmistress of the Melkite school in the al-Hāshimī district, which was part of this program, raised a number of difficulties encountered in the reception of these pupils within her school, starting with the lack of training of her staff to tackle the traumas of these children. She said that she received about fifty children every year, some of whom speaking only Aramaic and not Arabic. The project was funded by the Pontifical Mission and dedicated only to Christian children with the idea of preparing them for resettlement in Iraq or, if that was not possible, for staying and building their lives in Jordan. In this context too, the lack of fixed funding for this project also made it precarious in the long term. This policy generated debate, with some criticizing Caritas for not fully taking into account the voice and situation of Iraqi refugees, particularly their lack of resources. In this respect, the mere payment of school fees was not enough to guarantee the enrollment of children in school, as transportation costs, for example, could not be covered by the families. The realities on the ground put these criticisms into perspective, as most school directors found financial support to cover the costs of transportation, uniforms, and books for the children enrolled. The refugees themselves insisted that it was impossible for them to return to Iraq because of the violence and dispossession they had suffered. The Caritas Iraqi project managers were obviously familiar with these issues and had few illusions about the possibility of people returning to their country.

In another interview, in 2019, the head of the program dedicated to Iraqi refugees noted that ambiguity. Caritas, while implementing the project of preserving Christianity in the Middle East, was well aware of the complexity of the situation in the Iraqi case. According to him, only the older people would probably volunteer to return to Iraq. He was following closely the church's debates concerning the policy of return, especially those on raising funds for the reconstruction of Christian towns and villages there. In this perspective, the Caritas position would be to oppose both emigration and resettlement. The idea here was to advocate for the rights of Iraqi people, especially Christians, to the Iraqi State to ensure their property and protection. He stated that the emergency was to negotiate with the political authority in Iraq and especially in Kurdistan to find agreements and compensation for the Christians who had to leave the country. In the meantime, as he stated, a "livelihood approach" was chosen by Caritas, as attested to by the school policy, but also a series of initiatives in favor of the professionalization of adults. It was therefore primarily a policy of adaptation to the situation that was developed, according to this testimony, through the livelihood concept: schooling, training, and primary assistance.

Caritas organized workshops in several cities in Jordan, for example, a mosaics workshop in Madaba and workshops for leather and agricultural work in al-Karak, in order to encourage Iraqis—men and women—to work and find means of subsistence in their country of settlement. These projects were supported by the Ministry of Tourism to train refugees in what were considered to be "traditional" craft techniques. Several projects of this type were developed with the support of Caritas, such as the Our Lady of the Peace center in Nāʿūr, which specialized in the production of herbal products, soaps, and pallet wood furniture and involved between thirty to forty people.

Thus, the Iraqi refugee problem became a central issue for the churches themselves in terms of the official hosting policy and social projects in the long-term. It led to antagonistic projects and perspectives between those implemented by the priests, Caritas, and the Latin Patriarchate. Moreover, contradictory narratives developed concerning the solution to be brought to the situation of these migrants. In addition to discordant projects, a gap has clearly formed between the will of the migrants themselves, their projects, itineraries and the churches' framework, hosting policies, and assistance response that has arisen in Jordan in the Iraqi case. This is all the truer as representatives of the churches and associations involved in the assistance of these migrants, including Caritas and representatives of the Vatican and the Messenger of Peace, were gradually asked by the UNHCR authorities to represent these migrant populations during meetings. Churches, clerics, and faith-based associations or NGOs played a key role during the negotiation with UNHCR and imposed themselves as major actors not only within the process of assistance to migrants but also within the hospitality or welcoming policy strategy. This growing importance within the decision-making processes called for regular coordination between the various Catholic bodies, which was gradually put in place under the supervision of the Vatican Embassy. It raises the question of how migrants are represented in international institutions and how these fit in with their needs and expectations.

3.2. Competing Projects?

Thus, the church and faith-based charities, the traditional actors in assistance policies, became essential partners of the international organizations in charge of managing the migratory issue. In the case of Iraqi Christian refugees, as mentioned above, there was a prevailing tendency to distinguish them from the situation of other Iraqi refugees. Reception and assistance policies became a real space of power and affirmation of the authority of clerics and several initiatives—sometimes antagonistic—developed. Priests asserted their authority on their ability to raise funds and mobilize international networks to ensure assistance to refugees. As Ann Christine Wagner (now Zuntz 2018a) posits in the case of the Evangelical churches of Mafraq and the reception of Syrian refugees, while research has focused on the influence of Islamic charities, the post-2011 period must be seen as a time of major reconfiguration of Christian assistance in terms of discourse, prerogatives, and implementation on the ground. In the case of Iraqi refugees, the initiatives mentioned earlier indicate a rapid development of Christian action in terms of territorial imprint, of involvement of new actors and of development of activities and fields of competence. Is there some competition (Fiddian-Qasmiyeh 2015) between those dynamics? While the actors on the ground deny it, one can nevertheless decipher attempts to channel the most independent actors of the church. Their independence, made possible by the involvement within the associative networks, was often seen as problematic or a threat by ecclesiastic authorities.

In this context, new figures appeared in the field of Christian humanitarianism, with dynamics that can be perceived as competitive in several respects: both in terms of their fields of activity and of mirroring power struggles within the church and in particular the Latin Patriarchate of Jerusalem. Thus, in 2015, Fr. Mario Cornioli moved from Palestine to St Joseph's parish in Jabal Amman, a move he presents as emanating from a desire on his part to come to the assistance of refugees fleeing persecution by ISIS, largely taking up the rhetoric positing these refugees as an image of contemporary Christian martyrdom.

The activities developed by Fr. Cornioli were first carried out by his association Habibi Valtiberina, founded in 2013 by some of his relatives and based in Italy. The first activities supported by the association in Jordan concerned the professionalization of Iraqi refugees. As mentioned earlier, these projects were quite traditionally conceived in a non-mixed gender way. Fr. Cornioli opened a sewing workshop on the top floor of the building adjacent to the church in Jabal Amman. The idea was to train refugee women not only in sewing but also in the design of fashionable clothing. This project was associated with the Rafedin brand and was established in collaboration with the Keffieh factory in Hebron, whose fabrics are integrated into the creations of the workshop. Silk was imported from Italy. The association's projects then developed around catering activities, with the opening of a pizzeria on the ground floor of the parish hall, and with the production of raw materials, cooking, and training in service trades, particularly for men. Beyond these initiatives, it was craft trades that, as in other cases mentioned earlier, were promoted with the opening of leather, mosaic, and ceramic workshops in Amman.

Beyond these initiatives, in 2019, Fr. Mario Cornioli was entrusted with the opening of a school, under the tutelage of the Latin Patriarchate, for young Iraqi refugees in al-Hāshimī al-Shamālī, a district, as we have seen, where large numbers of Iraqi refugees settled. In November 2019, during an interview, Fr. Cornioli summarized the project as follows. He had been able to raise funds for the opening of a school for refugees and had drawn up a project in coordination with Wisam Mansour, the head of the Latin

Patriarchate's schools in Jordan. From September 2019, the school welcomed around 350 children in the afternoons, with a majority of Iraqi teachers and a pedagogical project mainly focused on foreign language learning, particularly English. The curriculum adopted was described as "international" and the Iraqi teachers were recruited by a committee of priests of different confessions (Chaldean, Latin, Syriac Orthodox, Syriac Catholic) who supported the school's educational project. This school, described as informal, was intended, in Fr. Cornioli's view, to prepare young children for Western culture, in the context of a migration project that would most likely take them to North America, Europe, or Australia. "Nobody wants to stay here and they do not want to go back," said Fr. Cornioli. The children came from both the al-Hāshimī neighborhood and Jabal al-Ḥusayn, from where buses had to be chartered. To carry out this project, he counted on the support of the Vatican Embassy in Amman, a British NGO, the support of the French Embassy, and the Latin Patriarchate, with the imperative of renewing this financial arrangement annually. This initiative, which began just before the beginning of the Covid-19 health crisis and the closure of schools in Jordan, was short-lived, largely because as of the beginning of the school year 2021, the Jordanian law changed and public schools were opened to Iraqi children. However, the initiative reveals changing perspectives within the reception policy strategy developed by the Catholic Church in Jordan, with the obvious *laissez-faire* of the Jordanian authorities.

From 2019 onward, there was a shift in the assistance policies relating to Iraqis in Jordan, with, firstly, less financial support for schooling projects launched by Caritas on behalf of the Pontifical Mission and, secondly, financial and official support for initiatives to help these populations leave and settle outside the Middle East. These developments do not indicate a radical change in the discourse of either the Vatican or the Iraqi churches, rather they are an adaptation to the realities on the ground. However, these new policies met a desire to control these informal school initiatives by a new creation which was perceived by Fr. Khalil Ja'ar as a form of competition or rivalry with his school. In fact, the headmistress of the Mārkā school left her post to join the al-Hāshimī school, as did part of the teaching staff. The functioning of the school in Mārkā had to adapt to the new situation. This paradoxical situation can be explained by the competitiveness of humanitarian projects for the same audiences by members of the clergy. In a context where the role of priests and their networks is decisive, Fr. Mario Cornioli appears to have powerful connections in Europe as well as in the Middle East, especially since the arrival of the Italian Patriarch Pierbattista Pizzaballa as head of the Latin Patriarchate in 2020. Thus, for the church, the enrollment of its clerics in the associative networks constituted an opportunity to quickly develop its field of activity and competence in order to adapt to the emergency situation. It represented an independent activity that was viewed with some caution as the economic stakes involved in raising funds were seen as delicate. The asymmetry and timelessness of the modes of support reveal a desire to keep control of humanitarian actors, action, and assistance and the need to adapt to reality in the field for a church which imposed itself within the migration policy field as a key actor at a local, national, and international level.

Conclusion

The case of Christian Iraqi refugees settled in Jordan following King Abdullah II's appeal in 2014 provides a privileged observatory for the confessionalization of the humanitarian assistance field in a migratory context, firstly from the perspective of the public and the targeted beneficiaries, with a relatively unprecedented confessional focus on Christians in the region by both faith-based charities and the churches. Furthermore, this case study reveals the contemporary restructuring of faith-based humanitarian aid in the post-2011 period, which undermines the hypotheses of secularization of humanitarian field (Ager and Ager 2015). It also highlights the powerful networks of Christian humanitarian actors, whether based on associations, clergy, diplomats, or state and international institutions. In the interweaving of these networks lies the capacity for action of Christian humanitarian actors, particularly clerics. From Mārkā outwards, it is from the settlement spaces of previous waves of migrants that radiate refugee-to-refugee assistance, in a deterritorialized perspective, for example. The spiritual and social needs of the refugees call for internal migrations within the church; the contemporary dynamics of reception and assistance are recomposed around both earlier and later networks of migration.

Secondly, this case study reveals the logic behind refugee-reception policies. The positions taken by the Vatican, which go against the aspirations of its flocks, have in fact helped to shape not only resettlement policies but also a clear definition of reception policies. While these lines and directives may evolve over several years, there seems to be a desire on the part of the international and religious institutions to control faith-based humanitarian expression. On the part of the clergy, the associative networks provided them with an unprecedented independence from the ecclesiastical authorities. Thirdly, within the structures and coordination of international organizations, these actors have established themselves as key players in the migratory field. Although this has required them to make an effort to coordinate, this intermediary role has directed their activities towards increased advocacy and the defense of refugees' rights, in addition to emergency action on the ground.

Bibliography

Al-Rasheed, Madawi (1998), *Iraqi Assyrian Christians in London: The Construction of Ethnicity*, Lewiston: The Edwin Mellen Press.

Achilli, Luigi (2015), "Syrian Refugees in Jordan: A Reality Check," Policy Brief, European Universty Institute. http://cadmus.eui.eu/bitstream/handle/1814/34904/MPC_2015-02_PB.pdf?sequence=1.

Ager, Alastair, and Joey Ager (2015), *Faith, Secularism and Humanitarian Engagement*, New York: Palgrave.

Ali, Ali (2011), "Displacement and Statecraft in Iraq: Recent Trends Older Roots," *International Journal of Contemporary Iraqi Studies*, 5 (2/28): 231–45.

Bakewell, Oliver (1999), "Can We Ever Rely on Refugee Statistics?" *Radical Statistics*, 72. Available online: www.radstats.org.uk/no072/article1.htm.

Borchgrevink, Kaja, and Marta Bivand Erdal (2017), "With Faith in Development: Organizing Transnational Islamic Charity," *Progress in Development Studies*, 17 (3): 214–28.

Chatelard, Géraldine (2002), "Jordan as a Transit Country: Semi-protectionist Immigration Policies and Their Effects on Iraqi Forced Migrants," *New Issues in Refugee Research*, 61. Available online: http://www.unhcr.org/research/RESEARCH/3d57aa757.pdf.

Chatelard, Géraldine (2004), "Iraqi Forced Migrants in Jordan: Conditions, Religious Networks, and the Smuggling Process," in G. Borjas and J. Crisp (eds.), *Poverty, International Migration and Asylum*, 341–70, Helsinki: UNU/WIDER.

Chatelard, Géraldine (2008), "Jordan's Transient Iraqi Guests: Transnational Dynamics and National Agenda," in *Viewpoints*, special issue *Iraq's Refugee and IDP Crisis: Human Toll and Implications*, modified version (2009), "Iraqis in Jordan: elusive numbers, uncertain future."

Chatelard, Géraldine, and Doraï Kamel (2009), "La présence irakienne en Syrie et en Jordanie. Dynamiques sociales et spatiales, et modes de gestion par les pays d'accueil," *Maghreb-Machrek*. Available online: http://halshs.archivesouvertes.fr/docs/00/33/84/03/PDF/Maghreb_Machrek_Chatelard_Dorai.pdf.

Danıs, Didem (2004a), "Attendre au purgatoire: les réseaux religieux des migrants chrétiens d'Irak en transit à Istanbul," *Revue européenne des migration internationales*, 22 (3): 109–34.

Danıs, Didem (2004b), "Iraqi Christian Women in the Domestic Service Ladder of Istanbul: Solidarity or Exploitation?" *Journal of Ethnic and Migration Studies*, 33 (4): 601–15.

Danıs, Didem (2008), *Pour une sociologie du transit dans les phénomènes migratoires: Le cas des réseaux des migrants irakiens en transit à Istanbul*,PhD thesis, EHESS, Paris.

Doraï, Kamel (2011), "Iraqis in Exile: Migratory Networks as a Coping Strategy," *International Journal of Contemporary Iraqi Studies*, 5 (2): 215–29.

Duriez, Bruno, François Mabille, and Kathy Roussel (eds.) (2007), *Les ONG confessionnelles. Religions et action internationale*, Paris: L'Harmattan.

El Nakib, Satha, and Alastair Ager (2015), "Local Faith Community and Civil Society Engagement in Humanitarian Response with Syrian Refugee in Irbid, Jordan," Report to the Henry Luce Foundation, New York: Columbia University.

Fattah, Hala (2007), "Les autres Irakiens : émigrés et exilés d'avant 2003 en Jordanie et leurs récits d'appartenance," *Revue des mondes musulmans et de la Méditerranée*, 117–118: 127–36.

Ferris, Elizabeth (2011), "Faith and Humanitarianism: It's Complicated," *Journal of Refugee Studies*, 24 (3): 606–25. https://doi.org/10.1093/jrs/fer028.

Fiddian-Qasmiyeh, Elena (2011a), "Faith-Based Humanitarianism in Contexts of Forced Displacement," *Journal of Refugee Studies*, 24 (3): 429–39. https://doi.org/10.1093/jrs/fer033.

Fiddian-Qasmiyeh, Elena (2011b), "The Pragmatics of Performance: Putting 'Faith' in Aid in the Sahrawi Refugee Camps," *Journal of Refugee Studies*, 24 (3): 533–47. https://doi.org/10.1093/jrs/fer027.

Fiddian-Qasmiyeh, Elena (2015), "Conflicting Missions? The Politics of Evangelical Humanitarianism in the Sahrawi and Palestinian Protracted Refugee Situations," in Alexander Horstmann and Jin-Heon Jung (eds.), *Building Noah's Ark: Refugee, Migrant and Religious Communities*, 157–79, London: Palgrave Macmillan.

Fiddian-Qasmiyeh, Elena (2016), "Refugee-Refugee Relations in Contexts of Overlapping Displacement," *International Journal of Urban and Regional Research*, Spotlight on "The

Urban Refugee 'Crisis.'" Available online: http://www.ijurr.org/spotlight-on-overview/spotlight-urban-refugee-crisis/refugeerefugee-relations-contexts-overlapping-displacement/.

Furniss, Jamie, and Daniel Meier (2012), "Le laïc et le religieux dans l'action humanitaire, une introduction," *A contrario*, 18 (2): 7–36.

Graham-Brown, Sarah (1999), *Sanctioning Saddam: The Politics of Intervention in Iraq*, London and New York: I.B. Tauris.

Gurak, Douglas T., and Maria F. Caces (1992), "Migration Networks and the Shaping of Migration Systems," in Mary M. Kritz, Lin Lean Lim, and Hania Zlotnik (eds.), *International Migration Systems: A Global Approach*, 150–76, Oxford: Clarendon Press.

Hashemi, Nader, and Danny Postel (2017), *Sectarianization: Mapping the New Politics of the Middle East*, Oxford: Oxford University Press.

Ismael, Tareq, and Max Fuller (2008), "The Disintegration of Iraq: The Manufacturing and Politicization of Sectarianism," *International Journal of Contemporary Iraqi Studies*, 2 (3): 443–73.

Løland, Ingrid (2021), "War, Displacement, and Refugeehood: Existential Encounters of Religion in the Syrian Refugee Crisis," *Entangled Religions*, 12 (1): 3. https://doi.org/10.46586/er.12.2021.8892.

Marfleet, Peter (2007), "Iraq's Refugees: 'Exit' from the State," *International Journal of Contemporary Iraqi Studies*, 1 (3): 397–419.

Mason, Victoria (2011), "The Im/mobilities of Iraqi Refugees in Jordan: Pan-Arabism, 'Hospitality' and the Figure of the 'Refugee,'" *Mobilities*, 6 (3): 353–73. https://doi.org/10.1080/17450101.2011.590035.

Neveu, Norig (2010), "La sacralisation du territoire jordanien. Reconstruction des lieux saints nationaux, 1980–2006," *Archives de sciences sociales des religions*, 151: 107–28.

Ozkan, Mehmet (2011), "Transnational Islam, Immigrant NGOs and Poverty Alleviation: The Case of the IGMC," *Journal of International Development*, 24 (4): 467–84.

Petersen, Marie Juul (2012), "Izlamizing Aid: Transnational Muslim NGOs After 9.11," *Voluntas*, 23: 126–55.

Prud'homme, Claude (2007), "De la mission aux ONG de solidarité internationale. Quelle continuité?" in Bruno Duriez et al. (eds.), *Les ONG confessionnelles. Religions et action internationale*, 55–70, Paris: L'Harmattan.

Rahe, Jens-Uwe (2002), "Iraqi Shi'is in Exile in London," in Faleh Abdul-Jaber (ed.), *Ayatollahs, Sufis and Ideologues: State, Religion and Social Movements in Iraq*, 211–19, London: Saqi.

Robbins, Michael, and Lawrence Rubin (2013), "The Rise of Official Islam in Jordan," *Politics, Religion & Ideology*, 14 (1): 59–74.

Ruiz de Elvira, Laura, and Sahar Aurore Saeidnia (eds.) (2020), *Les mondes de la bienfaisance. Les pratiques du bien au prisme des sciences sociales*, Paris: CNRS éditions.

Sasoon, Joseph (2008), *The Iraqi Refugees: The New Crisis in the Middle East*, London: I.B. Tauris.

Shryock, Andrew (2008), "Thinking about Hospitality, with Derrida, Kant, and the Balga Bedouin," *Anthropos*, 103 (2): 405–21.

Shami, Seterney (1996), "Transnationalism and Refugee Studies: Rethinking Forced Migration and Identity in the Middle East," *Journal of Refugee Studies*, 9 (1): 3–26.

Shoeb, Marwa, Harvey Weinstein, and Jodi Halpern (2007), "Living in Religious Time and Space: Iraqi Refugees in Dearborn, Michigan," *Journal of Refugee Studies*, 20 (3): 441–60.

UNHCR (2018), "External Statistical Report on UNHCR Registered Iraqis as of 30 September 2018," Available online: https://data.unhcr.org/en/documents/details/66125.

UNHCR (2020), "Jordan: Statistics for Registered Iraqi Refugees (as of 31 July 2020)," Available online: https://data.unhcr.org/fr/documents/details/78094.

Verdeil, Chantal (2016), "Martyrs de la foi catholique, combattants de l'Eglise romaine: les héros du théâtre de l'Université Saint-Joseph de Beyrouth (1875–1914)," in Julia Hauser, Christine Lindner, and Esther Möller (eds.), *Entangled Education. Foreign, National and Local schools in Ottoman Syria and Mandate Lebanon (19–20th century)*, 181–99, Beirut: Orient Institut Beirut.

Vieillard-Baron, Hervé (2013), "Le nouveau paysage religieux de la banlieue parisienne," *Carnets de géographes*, 6. https://doi.org/10.4000/cdg.923.

Wagner (now Zuntz), Ann-Christin (2018a), "Remapping the Holy Land from the Margins: How a Jordanian Evangelical Church Juggles the 'Local' and the 'Global' in the Syrian Refugee Response," *Contemporary Levant*, 3 (2): 95–109. https://doi.org/10.1080/20581831.2018.1532573.

Wagner (now Zuntz), Ann-Christin (2018b), "Giving Aid Inside the Home. Humanitarian House Visits, Performative Refugeehood, and Social Control of Syrians in Jordan," *Migration and Society: Advances in Research*, 1: 36–50. https://doi.org/10.3167/arms.2018.010105.

Zaman, Tahir (2016), *Islamic Traditions of Refuge in the Crises of Iraq and Syria*, London: Palgrave Macmillan.

12

Youth-Oriented Spaces in Amman

Inclusion of National and Refugee Youth

Oroub El Abed, Zoë Jordan and Yasmeen Shahzadeh

Young people have become an issue of global concern. Young people are increasingly prominent on international, regional, and national agendas, as evidenced by specific youth-oriented indicators in the Sustainable Development Goals (SDGs), regional youth initiatives (see for example the Arab Youth Report (UNDP 2014), and national level policies such as the Jordanian National Youth Strategy 2019–25. In recent years, this interest in youth has been accompanied by a soaring interest in refugee youth from policy, practice, and research actors. These actors are paying growing attention to the education, employment, and inclusion of young refugees as partners in the development process. In Jordan, this has been reflected through its commitments to youth in the Jordan Response Plan for the Syria Crisis (including the most recent JRP 2020–2), for example, highlighting youth as a priority group across multiple sectors. Yet within this plethora of youth-oriented activities and initiatives, the voices and actions of youth themselves often remain overlooked and under-emphasized, despite evidence of strong impulses toward engagement and activism expressed by young people in our research.

In this chapter, we explore the role of youth-oriented spaces such as cultural associations, NGOs, and youth-created initiatives in the inclusion of Palestinian and Syrian refugee youth (aged 15–29) in Amman. We seek to situate the youth in the wider context, defining their needs and their ways to represent themselves. We study the spaces shared by both locals and refugees to understand how young people voice out their generation's needs, and the presence of refugee youth voices within this. We work through the production of social spaces conceptually, including how they are given meaning, and the different activities and relationships that unfold through these spaces (Peteet 2005; Appadurai 1996; Pryor and Outley 2014) which are produced through everyday social relations and practices (Peteet 2005: 94). It is the social activity, as put by Appadurai (1996: 186) that produces a locality—such localities are "not only context driven but also context generative," productive for youth's own spatial practices and discursive policy.

In doing so, we consider three related questions. Firstly, what are the needs that young people identify in their lives in Amman? Secondly, why have young people in Amman created specifically youth-oriented spaces and what are their objectives? Finally, what is the impact of these spaces and practices on the inclusion of young refugees in Amman? We argue that through these spaces youth of different nationalities have worked together to carve out room to jointly confront the challenges and gaps in services they experience as young people living in Amman. However, the impact of these activities on refugee inclusion remains limited by broader bureaucratic, legal and social constraints. Building on interviews we have conducted with Jordanian, Palestinian, and Syrian youth over the last two years (2019–2020) studying their trajectories, we shall explain how the structure of the state shapes the way youth with different legal statuses and nationalities can represent themselves and how it often limits their presence in certain areas. This research forms part of a larger study into the trajectories from education to employment of young people living in Jordan and Lebanon. As part of the preliminary research in Amman, we completed a mapping of bodies working with young people on education and employment (encompassing formal, non-formal, informal, entrepreneurship, and creative initiatives). Subsequently, we conducted institutional interviews with forty-nine organizations,[1] in which we asked representatives to reflect on the role of their spaces for young people. A survey with 1,400 young people explored the relationship between their education and employment outcomes in relation to their legal status, socioeconomic background, and gender.[2] Following the survey, 145 young people in Jordan participated in individual interviews to provide an in-depth understanding of their trajectories from education to employment.[3] We use this qualitative material to understand how young refugees understand their position in Amman, the constraints and options they perceive, and their reflections on the impact of youth spaces on their ability to negotiate uncertainties and constraints, and on their connection to their places of displacement. In doing so, we highlight the diversity within Jordan's refugee population and the impact of different backgrounds on refugees' understanding of youth and their experiences of inclusion via these spaces.

In this chapter though we take an age-based starting point in our approach to youth; we understand youth as a multifaceted and socially constructed status that encompasses social, economic, and age-based markers and multiple intertwined transitions, some of which may never be "complete." There is little consensus on the meaning of "youth" and its conceptual use. According to the 2016 Arab Human Development Report, youth are individuals between the ages of 15 and 29, and many governments across the world follow a similar age-based categorization (UNDP 2016).[4] Somewhat similarly, some

1 Organizations working in the education or employment sector with youth populations, including nationals, and/or refugees. This included international NGOs, national NGOs, community-based organizations, youth-led initiatives, entrepreneurship and start-up incubators, and relevant government ministries.

2 Results of the survey are forthcoming.

3 In this chapter, we refer to the young people by pseudonyms to protect their anonymity.

4 Though many countries follow similar age-boundaries with most definitions falling somewhere between 12 and 35, specific definitions vary widely and make cross-country comparison challenging. In Jordan, the definition of youth as per the national youth strategy 2005–2009 of Jordan defines youth as between 12 and 30 years. The research this chapter is based on took the age-category 15–29 as its starting point in defining youth.

have identified youth as a biological and psychological developmental stage (Backes and Bonnie 2019). However, age-based understandings of youth are insufficient (Hart 2014; Furlong 2016). As per our fieldwork with youth in Amman, their self-perception of youth varied: some within our age-based category of 15–29 defined themselves as youth, some younger youth perceived themselves as adults, while other older youth still felt like young people.

Moving away from linear models of progression, others have recognized the construction of youth as a social category (Punch 2002; Valentine 2003; Jeffrey 2010; Hart 2014, Furlong 2016). In such an understanding, the definition of youth relies less on biological markers and more on a socially constructed understanding of who youth are and what youth do. In this way, youth is not only a biological or age-based status but encompasses economic positions, social status and generational relations, and encompasses multiple transitions, including moving from education to work, forming a family and increasing responsibility for oneself and others. This is not a neat or unilineal process but identifies youth as a period of transition. However, the focus on understanding youth in terms of "becoming" rather than as beings in their own right has also been criticized for undervaluing youth's lives and influence in the present (Herrera 2010; Costa and Kallick 2001; Driscoll 2002; Havighurst 1953) and for focusing on young people as victims of social and economic processes, rather than their active role in negotiating such circumstances (Kennelly et al. 2009). The 2014 Arab Youth report echoes this "becoming" approach, defining youth as the transitory period in an individual's life, during which a social passage occurs from childhood to adulthood. During this period, young people face the new roles required of them in the next stage and begin to form a new identity based on the achievement of embodied symbols of integrity, idealism, and life continuity (UNDP 2014: 49). In this chapter, we focus on youths' present-day agency, paying attention to how their actions to create youth spaces in the present respond to both their current realities and the futures they aspire to.

1. Understanding Youth Perspectives on Their Needs and Identity in Amman

Amman in the early twenty-first century has undergone rapid physical and social change (Al-Husban and Al-Shoman 2013). While in 2004, the capital was home to 38 percent of Jordan's population (2.5 million) and had a steady growth rate at about 3 percent (Department of Statistics 2004; Mango 2014), the population of Amman is currently estimated at over 4.5 million people, making it the highest populated governorate in Jordan (El Abed 2017; Mango 2014). Much attention has been given to the large-scale development and construction in Amman, driven by the interests of capital which may serve to interrupt residents' access to and participation in public spaces (Daher 2014; Ababsa and Daher 2011; Ababsa 2013; Mango 2014). However, our research shows that young people are still managing to find and create spaces in the map of Amman that reflect their priorities.

Amman has also hosted multiple waves of refugees in the twentieth and twenty-first centuries, including Palestinians displaced in 1948 and 1967, return movement of Jordanians and Palestinians during the First Gulf War (1990–91), and again since the 2003 US-led invasion of Iraq, and most recently, a large Syrian population since the outbreak of conflict in 2011 (Alnsour 2016). Approximately 30 percent of the city's population are now refugees (Turnball 2019; El Abed 2017). Among them, Palestinian refugees have a long-term presence in Amman and Jordan more widely, and the majority of Palestinian refugees hold Jordanian nationality. Those who do not hold the Jordanian nationality—primarily West Bankers and those from the Gaza Strip—are barred from many public services, employment professions, and public universities. As the displacement of Palestinians has persisted and become the most long-standing protracted refugee situation, Palestinians have not limited themselves to the camps, but moved beyond their limits, with most areas neighboring the camps now having become de facto part of the camps (Tiltnes and Zhang 2013). Due to their socioeconomic integration, the majority of the original camp dwellers have been able to move out. Thus, the camps have not been limited only to Palestinians but have been hosting migrant laborers and Syrian refugees who have moved into the camps in search of cheaper accommodation.

As with Palestinians, Syrian refugees have mainly established themselves in urban areas. In January 2021, there were 195,107 Syrian refugees registered in the Amman governorate (UNHCR 2021). Despite the presence of large refugee camps for Syrians in the north of the country, over 84 percent of Syrian refugees live outside of camps (Al-Tal and Ghanem 2019; El Abed 2017). The following chart shows the distribution of Syrian refugees in Amman (El Abed 2017). A larger proportion of Syrian households are clustered in central and East Amman, though Syrian households can be found across the governorate.

Both the Jordanian and refugee population is remarkably young, with people under 30 years forming more than 60 percent of its population (USAID 2020), and young

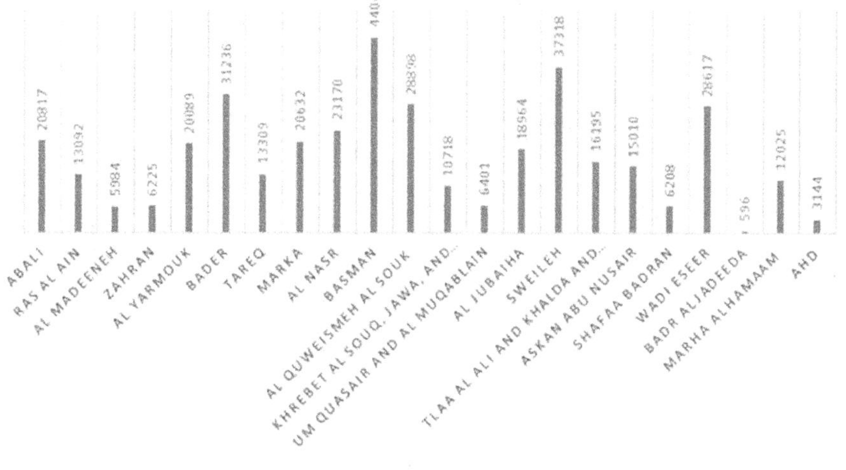

Figure 12.1 Number of Syrian refugees per district of Amman (El Abed 2017).

people between 10 and 24 making up 29.56 percent of the population (El Abed 2017).[5] As of June 2020, 43 percent of all refugees in Jordan are between the ages of 12 and 35 (UNHCR 2020b). In our research, we worked with youth who self-identified as Jordanian, Palestinian, or Syrian. This was nuanced by additional questions relating to family heritage and documentation held. For clarity, in this chapter, when we refer to Jordanians, we are referring to those who hold Jordanian nationality (a Jordanian national number).[6] This group encompasses both Jordanians and Jordanians of Palestinian origin who hold Jordanian nationality as per the citizenship law of 1954 (UNRWA 2021). All of the interviewees identifying as Syrian in our research are refugees. Though five of the forty-nine Syrians in our sample arrived in Jordan before the conflict, they are currently unable to return and all hold UNHCR registration.

Jordan has attempted to capitalize on the young demographic boom in their 2016–2025 National Strategy for Human Resource Development (2015), which highlights the importance of youth development and engagement. Key priorities of the strategy include increasing the numbers of youth and adults in technical and vocational education, supporting their entry to employment, as well as strengthening the engagement and involvement of youth in dialogue to have their voices heard within the higher education sector.

Despite the launch of this strategy over five years ago, youth in our research report that they do not feel well integrated into society, in public or private spheres. For example, Jordanian youth in our research highlighted the challenges they face in finding employment and the resulting limited or uncertain income, a lack of mentoring, limited possibilities for substantive engagement in politics, and a lack of opportunities that would enable youth to develop themselves. This culminates in a perceived inability to move forward with their lives. As summarized by Ahmed, a 28-year-old Jordanian man from a middle-class background, currently working in the creative industry:

> We [the youth] cannot separate our economic and political situation from anyone . . . you are talking about an environment that does not have job opportunities, and even the job opportunities that exist, do not build for the future, and at the end of the day, you want to live your life, not living it as in meaning to have fun, but to survive. The biggest ambition for anyone is to get married and have kids, and repeat the experience of their parents, and to do a cloning of it and this is the ambition, the successful do that.

Further, those opportunities that do exist are perceived as seldom under the direction of young people themselves. In the words of 27-year-old Fatima, a Jordanian woman currently volunteering with a local women's association in her neighborhood, while looking for work:

> Eastern Amman includes huge youth potential and I was among these [people with] potential[s]. I liked to somehow organize these youth [with potential]

5 A further 30.65 percent of the city's population is aged between 25 and 44 (El Abed 2017).

6 This decision reflects the focus of larger research projects on the impact of legal status on trajectories from education to employment.

> more, we worked with youth and volunteering and we started with this idea. We don't find a job but we can develop ourselves and find opportunities. . . . They are exploiting youth in general whether for political issues . . . volunteering is an investment for youth's potential but it should be in a better way.

The intersection of different identities and statuses produces unique social positions and exclusions, challenges which young people experience and respond to in different ways.[7] For instance, the social, political, and economic processes that marginalize women in Jordan contribute to their weak workforce participation (at just 14 percent (Al-Khatib 2020), their exclusion from political processes and (forced) entry into the private sphere (Mango 2017). For refugee women, these challenges are further compounded, for example, with the lack of work permits rendering the search for appropriate work more challenging; the increased risk of potentially harmful coping strategies such as early marriage; and restrictive gender norms that prevent participation in the public sphere (IPSOS Group SA 2018). Similarly, socioeconomic class has been shown to have a major impact. The neoliberal economic system in Jordan since the 1990s has strengthened class stratification and widened the disparities among people from different socioeconomic classes. As with gender, these exclusions are reinforced in interaction with legal status and nationality: refugees are typically more likely to be unemployed, underemployed or to be involved in informal and casual labor. Both Syrian and Palestinian refugees highlighted similar concerns to Jordanian nationals with regards to access to education and employment. However, while they similarly mentioned financial and social resources as determinants of access to education and employment, they also highlighted the importance of legal status and documentation.

As explained by Mahmoud, a 28-year-old Palestinian man from Syria, who holds both an Algerian passport and Syrian Palestinian travel documents: "I don't bring out a single paper here (in Jordan) that states I'm Palestinian, I go with my Algerian passport, which made my life easier, had I not obtained the Algerian passport I probably wouldn't have been allowed so many choices in life."

Similarly, Mariam, a 26-year-old Syrian woman, told us: "I searched at health centres, at volunteer organisations everywhere really but couldn't find anything, it was always the same answer even though I have the identity card for '*abna*' al-ʾurduniyyāt [Children of Jordanian mothers] but they still always said that my nationality is Syrian and others would say that they would call back but they never did."

Going beyond this, those with refugee status also reported more extensive social exclusion based on their perceived nationality and origin. For example, Amal, a 15-year-old Palestinian-Gazan woman with a two-year Jordanian passport and Jordanian mother ID,[8] told us about her experience in school:

7 This chapter is unable to address fully the intersectional interaction of legal status challenges with nationality, race, gender, and social class in the context of Amman. In this chapter, we focus on the experiences of Palestinian and Syrian refugees, the two largest refugee groups.

8 Palestinians from Gaza do not have access to the Jordanian nationality; however, they are able to apply for a two-year Jordanian passport. This allows for travel, but does not entail citizenship rights. Currently, under Jordanian law citizenship is passed through the father. However, since 2014 some restrictions have been eased for non-citizens with Jordanian mothers and this status is affirmed through a special identification card. However, challenges remain in obtaining and using the

Amal: It was from the teachers. . . . I felt that I didn't have the right to learn. "You are Gazzawi. You don't have the right to learn. Go and learn outside [in Palestine], you don't have the right to learn here." . . . But how? You are also Palestinian. When I knew that the teacher was from H family, she is Palestinian. How don't I have the right to learn? As long as you have the right then I also have the right.

Interviewer: So the difference is that she has a national number while you don't have a national number?

Amal: Correct.

While the majority of Syrian and Palestinian refugees shared such experiences, it is important to note that a minority of recipients did not identify their nationality or legal status as influencing their life so far, or not as the primary influence. For example, Hanan, a 28-year-old Palestinian woman working in the formal private sector told us: "Listen! In Jordan—if you have a national number or if you don't have a national number, if you have a *wasṭa*, then you work. If you don't have *wasṭa* then you don't work. And it actually happens."

These challenges concerning education and employment point to a generation that is struggling to define its place in society. Nonetheless, equally present was a depiction of young people as determined and ambitious agents in their own lives and societies. Ibrahim, a young Jordanian, summarized the position of many of the youth we spoke to, defining a youth as "someone with an idea, or a goal, and works towards it. . . . You can summarise the difference as either a person has something to give, or a person is just satisfied sitting around doing nothing about—it." Like others, he identified those who did not take action to meet their goals as non-youth. Further, Samira, a Jordanian woman expanded on this idea, saying "Youth is defined with being active, anybody who is active . . . with an impact on himself or two or three people around him." Repeatedly evident in our conversation with young people about the meaning of youth was this emphasis on energy and working toward a goal that would improve the situation—personally and collectively. Young Syrians and Palestinians share similar ideas, with Wafa, a 20-year-old Syrian, saying: "I think anybody with an idea or ambition, regardless of age, would be youth, even if they were 60" and Mariam saying: "Some people are young from inside and find nothing impossible and are able to confront difficult circumstances. Nothing is impossible, he who has a will, can make it"; and Halima, a 26-year-old Palestinian, telling us: "Last year when I was able to do something, I felt I was something. I feel the youth. I still try to push myself forward."

While Syrians and Palestinians largely defined youth in similar terms to Jordanians, they were more likely to reflect on their own rapid accumulation of responsibility and their lost or curtailed youth due to the associated impacts of their displacement. For example, Hana, a 26-year-old Syrian woman, shared her changing experience of youth, saying:

Jordanian Mother ID card, with young people in our research reporting an issue with recognition and understanding about their status as children of Jordanian mothers.

> Yes, it changed, in Syria I had a family, home, security. The financial situation is what changed my understanding of the concept of youth and not my move from Syria to Jordan. Going from being "wow" to slipping under. . . . When I came to Jordan, because of the financial situation, as a youth, I had to rely on myself, be independent, work, earn money, take care of my parents and be responsible for my little siblings as well if they ask for something, worry about buying my own phone and phone credit, in this situation as a youth it is required rely on one's self.

Others spoke of their youth identity as a divider or separation from older generations. Basma, a Palestinian woman from Gaza, expressed frustration at the contradictions between the image she sees of young people and the assumptions of older generations. She says:

> What annoys me most is when the older generation say that all we do all day is spend time on our phones, that we are not serious and that we are lazy and rely on our parents. . . . I think that the older generation have the wrong picture of us. . . . We are more prepared for the world than those who are older than us but we are being blamed for something that is not our fault, blamed because there are no jobs, we are here and ready to work but it is the older generation's fault that did not allow us to have jobs. I feel that they want to blame the youth for their mistakes and that we will fix their mistakes.

Interestingly, Ali, a 27-year-old Syrian, identified establishing one's own space as an important part of being a youth and moving toward adulthood. He said: "I see that I am still in chaos. And I want to secure myself. It is time to dissociate oneself from family and have my own space."

What is shared across these young people's words is a sense of youth as active, engaged in the world beyond themselves, and seeking to build opportunities for their generation, despite the challenges they confront. Existing literature has already emphasized the critical role youth play in society, and the importance of their integration (USAID 2020; WANA 2017; Peteet 2005). There are several layers to youth exclusion in Jordan, including high unemployment and economic marginalization, and political exclusion and limits to civic engagement (Milton-Edwards 2018).

Unemployment in Jordan has steadily been increasing in recent years, given recent economic and political instability in the region. The overall unemployment rate in the second quarter of 2020 reached 25 percent (22.6 percent males, 32.8 percent females), rising from 19 percent in the same quarter in 2019 and 15.3 percent for the year in 2016 (Department of Statistics 2017b, 2019, 2020). Unemployment and underemployment rates are high for refugee youth, particularly those whose legal status does not allow working in specific professions, or at all. Despite the relative success of the Jordan Compact and the transformation of Syrian participation in Jordan's labor market from a taboo topic to a policy goal (Lenner and Turner 2018), Syrian participation in the formal labor market remains low due to the limited sectors Syrians are permitted to access. Palestinian youth have different access to the labor market dependent on the documentation they hold. Palestinian refugees or who hold provisional Jordanian Travel Documents are given limited rights to higher education and private-sector jobs or informal sector jobs. Until 2016, Palestinians with provisional travel documents had been able to work in the private sector, provided that they got security clearance from the authorities. As a result of the Jordan Compact 2016 and the requirement for a work permit imposed on all non-Jordanians, the ex-Gaza refugees and West Bankers had to abide by the new classification of their status, being treated like the refugee newcomers.[9] As a result, the closed jobs announced as part of the Jordan Compact and the limited jobs open for non-Jordanians excluded ex-Gaza refugees and West Bankers from professional jobs that they used to work in before the decision. Gazan youth in particular experience a high unemployment burden. They are not allowed to register in professional societies or unions, establish their own offices or clinics, or easily work in the private sector (El Abed 2017). Both refugee and national youth experience a lack of political representation, and socio-cultural exclusion based on the perception of young people by others. Moreover, in many cases, youth are not taken seriously and are not seen as capable of directing their own lives. For example, the 2019–25 National Strategy for Youth challenges a prevalent depiction of young people as dominated by a culture of shame, a passive waiting for government employment rather than an active pursuit of work, and a desire to emigrate common among both Jordanians and refugees. This is in stark contrast to the conceptualization of youth described in the introduction to this chapter, where youth was identified as a period of dynamic transitions, of the assumption of greater responsibility, of the forging of new identities, and movement toward employment that would allow them to meet these new responsibilities. As argued by Linda Herrera (2010: 127): "They [youth] have been allowed little scope to question, reject, or offer alternative visions, demands, and arrangements for societal change and economic and social justice."

For Jordanian youth, key elements of socio-political exclusion relate to their civic engagement and representation. Since signing the Millennium Declaration 2000,[10] there has been an emphasis in developing countries on catering for the special demands of youth, women and children. The Sustainable Development Goals which followed in 2015, sought to integrate the goals in the everyday life designed to bring the world to several life-changing "zeros," including zero poverty, hunger, and discrimination against women and girls. Approaches to achieving the goals have provided support to bottom-up initiatives, which has widened the space for the active civil society bodies

[9] See Al Husseini and kvittingen in this volume.

[10] The Millennium Declaration reaffirms international commitment to a peaceful, prosperous, and just world, through the agreement of over sixty goals relating to peace, development, and poverty reduction, the environment, human rights, democracy, and good governance, protecting the vulnerable, meeting the special needs of Africa, and strengthening the United Nations. The text of the declaration approved by the UN General Assembly can be found here: https://www.ohchr.org/EN/ProfessionalInterest/Pages/Millennium.aspx

to be creative and engage with the members of society to achieve the SDGs in every context (UNDP 2015). The success of development and participatory governance depends on both a robust state and an active civil society with healthy levels of civic engagement. Priority of funding has been allocated ever since to the empowerment of the social groups giving them the space and the opportunity for inclusive growth and national ownership.

Despite the progress made in Jordan, there are still some challenges in democratic governance. Public participation in the decision-making process and the role of civil society institutions still need to be strengthened further (UNDP Jordan 2020). A recent UNESCO (2017) report explains how Jordanian youth lack civic engagement: youth do not enjoy any nationwide student unions or other forms of representation on such a level. Although youth are allowed to vote in elections at the age of 18, there are no interventions that support or encourage youth to take part in elections or to consider participating in them as candidates. In general, the relationship of Jordanians with political elections is weak as a result of limited debates and engagement. However, the lack of outreach and engagement with youth is particularly evident and means that youth voices are further stifled.

Refugee youth are legally excluded from nearly all forms of formal political inclusion. This exacerbates their social exclusion, which is evidenced by their exclusion from the social system, lack of social status, increased rates of unemployment and financial difficulties associated with low levels of services, and the social containment (Mencütek 2019; Shahzadah 2021). Many institutions have launched initiatives intended to ameliorate social interaction and inclusion of youth from different backgrounds. Notably, few have been able to go so far as to include refugee youth in the design, planning, and leadership of such initiatives.

While much research and programming has focused on combating nationality-based social divisions and tensions, young people in Amman share common characteristics: they have energy, aspire for leadership, the ability to acquire knowledge and skills, a vision toward the future, the desire to accomplish valuable actions in life and have vitality and are willing to take risks (UNDP 2014: 49). Despite these connotations with youth, in reality, young people are also confronted with substantial constraints, such as high unemployment, social exclusion, and uncertainty about their present and the future. In light of this, young people are searching for space for themselves.

2. Conceptualizing the Spaces of Youth in Amman

Young people in Jordan—of all nationalities—face an increasingly challenging and restrictive environment in which youth have little dedicated space, politically, economically, and—in the urban context of Amman—spatially. While the challenges to "achieving" the transition to adulthood are common across much of the youth population of Amman, there are additional challenges and specific experiences of youth-hood in Amman for those from different refugee backgrounds, young women and young people from lower socioeconomic classes. The lack of employment opportunities, precarious legal positions, and socio-cultural exclusion have pushed young people to create their own social spaces, in which they can express and develop their various identities as young people and work to create their futures—individually and collectively.

Here, we focus on how young people carve out a space for themselves and the potential for the inclusion of refugees contained within these efforts. As argued by Pryor and Outley (2014) youth spaces and recreational facilities can provide an important resource for developing self-awareness and critical consciousness. Such spaces in Amman include corners in coffee shops, study rooms, youth-led platforms such as Jadal for Knowledge and Culture, Liwan, and public spaces popular among young people such as the square overlooking Downtown on Rainbow Street, the parks and cafes of Jabal al-Luwaybda, and 7Hills Skatepark. Beneficial for personal development, self-identity, and social transformation, youth spaces can be a "mode of survival" and sites of resistance that allow young people to assert meaningful identities (Breitbart 1998; Pryor and Outley 2014). Magana (2017), in his study of spaces of resistance in Oaxaca, Mexico, shows how youth spaces can provide an alternative to the dominant system. Through young people's efforts to claim urban space and assert their right to occupy, use, and alter space, such spaces allow for the participation of young people in the state and with each other, beyond the narrow confines of formal citizenship.

We understand place as socially constructed by a dynamic confluence of external forces, structural constraints, and human agency, as a particular articulation of social relations (Peteet 2005: 27). People, whether locals or refugees, co-produce place. The place shaped their identities, a process of mutual construction constrained and enabled by power (Peteet 2005; Hirsch and O'Hanlon 1995; Ghannam 2002). Understood in terms of social relations, the connection between place and refugee inclusion becomes more apparent.

Inclusion refers to the opportunities in society to enhance one's life chances (Kelly 2010), such as employment, housing, education, social services, and social protection (Smyth 2008 in Cheung 2013). Jenson (1998) identifies five dimensions to social inclusion: (1) affiliation/isolation, (2) insertion/exclusion, (3) participation/passivity, (4) acceptance/rejection, and (5) legitimacy/illegitimacy. These opportunities are reflected in an individual's daily life experience and, as such, working to expand inclusion requires a transformation in culture, policy, and practice to accommodate difference and remove the barriers to an individual's participation. Focusing on social inclusion as social cohesion, Chan, To, and Chan (2006) argue that social cohesion concerns the vertical (with the state) and horizontal (with one-another) interactions among members of society, and includes trust, a sense of belonging and the willingness to participate and help, as well as other behaviors (in Klein 2013). Hülse and Stone (2007) also identify social cohesion as a "bottom up" voluntary process in which people and social groups play a major role, with government as an enabler and facilitator (in Klein 2013). In our work, we pay attention to how young people through these bottom-up, voluntary processes have established trust, shared common values, and created youth-oriented spaces.

Since the 1990s, space has become a central dimension of social theory and social sciences (Brun 2001). In this chapter, space is understood as constructed from the multiplicity of social relations across all spatial scales, with place understood as a particular articulation of those relations, a particular moment in those networks. This highlights the importance of social relations in the creation of space and place, emphasizing the intricate relationship between space and inclusion and belonging. Place and space are mutually interactive and constitutive, with their focus on meaning, practice, and agency (Peteet 2005). It is through the interaction of social relations at a particular time and space that individuals develop a sense of belonging (Crang 1998) and a relationship to place, understandings which situate the refugees in the national order of things, as put by Malkki (1995). The youth spaces considered in this work can therefore be understood as specific constellations of social relations, with attached meanings and significance to those involved. As explained by Kibreab (1999) the sense of place becomes bound up with peoples' social and individual identity. Conceptual debates, especially in refugee studies, have endeavored to tease out the relationship between people, space, and identity (Kibreab 1999; Malkki 1992, 1995; Stepputat 1994; Turton 2005; Zetter 1994). Similar work has highlighted the importance of space in the formation of youth identities (Holloway and Valentine 2000; Matthews and Limb 1999; Kibreab 1999; Peteet 2005; Pryor and Outley 2014). In the late nineteenth century and early twentieth century, the Arab World was known for its cultural salons (where literature and politics used to be discussed), with the participation of young intellectual Arabs in Greater Syria and Egypt such as Rifaʿa al-Tahtawi, May Khoury, Butrus al-Bustani, Francis Marrash, Taha Hussein, and Naguib Mahfouz. These salons are referenced as key venues for the youth to voice out their needs and thoughts in the age of the Arab Renaissance. In the twentieth century, youth clubs, such as those in Lebanon and Egypt, were important political venues for youth to meet and discuss liberal ideas to stand against colonial power representative of the Ottoman Empire and of the British Mandate. However, as yet little work has looked at twenty-first-century youth-oriented refugee spaces, particularly in non-Western countries (Young 2003).

The context established by the state, by-laws, regulations, and policies, limits the ability of young people, especially non-Jordanians, to establish their own space. While aware of this, we seek to understand the means young people have used to express their needs in their own space, against policy, financial, traditional, and familial constraints. In this chapter, we consider the importance and interconnectedness of youth spaces with young people's identities and their struggles for economic and social inclusion within different youth spaces with varied characteristics.

There is a substantial body of work from refugee studies relating people to place, and considering the role of place in the development of identities. Malkki's (1992) work shows the role of place as an influence on the forms and dynamics of these identities. She argues that "identity is always mobile and processual, partly self-construction, partly categorization by others, partly a condition, a status, a label, a weapon, a shield, a fund of memories, et cetera. It is a creolized aggregate composed through bricolage" (1992: 30). While memories and claims to places displaced persons can no longer inhabit are a key component of their relationship to places of displacement, identities—including refugee identities—are not fixed. They are heterogeneous, related to the context of the host environment, and are multi-layered through the intersections of various social positions, including gender, age, class, and status (Appadurai 1996). Refugee identities are not cohesive or homogenous but are often marked by internal differences and divisions (Kibreab 2000; Sommers 2001). For example, in Jordan, there are considerable differences in the experiences and status of refugees from different nationalities. While on an individual level many young refugees of different nationalities form close friendships, there is relatively little common identity as refugees. For example, we had the following conversation with Yousef, a 22-year-old Palestinian (ex-Gazan) man:

> Interviewer: You identified the "dirty guys" as Palestinians, and the ones who became your friends as Jordanians, correct?
>
> Yousef: Yes, and the others were Jordanians. I: Did you not feel that it was easier to connect with other Palestinians? Yousef: No. I don't care about nationalities at all, I have a friend who is Ukrainian and I tell her secrets that I don't tell to my mother, imagine and she is not Muslim, a Christian. For me, I don't mix nationality or religion in any kind of relationship.
>
> I: One would think that perhaps you had shared or similar experiences with them since you do not have a national ID, but it seems that was not the case for you?
>
> Yousef: No, that wasn't the case for me.

Similarly, when we asked Rana, a 15-year-old Syrian girl, if she had ever been made to feel different from other young people due to her Syrian identity, she said: "No, not at all. I deal with Jordanians so that they treat me better than Syrians. I feel more comfortable with Jordanians."

As forced migrants, young people may be searching for security and a place where they do not risk being "invisible" and excluded (Peteet 2005). As they move, they invent places of habitual residence and belonging in the absence of territorial, national bases to which they relate as their home. Consequently, a naturalized identity between people and place is nurtured and created in the course of other, non-discursive practices, supporting community and diverse identities. Despite their differences, young people in Amman have nonetheless identified and created spaces in which they share a common sense of youth identity. By way of example, Omar explained to us how his participation in a sports club had led to a shared development in ways of behaving. In his words: "It was sports that got us together, and there is no animosity between any of us. . . . It all comes down to manners, and also sports got us together and united us."

Spaces are given meaning through the activities that take place within them and how people relate to and conceive of the spaces. It is through these processes that the most mundane of spaces can take on important significance for certain groups or individuals at certain times, including coffee shops or gaming centers. Places become localities where they "impose their own imprint . . . they are producing by and productive of everyday social relations and practices" (Peteet 2005: 94). As argued by Appadurai (1996), localities are distinct from neighborhoods, in that they encompass a sense of place, and are not "just there," but require regular and hard work to produce and maintain. For example, Liwan, based in Abdali in central Amman, was founded by a council of Jordanian youth created in 2018. The council was created through a partnership between Tammey[11] and Action Aid.[12] The Jordanian youth selected for this council were given the task of determining the purpose of the space, its mandate, and how it would operate. They researched spaces that exist in Amman, features that are lacking or important, and ways to create a space that is as open and inclusive as possible. Through a process they dubbed participatory action research, they were able to come up with the main mandates of Liwan. It is a youth space that was created through a youth-led participatory action project; it fosters creativity, provides a safe space for youth to work and connect, offers learning opportunities, and it acts as an accessible gathering space for all youth. As a participatory venue for better integration, Liwan offers meeting spaces that can be rented or reserved by organizations and initiatives. The space is open to all youth of all backgrounds. Youth do not have to pay when they come to the space: they either volunteer ten hours of their time over the next four months in cleaning or being present at the space, pay a small fee, or offer resources that they have and that are needed by the center. These resources can be tangible, such as stationary, or running workshops on specific skills that are in demand. In committing their resources—whether money, time, or skills—the young people who use this space demonstrate their ongoing commitment to maintaining the space.

Through culturally grounded practices of ordinary living, localities impose their social identity and presence. Social relations within a particular space are therefore central to the production of place. However, as indicated above, there is also a close interaction between space, social relations, and belonging or identity. Young refugees' identities and their relationship to place therefore must be understood through the interaction of past and present places, positions, and social relations. For example, Ola, a 17-year-old Syrian girl living in al-Naṣr told us about the importance of the Yazan center in her life. She attends to learn the Quran, volunteer and attend training sessions. While she is no longer attending school as she is needed to take care of her young siblings while her mom works, her friends bring their homework to the center to study together with her and receive help with their schoolwork from the center staff. When we asked her about the most important turning point in her life, she mentioned registering in the Yazan center as the key moment. She told us that after registering she started wanting to learn new things, that it gave her a sense of purpose and improved her mental health. Most importantly, attending the center changed her perspective on life and her sense of her place, in her words: "I used to [feel like a stranger]. But now no."

Young Jordanians and non-Jordanians frequenting youth spaces respond to their situation through pursuing strategies that are grounded in their youthfulness and the cultural politics of their generation (Herrera 2010).[13] For the spaces described in this

[11] Tammey is a social enterprise with expertise in working with youth and in community development. https://tammey.org/

[12] Action Aid is an international organization that has been working in Jordan since 2005. One of the key areas of focus is supporting youth participation in politics, alongside humanitarian response to refugees and supporting women's rights; https://www.actionaid.org.uk/about-us/jordan

[13] Herrera (2010) focuses on the role of internet access in young Egyptian people's response to their situation. While the spaces analyzed in this chapter all have an online presence, mainly through Facebook, we focus on the physical space and young people's interactions within and relations to these spaces, rather than their digital interactions.

chapter, three major strategies or objectives emerge. For some, they are a deliberate attempt to network, develop skills, and (hopefully) access education or employment opportunities. Other spaces are an attempt to claim space in the city to share experiences and identify common goals. Yet others provide a base for young people to develop their voice and agitate for representation. Despite these different objectives or strategies to combat the marginalization of youth in urban Amman, the spaces shared certain common features.

The use of youth spaces to develop skills, access education and employment opportunities, and network is evident in the work of Eye on the Future. Established in 2011 through the Jordan University (JU) student's union, Eye on the Future targets secondary school students from grade 10 onward to help them decide and select their specialty and major. Since 2018, they have also targeted university students, offering advice on the job market and the skills and qualifications needed. Attracting students through social media, word of mouth, and connections with schools, they have provided advice to approximately 10,000 students across the governorates of Amman, ʾIrbid, al-Zarqāʾ, al-ʿAqaba, and Karak. All activities are led by volunteers, who are themselves near- or recent university graduates.

The second use of youth spaces is to claim space and build a shared sense of youth identity. Youth spaces are founded from and allow for an articulation of youth identity, based on perceived common experiences of youth exclusion and shared attitudes to actively strive toward their futures. For example, Jadal is a youth space in the heart of the city center of Amman, which was opened in late 2012 in the wake of the Arab Spring. It is intended as a safe space to support youth initiatives, connect and network youth, and raise awareness about socioeconomic issues such as unemployment, drug misuse, and gender relations within the context of the rapid social change that was, and continues to be, occurring in the region. Jadal currently functions as a cultural center hosting events and speakers, a cafe, and a meeting or study space for youth in Amman to gather. The space is meant to be inclusive for all youth, and a hub for youth to meet and speak together. The founder, Fadi, a young man of Palestinian origin, identified a negative trend among youth in the country, with high unemployment and a lot of youth aiming to migrate for better lives. He explained that Jadal serves as a safe space for youth to air out their grievances, but also for them to attend workshops that could improve their livelihoods: several attendees of workshops at the center who were able to learn a new skill or language said they were able to find employment as a result.

Finally, youth spaces serve as focal spaces for young people to develop a voice, agitate for representation, and increase their political participation. Returning to Liwan, from its conception, it was intended to serve as a physical space for young people. In our interview, members of the Liwan council noted that Action Aid has worked with youth for a long time, but had not previously established a space in which to engage youth; as a guiding priority, they believe that it is important for youth to understand their role in the greater civil and political community and to gain a higher sense of self-awareness. For example, young Jordanian activists, university-graduates Qusai and Shoroq were two members of the council at Liwan Youth Space who continue to be active at Liwan, and frequent the space to do their own work, attend panels, and gather with their peers. Shoroq, who participated in the founding of the center, mentioned the space, connections, and resources for discussing different social issues and to identify action points as one of the key benefits of her participation in Liwan. Qusai and Shoroq both stressed that Liwan was meant to be a "space" and not a "center": when determining the mandate of Liwan, they decided to name it a space in reference to it being a safe space for youth, with doors wide open. Thus, Liwan became a space to host youth in educational opportunities like training, political participation, networking opportunities, skill-sharing and more, but also became a home and network for like-minded individuals and a hub for social innovation and mentorship. Qusai explained that existing infrastructure and resources in Jordan for youth are plenty, but they do not always operate well or do not suit current needs. For instance, existing Ministry of Youth centers only operate during business working hours (often only until 5:00 p.m.) and cannot offer youth a gathering space or activities in the evenings, which would better suit youths who work or study. The spaces are also often gender-segregated, and are not well-maintained, deterring youth from utilizing them.

The majority of youth we spoke to, while they highly appreciated youth-oriented services and enjoyed spending time in such spaces, identified substantial barriers to participation and limited success in leveraging their participation in the wider environment. Some youth centers, such as Liwan, fall under the institutional framework of either non-governmental bodies, profit or non-profit companies (known as social enterprise). Although this is a way to mobilize professionally and strategically plan for addressing issue-specific and knowledge-based structures that respond to donors' needs, such bodies are often overtaken by a policy-outcome oriented agenda (Ungsuchaval 2016). Ultimately, this could widen the objective of the youth center, where funding becomes an issue and responding to funding requirements becomes the concern.

As shown in the cases presented here, the creation and maintenance of youth spaces can be challenging. Organizations interviewed during our research identified funding and bureaucracy as the two main challenges they experienced in setting up their initiatives or spaces. For example, Qusai from Liwan explained that in setting up his start-up, he had to deal with the same level of bureaucracy and business competition as many of the larger corporations in the country, which he sees as unfair. He explained that the lack of institutional support for start-ups and small youth businesses has been a barrier to his work. Qusai and Ehab (discussed below) explained that funding has been a challenge. Some mentioned the fear that if they accept money from funders, they will become governed by donor conditionalities and obligations. Others mentioned the fact that the private sector in Jordan does not offer enough funding opportunities, and that NGOs in the country prefer to fund more established organizations making it difficult for new projects to get access to the resources they need.

3. The Impact of Youth Spaces on Refugee Youth Inclusion: The Relevance of Legal Status and Nationality

As is evident in the preceding discussion, economic and socio-political exclusions are compounded for refugees who hold precarious and at times uncertain legal statuses that restrict their full participation in society, including access to employment, and basic rights such as education and mobility. In addition to the challenges in accessing education and employment associated with different legal categories, young people's trajectories are further complicated by shifting requirements and the changeable enforcement of regulations. As argued by Hawkins, Assad, and Sullivan (2019: 4) "refugees experience an unclear status of belonging and citizenship, with only partial rights and obligations." The legal and social exclusion of youth from various areas of life in Amman has shaped their response. Our interviews with young women reflected how some tend to create their own niche when they fail to be part of the wider youth group, limited by cultural and traditional values which may restrict their movement across the city, familial attitudes to further education and employment, or the types of recreational and social activities they can engage in. Socioeconomic class also plays a role, with young people of East Amman, often categorized within a lower social class, creating activities and seeking out different ways of gathering from those within the more affluent Western part of the city. Harra,[14] a social initiative in East Amman, for example, invited all neighbors to eat on the side of the road in their area during the holy month of Ramadan, to connect and develop their community through the sense of solidarity and ownership of the place where they live. In contrast, in West Amman, some organizations or youth groupings such as Ahel for Community Organizing[15] and Liwan/Tammey[16] tend to focus on Sustainable Development Goals and get financial support from the international community and UN bodies to bring young people together.

Refugee organizations have a much lower profile and do not seek a high profile in their activities and their gatherings. For example, Souriyat Across Borders[17] was created to support those with injuries and disabilities and later expanded to include young Syrians, creating an outreach for them. Similarly, Sawiyan[18] brings together Jordanians, internationals, and refugees in their leadership board, but was only formalized after several years of operating as a volunteer network. Despite the low visibility of some refugee-led initiatives, all of these youth entities carve out their presence and voices. In other cases, the openness of youth spaces to refugee youth is more about the new identity of youth they are crafting as worldly and international, breaking down boundaries beyond nationality, rather than a specific political reaction to refugee exclusion, though there is some overlap. However, youth spaces cannot fully counter the exclusionary features of displacement and marginalization of young people, particularly for young refugees. This can be seen in the dynamics within youth spaces, in questions of access to spaces, and in the limitations of the national and municipal political/bureaucratic space, which fails to facilitate such initiatives, particularly in the case of non-nationals.

Ehab, a young Syrian refugee, highlighted the challenges facing non-Jordanians in maintaining initiatives. Ehab runs a successful initiative called Ibtaker Go (Innovate Go) focusing on teaching youth tech-based innovation and entrepreneurship skills and in developing a mobile app project for deaf children to learn basic literacy. He launched his project after participating in a workshop by the Norwegian Refugee Council on how

14 https://almaktouminitiatives.org/en/middle-east-exchange/story/sprucing-up-amman-neighbourhoods-for-the-greater-good
15 https://ahel.org/en/
16 https://tam mey.org/
17 http://souriyat.org/category/home/
18 https://sawiyan.org/

to start an initiative and receiving a small grant of JOD 500. His workshops have reached over 450 Jordanian, Syrian and Iraqi students across Amman. Despite this, as a Syrian in Jordan, he struggles to expand his non-profit initiative since he cannot easily register it due to his refugee status in Jordan. He explained that he struggles to make basic ends meet and is hoping to pass on his initiative to someone who can invest more time and effort into it. His case also highlights the limitations of NGO-led attempts to catalyze the creation of new initiatives and social development programs by refugee youth.

Even Jordanian youth have reported similar experiences of bureaucratic constraints. Fadi, of Jadal, mentioned some challenges in setting up the space, such as some members of the local community being against the center in its earlier days due to its political nature supporting the arrival of Syrian refugees and migrants of other nationalities to Amman. Fadi talked about the sporadic security checks, putting pressure on the center not to discuss certain topics, which he explained has a minor impact on the center's activities. The challenges of establishing civil society and non-governmental organizations for non-Jordanians has often been overlooked in the discussion of the flourishing third sector in Amman and wider Jordan, especially when legal responsibility for these spaces rests with Jordanian founders and leaders. In response, spaces such as Jadal have developed collaborative and non-hierarchical decision-making structures. Beyond this, young people have also, through their own bottom-up activities, made space for themselves in existing public spaces and private businesses, such as habitual daily meetings in coffee shops and study rooms.

Returning to Appadurai's (1996) theory of locality, the construction of a sense of place raises questions of power over the production of the specific sense of place. As highlighted in other theories of urban space production, space and place are not value-neutral, but rather reflect the identities and priorities of those who produce them. As has already been discussed above, the production of refugee and youth identities is intimately connected to their places of living, working, learning, and socializing. However, these identities also impact the construction and maintenance of the "sense of place" within these different spaces. The collective endeavor to create a space for young people in the city to articulate claims of belonging and to contest youth exclusion on multiple fronts has resulted in a growing sense of ownership and inclusion within the social, economic, and political fabric of Amman for young people. However, while youth spaces do result in a deepening relationship to place for young refugees displaced to Amman, external limitations have prevented young people—Jordanians and refugees alike—from fully identifying with their current place and many continue to dream of life elsewhere. Feelings of surveillance, lack of belonging, and frustration with the general socioeconomic and political circumstances have prevented youth from fully taking comfort in the spaces they have created.

Conclusion

In this chapter, we have sought to understand why young people create their spaces and the impacts of such spaces on refugee youth inclusion. To integrate effectively in life and society, these youth seek accommodating cultural and political structures that allow participation and integration, and support the acquisition of various roles and responsibilities equally. Whether through initiatives, youth groups, or volunteer groups, a youth platform like Jadal, in a study room, or a public space young people has come together to build cooperation, dialogue, and empowerment. By founding their own physical spaces and social groupings, youth in Amman, of different origins, legal statuses, and backgrounds, have been able to carve out room to gather, express themselves, and strive to reach their aspirations.

Young people engage in bottom-up work to create spaces in order to attempt to bridge the gaps between education or unemployment and the struggle to make themselves and their needs heard. These spaces provide a place for young people to establish trust with their peers, to find common causes and values, and be socially included while building a nascent sense of ownership within such spaces. These spaces provide a locality within which they can prove themselves, regardless of their status. As demonstrated through the success of these initiatives in challenging circumstances, the young people in our research have proven themselves by their active engagement in society, challenging depictions of refugee youth as passive or problematic recipients of assistance. The embodiment of a social and cultural venue represents a dynamic within the youth and is an example of how young people collectively negotiate uncertainties and constrained environments. Whether local or refugees, they have endeavored to express their needs and identities in these spaces as a way to integrate socially with peers against limitations, creating spaces with intersectional identities where they can learn new skills, network with peers who have similar interests, and build community with like-minded individuals.

Despite the many positive outcomes of participation in such spaces for refugee youth—recognizing the limitations of such spaces to fully engage with the different experiences of youth raises questions as to the commonality of experiences of "youthhood." As expressed by Fadi, "youth" can be seen as a social category, even as a phase that individuals experience as they move from dependence to independence, as they mature socially, politically, and economically. The young people participating in these spaces envision socially integrating into the wider communities. In creating youth spaces—producing these localities and shaping their identities—young people create a sense of belonging within these spaces, and a connection to the wider place of Amman. However, questions remain as to the interaction between and positions occupied by youth of different nationalities in such spaces and the extent to which these spaces and their attempts to be inclusive, collaborative, and based on mutual learning and understanding can challenge the exclusions present beyond their walls.

Bibliography

Ababsa, Myriam (ed.) (2013), *Atlas of Jordan: History, Territories, and Society*, Beirut: Ifpo.

Ababsa, Myriam, and Rami Daher (eds.) (2011), *Urban Practices and National Building in Jordan*, Beirut: Ifpo.

Al-Husban, Abdel Hakim, and Abdulla Al-Shorman (2013), "The Socioanthropological Dynamics of the Urban Evolution of the Contemporary Amman City," *Anthropos*, 108: 219–25.

Al-Khatib, Maram (2020), "Facilitating Female Employment in Jordan," *Youth Employment in the Mediterranean, YEM Blogs and Thinkpieces, UNEVOC-UNESCO*

(February). Available online: https://unevoc.unesco.org/yem/Female+unemployment+in+Jordan+YEM+Blog&context (accessed July 12, 2021).

Alnsour, Jamal Ahmad (2016), "Managing Urban Growth in the City of Amman, Jordan," *Cities*, 50: 93–9.

Al-Tal, Raed Salem, and Hala Hesham Ghanem (2019), "Impact of the Syrian Crisis on the Socio-spatial Transformation of Eastern Amman, Jordan," *Frontiers of Architectural Research*, 8: 591–603.

Appadurai, Arjun (1996), *Modernity at Large: Cultural Dimensions of Globalization*, Minneapolis: University of Minnesota Press.

Backes, Emily P., and Richard J. Bonnie (2019), *The Promise of Adolescence: Realizing Opportunity for All Youth*, Washington, DC: National Academies Press. Available online: https://www.ncbi.nlm.nih.gov/books/NBK545476/.

Breitbart, Myrna (1998), "Dana's Mystical Tunnel: Young People's Designs for Survival and Change in the City," in T. Skelton and Gill Valentine (eds.), *Cool Places: Geographies of Youth Cultures*, 305–27, New York: Routledge.

Brun, Catherine (2001), "Reterritorializing the Relationship Between People and Place in Refugee Studies," *Geografiska Annaler*, 83B (1): 15–25.

Chan, Joseph, Hong-Po To, and Elaine Chan (2006), "Reconsidering Social Cohesion: Developing a Definition and Analytical Framework for Empirical Research," *Social Indicators Research*, 75: 273–302.

Cheung, Chau-Kiu (2013), "Public Policies that Help Foster Social Inclusion," *Social Indicators Research*, 112 (1): 47–68.

Crang, Mike (1998), *Cultural Geography*, London: Routledge.

Costa, Arthur L., and Bena Kallick (2001), "Habits of Mind." Available online: http://www.habits---of---mind.net (accessed October 2, 2008).

Daher, Rami (2014), "Discourses of Neoliberalism and Disparities in the City Landscape, 'Cranes, Craters, and an Exclusive Urbanity,'" in Myriam Ababsa and Rami Daher (eds.), *Villes, pratiques urbaines et construction nationale en Jordanie*, 65-89, Beirut: Ifpo.

Department of Statistics (2004), "Population and Housing Census 2004." Available online: http://dosweb.dos.gov.jo/censuses/population_housing/census2004/census2004_tables/ (accessed January 20, 2021).

Department of Statistics (2017a), "Jordan Figures." Available online: http://dosweb.dos.gov.jo/DataBank/JordanInFigures/JORINFIGDetails2017.pdf.

Department of Statistics (2017b), "The Total Unemployment Rate for the Year 2016 is 1.6% Higher than in 2000." Available online: http://dosweb.dos.gov.jo/the-total-unemployment-rate-for-the-year-2016-is-1-6-higher-than-in-2000/.

Department of Statistics (2019), "19.0% The Unemployment Rate during the Fourth Quarter of 2019." Available online: http://dosweb.dos.gov.jo/19-0-the-unemployment-rate-during-the-fourth-quarter-of-2019/.

Department of Statistics (2020), "24.7% Unemployment Rate During the Fourth Quarter of 2020." Jordan Department of Statistics. Available online: http://dosweb.dos.gov.jo/unemp_q42020/.

Driscoll, Catherine (2002), *Girls: Feminine Adolescence in Popular Culture and Cultural Theory*, New York: Columbia University Press.

El Abed, Oroub (2005), "Immobile Palestinians," in Hana Jaber and France Métral (eds.), *Mondes en mouvements, migrants et migrations au Moyen-Orient au tournant du XXIe siècle*, Beirut: Ifpo, https://www.scribd.com/document/534470773/Amman-City-Migration-Profile.

El Abed, Oroub (2017), "Amman City Migration Profile," Mediterranean City-to-City Migration, (MC2CM), International Centre for Migration Policy Development (ICMPD), United Cities and Local Governments (UCLG) and UN-Habitat, funded by EU.

Furlong, Andy (2016), "Future Agendas in the Sociology of Youth," *Youth Studies Australia*, 30 (3): 54–9.

Ghannam, Farha (2002), *Remaking the Modern Space, Relocation, and the Politics of Identity in a Global Cairo*, Berkeley, Los Angeles, and London: University of California Press.

Hart, Jason (2014), "Locating Young Refugees Historically: Attending to Age Position in Humanitarianism," *European Journal of Development Research*, 26 (2): 219–32.

Hawkins, Allyson, Ruby Assad, and Denis Sullivan (2019), "Citizens of Somewhere: A Case Study of Refugees in Towns, Amman, Jordan," Feinstein International Centre, Tufts University. Available online: https://static1.squarespace.com/static/599720dc59cc68c3683049bc/t/5d52c54b18d85e0001b20f88/1565705548232/RIT+Report+Amman+Jordan.pdf.

Havighurst, Robert J. (1953), *Human Development and Education*, New York: Longman, Green, and Co.

Herrera, Linda (2010), "Young Egyptians' Quest for Jobs and Justice," in Linda Herrera and Asef Bayat (eds.), *Being Young and Muslim: New Cultural Politics in the Global South and North*, 127–44, New York: Oxford University Press.

Hirsch, Eric, and Michael O'Hanlon (1995), *The Anthropology of Landscape: Perspectives on Place and Space*, Oxford Studies in Social and Cultural Anthropology, Oxford: Clarendon Press.

Holloway, Sarah, and Gill Valentine (2000), "Children's Geographies and the New Social Studies of Childhood," in Sarah Holloway and Gill Valentine (eds.), *Children's Geographies: Playing, Living, Learning*, 1–26, London: Routledge.

Hülse, Kath, and Wendy Stone (2007), "Social Cohesion, Social Capital and Social Exclusion: A Cross-Cultural Comparison," *Policy Studies*, 28 (2), 109–28.

IPSOS Group SA (2018), "Unpacking Gendered Realities in Displacement: The Status of Syrian Refugee Women in Jordan," *UN Women*. Available online: https://reliefweb.int/report/jordan/unpacking-gendered-realities-displacement-status-syrian-refugee-women-jordan (accessed July 12, 2021).

Jadal for Knowledge and Culture. Available online: https://jadalculture.com/; https://www.facebook.com/jadal.amman/?ref=page_internal.

Jeffrey, Craig (2010), "Geographies of Children and Youth I: Eroding Maps of Life," *Progress in Human Geography*, 34 (4): 496–505.

Jenson, Jane (1998), "Mapping Social Cohesion: The State of Canadian Research," CPRN Discussion paper No F 03, Canadian Policy Research Network.

Jordan Response Plan for the Syria Crisis (JRP 2020–2022), MoPIC. Available online: http://www.jrp.gov.jo/Files/JRP%202020-2022%20web.pdf (accessed January 20, 2021).

Kelly, Laura (2010), "Social Inclusion Through Sports-Based Interventions?" *Critical Social Policy*, 31 (1): 126–50.

Kennelly, Jacqueline, Stuart Poyntz, and Paul Ugor (2009), "Special Issue Introduction: Youth, Cultural Politics, and New Social Spaces in an Era of Globalization," *Review of Education, Pedagogy, and Cultural Studies*, 31 (4): 255–69.

Kibreab, Gaim (1999), "Revisiting the Debate on People, Place, Identity and Displacement," *Journal of Refugee Studies*, 12 (4): 384–410.

Kibreab, Gaim (2000), "Resistance, Displacement, and Identity: The Case of Eritrean Refugees in Sudan," *Canadian Journal of African Studies / Revue canadienne des études africaines*, 34 (2): 249–96.

Klein, Carlo (2013), "Social Capital or Social Cohesion: What Matters for Subjective Well-Being?," *Social Indicators Research*, 110 (3): 891–911.

Lenner, Katharina, and Lewis Turner (2018), "Making Refugees Work? The Politics of Integrating Syrian Refugees into the Labor Market in Jordan," *Middle East Critique*, 28 (1): 65–95.

Liwan Youth Space. Available online: https://liwanspace.com/.

Magana, Maurice Rafael (2017), "Spaces of Resistance, Everyday Activism, and Belonging: Youth Reimagining and Reconfiguring the City in Oaxaca, Mexico," *The Journal of Latin American and Caribbean Anthropology*, 22 (2): 215–34.

Malkki, Lisa (1992), "National Geographic: The Rooting of Peoples and the Territorialization of National Identity Among Scholars and Refugees," *Cultural Anthropology*, 7 (1): 24–44.

Malkki, Lisa (1995), *Purity and Exile: Violence, Memory, and National Cosmology among Hutu Refugees in Tanzania*, Chicago and London: University of Chicago Press.

Mango, Oraib (2014), "The Impact of Real Estate Construction and Holding Companies: A Case Study of Beirut's Solidere and Amman's Abdali," PhD thesis, University of Essex.

Mango, Oraib (2017), "Uncertainty and Resistance in Jordanian Women's Perceptions of Their Positionings in Society," *Journal of International Women's Studies*, 18 (4): 218–32.

Matthews, Hugh, and Melanie Limb (1999), "Defining an Agenda for the Geography of Children: Review and Prospect," *Progress in Human Geography*, 23 (1): 61–90.

Mencütek, Zeynep Şahin (2019), *Refugee Governance, State and Politics in the Middle East*, London and New York: Routledge.

Milton-Edwards, Beverly (2018), "Marginalized Youth: Toward an Inclusive Jordan," Brookings Doha Center, Policy Briefing, June 2018. Available online: https://www.think-asia.org/bitstream/handle/11540/8351/June-2018_Beverly-Jordan_English-Web.pdf?sequence=1 (accessed July 12, 2021).

Ministry of Youth, Kingdom of Jordan (2017), "Jordan National Youth Strategy 2019–2025." Available online: http://moy.gov.jo/sites/default/files/jordan_national_youth_strategy_2019-2025_english_compressed_1.pdf (accessed July 12, 2021).

Peteet, Julie (2005), *Landscape of Hope and Despair, Palestinian Refugee Camps*, Philadelphia: University of Pennsylvania Press.

Pryor, Brandy N. Kelly, and Corliss W. Outley (2014), "Just Spaces: Urban Recreation Centers as Sites for Social Justice Youth Development," *Journal of Leisure Research*, 46 (3): 272–90.

Punch, Samantha (2002), "Research with Children: The Same or Different from Research with Adults?" *Childhood*, 9 (3): 321–41.

Shahzadah, Yasmeen (2021), "Youth Unemployment in Jordan, What are the Challenges and the Road Ahead?" Available online: https://www.paeradigms.org/post/youth-unemployment-in-jordan-what-are-the-challenges-and-the-road-ahead (accessed July 12, 2021).

Smyth, Paul (2008), "Closing the Gap? The Role of Wages, Welfare and Industry Policy in Promoting Social Inclusion," *Journal of Industrial Relations*, 50 (4): 647–63.

Sommers, Marc (2001), *Fear in Bongoland: Burundi Refugees in Urban Tanzania*, New York and Oxford: Berghan Books.

Stepputat, Finn (1994), "Repatriation and the Politics of Space: The Case of the Mayan Diaspora and Return Movement," *Journal of Refugee Studies*, 7 (2–3): 175–85.

Tiltnes, Age A., and Huafeng Zhang (2013), "Progress, Challenges, Diversity Insights into the Socio-Economic Conditions of Palestinian Refugees in Jordan," Fafo: 42. Available online: https://www.unrwa.org/sites/default/files/insights_into_the_socio-economic_conditions_of_palestinian_refugees_in_jordan.pdf.

Turnball, Elizabeth (2019), "Jordan Remains Second Largest Refugee Host Globally – UNHCR," *The Jordan Times*. Available online: https://www.jordantimes.com/news/local/jordan-remains-second-largest-refugee-host-globally-%E2%80%94-unhcr (accessed January 20, 2021).

Turton, David (2005), "The Meaning of Place in a World of Movement: Lessons from Long-Term Field Research in Southern Ethiopia," *Journal of Refugee Studies*, 18 (3): 258–80.

UNDP (2014), "Arab Knowledge Report: Youth and Localisation of Knowledge," United Nations Development Programme (UNDP), Mohammed bin Rashid Al Maktoum Foundation. Available online: http://www.arabstates.undp.org/content/dam/rbas/report/UNDP-GENERAL-REPORT-ENG.pdf (accessed July 12, 2021).

UNDP (2015), "What are the Sustainable Development Goals?" Sustainable Development Goals United Nations Development Programme. Available online: https://www.undp.org/content/undp/en/home/sustainable-development-goals.html.

UNDP (2016), "Arab Human Development Report (AHDR) 2016: Youth and the Prospects for Human Development." Available online: http://www.arab-hdr.org/Reports/2016/2016.aspx.

UNDP Jordan (2020), "Democratic Governance." Available online: https://www.jo.undp.org/content/jordan/en/home/ourwork/democraticgovernance/overview.html (accessed January 25, 2021).

UNESCO (2017), "Assessing the Broader Youth Environment in Jordan." Available online: http://www.unesco.org/new/fileadmin/MULTIMEDIA/FIELD/Amman/pdf/Assessing_broader_youth_environment_JOR.pdf.

UNHCR (2020b), "Jordan: Statistics for Registered Syrian Refugees (as of June 30, 2020)." Available online: https://data2.unhcr.org/en/documents/details/77434.

UNHCR (2021), "Syria Regional Refugee Response. Jordan. Amman Governorate. Total Persons of Concern." Available online: https://data2.unhcr.org/en/situations/syria/location/47 (accessed January 20, 2021).

Ungsuchaval, Theerapat (2016), *NGOization of Civil Society as Unintended Consequence? Premises on the Thai Health Promotion Foundation and its Pressures Towards NGOs in Thailand*, PhD thesis, University of Kent.

UNRWA (2021), "Where We Work: Jordan." Available online: https://www.unrwa.org/where-we-work/jordan (accessed January 20, 2021).

USAID (2020), "Youth." Available online: https://www.usaid.gov/jordan/youth (accessed December 18, 2020).

Valentine, Gill (2003), "Boundary Crossings: Transitions from Childhood to Adulthood," *Children's Geographies*, 1: 37–52.

WANA (2017), "Role of Civil Society Organisations in Promoting Youth Participation in Policy Dialogue: Summary." Available online: http://wanainstitute.org/sites/default/files/publications/Publication_YouthPolicyDialogue_EnglishSummary_0.pdf.

Young, Lorraine (2003), "The 'Place' of Street Children in Kampala, Uganda: Marginalisation, Resistance, and Acceptance in the Urban Environment," *Environment and Planning D: Society and Space*, 21 (5): 607–27.

Zetter, Roger (1994), "The Greek-Cypriot Refugees: Perceptions of Return Under Conditions of Protracted Exile," *International Migration Review*, 28 (2): 307–22.

Conclusion

Kamel Doraï

This book offers new and original insight on the current refugee situation in Jordan, putting in perspective different refugee groups, from the Chechens in late Ottoman times to more recent communities such as Syrians, Iraqis, or Yemenis. The Palestinians, often considered an exception, are here conceived and analyzed as a key group to understand the evolution of the Jordanian reception policy over time. It clearly shows the role of different actors, international institutions, state actors, local non-state institutions, and refugees themselves. It also explores the consequences of their long-term settlement in urban areas while analyzing the development of new refugee camps since 2012.

Since the end of the nineteenth century, Jordan has occupied a unique place in the Middle Eastern migratory system (Shami 2009; De Bel Air 2006). Jordan has emerged both as a host country for refugees fleeing conflict in the Middle East and migrant workers and as a country of departure for Jordanian citizens. It is also a transit country for many refugees coming from neighboring countries, on their trajectories to resettlement in third countries. Refugee populations are central actors in the Hashemite Kingdom, both from socioeconomic and political perspectives. Alongside the Palestinians who arrived in two main waves, in 1948 and 1967, many Iraqis (Chatelard 2010) and Syrians (Ali 2021) have settled in Jordan since the 1990s, as well as more marginal groups, such as the Yemenis or Sudanese (Davis et. al. 2016). Migrant workers also occupy an important place in the Jordanian labor market. There are indeed Egyptians, Bangladeshis, and Filipinos, many of whom are women, who hold many jobs in agriculture, catering, industry, or personal services (Caillol 2018; Lenner and Turner 2019). The Palestinian refugee question has also long been at the center of many studies on migration in Jordan and constitutes one of the main bases for analyzing the relationship between migration and nation-building in the region (Al Husseini 2004). The Palestinian experience constitutes the analytical filter from which most current refugee movements are studied, both on the determinants of the implementation of migration and asylum policies and on the modalities of the settlement of refugees. Jordan is well known for developing a rent-seeking strategy as a response to the massive influx of refugees into its territory (Kelberer 2017).

Different contributions analyze the specific role that international organizations play in Jordan in receiving and settling protracted refugees (cf. Lillian Frost). Particular attention is paid to minority refugee groups often little treated in the literature, such as the Palestinian refugees from the Gaza Strip (cf. Jalal Al Husseini and Anna Kvittingen) or the Yemenis (cf. Solenn Al Majali). While current debates are centered on the question of the future of Syrian refugees, the analysis developed in this book puts it into broader perspectives. While Jordan is not part of the 1951 convention on refugees and does not have a national asylum law, it has developed ad hoc policies for each refugee group hosted in the kingdom. The country has a long experience of hosting forced migrants and has adapted, sometimes boldly, its strategy in cooperation with international organizations and the international community. For example, with the implementation of the Jordan Compact in 2016, the kingdom became a central actor, in cooperation with European states and international donors, in the implementation of containment policies based on tools to control the mobility of Syrian refugees both at a national and Euro-Mediterranean levels (McConnachie 2016). The Compact questions the nexus between humanitarian action and development issues in a protracted refugee crisis, as it is addressed in this first part of the book.

Following the pioneering work of Seteney Shami (1996) on the role of transnational networks in the analysis of forced migration in the Middle East, this book attempts to analyze the role of networks of solidarity in their different dimensions. Studies conducted on transnational activities of refugees have contributed to a more comprehensive way of addressing the role of the state in shaping migrant networks and bringing the state back into most of these analyses. As noted by Richard Black, "focusing on the role played by refugees in transnational activities could help to dispel some of the more idealistic notions of transnationalism from below as a people-led process, which take advantage of processes of globalization and ease of travel in the modern world" (2001, p. 66). In this book, several approaches have been developed to account for the plurality of actors involved in the migration process. The institutions play a key role in the organization of the mobility of certain refugee groups, as is the case for the Iraqis (cf. Norig Neveu) but also the Syrians, even if many initiatives are taken by the refugees themselves in parallel to the response drawn up at the national level (cf. Valentina Napolitano). While religious solidarities can be structured by humanitarian institutions, as is the case for Christian refugees from Iraq, networks of solidarity are most often structured around groups of refugees on a local or family basis. These networks are based on solidarities that develop over the long term, as is the case for the Chechen community (cf. Gaspard Vial-Benamra), or for certain Syrians who had structured commercial networks between Syria and Jordan for several decades (cf. David Lagarde and Kamel Doraï). This long-term structuring also concerns many Palestinian refugees in Jordan, whose Jordanian citizenship has not prevented them from continuing to organize themselves with reference to their Palestinian origin, although the new generation built up new sociability spaces shared with refugees of other nationalities and local youth (cf. Oroub El Abed et al.). Conflicts are often moments when networks are restructured and adapted to help refugees. Other forms of networks emerge during exile leading to transnational reconfigurations of the family structure, with access to the labor market for women (cf. Ann-Christin Zuntz). These chapters provide a better understanding of the role of refugees in structuring their reception in Jordan. While the Hashemite Kingdom has for many years implemented specific policies for the different groups of refugees who have arrived since 1948, initiatives developed by the refugees themselves and non-state institutions play a central role in their reception. Different chapters of the book offer a new perspective on what Michael P. Smith (2002) called *"forced" transnationalism*, linking the fields of the forced mobility of refugees and transnational studies, with original case studies.

The role of refugees in the urban development of Jordan is also analyzed. The migrant and refugee settlement process in contemporary Jordan is central to understanding the urban growth of the main cities in the Hashemite Kingdom, and more specifically Amman (Ababsa 2011), which has been settled by several waves of Circassian migrants who created different neighborhoods, beginning in 1878 (Hamed-Troyansky 2017). The settlement of Palestinian refugees in 1948 and 1967 contributed then to the urban development of Amman. In 1918, Amman's population was less than 5,000 inhabitants. When, in 1921, Amman became the capital of the Emirate of Transjordan, its population was estimated at 10,500. In the early 1950s, Amman's population has more than doubled and reached around 100,000 inhabitants (Alnsour 2016). Since their arrival in 1948, refugee camps have deeply transformed eastern neighborhoods and gradually became part of the city (Hanania 2014). Middle- and upper-class Palestinians also settled in more privileged areas. Following Iraq's invasion of Kuwait in 1990, more than 200,000 Palestinians left Kuwait or were expelled by the Kuwaiti authorities because they were opposed to the Iraqi occupation and to escape the conflict. The involuntary return of Palestinians from Kuwait to Jordan, in the 1970s, had a significant impact on Jordanian society, given the numerical scale of the phenomenon (Van Hear 1995). It has contributed to the transformation of entire neighborhoods of West Amman. Returnees have been the main actors of the city's expansion. First, most of the returnees were well-off and rented or bought apartments and villas in the most privileged locations of Jabal Amman. Second, they have developed economic activities, many of them in the service sector but also in commercial activities and catering, with the opening of many restaurants and cafés. Other cities, such as 'Irbid or al-'Azraq, have been shaped by migrant and refugee settlement at different times.

More recently, refugee groups also settled in Jordan. Since the 1990s, and then after the fall of Saddam Hussein's regime in 2003, hundreds of thousands of Iraqi refugees arrived in Jordan, some of them settled in Amman (Chatelard et al. 2009). Jordanian authorities decided not to open refugee camps in order to avoid the emergence of new pockets of poverty and to limit the possibility of political organization on its territory. Thus, they were all labeled urban refugees. Most of the Iraqis who arrived after 2003 had an urban background and belonged to the middle class. They settled in Western Amman, and many shops, restaurants, and travel agencies developed. Others, belonging to underprivileged social classes, settled in impoverished neighborhoods of East Amman. Access to housing (cf. Myriam Ababsa) as well as the social transformation of Jordanian cities such as Amman and 'Irbid (cf. Héloïse Peaucelle) confirm the crucial role of migrants and refugees in the urban development in Jordan, and more specifically the new urban dynamics that emerged with the settlement of Syrian refugees. Since July 2012, Jordan has decided to open refugee camps for Syrian refugees. This partial shift in Jordanian settlement policy has led to the creation of three main refugee camps in the kingdom (cf. Ayham Dalal and Aline Fraikin). The protracted nature of the Syrian refugee crisis tends to transform refugee camps into de facto more permanent structures and contributes to the blurring of the distinction between camps and cities.

The contributions in this book offer an in-depth and diachronic analysis of different refugee settlements in Jordan, contributing to the debate on the future of refugee groups in the Middle East. It also highlights the specificities—and some commonalities—of Jordan in its regional context, opening possibilities for comparative research with other countries, such as Lebanon, Iraq, or Turkey. It also brings new and original research results to the different facets of how reception policies are shaped by different actors, opening the potential for a comparative reflection within the Euro-Mediterranean context, while Europe is facing new challenges with the development of refugee camps on its territory and the reorganization of migratory routes.

Bibliography

Ababsa, Myriam (2011), *Citizenship and Urban Issues in Jordan*, Beirut: Ifpo.

Al Husseini, Jalal (2004), "La question des réfugiés palestiniens en Jordanie entre droit au retour et implantation définitive," *Cahiers de l'Orient*, 75: 31–50.

Alnsour, Jamal Ahmad (2016), "Managing Urban Growth in the City of Amman, Jordan," *Cities*, 50: 93–99.

Ali, Ali (2021), "Disaggregating Jordan's Syrian Refugee Response: The 'Many Hands' of the Jordanian State," *Mediterranean Politics*, 28: 1–23.

Black, Richard (2001), "Fifty Years of Refugee Studies: From Theory to Policy," *International Migration Review*, 35 (1): 57–78.

Caillol, Daphné (2018), "The Spatial Dimension of Agency: The Everyday Urban Practices of Filipina Domestic Workers in Amman, Jordan," *Gender, Place & Culture*, 25 (5): 645–65.

Chatelard, Geraldine (2010), "What Visibility Conceals: Re-embedding Refugee Migration from Iraq," in Dawn Chatty and Bill Finlayson (eds.), *Dispossession and Displacement: Forced Migration in the Middle East and North Africa*, 17–44, Oxford: Oxford University Press.

Chatelard, Geraldine, Oroub El-Abed, and Kate Washington (2009), *Protection, Mobility and Livelihood Challenges of Displaced Iraqis in Urban Settings in Jordan*, Geneva: International Catholic Migration Commission.

Davis, Rochelle, Abbie Taylor, Will Todman, and Emma Murphy (2016), "Sudanese and Somali Refugees in Jordan," *Middle East Report*, 279: 2–10.

De Bel Air, Françoise (ed.) (2006), *Migration and Politics in the Middle East: Migration Policies, Nation Building and International Relations*, Beirut: Ifpo.

Hamed-Troyansky, Vladimir (2017), "Circassian Refugees and the Making of Amman, 1878–1914," *International Journal of Middle East Studies*, 49 (4): 605–23.

Hanania, Marwan D. (2014), "The Impact of the Palestinian Refugee Crisis on the Development of Amman, 1947–1958," *British Journal of Middle Eastern Studies*, 41 (4): 461–82.

Kelberer, Victoria (2017), "Negotiating Crisis: International Aid and Refugee Policy in Jordan," *Middle East Policy*, 24 (4): 148–65.

Lenner, Katharina, and Lewis Turner (2019), "Making Refugees Work? The Politics of Integrating Syrian Refugees into the Labor Market in Jordan," *Middle East Critique*, 28 (1): 65–95.

McConnachie, Kristen (2016), “Camps of Containment: A Genealogy of the Refugee Camp,” *Humanity: An International Journal of Human Rights, Humanitarianism, and Development*, 7 (3): 397–412.

Shami, Seteney (1996), “Transnationalism and Refugee Studies: Rethinking Forced Migration and Identity in the Middle East,” *Journal of Refugee Studies*, 9 (1): 3–26.

Shami, Seteney (2009), “Historical Processes of Identity Formation: Displacement, Settlement, and Self-representations of the Circassians in Jordan,” *Iran and the Caucasus*, 13 (1): 141–59.

Smith, Michael Peter (2002), “Preface,” in Nadje Al-Ali and Khalid Koser (eds.), *New Approaches to Migration? Transnational Communities and the Transformation of Home*, xi–xv, London and New York: Routledge.

Van Hear, Nicholas (1995), “The Impact of the Involuntary Mass ‘Return’ to Jordan in the Wake of the Gulf Crisis,” *International Migration Review*, 29 (2): 352–74.

Index

www.ingramcontent.com/pod-product-compliance
Lightning Source LLC
Chambersburg PA
CBHW071842270326
41929CB00013B/2075